Further praise for *The Tri............... ....al Class*:

'If books were on the Downing Street letter to Santa, I hope someone gave Mr Brown a copy of Peter Oborne's *The Triumph of the Political Class*. Oborne shrewdly analyses the reasons for the disconnect between the political class and the voters. He contends that the long tradition of integrity and duty that characterised British public life for much of the 19th and 20th centuries has now been abandoned and replaced by crony capitalism, casual corruption, venality, nepotism and mendacity. With an array of devastating evidence ... this book describes our current politics as a reversion to the 18th-century system'

Michael Brown, *Independent*

'Easily the most entertaining political book of the year is Peter Oborne's *The Triumph of the Political Class*. Never a man to ride a hobby horse unless he can thrash it point-to-point, Oborne charts the inexorable rise of professional politicians and their unhealthy engagement with the media'   Paul Routledge, *Tribune*

'A brilliant anatomisation of the reality of the contemporary situation'   Guido Fawkes, *www.order-order.com*

'Admirably comprehensive starting with the anatomy of this new [political] class, then going on to the ravages it has inflicted on British institutions, the capture of the media and a closing section on "manipulative populism"'

Samuel Brittan, *Financial Times Magazine*

'An extremely important new book ... exposes the damage done by professional politicians to the fabric of our democracy and traditional system of government'   Iain Martin, *Sunday Telegraph*

Also by Peter Oborne

Alastair Campbell: New Labour and the
Rise of the Media Class

Basil d'Oliveira: Cricket and Conspiracy –
The Untold Story

The Rise of Political Lying

THE TRIUMPH OF
THE POLITICAL CLASS

PETER OBORNE

POCKET
BOOKS

London • New York • Toronto • Sydney

First published in Great Britain in 2007
by Simon & Schuster UK Ltd
This edition first published by Pocket Books, 2008
An imprint of Simon & Schuster UK Ltd
A CBS COMPANY

10 9 8 7 6 5 4 3

Simon & Schuster UK Ltd
1st Floor
222 Gray's Inn Road
London WC1X 8HB

www.simonandschuster.co.uk

Simon & Schuster Australia
Sydney

A CIP catalogue for this book is available
from the British Library.

ISBN: 978-1-41652-665-0

Typeset by Rowland Phototypesetting Ltd, Bury St Edmunds, Suffolk
Printed and bound in Great Britain by
CPI Cox & Wyman, Reading, Berks RG1 8EX

To Virginia and the memory of Frank

Contents

PART IV: A NEW SYSTEM OF GOVERNMENT

Acknowledgements

I have acquired a very large number of debts while writing and researching this book. In particular I would like to express overwhelming gratitude to my researchers Tom Roberts, Tom Greeves, Harry Snook and Matthew Grimshaw. This book would simply not have been finished without their unstinting hard work, diligence, loyalty and insight. In addition, Jana Sparks has helped me understand the unique system of allowances in the House of Commons; Dominic Raab has provided a framework for understanding Political Class hostility to freedom; while Dr Peter Swaab has helped me link the ideology of the Political Class with wider currents of ideas. I am grateful to Matt Daniel for helping me explore modern political language. Anthony Barnett, and his 'Our Kingdom' website, has helped me come to terms with the peculiarities of British constitutional arrangements. Jon Cruddas gave me a masterclass in the collapse of the British party system, and its consequences. Dr Catherine Needham has focused my mind on the introduction of corporate practice into the public sphere, while Nicholas True has provided numerous insights into the workings of Parliament. Dr Glen Rangwala and Natalie Whitty have given expert guidance on how the Political and Media Class created a false narrative on Iraq. Andrew Gordon of Simon & Schuster (and now of David Higham Associates) has sustained me and given me brilliant guidance. I am extremely grateful to Channel Four television, and in particular Dorothy Byrne, for allowing me the opportunity to investigate some of the themes of this book in a series of films. Patrick O'Flynn, Simon Walters and Tim Knox read and commented on sections of the book. George Appleby and Laura Chisholm also carried out useful work. There is furthermore a very long list of people who contributed or helped in all kinds of ways, and words cannot express my gratitude. I have corrected two errors discovered in the hardback edition of this book published last year. I inadvertently accused Lord Evans of Temple Guiting of voting a mere 37 times in the 2005/6 session of Parliament. The true figure was far higher, and I apologise to Lord Evans. I falsely stated that the Treasury dropped the royal coat of arms from its logo and the initials HM from its official title. This measure was proposed, but never took effect. Finally, I would like to thank Paul Dacre of the *Daily Mail* for allowing me time to write, and Boris Johnson and Matthew d'Ancona of the *Spectator*, where as Political Editor I first started to ponder the menacing phenomena which are explored in this work.

PETER OBORNE
London, July 2008

Introduction

Sir Lewis Namier's classic study *The Structure of Politics at the Accession of George III* (1929) painted a devastating portrait of the British ruling class on the eve of the American Revolution. Sir Lewis sought to demonstrate how idealism, party division and disinterested public service had no relevance at the time. Public men sought office as a means of enriching themselves and rewarding their relations, clients and dependants. A change of government, such as the one brought about by the death of George II, did not merely mean a change of ministers. It brought about a wholesale transfer of public offices. Politicians sought power in order to pillage the state machine. For example the post of Paymaster-General, to be occupied with some distinction two hundred and forty years later by the Labour politician and businessman Geoffrey Robinson, was the foundation of at least one immense fortune.

This in some ways agreeable system of government persisted for many decades after the accession of George III and is still in use in many parts of the world today. Throughout much of Continental Europe, the Indian subcontinent and Africa, government is viewed, at least in part, as a method of personal enrichment. Even in the United States of America, where the Founding Fathers sought to copy the British system with the monarch left out, good old-fashioned jobbery is still a highly obtrusive feature.

Britain, however, departed from that path. For reasons that have still not been fully examined by scholars, the British state changed fundamentally in the course of the nineteenth century. This was not a matter of size, or even of function. It was mainly a matter of attitude. The governing class internalised the idea of public duty. It evolved a picture of the state which could not have been more different from the orgy of greed and concupiscence painted by Sir Lewis Namier. Our nineteenth-century ancestors gradually established a series of dividing lines between private and public, and between party and state. Once these boundaries had been put in place, through the creation of powerful cultural conventions and through Acts of Parliament, transgression often led to personal disgrace or jail. The great Victorians created the notion of the public domain, from which private interest had been banished, and where all were to be treated with fairness regardless of personal influence or connection.

As ever with revolutions in thought or affairs, this astonishing change in attitudes was the work of a relatively small group. Some of the reformers, like Edmund Burke and at a much later stage Benjamin Jowett, were classical scholars animated most obviously by the ambition to emulate Roman virtue. For others, like William Wilberforce and later on William Gladstone, evangelical Christianity seems to have been the primary spur. The Victorian education system, which imposed classical learning amidst an overpowering atmosphere of religious instruction, ensured that both classical and Christian traditions were powerfully present in the minds of most nineteenth-century public men.

Social and economic forces were also at work. During the course of the nineteenth century contemporary industrial development combined with traditional military rivalry to place a powerful competitive advantage in the hands of those states with the strongest structures of public integrity.[1] It is probably no coincidence that Britain and Germany, the two countries that acted most rigorously to exclude private interests from government, were the two dominant military powers within Europe by the end of the nineteenth century.

In both countries a self-confident middle class had increasingly come to resent the way in which the old landed and financial elites treated the machinery of state as their private fiefdom. At one level nothing more complex was going on here than a classic struggle between aristocrat and bourgeois. But the over-riding achievement of Victorian reformers like Gladstone was to lend their side of the argument such an ethical imperative. Sceptics like the Whig Prime Minister Lord Melbourne, the satirist W. S. Gilbert or the popular novelist Anthony Trollope had nothing more potent than ridicule or languid indifference with which to combat this national outbreak of earnestness. Gladstone and his allies invented the idea of clean government, overseen by a new class of benign and above all disinterested administrators. These zealous guardians of the Victorian state could not be bribed, suborned or influenced. They rejected the ancient ties of custom, connection or family favoured by their opponents. They converted the civil service from a system of indoor relief for the dependants of great men into a professional elite which recruited through open public examination. As Gladstone's biographer H. C. G. Matthew describes it: 'Whereas, Gladstone thought, the seventeenth century had been an age of rule by prerogative, and the eighteenth by patronage, the nineteenth would become a rule by virtue.' It became fashionable in the second half of the twentieth century to mock this Victorian idealism. But such irreverence flowed from a failure of vision. The Victorians had created something extremely unusual in the long history of political society: the idea of an unselfish public domain and an altruistic governing class.

In almost every area they set in place a new system. They abolished the purchase of commissions in the armed forces, streamlined recruitment in the Foreign Office and home civil service, rooted out bribery and corruption from the ballot box, and set new standards of public regulation through the factory acts and other public works. A parallel process took place in the private sector. The nineteenth century saw the emergence of the great self-regulating professions: medicine, the law, auditors, architects, engineers.

It is the central thesis of this book that in recent years the achievements of the Victorian reformers have been cut through and in some cases destroyed. The stringent and morally onerous Victorian dividing lines between public duty and private interest survived and often strengthened deep into the twentieth century. But they have been deliberately undermined by a new generation of 'modernisers' over the past twenty-five years. The so-called modernisers always claim to be bringing British politics up to date by introducing competence and integrity, for instance by introducing market disciplines into the public sector. In practice they often turn out to have achieved the exact opposite, and to have helped the governance of Britain revert in a variety of important ways to something close to the situation described by Sir Lewis Namier. At the start of the twenty-first century British public life is once again dominated by a tight political elite which pursues its own sectional interest oblivious to the public good. The rhetoric of public virtue persists – indeed, has rarely been more emphatic – but the old barriers against factionalism, patronage and corruption have been for the most part broken.

Of course, this new Political Class has scant connection with the old landed aristocracy – indeed, it is metropolitan in orientation. But it shares important structural features with the pre-modern elites that dominated politics in Britain and most other European countries before the arrival of mass democracy. The new Political Class is set apart from the rest of society. As I demonstrate in Part I, it has its own manners, morality, habits and specific behavioural codes which place it at a sharp angle to mainstream society. More striking still, it has its own methods of communication. It is normal that crafts, professions and all other specialised forms of activity should have their own private language. But a healthy political system should reflect the life of the nation in its fullest extent, and be readily comprehensible to the country at large. I demonstrate in this book how, within a very short space of time, the Political Class has come to communicate in a peculiar, false and barely comprehensible fashion, full of specialised jargon and phrases that bear an application only within the very restricted media/ political caste that governs twenty-first-century Britain. Their coded language, which is impenetrable except in a very superficial sense to outsiders, is often intended to mislead.

The Political Class has come to acquire one of the defining characteristics of a social class: a common economic base. Politicians are now fundamentally dependent for funding and prestige upon the British state. Indeed many members of the Political Class abuse their financial and other privileges, then collaborate with each other, even across traditional party lines, to prevent themselves being found out. The real divide in British public life is no longer between the main political parties, but between the Political Class and the rest.

All this means that the Political Class is not merely separated from ordinary people and common modes of life: it is actively hostile. It is in the nature of special interest groups to seek influence at the expense of the rest of the community. Just as farmers want subsidies and brewers argue for cuts in excise duty, so the Political Class now asserts special privileges that are not available to voters. Indeed it possesses an advantage which is not available to any other vested interest. The Political Class not only determines its own regulations, pay-rates, pensions and so forth. It also sets the rules of conduct which everybody else must obey. This power is exceptionally dangerous because the Political Class possesses a structural hostility to ordinary freedoms, independent institutions and all public rituals and ceremonies which lack an explicit political dimension or meaning. It refuses to acknowledge that some of the most important areas of our national life, like the civil service or the universities, are not political at all in the proper sense of the word.

Part II of this book is devoted to describing in detail the long, sustained attack that the Political Class has launched against the traditional institutions of British civil society and the state: the judiciary, the monarchy, the diplomatic and intelligence services, public standards, Parliament and Cabinet government. It will show that in very recent times British politicians have sought to govern in a novel way, obliterating the organisations and methods of representative democracy and instead using the press and broadcast media as the key method of communication between ruler and ruled.

This means that any examination of how Britain is governed nowadays is incomplete without taking the presence of the media fully into account. In Part III I challenge the conventional view taken in the bulk of academic and mainstream literature that the media is extraneous, nihilistic and hostile to politics and politicians. I will argue that the media can more accurately be described as the auxiliary brigade of the new Political Class and an organic part of a courtier-based system of populist rule. In postmodern political society the media can most usefully be understood as an instrument of power. Throughout the 1980s it played a role in maintaining Margaret Thatcher's Conservative Party as the party of government. From the mid-1990s onwards it collaborated with New Labour in opposition and after the 1997 election sustained New Labour in government. Once again the relationship was corrupt. Only very rarely does the print and broadcasting media form a general alliance with opposition parties, as it did between 1994 and 1997 and to some extent before the Conservative victory of 1979. Still more rarely does the mainstream media act in a way that could be described as independent of the Political Class or related corporate interests.

This fusion between the media and political domains defines British politics today. In a stunningly short space of time it has come to produce a new system of government, which has been beautifully christened 'manipulative populism' by the constitutional expert Anthony Barnett. In the fourth part of the book, I devote space to describing how this debased system of government works. I show that very few utterances by front-rank politicians have any meaning, and fewer still correspond in even a rudimentary way to the truth. The same is the case with the reports sent back to head office by political reporters once these utterances have been made. Their 'stories' are in essential respects elaborate fictions, which can only be appreciated once it is grasped that they are not an attempt to describe the truth and certainly not to inform the reader, but rather manifestations of power.

In the concluding chapter I argue that the contemporary political system as set out in this book is a transgression. The techniques of manipulation, deception, smear and institutional capture have taken power away from ordinary voters and placed it in the hands of the Political Class. But this means that democratic politics in

Britain no longer does the job most people want it to do. Rather than resolve conflict, it suppresses it. Rather than inform voters, it deceives them. Rather than place a check on the power of the executive, it celebrates it. This is a fantastically dangerous structure. The destruction of the mediating institutions means that swathes of ordinary people and whole sections of civil society have been excluded from meaningful democratic participation.

The book is based on my fifteen years' day-to-day experience as a reporter and, more recently, political columnist, in the press gallery and lobby of the House of Commons. This is an incomparably privileged job, giving one front-row seats in the great political theatre of the day, as well as intimate access to politicians and their senior staff, many of whom I have come to know extremely well.

After I had been doing this job for a number of years I started to gain a sense that something was wrong. I noticed that the reports of political events put out to the public through newspapers and the broadcasting media were in large part either meaningless or untrue. As I probed further I gradually became aware that the conventional narrative structure which is used to give sense and meaning to British politics was extremely misleading. Though the public is always told that Tory and Labour are in opposition, that is not really the case. They are led to believe that the Liberal Democrats are an insurgent third party, but that is not the case either. It has come to seem to me that their strongest loyalties are to each other. For the greatest part of my time as a political reporter the most bitter rivalries at Westminster have involved factional conflicts within individual parties rather than collisions of ideology and belief.

About five years ago I spent some time in Zimbabwe reporting on the way that President Mugabe was brutalising his people, in part thanks to the inertia and complicity of the British government. After I returned, Sir Patrick Cormack, a Conservative Party backbencher, invited me to his room to ask what questions he should put to a government minister who would soon be giving evidence on Zimbabwe to the Foreign Affairs Committee of the House of Commons, of which he was a member.

So I told Cormack about a strange event that had occurred the previous month. President Mugabe had been invited to Paris by President Chirac for a summit meeting. This evidence of European approval of a barbarous dictator caused uproar. When Downing Street was asked about the episode at the morning press briefing, it gave the impression to reporters that it had neither been consulted nor informed, while government ministers spoke out angrily against the invitation. In fact I was able to show Cormack evidence that the British government had known all along about the invitation, raised not the slightest objection, that its protest-ations of ignorance were false, and that the angry pronouncements by ministers were a cynical device. I suggested to Cormack that he should raise this wretched business at the Foreign Affairs Committee, and offered to draft him a list of questions.

Sir Patrick gazed around his large and beautifully appointed Commons office. He looked appalled. 'Oh, I could never do that,' he stated. 'It might embarrass the government.' Since then I have often noted Sir Patrick nod with vigorous approval from the Conservative side as Tony Blair spoke from the dispatch box. I have seen him cross the floor of the House to offer sympathy and support to a government minister in trouble. I have also been reliably told that he wrote a letter of rebuke to a younger Tory MP in a neighbouring constituency who attacked the government. 'That is not the sort of thing we do in Staffordshire,' declared Cormack.

Cormack has his fans who believe that he represents a 'civilised' kind of politics. I cannot agree. Voters put their MPs into Parliament to represent their interests, and articulate their anger, not to form part of a comfortable club, or to collude with oppos-ition parties. In early 2007 it came as little surprise to learn that members of Cormack's constituency association had launched a move to deselect him. This development was greeted with horror in the Commons – if this kind of disaffection caught on, where might it lead? – and no fewer than eighty-two of his Conservative colleagues signed a letter to his constituency associa-tion offering support and warning that Sir Patrick's loss 'would be an irreparable blow to our team in the Commons'.[2] In due course, thanks to a technicality, Sir Patrick (who will be seventy at the likely time of the next election, some five years past the normal national retirement age) was saved to fight another day.

Sir Patrick's four decades as an MP have left him comfortably off, and he can look forward to a generous and secure state pension when he retires. He is one of hundreds of Members of Parliament who now belong to a Political Class that has become entrenched at the centre of British politics, government and society. This manifestation of elite rule has sprung into existence only over the last few decades, and amounts to a denial of democracy. This book attempts to expose how it works, what it does and who belongs to it. I also found, as I was setting about this task, that I was discovering how Britain is really governed, and the discovery was very frightening indeed.

PART I

THE ANATOMY OF THE POLITICAL CLASS

1

THE ARCHITECTURE OF THE POLITICAL CLASS

'In practical life we all recognise the existence of this ruling class (or political class, as we have elsewhere chosen to define it). We all know that, in our own country, whichever it may be, the management of public affairs is in the hands of a minority of influential persons, to which management, willingly or unwillingly, the majority defer' – Gaetano Mosca, *The Ruling Class*

'Political Class: The class, increasingly important in modern democratic politics, of people who have made a career in political and administrative institutions, but who have not had any experience of the ordinary workplace' – Roger Scruton, *The Palgrave Macmillan Dictionary of Political Thought*

The new Political Class is above all a manifestation of the state. It depends directly or indirectly on the state for its status, special privileges, career structure and increasingly for its financial support. This visceral connection with the state distinguishes it from all previous British governing elites, which were connected much more closely to civil society and were frequently hostile or indifferent to central government. Until recent times members of British governing elites owed their status to the position they occupied outside Westminster. Today, in an important reversal, it is the position they occupy at Westminster that grants them their status in civil society.

Though still comparatively limited in numbers, the Political Class is now expanding all the time and with dazzling speed.

It comprises most – though by no means all – of the 646 MPs in the House of Commons. The small army of assistants and researchers who now service these MPs are without exception cadet members of the Political Class. The House of Lords, with its formidable contingent of judges, bishops, generals and hereditary peers, was until very recently a bastion of resistance against Political Class values and influence. But recent changes to the Lords, and above all the arrival of a surge of placemen since 1997, have changed its character. It is now on the way to becoming another Political Class stronghold.

The Parliament in Scotland and the Assembly in Wales – 129 MSPs and 60 Assembly members respectively, plus hundreds of auxiliary workers – have provided a fresh tranche of opportunities for the Political Class. The European Union has also provided a rare source of very well-paid employment, not merely for the 78 Members of the European Parliament who represent United Kingdom voters, but also the large number of additional staff hired by these MEPs. Proposals for elected regional assemblies in England can partly be understood as another audacious scheme to create thousands of new jobs for the Political Class.* However, in a rare setback, the scheme was rejected by the voters.

In recent years the Political Class has extended its membership and influence well beyond the strictly political domain. As government has grown more powerful, it has become essential for large corporations to influence decision-making. As a result a vast commercial lobbying industry has grown up, whose role is to link the business sector to central government and the political parties. This phenomenon has thrown up fresh and profitable opportunities for the Political Class.

Lobbying provides well-paid temporary billets for ambitious politicians as they search for a constituency – and a permanent career for those who fail for whatever reason to enter Parliament.

---

* It should be borne in mind that appointed regional assemblies already exist on a modest scale. These lack an organic link with the areas they represent and are a pure manifestation of Political Class domination.

It also provides a default position for MPs who lose their seats at General Elections, are forced to resign for some other reason, or reach the end of their career.

This linking role does not merely apply to large corporations. The voluntary sector urgently needs to employ members of the Political Class. Most large charities have become arms of the state in recent years, pursuing politically determined objectives in return for funding from central government. Senior work inside the charitable sector has thus become a core Political Class activity. Some charitable organisations have become embedded as an intrinsic part of the Political Class career structure. The Smith Institute, to give one example, is an important part of Gordon Brown's extra-parliamentary machinery, providing a linking role between private business and the government.

The Institute employed the Brownite apparatchik Edward Balls* during the brief interlude when he had ceased to work for the Treasury and before he entered the House of Commons as MP for Normanton. Likewise, the Institute for Public Policy Research (IPPR) has provided a comfortable billet for numerous cadet members of the Political Class as they seek jobs as special advisers to Cabinet ministers or as MPs. While working for the IPPR they supply research papers for politicians, host occasions where Cabinet ministers can test or fine-tune their ideas, and provide a

---

* Rising star in the Brown administration whose brief career already features numerous hallmark Political Class characteristics. Ed Balls read Philosophy, Politics and Economics (PPE) at Keble College, Oxford, then spent a brief period as a journalist for the *Financial Times*. In 1994 he was hired as adviser to Gordon Brown, who was then shadow Chancellor. As special adviser at the Treasury after 1997 Balls carried far more weight than the Permanent Secretary, undermining usual civil service procedures and orders of precedence. In a transgressive development, Balls was soon installed in the mainstream civil service position as Chief Economic Adviser to the Treasury. Now the first Secretary of State for Children, Schools and Families in the Brown government, and considered to be Gordon Brown's chosen heir. Married within the Political Class to Yvette Cooper, MP for the neighbouring constituency of Pontefract. Like her husband, Cooper studied PPE at Oxford, and worked in journalism and as a Labour researcher before becoming an MP. Balls and Cooper now form the first ever instance of two Cabinet ministers being married to each other.

secondary marketplace for political discussion. (The IPPR has played a very important role, for example, in legitimising the Political Class attack on the traditional civil service.) Crucially, these discussions are often paid for by private-sector firms or individuals anxious to influence government policy or gain access to ministers and senior politicians.

The print and broadcasting media have come to play a similar role for the Political Class. Theoretically independent of government, in Britain the media is in fundamental respects an ancillary arm of the Political Class. In recent years the new phenomenon of the Political Class journalist has emerged. This individual's loyalty to the newspaper or broadcasting organisation for which he or she works is illusory. In reality he or she is an operative of the Political Class, given temporary accommodation before formally enrolling themselves in a governmental or party role.

The Political Class is distinguished from earlier governing elites by a lack of experience of and connection with other ways of life. Members of the Political Class make government their exclusive study. This means they tend not to have significant experience of industry, commerce, or civil society. The Tory Cabinet minister Michael Portillo* lasted a very short time working for a shipping company where he developed a 'deep distaste for his clerical and administrative duties'.[1] The Mayor of London Boris Johnson worked as a management consultant after leaving university. 'Try as I might,' he later stated, 'I could not look at an overhead projection of a growth/profit matrix, and stay conscious.'[2] The only Cabinet minister in Tony Blair's 1997 administration known to have had any experience of work in the commercial sector was the

---

* Pioneering Political Class figure whose glittering early career paved the way for a generation of successors. After reading History at Cambridge University's Peterhouse College, a seminary for right-wing members of the Political Class, Michael Portillo soon made the move to the Conservative Research Department, becoming a special adviser after the 1979 election victory. He worked for the oil company Kerr McGee as a temporary expedient before becoming an MP in 1983, and then embarking on a spectacular ministerial career. Much later Portillo became disillusioned with the Political Class and joined the Media Class instead.

Deputy Prime Minister John Prescott, who had been a ship's steward in the 1950s. He was joined in the Cabinet in due course by Alan Milburn, whose commercial experience was limited to a brief period running Days of Hope, a Marxist bookshop known to its patrons by the spoonerism Haze of Dope. Milburn was nevertheless handed the task of running the National Health Service, the largest employer in the world outside Indian Railways and the Red Army. When Milburn left the government he was succeeded as Health Secretary by John Reid, whose private-sector experience was confined to a brief spell in the insurance industry during the 1970s. So far as could be discovered, not one of the Gordon Brown Cabinet formed in June 2007 had any commercial experience.

Such experience as the Political Class does enjoy in commerce tends to be at a far remove from the productive side of the organisation for which they work, and rather in the field of government lobbying or communications. Thus David Cameron at Carlton Communications was engaged in strategy, lobbying and press handling rather than the core company business of TV production.* The Political Class generally lacks what Denis Healey, Chancellor of the Exchequer in the 1970s and beachmaster for the British assault at Anzio in January 1944, calls 'hinterland'. The professional nature of their political activity has come to mean that the concept of disinterested public service is baffling to the Political Class.

It is reasonable to speculate that one of the reasons why Tony Blair was later so ready to take the ill-informed and disastrous decision to commit British soldiers to Iraq was the total lack of military service among the political directorate. The writer Martin Amis caught something of this in his attentive article on Tony Blair's final world tour as Prime Minister, describing a meeting between the then Prime Minister and British soldiers in Basra:

---

* There are some exceptions. The Conservative MP Brooks Newmark made a massive fortune in the private equity business before entering Parliament as MP for Braintree in 2005. The Conservative chief whip, Patrick McLoughlin, was a coal-miner.

Blair then repaired to a side room, for a closed session with the padre, several officers and about twenty-five young soldiers. And something happened.

There was talk from the senior men about 'the hard and dark side' of recent events at the camp (losses of life and limb), about transformative experiences, about the way 'these young people have to grow up very quickly'. And when it came to Blair, all the oxygen went out of him. It wasn't just that he seemed acutely underbriefed (on munitions, projects, tactics). He was quite unable to find weight of voice, to find decorum, the appropriate words for the appropriate mood. 'So we kill more of them than they kill us . . . You're getting back out there and after them. It's brilliant, actually . . .' The PM, it has to be said, appeared to be the least articulate man in the room. The least articulate – and also the *youngest*.[3]

Likewise the culture of incompetence which has become a special hallmark of modern British government may be linked to the lack of any meaningful managerial experience among the Political Class. Very serious decisions are made with an absence of elementary preparation or understanding on a scale which would be completely shocking in the private sector. Recent examples include catastrophic IT failures in Whitehall departments; the failure to prepare for the *post-bellum* situation in Iraq (an act of gross negligence of historical magnitude, with the bulk of the blame falling on the United States government); the 2003 Cabinet reshuffle; the nationalisation of Railtrack; the mismanagement of NHS reforms; the Millennium Dome; the collapse of the Home Office as a functional organisation in 2006; the shambles over Home Information Packs; and the handling of the Foot and Mouth crisis.*

---

* In a very competitive field, the 2003 Cabinet reshuffle is perhaps the *pièce de résistance*. It was supposed to abolish the historic post of Lord Chancellor. This decision, made without consultation, was reversed within hours. It turned out that the Lord Chancellor had an existence in statute law that could not simply be

With relatively few exceptions the members of the Political Class have pursued politics as a vocation. One consequence of their limited experience is that their outlook is often metropolitan and London-based. They perceive life through the eyes of an affluent member of London's middle and upper-middle classes. This converts them into a separate, privileged elite, isolated from the aspirations and the problems of provincial, rural and suburban Britain. This very restricted perspective on life is made very much worse by the tendency of members of the Political Class to marry or form partnerships with each other. Previous generations of political spouses – Denis Thatcher, Audrey Callaghan, Mary Wilson – normally came from outside politics, and thus brought a touch of perspective into domestic life.

The classic career path of a Political Class member begins with political involvement at university. Occasionally he or she will affiliate to more than one political party. The most committed shun the usual vacation activities of their fellow students to instead volunteer in the party and election apparatus in the hope of being noticed. After graduation formal employment will be sought as researcher to an MP, or as a party operative. Talented members of the Political Class soon get picked out to work as special advisers to ministers or researchers for members of the shadow Cabinet. The post of special adviser is very highly cherished among the Political Class. Being singled out as a 'SPAD' to a Cabinet minister is equivalent to being appointed a staff officer in the armed forces. It means that you have become a member of an elite cadre, and will receive future promotion. Before being appointed these special advisers are carefully screened within the party machines for reliability and for ideological soundness. David Cameron*

---

over-ridden by the Royal Prerogative, as Tony Blair and Charlie Falconer were trying to do. The Cabinet Secretary, Sir Andrew Turnbull, was informed half an hour before the announcement. *Plundering the Public Sector*, a work of first-rate importance by the journalists David Craig and Richard Brooks, itemises the long series of IT disasters.

* Cameron is an unusual figure because he combines elements both of the old and new governing elites. For instance Cameron is a member of White's Club in

worked as a special adviser first for Norman Lamont when he was Chancellor of the Exchequer and later for Michael Howard as Home Secretary. Almost all of the rising stars inside the New Labour government were special advisers – Ed Balls, Ed Miliband and others for Gordon Brown;* David Miliband† for Tony Blair;‡ Kitty Ussher§ for Patricia Hewitt.** And so on. This is not a

St James's, frequented by members of the former ruling class, or British Establishment. He supports Establishment sports such as hunting and shooting, was notoriously educated at Eton, and married outside the Political Class to Samantha Sheffield, a director of a Bond Street stationery firm. However, Cameron also displays numerous Political Class characteristics: background as a special adviser, modernising credentials, warm cross-party affiliations, and so on.

* Prime Minister. Politically active since university days, Brown spent a brief period working in current affairs for Scottish Television before entering Parliament aged thirty-two. Married inside the Political Class to Sarah Macaulay, a public relations expert. Gordon Brown is a core member of the Scottish branch of the Political Class, itself an interesting study which unfortunately lies beyond the scope of this book. The Scottish Political Class is even tighter and more collusive than its English equivalent. Owing to various accidents of history – among them the partial wipe-out of the English Labour Party in the 1980s and the ancient superiority of the Scottish system of state education – it has provided an exceptionally high proportion of senior British politicians over recent decades.

† The brothers David and Ed Miliband, sons of the Marxist theorist Ralph Miliband, both read PPE at Oxford University. David undertook further postgraduate study at MIT in the United States; Ed at the London School of Economics. After 1997 David worked as a Special Adviser to Tony Blair. As education minister, he would annually insist that rising grades in public examinations reflected rising standards rather than grade inflation – a classic example of the parallel reality experienced by the Political Class mind. Now both Milibands are in the Cabinet: David as Foreign Secretary, Ed as Cabinet Office minister – the first case of siblings serving in the same Cabinet since Neville and Austen Chamberlain were members of the National Government of the early 1930s.

‡ Prime Minister of the first fully fledged Political Class government. Nevertheless, Tony Blair himself possessed certain non-Political Class characteristics which accounted for much of his popular appeal. He was not involved in politics at university and worked, admittedly fleetingly, as a lawyer before becoming an MP in 1983, aged twenty-nine.

§ Second-generation Political Class. In common with many members of the ruling elite in the era of both the old British Establishment and also the modern Political Class, Kitty Ussher read PPE at Oxford. Then followed a career progression as economist, researcher and special adviser until becoming MP for Burnley in 2005, aged thirty-four. Like many members of the Political Class, Ussher included support for a football club (in this case Burnley FC) as an unlikely leisure interest coincidence. Singled out for preferment in their twenties, they have been trained like racehorses for the unique demands of ministerial office in the era of the Political Class.

Once the special adviser makes the decision to find a constituency, the party machine is commandeered to secure him or her a safe seat. Very often a sitting MP is bribed with a peerage or some other inducement, or pressured in some way, into giving up his constituency, while strong local candidates are discouraged from standing or sometimes sabotaged by the high command. In this way the Political Class makes ruthless use of the party machinery as a tool against the local regime, almost always with success, though there is still the danger of rebellion. Special advisers have a familiarity with the system, and are automatically written up as rising stars. Their number has risen sharply from around thirty-five at the time of the fall of the Major government in 1997 to more than eighty at the start of 2007. There is sometimes an uncomfortable lull, which can last several years, between ceasing this kind of work in government or opposition and arrival in the House of Commons. This gap may well be filled by certain types of work in the commercial sector, the method chosen by the young Tory leader David Cameron during the six-year interlude between his ceasing to be a special adviser in the John Major government and his arrival in the House of Commons as MP for Witney in 2001.

Membership of the Political Class is not connected to schooling or social background. David Cameron attended Eton and the Labour leader Gordon Brown went to Kirkcaldy High School, yet each display over-riding Political Class characteristics. Essentially

---

in her *Who's Who* entry. Cousin of the Tory former minister Peter Bottomley. ** Like many first-generation members of the Political Class, Hewitt cut her teeth in far-left politics. She was an early supporter of Tony Benn, and publicly condemned those left-wing MPs who failed to vote for Benn in the famous Labour deputy leadership contest of 1981. Soon she changed tack, becoming a core part of the Neil Kinnock leadership team before entering Parliament in 1997. Hewitt proved unequal to the task of running the NHS after her appointment as Health Secretary in 2005.

politics has become a trade or profession, with its specialist knowledge, rules and rites of entry. Like other professions, the Political Class has its own career structure and sense of distance from outsiders.

It is important to remember, however, that elected politicians are not by definition members of the Political Class. Indeed those MPs who carry out their constitutional role of representing voters and above all of challenging decisions made by the executive arm of government cannot be regarded in this way. Only those who betray these grave responsibilities and become creatures of the executive or their party machines, enter into cross-party conspiracies, or use Parliament as a method of self-enrichment or for personal advancement can be properly regarded as members of the Political Class. Unfortunately, these categories account for the very substantial majority of MPs working at Westminster. There are some exceptions, and they deserve to be celebrated. Tam Dalyell, who retired from Parliament at the last election after a career devoted to harassing ministers, is one outstanding case. So is the Labour back-bencher Andrew Mackinlay. Douglas Hogg, a rare Tory MP to have opposed the Iraq invasion, possesses an exceptionally clear understanding of the duties of a parliamentarian, fastidiously avoiding cross-party fraternisation while scrupulously using parliamentary procedures to hold the executive to account. This vocation, however, is hard to reconcile with affiliation to any of the major Westminster party machines as presently constructed. So MPs who do take the traditional attitude to their job either make little headway, or face ostracism inside Westminster. The first was the fate of the anti-sleaze MP Martin Bell, while George Galloway, the former Labour MP, was turned into a House of Commons pariah after he won the Bethnal Green and Bow seat off Labour in the 2005 General Election.

Meanwhile politicians who play by the rules of the Political Class have come to resemble one another very closely. MPs from different parties have far more in common with each other than they have with voters. Normally they will have known each other since an early age. They seek to protect one another, help each other out.

The House of Commons is no longer really a cockpit of debate where great conflicts of vision are fought out across the chamber. It has converted instead into a professional group, like the Bar Council or the British Medical Association. In all the Political Class contains approximately 5,000 fully fledged members – most MPs, peers, MEPs, MSPs, lobbyists, quangocrats, researchers and special advisers. This number, which is growing all the time, is comparable to the 'top 10,000' who governed Britain in the nineteenth century, before the arrival of universal suffrage.

The Social Anthropology of the Political Class

When I was still fairly new and raw as a political journalist, my wife and I received an invitation from Peter Lilley, then a Cabinet minister in John Major's government, to stay in his French country house for the weekend. I was amazed and thrilled to get such an invitation, and accepted in part because I saw it as a way of getting to understand the habitat and the species which it was my daily business to report.

It was a thoroughly congenial weekend. Gail Lilley was a wonderful cook, and both she and Peter were marvellous hosts. Michael Brown, then a junior government whip and later a political writer for the *Independent*, dispensed the drinks with tremendous brio and enthusiasm. Peter Lilley, unlike his Cabinet ally Michael Portillo, was definitely not a member of the Political Class. He had a career as a stockbroker before entering politics, and some of the house-party guests worked in the City. No pressure was ever put on me, either at the time or subsequently, to write anything kind about Peter Lilley, nor did he ever divulge to me a Cabinet secret. Nevertheless, the weekend probably proved professionally useful. It is likely that word got around I had been there, making serious Tory politicians more likely to confide in me. It was a weekend I looked back on only with pleasure.

However, after I had had rather more experience in political journalism, I came to the conclusion that I had been wrong to go.

The relationship between journalist and politician is an extremely complex one. Sometimes it is so close that it is like being a priest in a confessional. Politicians pour out secrets you might have expected them to take to the grave. Sometimes it is like the connection between executioner and victim. As a reporter you are compelled to break news to a politician about some scandal or abuse that you know will end his career. Often it is mutually disreputable: politicians, or aides acting on their behalf, hand reporters unsavoury information designed to damage rivals, normally those of his or her own party. Of course the journalist collaborates in two ways: first by carrying out his professional duty and publishing the story and second by going to some lengths (sometimes by including misleading information) to protect the source. There are certain politicians who mysteriously get a far better press than they deserve. Normally it is because occult transactions of this sort have won them allies in the media.

After a while I concluded that all informal connections between journalists and politicians were in some way corrupting. MPs, ministers and their political aides are always trying to draw you into the Political Class, and to make you one of them, and part of their world. Often we succumb. In 2006, at the height of the scandal surrounding Tessa Jowell and the corruption charges being levelled against her husband David Mills by the Italian authorities, one political editor told me he was on the side of the Jowells. 'I've played golf with David, he's straight.' David Mills has never been convicted of any crime. Nevertheless, the political editor was allowing his professional judgement to be affected by personal friendship. This is a luxury which genuine reporters cannot afford. Graham Greene said that every novelist needed a 'splinter of ice' in his heart. The same applies to reporters who want to tell their readers the truth.

This book is an attempt to draw back from the Political Class, and to see it as objectively as I can. I will try to escape the values and judgements of Westminster and Whitehall, and apply instead the wider and more down-to-earth morality of the ordinary woman or man going about her or his normal business in life. This is important, because the main rules that govern the Political Class are often the reverse of those which hold good in civil society.

For members of the Political Class everything exists for a purpose. Very little can be enjoyed for its own sake, except of course power. Leisure activities are an example of this. Football has assumed an overwhelming position as the favoured sport of the Political Class, even among those who are privately indifferent to the sport. This is because it is thought to afford an easy way of communicating with voters. Along with the phenomenon of politicians disguising their natural governing-class accents when attempting to attract voters (explored more fully in the next chapter), this is a manifestation of one key characteristic of the British political elite: the price for membership is the simulation of anti-elite sentiments, characteristics and habits.[4]

The Political Class finds it hard to understand friendship, at any rate as it should surely be understood and practised. C. S. Lewis said of friendship that it 'has no survival value, rather is one of those things that give value to survival'. The pure and disinterested quality which lies at the heart of friendship is alien to the Political Class. People become useful in order to fulfil a certain function, and then they are dropped. Personal courtesies do exist, but they are tailored to power. I once met a man who said he had known Tony Blair quite well at university. He told me how he had bumped into the future Prime Minister several years later, when they were both still practising at the Bar. Blair scarcely acknowledged his greeting.

All ambitious politicians – in other words, all politicians – have a tendency to behave in this focused way. They start at the bottom, and try to battle their way to the top. This means forming various kinds of alliance along the way. Many of these connections become tedious or embarrassing once they have served their purpose. For this reason politicians feel the need to suddenly drop people with whom they briefly appeared to be friends. This basic falseness lurks underneath the surface warmth of most kinds of political transaction.

A nice example of this is the use of personal notes. After a new

MP has made his first speech in the House of Commons he will inevitably find his pigeonhole in the Members' Lobby stuffed with letters of congratulation from people he has never met. These letters will compliment his oratory, regardless of the real merit of the speech in question. A proportion of these will be from ministers, eager to obtain the allegiance of the new arrival with an eye on future leadership battles and other power struggles, or merely as a precaution. A variant of this is letters written to ministers who have been dismissed. There are rising politicians who write a letter of condolence to all sacked ministers, even those they hardly know or may privately despise. This is because they are hoping to gain their support from their position of exile in the back-benches and to fuel their rancour against the party leader who has sacked them. Gordon Brown, during the long years when he was Chancellor of the Exchequer, and hungrily ambitious for Tony Blair's job, would send letters of this kind to former ministers.

On the other hand representatives of the Political Class, who are over-solicitous about niceties when it comes to dealing with people who can be useful to them, are often negligent when it comes to acts of personal courtesy to people of no utility. One year I kept a count of the number of thank-you letters I received after taking people to lunch or dinner. This is a customary gesture of thanks in normal society, but very unusual among the Political Class, as my research confirmed. Of the fifty-six people I lunched or dined that year, some forty-nine could reasonably be classified as members of the Political Class. Of them just eleven wrote a thank-you letter. I also had meals with a number of people who came from outside politics. Each one of them – seven out of seven – wrote me a bread-and-butter note.[5] The Political Class values only success. It rarely finds time for those who fail to measure up to these standards. Here is the *Sunday Times* writer David James Smith describing the funeral of Fiona Jones, who drank herself to death after being Labour MP from 1997 to 2001:

> There were no MPs at Fiona Jones's funeral, not a single one. Some I spoke to said they hadn't been told and couldn't find out

when it was. Others said they wanted to go but had prior commitments they couldn't break. Giles Radice was there, but he is a peer, a former MP, and he was the only senior figure from the Labour Party in attendance.[6]

The Political Class is a callous and lonely place. Human values, where they exist, get distorted. Members of the Political Class always profess generous democratic sentiments which are often belied by their personal behaviour. They use the power of their office to intimidate and are often privately contemptuous of what Leona Helmsley, widow of the New York real-estate tycoon Harry Helmsley, referred to dismissively as the 'little people'. Those lacking in either significance within the Political Class, influential patrons or special wealth are treated as insignificant and even beneath contempt. Lord Chancellor Derry Irvine, a political godfather of Tony Blair, employed a servant to peel his oranges. Irvine, with his conspicuous grandeur and habitual disregard for the distinction between the public and the private sphere, displayed in grotesque form many of the least attractive mannerisms of the Political Class character. Cherie Blair would dispatch officials and diplomats – often quite senior ones – on shopping expeditions and other menial chores. A particularly telling example of this Political Class contempt for ordinary people concerns the attitude taken by Gordon Brown's close adviser Shriti Vadera to small shareholders as the government contemplated the renationalisation of Railtrack in the summer of 2001. Ms (now Baroness) Vadera was unwilling to give them compensation, and small shareholders came to be contemptuously described in Whitehall shorthand as 'grannies'.

Gordon Brown repeatedly fails even to acknowledge civil servants and others who work for him, an elementary failure of courtesy amounting to extreme personal rudeness. Brown presents an extreme version of this unattractive Political Class indifference to people lacking in political utility, as the following anecdote demonstrates. During the mid-1990s, while Brown was shadow Chancellor and had not yet entered government, he had an office in the so-called 'shadow Cabinet corridor', a collection of MPs' offices near Westminster. There was a reception area with a small rack of daily newspapers for constituents and others to read as they waited to meet their MPs. People arriving for work at 8.30am or even earlier would notice that the papers had gone missing. In due course one Labour political aide, happening to go into the shadow Chancellor's office on business, discovered Gordon Brown at his desk with newspapers spread out in front of him. He was wholly unabashed to be caught red-handed in this act of misappropriation.[7] The diaries of Alastair Campbell record a comparable account of abnormally selfish behaviour, this time from Tony Blair. Campbell describes how the Prime Minister arrived at an election event during a downpour. The organiser, Jess Tyrell, was holding an umbrella: 'TB just took it out of her hands and walked on, leaving her to get wet,' records Campbell. His diaries show that such behaviour from Tony Blair was by no means unusual.[8]

It has become commonplace for ministers, when finding themselves in political trouble, to divert the blame on to people who are unable to speak up for themselves. Modern party political machines, when under pressure, are prepared to exploit, humiliate or smear political non-combatants. Both the Conservative Party and New Labour did this in the case of Rose Addis, the 94-year-old widow taken to the Whittington Hospital in north London after a fall. The Tories set the story rolling when they turned the case of Mrs Addis, allegedly left untended and confused for hours on end, into a national issue. Labour then hit back by hinting that Mrs Addis's problem had come about because she was racist.

This dismissive and instrumental approach to people who do not carry influence contrasts very sharply with the sycophantic attitude taken by members of the Political Class to powerful or very rich people. Casual acquaintances with something to offer – holiday villas to stay in, celebrity endorsements, expensive gifts, or cash for party machines – are rapidly treated as close friends. I remember once, before the 1997 General Election, listening to the soon-to-be Cabinet minister Mo Mowlam tell me that she found herself in a predicament that she had not expected. Thanks to some passing political crisis Mowlam had been forced to abandon her holiday plans. The alarm was now over, and Mowlam had nowhere to go. At that stage Mowlam was Labour's spokesperson for the City of London, and various tycoons had instantly stepped in and offered her the use of their holiday villas. But Mowlam sorrowfully told me that it would be wrong to take up these generously meant offers because they would cross a boundary and create a sense of future obligation. In the end she took a cheap last-minute package in the Mediterranean. This scrupulousness was comparatively unusual, and certainly not shared by Tony Blair, who made a regular practice of using the allure of his position as Prime Minister to scrounge lavish holiday accommodation from chance acquaintances.

Friendship in the Political Class does not mean friendship as understood among ordinary people. The 'friends' of a Cabinet minister are the congregation of allies attached to him at any one time and almost certainly include a number of people he cordially detests. Alternatively, these so-called friends might be members of the Whips' Office who are manoeuvring behind the scenes to entrench the Cabinet minister's position, supportive back-benchers he privately despises or Cabinet colleagues whose real ambition is to supplant or destroy the individual they are embracing as a friend. It goes without saying that this inner ambivalence is reciprocal.

The number of friends a Cabinet minister has around him at any given moment is directly related to his political standing. Nobody is more lonely than an out-of-favour politician. They are avoided by other members of the Political Class as if they possessed some kind of infectious illness or had a personal hygiene problem. This is why parties attended by the Political Class are demeaning and inhumane affairs. These events are not a manifestation of friendship or bonhomie. They are simply an expression of naked power. The largest circle of 'friends' automatically assembles around the dominant person in the room. However conventional or humourless he or she in reality is, it can be guaranteed that party guests will find their remarks more interesting than anyone else's. This syndrome explains why even very dull or obvious jokes made by really powerful men are always met by gales of respectful laughter. Eighty years ago the novelist E. M. Forster shockingly remarked that he would rather betray his country than his friends. The problem with this comment was that Forster was confusing the values of the private world in which he flourished with the values of the public sphere. The Political Class makes the identical, though opposite, confusion.

Really serious members of the Political Class do not want friendship. It is compromising and obliges them to make decisions for reasons which do not advance their personal or political interests. They seek out dependence, which is a different thing. The inner circle that has congregated around Gordon Brown is an extremely good example of this. I have spoken to a very large number of people in the vicinity of the Prime Minister, and they mostly make the same observation. It is extremely difficult to become part of the inner circle, and a certain number of tests must be passed in order to break in. The aspirant members of the team around Brown must show total loyalty. This means standing by their man whether he is right or wrong. There is no room for divergent voices and people who speak out or challenge him. This is one important reason why so many of Brown's policies when Chancellor – tax credits is an outstanding example – have ended up being badly planned. In practice, Gordon Brown is not seeking to pursue friendship, a relationship in which the two people involved must regard each other as equals. In fact Brown's record as Chancellor would suggest that he seems to find it hard to endure the kind of equality which friendship implies.

The Theory of the Political Class

The concept of the Political Class – or *'classe politica'* – was first used in academic debate by the Italian lawyer and social theorist Gaetano Mosca. Mosca's major work, *Elementi di Scienza Politica*, was published in 1896 and translated into English as *The Ruling Class* some forty years later. This book, today viewed by some historians as a theoretical precursor to the fascist ideology that was soon to take root in Italy and elsewhere, paid close attention to the abyss which divided a governing elite from the wider population. In turn, Mosca derived a large part of his inspiration from the great French historian Hippolyte Taine, and his analysis of the causes of the French Revolution. Taine located the collapse of the pre-revolutionary French monarchy in the decadence of the governing class. In Mosca's words: 'Taine gave a masterly explanation of the origins of the great French revolution, holding that it resulted from the need to substitute a new ruling class for an old ruling class which had lost its original capabilities of leadership and had not succeeded in acquiring the capacities that a new era demanded.'[9]

Mosca's term never became current among political scientists. This was partly because the idea of class in political or social analysis was dominated by Marxist thought during the bulk of the twentieth century. Mosca's notion of a Political Class challenged Marxist ideas of class structure, which were grounded in economics. Indeed, Mosca's motivation was partly to provide a realistic alternative to what he viewed as Marx's partial and inadequate understanding of the human condition.

Mosca's ideas did not just clash with the Marxist school. His insistence on the estrangement of the Political Class and hints at a common consciousness and parasitic dependence on the state had subversive implications which unsettled thinkers who sought to celebrate Western democracy, particularly in the decades after the Second World War and the victory over fascism.[10]

But the most important problem with Mosca's concept was that it was out of sympathy with its time. It may have been partially applicable to nineteenth-century Italy, an artificial state which had been invented by a centralising clique, but the idea of a Political Class had only limited application to other European countries in the late nineteenth century. In Britain the political elite had its roots outside Westminster, and there was little or no common awareness. The ruling class of a century ago was entrenched, in a way that is not duplicated today, in the nation in its full sense. The north, the manufacturers, the agricultural interest, the Nonconformists, the trade unions and the working man, all had their representation in Parliament.

Mosca defined the Political Class through its professionalisation, and dependence on the state for what he called 'material subsistence', or the ability to earn a living. But the British ruling caste possessed little of the internal coherence that is the defining characteristic of the Political Class. The Labour Party, for example, retained for many years the structure and outlook of an extra-parliamentary organisation. Its leaders were accountable to its ordinary members through mechanisms like an Annual Conference and the National Executive Committee, to which the parliamentary party was subordinate. Early Labour MPs were hostile to Westminster and what it stood for. Labour's first leader, Keir Hardie, stood aside from parliamentary intrigues, which he regarded as corrupt. Parliament made many attempts to domesticate Hardie. He was offered cash, status and deals with other parties. Hardie turned it all down because he felt that his sole accountability was to working people.

The Conservatives, too, were a stolidly provincial party. At its core were businessmen, farmers, landowners, doctors, retired officers, organised at a local level. All towns of any significance had their Conservative Club, which played a central role in civil society. Stanley Baldwin, who inspired the 1922 coup against David Lloyd George* and led the party through most of the interwar years, was an iron-founder from Worcestershire. Margaret Thatcher, the daughter of a Lincolnshire grocer and always an outsider at Westminster, gained massive strength from her unfashionable, lower-middle-class, provincial background. While she

---

* Lloyd George's late premiership was a fascinating anticipation of the post-democratic politics of the twenty-first century. He governed through sheer force of personality, close links with press barons, and a defunct political party. He made up for the absence of a political base with corruption on a massive scale. Lloyd George smashed through the structures of Parliament and Cabinet, and treated party with contempt.

was British Prime Minister divisions between the government and opposition parties were unambiguous. The Thatcher premiership preserved ideological distinctions in Britain during a period when they were collapsing elsewhere, and delayed the emergence, or at any rate arrested the symptoms, of a British Political Class.[11]

In Europe, however, the concept of a Political Class, absent from academic discourse for half a century, began to creep back into use in the 1970s. It was journalists and not political scientists (many of whom were still stuck in hidebound Marxist terminology and intellectual method) who rescued the phrase from oblivion. Correspondents on French and German newspapers tentatively began to use the term in an attempt to find a language that would describe the new political structure that was taking shape in Western Europe.

They were struggling to find an empirical term that would describe the emergence of a new type of political party, and with it the arrival of a new type of politician. Politicians were ceasing to operate as traditional democratic theorists assumed they should. They no longer provided the essential link between citizens and the state. Instead of representing the voters, they had begun to represent themselves. This led directly to the collapse of opposition politics. The fundamental pattern of party engagement across Western Europe ceased to be based on confrontation, but co-operation. The ruling elite was no longer engaged in ideological struggle, but instead joined forces in a common endeavour to share out the rewards of power. In Germany, France and other European countries, this novel kind of politics has led to corruption on a prodigious scale.* By the turn of the twentieth century Gaetano

---

* The highest-level example of Political Class corruption on Continental Europe concerns the relationship between Chancellor Kohl of Germany and the French President François Mitterrand. Mitterrand used the state-owned oil company Elf Aquitaine as a method of financing Kohl's Christian Democratic Union, the same basic technique used by the French government to finance client political parties in Africa. Kohl and other politicians involved in the scandal did not deny the payments. Rather they defended themselves with the claim that the funds had been used to promote reconciliation between France and Germany.

Mosca's concept of a Political Class – self-interested, self-aware and dependent for its economic and moral status on the resources of the state – was no longer an archaic and quaint idea. Instead it had become the most lucid explanation of how politics worked today not just in Europe, but also in Britain.

2

THE POLITICAL CLASS AND THE DESTRUCTION OF THE BRITISH ESTABLISHMENT

'An elite, if it is a governing elite, so far as the natural tendency to pass on to one's offspring both power and prestige is not artificially checked, will tend to establish itself as a class' – T. S. Eliot, *Notes Towards the Definition of Culture* (1948)

The Political Class has come to occupy the same public space that the Establishment was supposed to do until the end of the twentieth century. Like the Establishment, the Political Class stands at the pinnacle of the British social and economic structure. It sets social conventions, and demarcates the boundaries against which both public and private behaviour are defined. Even more than the Establishment, the Political Class is a closed group, un-receptive to new methods of thought and fresh ideas. It articulates the official national mood, and forms the pool of talent from which important positions in the state and public bodies are drawn.

According to Jeremy Paxman in *Friends in High Places*, his masterly survey of British governance published in 1990, the term 'Establishment' was first used by the historian A. J. P. Taylor, who wrote in 1953 that: 'The Establishment talks with its own branded accents; eats different meals at different times; has its privileged system of education; its own religion; even, to a large extent, its own form of football. Nowhere else in Europe can you discover a man's social position by exchanging a few words or breaking bread with him.' Taylor equated the Establishment with 'the Thing', the term used by radical journalist William Cobbett in his campaigning newspaper the *Political Register* during the early part of the nineteenth century. However, one of the purposes of this book is to argue that the comparison of the 1950s Establishment and Cobbett's 'Thing' is misleading. Cobbett's 'Thing' was dominated by money-men, government patronage, a corrupt press, and inter-party collusion. It is much closer to today's Political Class than the Establishment as described, rather loosely, by Taylor.

The phenomenon had in fact flourished for many decades before the 1950s, and was perhaps at the height of its very formidable power and influence around the time of the 1936 Abdication Crisis. Henry Fairlie, political editor of the *Spectator*, wrote the classic article on the subject in 1955:

> By the 'Establishment' I do not mean only the centres of official power – though they are certainly part of it – but rather the whole matrix of official and social relations within which power is exercised. The exercise of power in Britain (more specifically in England) cannot be understood unless it is recognised that it is exercised socially. Anyone who has at any point been close to the exercise of power will know what I mean when I say that the 'Establishment' can be seen at work in the activities of, not only the Prime Minister, the Archbishop of Canterbury and the Earl Marshall, but of such lesser mortals as the chairman of the Arts Council, the Director-General of the BBC, and even the editor of the *Times Literary Supplement*, not to mention divinities like Lady Violet Bonham Carter.*

---

* Henry Fairlie, *Spectator*, 23 September 1955. Certain of its references are obscure today. The Earl Marshal is a royal office-holder, charged with organising corona-tions, and the State Opening of Parliament. The post is hereditary and is always held by the Duke of Norfolk. Lady Violet Bonham Carter was the daughter of the Liberal Prime Minister H. H. Asquith. Her granddaughter, Jane Bonham Carter, was in 2005 made a Liberal Democrat baroness in a move which suggests that the Establishment retains a vestigial power within the British state.

Henry Fairlie's Establishment was bound together by certain similarities of outlook, accent, social class and education. The same applies to the Political Class. It is instructive to compare these affinities in more detail.

Accent and Speech

The Establishment favoured the Queen's English, a method of pronunciation which had come into being during the nineteenth century and was designed to convey no information about the speaker's regional origins. It was so powerful that aspiring politicians and socially ambitious people who failed to naturally conform to it went to great lengths, including elocution lessons, to change the way they talked.* For example, the Tory Prime Ministers Edward Heath and John Major, who both came from lower-middle-class backgrounds, worked hard to disguise their accent at massive cost to their authenticity as politicians and human beings. However, speaking the Queen's English has now become, if anything, a barrier to advancement within the Political Class.

'Estuary English', identified by the British linguist David Rosewarne in 1984, has become the default pronunciation of the Political Class.† This is a compromise form which incorporates

---

* There still exists in Britain an atavistic section of British upper-class society which uses a form of speech that pre-dates the emergence of 'received pronunciation'. Sir Mark Prescott Bt, the racing trainer, is an interesting study. Living in the closed Newmarket racing centre, Sir Mark uses a characteristic form of speech incorporating upper- and lower-class vowel sounds which does not fit into any other modern speech pattern.
† Rosewarne's famous article 'Estuary English' was published in the *Times Educational Supplement* on 19 October 1984. Rosewarne noted that Estuary was a 'continuation of a long process by which London pronunciation has made itself felt ... Because it obscures sociolinguistic origins, "Estuary English" is attractive to many. The motivation, often unconscious, in those who are rising and falling socio-economically is to fit into their new environments by compromising but not losing their original linguistic identity.'

elements of the old received speech, but also embraces local usages, above all cockney. It is accessible both to upwardly mobile members of the working classes, and also to privately educated men and women seeking to emphasise their easy and confident familiarity with fashionable urban and especially youth culture. It has paralleled the development of the main British political parties, which have treated their core voters with contempt in a drive to conquer the centre ground. Estuary serves the useful function of obscuring social or class identity, and many experts believe that it will soon establish itself as the modern equivalent of received pronunciation.*

Among the Political Class, Tony Blair is an example of a speaker of the Queen's English who adopts Estuary. The rising Cabinet ministers Ed and David Miliband exhibit the same affectation. So do many others. The Cabinet minister Alan Johnson, who has retained a Whitehall version of his original London accent, is an example of somebody moving in the opposite direction. Estuary English can now be heard on the front and back benches of the House of Commons, and also in the House of Lords, among both life and hereditary peers. It is widespread among the media, the civil service and the advertising industry.

Though the British ruling-class accent has become more demotic and less patrician, the forms of words used by the political directorate have moved a very long way in exactly the opposite direction. Interviews with Establishment politicians and others dating back to the 1960s and before often seem droll. This is because they are using ordinary methods of serious conversation, with all the eccentricity and quirkiness that involves. The Political Class, however, has deliberately cast aside this homeliness of language.

It has now evolved two novel methods of communication, both

---

* An Australian academic study has even claimed the Queen's own accent is already showing signs of Estuarisation. See 'Is one speaking Estuary?', *Daily Mail*, 21 December 2000 and 'Who cut off the Queen's vowels?', *Daily Telegraph*, 5 December 2006.

of which are unintelligible to the ordinary person, and therefore estrange the Political Class from the voters they are supposed to represent. The first is the kind of language used when the Political Class talks among itself. This has become arcane, often concerned with the techniques of voter manipulation and relying on the anti-democratic assumption that there are matters which ordinary people are either incapable of understanding, or which it would be too dangerous for them to know. In a speech to the Policy Exchange Think Tank in early May 2007, the Conservative Party policy chief Oliver Letwin* made a notoriously opaque speech in which he spoke of the need 'to identify externalities that participants in the free market are likely to neglect, and then seek to establish frameworks that will lead people and organisations to internalise those externalities'. This cumbrous formulation drew comparison with Gordon Brown's own excursion into 'post-neoclassical endogenous growth theory' before the 1997 election. Examples of obscure or misleading language are extremely numerous, the main reason why British political discussion has ceased to form part of ordinary public culture the way it naturally did half a century ago.[1]

These kinds of conversation, while self-referential and hard to understand, at least have the justification of being an attempt at policy debate or construction. The same cannot be said of the language used by modern political leaders when they talk direct to the voters. The emergence of the Political Class has coincided with the rise of the soundbite, which can be defined as a short and

---

* Former special adviser in the Thatcher government and key member of the inner core of modernising Conservatives surrounding David Cameron. Nevertheless, Letwin embodies a number of pre-Political Class characteristics. He has a disinterested interest in ideas for their own sake, a trait which has led him into political trouble on occasions. Furthermore he retains his links outside the political centre. Letwin works most mornings at the merchant bank Rothschilds, opening himself up to the Political and Media Class criticism that he is neglecting his parliamentary duties. Letwin's engagement with the outside world would have been understood as a strength in the era of the British Establishment. The future Liberal leader H. H. Asquith, to give one example, combined practice at the Bar with his duties as shadow Home Secretary to no ill-effect.

often verbless sentence which creates in the mind of the voter the impression of being easy to understand, but is normally designed to mislead. The soundbite has become one of the most effective weapons in the hands of the Political Class, used unsparingly by the Tories and Labour alike. It contrasts sharply with the muddled and hesitant public speech used by ruling elites in the era of the Establishment. In the words of the political scientist Colin Crouch:

> We have become accustomed to hear politicians, not speaking like normal people, but presenting glib and finely honed statements which have a character all of their own. We call these 'sound bites', and having dismissively labelled them think no more about what is going on. Like the language of tabloid newspapers and party literature, this form of communication resembles neither the ordinary speech of the person in the street, nor the language of true political discussion. It is designed to be beyond the reach of scrutiny by either of these two main modes of democratic discourse.[2]

Political Class Clothing

The British Establishment is supposed to have been notoriously prescriptive in matters of dress. Its male representatives were reputed to wear tailor-made suits, carry umbrellas and – until the social revolution of the 1960s – sport bowler hats when in London. However, the sumptuary laws of the Political Class are no more relaxed, and in certain intriguing respects even more formal, than the conventions formerly observed by members of the Establishment. Political leaders in the era of the Political Class continue to wear suits (and women members of the Political Class almost universally wear the same workplace uniform as high-level business executives). Furthermore, they are notably more smartly turned out than the pre-Political Class generation of leaders. It is only necessary to compare Tony Blair or Gordon Brown to Harold

Wilson, or David Cameron to Edward Heath, to see that party leaders in the era of the Political Class take far more trouble about personal appearance than the earlier generation.

This point becomes clearer still when one examines the casual dress of the Political Class. Off-duty members of the Establishment might have worn baggy corduroy trousers and scruffy old jumpers. But the Political Class, even when not at work, finds it hard to relinquish official sartorial codes. Many male members of the Political Class choose to indicate informality by continuing to wear an office suit, but simply removing a tie. This very interesting phenomenon of tielessness, which started to emerge only in the first decade of the twenty-first century, is a symptom of two conflicting attitudes. On the one hand it hints at a daring and independent-minded refusal to conform to traditional standards. This kind of statement is indeed characteristic of the self-conceit of the Political Class, which has emotional and moral roots in 1960s student agitation. On the other hand the readiness to adopt official clothing even in casual situations indicates the exact opposite: an unhealthy attachment to official forms of behaviour. It also hints at the collapse of the distinction between private and public which is a feature of Political Class cultural dominance.

A very early example of this general approach concerns the Prime Minister Gordon Brown. In the late 1980s the *Daily Mirror* journalist Fiona Millar* went to interview Brown, then a rising Labour Party star, in his Edinburgh flat. Her assignment was to present Brown in a homely and domestic light. Brown, however, posed in front of the photographer in a formal, dark suit. When gently asked to put on something more casual, Brown slipped into his bedroom and returned having changed his tie.[3] In 2006, in an attempt to demonstrate man-in-the-street credentials, Gordon Brown's press advisers arranged for some newspaper reporters to watch a football match with the then Chancellor in his flat on

---

* Later to become Downing Street handler for Cherie Blair; long-term partner to Alastair Campbell, press adviser to the Prime Minister from 1997 to (officially) 2003.

the top floor of Downing Street. Once again, he wore a suit. On a sweltering trip to India in early 2007 he wore a suit in casual situations where informal garments were more appropriate. The Prime Ministerial preference for the clothing of the corporate elite even in a domestic environment is characteristic Political Class behaviour which deserves further analysis.

While Brown is happy to wear a suit at home, he is notorious for not dressing up in formal clothing for public events. As Chancellor of the Exchequer he would refuse to observe tradition by putting on White Tie, the most elaborate and stylised form of masculine evening dress, in order to attend the Lord Mayor's Banquet. Here Gordon Brown was displaying the fundamental duality that lies at the heart of the Political Class method of expressive public behaviour. On the one hand it is in rebellion against established customs, traditions and modes of social control which challenge its own dominance. On the other hand the Political Class, by adopting its own very severe dress code, is showing an awareness of the need to assert its own authority, and distinguish itself against the ambient population. Of course this same desire to symbolise public dominance may have lain behind the lavish public displays of the now discredited Establishment, whether the robes and wigs of the judiciary, the flummery of formal regimental dress, the red coats of the hunting field, the morning suits on display at Royal Ascot and so forth. The difference is that the Establishment used clothing as a way of signalling its engagement in a very wide variety of social, economic, judicial and other public and private roles. By contrast the Political Class insistence on the dark suit, the daily uniform of corporate life in the Western, capitalist world, gives away its preference for conformity, homogeneity, and control.

The Status of the Political Class

This Political Class preference for a single official mode of dress results from its insistence upon emphasising its own position or standing in relation to ordinary people. Previously politicians mainly felt that their identity was located in who they were rather than what they did. When they went home at the weekends, for example, they did not rely on the fact that they served as a member of the government or chairman of some important public body in order to play a grand role in their locality. They were often assimilated into their communities as trade union representatives, landowners, parents, church-goers, and so on. This is not often the case with the Political Class, which self-consciously derives its social status, and normally its economic livelihood as well, from proximity to power.

In general, the members of the Political Class are very much more conscious of their importance than the defunct British Establishment. This self-awareness is demonstrable in a number of ways. There is a powerful weight of anecdotal evidence showing members of the Political Class using their rank to extract advantage or exert authority in ordinary situations. MPs seem to think that their status demands special treatment at airports, upgrades on flights, advantageous treatment from commercial firms, while allowing them to display uncalled-for rudeness to ordinary people. The author has private information, for example, of shatteringly rude and arrogant conduct by MPs denied upgrades to the first-class compartment on overseas trips. For another manifestation of the self-importance of the Political Class, see the Labour MP Geraldine Smith's own account of her dispute with a ticket inspector, as recorded in the blog of Tory journalist Iain Dale:

Having listened to what I had to say the train manager asked me for my name and address. I replied Geraldine Smith, House of Commons, London on the basis that any payments due to be made or any refund on unused tickets would have to go through the House of Commons procedures. He responded by stating that he could not accept the House of Commons as my address and that he required my home address. I realised at point [sic] that it was his intention to issue me with an invalid travel notice (even though I had already presented him with a valid ticket that he had accepted) and not to my member of staff whose ticket he had rejected. I came to the conclusion that any further dialogue with the train manager was futile and informed him accordingly. I also informed him that I would be contacting a senior manager at Virgin trains headquarters as soon as I was able to do so . . .[4]

The Political Class in general is far more attached than the Establishment to the paraphernalia of office. This was perhaps in part because many Establishment politicians possessed their own country houses and estates, employed private chauffeurs, owned flats in the best parts of London and so forth. This meant that the grandest Establishment figures gained no benefits in terms of material comfort or status – if anything rather the reverse – by becoming a minister. Many members of the Establishment believed that their motive for entering public life was public duty, and nothing else. When Sir Alec Douglas-Home became Prime Minister in 1963, he sacrificed an earldom and a leisurely life on his Scottish estates in order to do so.

An early instance of the Political Class obsession with the benefits of office came from Geoffrey Howe after he was sacked as Foreign Secretary in July 1990, and awarded a more junior Cabinet position. Howe reluctantly agreed to stay in the government but fought to retain the use of Chevening, the country house which is traditionally available to the Foreign Secretary. This obsession with the peripheral benefits of power was to be repeated many times after New Labour secured victory in 1997. David Blunkett clung on to the Belgravia flat lived in by Home Secretaries long after leaving office. In the dying days of the Blair government Lord Chancellor Falconer accepted the use of a grand flat in Admiralty House, even though he had a pleasant home in fashionable Canonbury.[5] Tony Blair stayed on at Chequers after ceasing to be Prime Minister, in a sharp departure from normal practice.

Another contrast concerns the conduct of Prime Ministers after leaving office. Prime Ministers during the era of the British

Establishment, for example Jim Callaghan and Harold Wilson, tended to return to normal life as it had been lived before the interruption of Downing Street. Sir Alec Douglas-Home, whose mother remarked upon his appointment as Prime Minister that it was 'awfully good of Alec' to take the job, went back to live in his home in the Scottish borders.[6] Stewart Steven, a political correspondent in the 1960s and later editor of the *Mail on Sunday* and *Evening Standard*, once told me how as a junior reporter he rang Sir Alec's Berwickshire home to gain confirmation that he was planning to resign as Conservative Party leader. Sir Alec answered the phone, and dealt courteously and honestly with all questions, thus granting Stewart Steven an important scoop.

This kind of transaction is inconceivable today. Senior members of the Political Class, even in retirement, are protected by a small army of henchmen and would be inaccessible to junior correspondents, as Stewart Steven was then. Even if an enterprising reporter had audaciously broken through the inner ring that now guards former Prime Ministers, it is hard to imagine that he would receive an honest answer. I once spotted Sir Alec Douglas-Home, very late in life, on his own and battling through a rush-hour crowd at Waterloo Station, suitcase in hand. This too would be inconceivable in the era of the Political Class. Ex-Prime Ministers now take the same attitude to their life in retirement as former US Presidents, expecting to be treated in effect as royalty, continuing to be as well protected from the indignities of normal life as they were when holding high office. Margaret Thatcher, for example, took with her several members of her personal staff after resigning as Prime Minister. She established a very well-funded Thatcher 'foundation', and continued for some years to conduct herself as an international stateswoman. Tony Blair has followed this example and taken it much further. There was a tradition dating back to the eighteenth century that resigning British Prime Ministers quit office at once. This custom lasted right up to the end of the twentieth century, with John Major out of Downing Street by lunchtime on the day of the 1997 General Election, and Margaret Thatcher quitting with equal lack of ceremony seven years earlier.* Though undignified and painful, there was something magnificently democratic and even primitive about this procedure. Tony Blair, however, arranged for himself a transitional period of grace of a kind that has always been available to US Presidents but not British Prime Ministers, thereby creating a novel constitutional role for Gordon Brown as 'Prime Minister-in-waiting'.†

Rites of Entry

Membership of the Establishment, though much more open to outsiders (so long as they were ready to adapt to conventional methods of thought and behaviour) than widely understood, was to a significant extent hereditary. The Tory grandee Oliver Poole remarked in 1961 that 'the Tory party is run by about five people who all treat their followers with disdain. They're mostly Etonians, and Eton is good for disdain.'⁷ The same observation can be made against David Cameron's Conservative Party, but this undeniable Etonian connection has now become an embarrassment.

For the Political Class university rather than school or social background is likely to be the crucial recruitment point. In this – as in many other respects – the Political Class is like a large corporation. At this stage of its development its entrance criteria are only loosely based on connections or class background. The key qualification is the ability to show a fairly high level of educational

---

* Defenders of Tony Blair are probably entitled to claim that his situation was most analogous not to Major or Thatcher, but Harold Wilson, who resigned in 1976, in between General Elections. The contrast between Blair and Wilson, however, is even more striking. Wilson stayed on solely for the two or three weeks necessary for the Labour Party to find a replacement, then at once left office after submitting his resignation to the Queen. Tony Blair lasted six weeks after Gordon Brown had been chosen as his successor, time he spent in a series of sometimes tearful speeches and farewell visits.

† The Labour Party and media called Brown 'Prime Minister elect' during this period. But Prime Ministers under the British constitution are appointed by the monarch, and in any case Brown had not been elected.

attainment, and to demonstrate the potential to fit naturally into a mainstream business environment. Once an individual signs on the dotted line at the start of his or her career, he or she is almost bound to become a member of the corporate elite for life, barring some dramatic change of heart or catastrophic accident.

These transformations do occur in the Political Class, as in the corporate world. The decision announced early in 2007 by the Labour MP Alan Simpson to step down at a relatively early age to become an environmental campaigner was in part an acknowledgement of the futility of conventional political life. The former Cabinet minister Tony Benn claimed before the 2001 election that he was retiring from the House of Commons in order to 'devote more time to politics', a remark which contained a great deal of truth.

The central defence of the Political Class is that its structure of government, unlike the nepotistic elite which allegedly preceded it, is meritocratic, or open to all talents. All members of the Political Class, both right and left, make this assertion. John Major – admittedly a transitional Prime Minister with few Political Class credentials – taking over from Margaret Thatcher as Prime Minister in 1990, announced his determination to turn Britain into a 'classless society'. His first act in government, however, was to award a baronetcy to Sir Denis Thatcher, the final time that an hereditary honour was awarded.[8] Tony Blair's pledge to get rid of the old Establishment which allegedly ran Britain, and replace it with a new elite, was a core part of his platform for office. Before winning power he promised a new One Nation radicalism which meant 'sweeping away the vested interests of the old Establishment and ensuring that Britain becomes a truly meritocratic country'.[9] In April 1997 he observed that 'I want a society based on meritocracy'.[10] Two years later he noted: 'Slowly but surely the old Establishment is being replaced by a new, larger, more meritocratic middle class.'[11] Gordon Brown also went out of his way to frame the argument that New Labour was the party which drew on all types of background. 'The modern economy must draw on the widest pool of talent, so the dynamism we need requires opportunity for all,' he stated in a speech to executives at Rupert Murdoch's News Corporation annual gathering in July 1998, adding that 'there can be no room in a society that values work, effort and merit for perpetuating old Establishment elites that unfairly hold people back and deny opportunity'.

There is some truth in this constantly reiterated Political Class claim that it has opened up British political structures. When the British Establishment was at its most dominant the ruling elite was overwhelmingly white and male. One of the major achievements of the progressive wing of the Political Class has been to challenge the ethnic and gender composition of the British governing strata through imaginative devices such as the intro-duction of a quota system for aspiring members. This method of so-called positive discrimination was extremely effective until successfully challenged in the courts.

Nevertheless it is misleading to suppose that the Political Class is necessarily more open than the British Establishment. The rise of the Political Class has coincided with a decrease of social mobility and sharp widening of the gap between rich and poor. Its leading members, most of whom were at school in the 1950s and 1960s, have benefited from the exceptional fluidity of post-war British society. Michael Young, the social theorist who coined the term 'meritocracy' almost fifty years ago – although his book was intended as a satirical guide to the future, not as a cele-bration of the phenomenon – wrote movingly just a few months before his death in January 2002 about the consequences of meritocracy. 'It is good sense to appoint individual people to jobs on their merit. It is the opposite when those who are judged to have merit of a particular kind harden into a new social class without room in it for others.' Young, who also drafted Clement Attlee's 1945 General Election manifesto *Let's Face the Future*, went on to say:

With the coming of the meritocracy, the now leaderless masses were partially disenfranchised; as time has gone by more and more of them have been disengaged, and disaffected to the extent of not even bothering to vote. They no longer have their own people to represent them.

To make the point it is worth comparing the Attlee and Blair Cabinets. The two most influential members of the 1945 Cabinet were Ernest Bevin, acclaimed as Foreign Secretary, and Herbert Morrison, acclaimed as Lord President of the Council and Deputy Prime Minister.

Bevin left school at eleven to take a job as a farm boy, and was subsequently a kitchen boy, a grocer's errand boy, a van boy, a tram conductor and a drayman before, at the age of twenty-nine, he became active locally in Bristol in the Dock Wharf, Riverside and General Labourers' Union.

Herbert Morrison was in many ways an even more significant figure, whose rise to prominence was not so much through the unions as through local government. His first job was also as an errand boy and assistant in a grocer's shop, from which he moved on to be a junior shop assistant and an early switchboard operator. He later became so influential as leader of the London County Council partly because of his previous success as Minister of Transport in the 1929 Labour government.

He triumphed in the way [Ken] Livingstone and [Bob] Kiley hope to do now, by bringing all London's fragmented tube service, buses and trams under one united management and ownership in his London passenger transport board. It also made London's public transport the best in the world for another 30–40 years and the LPTB was also the model for all the nationalised industries after 1945.

Quite a few other members of the Attlee Cabinet, like Bevan and Griffiths (miners both), had similar lowly origins and so were also a source of pride for many ordinary people who could identify with them.

It is a sharp contrast with the Blair Cabinet, largely filled as it is with members of the meritocracy. In the new social environment, the rich and powerful have been doing mighty well for themselves. They have been freed from the old kinds of criticism from people who had to be listened to. This once helped keep them in check – it has been the opposite under the Blair government.

The business meritocracy is in vogue. If meritocrats believe, as more and more of them are encouraged to, that their advancement comes from their own merits, they can feel they deserve whatever they can get. They can be insufferably smug, much more so than the people who knew they had achieved advancement not on their own merit but because they were, as somebody's son or daughter, the beneficiaries of nepotism. The newcomers can actually believe they have morality on their side.[12]

Meanwhile the Political Class is already showing hereditary tendencies which, human nature being what it is, are certain to increase very rapidly. Michael Young's claim, made in 2001, that the Political Class advanced on its own merits, gets more and more dubious with each General Election. The Cabinet ministers Ed and David Miliband, sons of a celebrated Marxist professor, are hereditary members of the Political Class, as is Hilary Benn, the third successive generation of his family to serve in the Cabinet.

The Leadership Style of the Political Class

Before the emergence of the Political Class the conventional mode of national leadership was based on a vestigial idea of gentlemanly conduct. The style had been laid down by the Duke of Wellington in the early nineteenth century, both as a leader of men on the battlefield and later as Prime Minister and national icon.[13] It was based on understatement, sobriety both in personal conduct and in speech, self-sacrifice, restraint. In sharp contrast to Napoleon, his great rival, Wellington eschewed displays of private emotion, downplayed his personal achievements, and showed a studied indifference to public opinion. Wellington was massively influential at the time and later. He was consciously or unconsciously copied by successors dating from Robert Peel in the 1840s through

Clement Attlee right up to Harold Wilson and Jim Callaghan (though with certain famous exceptions, such as Winston Churchill in his apotheosis as war leader, or the exotic Benjamin Disraeli). These Prime Ministers from the time of the British Establishment would often deprecate their own work, typically acknowledge the contribution of Cabinet colleagues, and were clear about the dividing lines between public and private life.

In certain of her leadership techniques, such as the use of methods and personnel drawn from commercial advertising, and a routine emphasis on the dramatic flourish, Margaret Thatcher marked a turning point. Her successor John Major attempted to revert to an earlier style, and was not successful. Tony Blair, however, was the first national leader to wholeheartedly turn his back on the style of national leadership that had been normal during the period of institutional dominance.

He exchanged the gentlemanly school of leadership for the contrasting false heroic, renouncing the Establishment style of the stiff upper lip in favour of a Political Class methodology which favoured display, self-promotion, knowingness and ostentation. The Political Class leader invites the public to share the tragedies and triumphs of his private life. It is automatic for a member of the Political Class to exploit family and friendships in order to sell his political career. With the arrival of the Political Class the term 'back story' has entered British politics, the insider's term for the elaborate construction of an attractive version of a politician's life outside Westminster for public consumption. The carefully sanctioned accounts of Tony Blair's career offer a fascinating example of this political myth-making. There was no early struggle out of poverty, or act of heroism. Nevertheless the professional image makers laid stress on Blair the family man, the church-goer, and a figure of basic human decency.

Photographs of the future Prime Minister with his wife and children were made freely available. He was pictured at prayer, while one favoured political editor was allowed to take shots of Tony Blair playing football in the park with his children. As time passed the model changed and emphasis was laid instead on Blair the man of conviction, or (at the time of the Iraq invasion) Blair the battered war leader. Blair's transformative moment of sheer genius, however, remains his reaction to the death of Princess Diana in the autumn of 1997. His ostentatious suppression of raw emotion, and careful stress on his personal connection to the dead woman, was a massive breakthrough in British political culture, handled with exemplary poise by the Prime Minister. All major politicians have since sought to emulate Tony Blair's artistry, above all the new Conservative leader David Cameron, none with such success.

This form of celebrity politics is a crucial part of the Political Class governing method.* It enables political leaders to enjoy a direct link with the public that is more immediate and powerful than anything enjoyed either by parties or by governing institutions. This gives them the ability to sideline, subvert or to over-ride mainstream political structures, thus converting the business of government to a form of personal connection between ruler and ruled.

Senior members of the Political Class now place their private lives at the disposal of their public careers in a remorseless and systematic way. This confusion of categories is just one manifestation of the way the Political Class has come to exploit private life as a tool rather than something to be enjoyed as an end in itself. In effect we are seeing a reversion to a pre-modern mode of leadership where the life of the sovereign, often down to the most intimate details, is lived out in full view of his subjects. Charismatic or celebrity rule of this type has accompanied the rise of the Political Class, and marks a definite break with the normal procedures of governance as practised over the last two centuries.

---

* Gordon Brown claimed to be opposed to 'celebrity politics' at the start of his 2007 Labour leadership campaign. Within days he cast doubt on the sincerity of this pledge by being interviewed by the broadcaster Mariella Frostrup, and intervening in the Portuguese police investigation into the disappearance of Madeleine McCann.

Structures of Belief

The British Establishment was founded on the Christian religion. With relatively few exceptions, members of the Establishment were baptised, confirmed, married and in due course buried within the Church, above all the established Church. Religion did not merely give this immensely powerful narrative for private and family life, it also provided the over-riding justification and legitimacy for the social and moral order of the British state during the era of Establishment dominance. This applied even for the many members of the Establishment who privately did not believe in God.

As a result, members of the Establishment understood and surprisingly often sought to live up to the Christian values of humility, duty, forbearance, truthfulness and service. They also accepted Church teaching about male dominance, often accompanied by an implicit doctrine of racial supremacy, leading to the exclusion both of women and of ethnic minorities from the ruling elite. These Christian teachings equipped members of the Establishment (and the British people at large) to make sacrifices of such an extremity that they now seem baffling. Widespread acceptance of the great doctrine of personal subordination to what was regarded as a national good was one of the reasons nearly a million young men died on the Western Front in the First World War.

The Church plays no meaningful role, except perhaps a negative one, in the formation of Political Class beliefs. Although a number of individual members of the Political Class believe in God, they are careful to place a barrier between their faith and their political convictions. When he was Prime Minister Tony Blair was a very clear example of this fastidiousness. He was adamant in his refusal to allow religious teaching to affect the actions he took in government, obeying an injunction from his press adviser Alastair Campbell not to 'do God'. When the issue of abortion became significant early in the Blair premiership, the Prime

Minister insisted that while privately he was against abortion, as a 'legislator' the question was not about personal belief. He argued instead that it was about 'whether in cases where women face very difficult and agonising decisions the criminal law is the right instrument to make that decision for them'.* Furthermore, he treated with disdain the pleas of the leaders of both the Church of England and the Catholic Church to avoid war in Iraq. Despite this opposition from the Pope, the Archbishop of Canterbury and other religious leaders, Downing Street press handlers, as well as many Blair apologists, continued to assert that Tony Blair's religious beliefs lay behind his decision to invade.

In general, members of the Political Class are encouraged not to hold strong or passionate religious beliefs, and to conceal them if they do. Thus Cabinet minister Ruth Kelly's membership of the devout Roman Catholic pressure group Opus Dei has constantly brought her embarrassment. Basically the Political Class and Opus Dei represent two opposite principles, and it is likely that at some stage of her career Kelly will be obliged to choose between her contradictory allegiances. However muddled and self-serving it may often seem, the philosophy of the Political Class is always based on a basic assumption about the supremacy of human reason and the human will. The Establishment, in sharp contrast, subscribed to a system of thought which stressed the fallibility of human beings, and emphasised that there were limits beyond which the human intellect finds it unable to stretch. The Establishment felt confident that its hegemony was sanctioned, at any rate in formal terms, by Almighty God.

---

* The former Prime Minister never once voted with the pro-life lobby and has voted fourteen times for the pro-choice lobby in Parliament. In 1990, during the debates leading up to the Human Fertilisation and Embryology Act, he voted on three occasions to extend the time limit for abortion to birth on grounds of handicap. In December 2000 he gave personal backing to regulations permitting stem-cell research on human embryos; and his government enthusiastically promotes the morning-after pill. See Peter Oborne, 'The Special Relationship between Blair and God', *Spectator*, 5 April 2005.

Political Class Values and the 1960s Counter-Culture

The values of the Political Class, which are still in the process of formation, are more difficult to categorise than those of the Establishment. A variety of intellectual, moral and political traditions have converged to create the mental framework of the Political Class, and they are still in the melting pot. On the progressive wing numerous strands of Marxism, late twentieth-century management theory, Fabianism, and most recently of all a loose doctrine of consumer gratification (an offshoot of the 1960s cult of self-realisation) contend for supremacy. On the right wing elements of free-market liberalism, libertarianism and naked power worship of a type more usual on the Continental than the British right are all to be found. Also present in the mix is a raw populism reminiscent of the totalitarian movements which rose to power in Europe, and never before seen in Britain. Some of these elements have partially merged into the Political Class cult of modernisation, an unstable phenomenon of great importance which receives its separate treatment in Chapter 5.

Certain generalisations can nevertheless be made with reasonable confidence. The Political Class rose to power in self-conscious opposition to the Establishment, the direct result of a brilliantly successful project to undermine and destroy its public legitimacy. Most of the current leadership of the Political Class, both in respect of its political enforcers and public apologists, began their adult life in the 1960s and 1970s. During these decades the Establishment was repeatedly and systematically savaged, partly through ridicule and partly through direct attack. It was held up as hypocritical, rancid, out of date, conservative, elderly and morally bankrupt. This assault started with ridicule in the social revolution of the early 1960s, and came to an end with the savage attacks mounted by the media on the royal family and Conservative Party Cabinet ministers in the middle of the 1990s. At no stage did the Establishment, which had been practically unchallenged in British public life when Henry Fairlie wrote his famous article in 1955, mount a serious defence. There was a moment of romantic counter-revolution in the early 1980s, the main Establishment triumphs being the royal wedding of 1981 and the Falklands War the following year, when it seemed as if there was a hint of a Restoration in the air. But it was not followed up and proved short-lived.

The Establishment simply collapsed under combined attack from economic radicals on the right and social and cultural revolutionaries from the left. Looking back it is possible to pinpoint almost exactly the dates the first and last shots were fired in this one-sided war. The Profumo Affair of 1963, cleverly portrayed as the first public revelation of the hypocrisy and corruption of the old ruling class, marked the moment when the post-war order first came under direct attack.* Thirty-four years later all remaining resistance was flushed out when guitar-strumming Tony Blair brilliantly mobilised the forces of youth, modernity, meritocracy and optimism in his campaign to secure power. Tony Blair's triumph was based on the explicit claim that his government was new, different and represented a fresh start after the harm inflicted on the British nation by a corrupt Establishment. In other words the 1997 election victory marked the triumph for a series of moral, social and political ideas which had been part of the British counter-culture in the 1960s and 1970s.

There were two major elements to this counter-culture. The first was political. The majority of the members of the current political directorate were active in the far left in those decades. Several are former members of the Communist Party, and very few had avoided contamination from the various strands of Marxist organisation and belief that were current from the 1960s. Although by the time they arrived in government they had abandoned most orthodox Marxist beliefs, they nonetheless remained wedded to

---

* John Profumo resigned as Defence Minister in 1963 after admitting to lying to the House of Commons. Ministers in the age of the Political Class have never followed suit.

the organisational doctrines of the far left, and the methodology of centralised control.*

The second element of the counter-culture was not political but personal. It stressed the overwhelming importance of personal fulfilment, and taught that the path to self-realisation was blocked by the institutions of bourgeois society, such as schools, churches, the police, all sources of authority, and so-called patriarchal structures of which the family was often held to be the most invidious. During the 1960s all this manifested itself in various ways including 'flower power'; the hippy movement; the teachings of the psychiatrist R. D. Laing, who lifted responsibility for psychological problems off the shoulders of the individual and attributed it instead to the malign effect of the family and society; the songs of John Lennon; the sudden rise to fashion of the Bloomsbury set with its remorseless attention to the niceties of private life; the popularity of the novels of writers like Hermann Hesse; and the influence of Far Eastern religions with their insistence on inner spiritual growth combined with a studied indifference to the social order, and stress on the search for true knowledge of the inner self. Just as much of the political wing of the 1960s counter-culture could be traced ultimately to the theories of Karl Marx, so this more inward-looking expression of the 1960s counter-culture owed something to the writings of Sigmund Freud and the psychiatric profession which he founded at the start of the twentieth century. However, Buddhism, pop music, radical

---

* Although communism has enjoyed barely any electoral success in Britain during the last 100 years, its influence has been exceptionally strong among the governing elite, both in politics and other spheres. Two of Tony Blair's most cherished Cabinet ministers, John Reid and Peter Mandelson, had both been active members of Communist organisations. When asked about his involvement, Reid would say that he 'used to believe in Santa Claus'. Nevertheless, Reid was a member of the CP, which was controlled by Soviet Russia, well into his adult life, and long after the truth had been published about Stalin's death camps. The CP influence was even stronger among New Labour intellectuals. The CP and the various Marxist factions played a very large part in the education and intellectual construction of numerous members of the Political Class, a phenomenon which cries out for further study.

feminism and perhaps above all the Western advertising industry and its cult of consumer gratification were all extremely important as well.

These two movements – one praising collective structures as the solution to human exploitation, the other targeting them as the proximate cause of human alienation – were fundamentally contradictory. However, this contradiction rarely loomed large at the time. This is because all wings of the 1960s counter-culture were able to agree on a common enemy: the basic rottenness of the existing structures of the state, and the evil done by its institutions.

While the doctrine of radical individualism challenged institutions because they suppressed human potential, the Marxist left hated them because they were instruments for class domination. Karl Marx and Friedrich Engels had noted in the *Communist Manifesto* that 'the executive of the modern state is but a committee for managing the common affairs of the whole bourgeoisie'. Included in this casual dismissal were the system of justice, Parliament, the law and order 'apparatus', as well as apparently autonomous institutions like universities. Communism was opposed to all organisations that represented a sense of life, thought or identity that was not dependent on the state. This list included the family. As Anatoly Lunacharsky, the Soviet Commissar of Education, noted in the early 1930s, 'Our problem now is to do away with the household and to free women from the care of children.'[14]

The Attack on Institutions

It is the attitude towards institutions which, more than anything else, separates the Political Class from the British Establishment. The Political Class despises them; the Establishment revered them. The most significant point about the Establishment was that it mainly existed through institutions. The attack on the Establishment and the assault on institutions that began at the start of the 1960s and gathered pace thereafter were identical. Judges, ambassadors, civil service mandarins, bishops, generals, the Queen, the secretary of the MCC were all by definition Establishment figures. In certain essential respects so were trade unionists, referred to by Winston Churchill in 1947 as 'pillars of our society'.[15]

The powerful presence of these institutions deprived the British Establishment of a common identity, whereas it can certainly be said that the Political Class has a common identity. It is true that many members of the Establishment shared certain patterns of speech, background and assumptions about the structure of society. But their allegiance to powerful institutions obliged them to have separate identities, duties and loyalties. For example judges were there to uphold the law, but the Cabinet Secretary did his best to secure the efficiency of the executive arm, objectives that were sometimes impossible to reconcile. One of the most interesting findings of Anthony Sampson's famous survey of how Britain was governed, *The Anatomy of Britain*, published in 1962, was the demonstration that the British Establishment was by no means monolithic and lacked anything much in the way of a common consciousness. 'The rulers are not at all close-knit or united. They are not so much in the centre of a solar system, as in a cluster of interlocking circles, each one largely preoccupied with its own professionalism, and touching others only at one edge,' wrote Sampson, adding the vital observation:

They are not a single Establishment but a ring of Establishments. The frictions and balances between the different circles are the supreme safeguard of democracy. No one man can stand in the centre, for there is no centre.[16]

This fundamentally heterogeneous and decentralised structure of British government has since come under brutal attack from the Political Class. One of the central purposes of this book is to demonstrate how the Political Class has at all times resented and sought to destroy the free-standing status of British institutions, a subject of the highest importance which will be dealt with in great detail in Part II. For instance, the Political Class is deeply hostile to the rule of law, instinctively preferring to govern through executive fiat, repeatedly showing anger when the judges thwart illegal decisions made by ministers. Likewise the traditional civil service insistence on the necessity of due process, note-taking and the importance of precedent fills the Political Class with rage. The Political Class is infused by an unbending hostility to all centres of power or values which it cannot control or manipulate.

The Political Class hostility to institutions means that it has chosen an entirely different methodology of government to the Establishment. Under the Establishment the home civil service, the diplomatic service, Parliament, the armed forces, the judiciary, trade unions, the monarchy and the even the Anglican Church were all part of the machinery of government. Each of these organisations had its own independent status, public standing and discrete set of values. Between them the longstanding institutions of the British government, far from being hostile to freedom as critics claimed, provided an extremely powerful protection for the individual against the overbearing state.*

While it is possible to describe very clearly which institutions and organisations embodied Establishment values, it is also important to note which did not. The press and broadcasting media (with the significant exception of *The Times* newspaper) stood outside the Establishment. The advertising and marketing professions were unacceptable, and so was the nascent public relations field. For the most part the world of business, whether in the form of large corporations or self-made entrepreneurs, was not compatible with the Establishment, which considered genteel poverty to be a more honourable condition than new money. (Exceptions were made for certain City of London banks, stockbrokers and discount houses of an almost morbid conservatism, all

---

* As the political philosopher Roger Scruton noted: 'A state may also be defined as totalitarian on the grounds that it does not permit autonomous institutions in any sphere in which the state has an interest – e.g. in education, trade union organisation and so on.' See Scruton, *The Palgrave Macmillan Dictionary of Political Thought*, p. 264.

swept away by the structural changes that followed Big Bang in 1986.) This hostility to wealth creation was an endemic feature of the British Establishment, blamed by theorists of the time for apparent national economic decline.

The Political Class operates on an entirely opposite basis. It prefers to work through the commercial or service sector, either keeping the institutions of the British state at bay or turning them into client organisations. The media, kept on the outside by the Establishment, has emerged as the defining Political Class activity. Likewise advertising and public relations, considered by the Establishment as low-grade and not worthy of notice, have become a core part of government. These professions are central to the key Political Class methodology of electoral manipulation, and no modern political leader feels comfortable operating without advertising, media and PR experts in his inner team. Margaret Thatcher favoured Maurice (now Lord) Saatchi. Tony Blair used the consultant Philip (now Lord) Gould and others. Steve Hilton, formerly of Saatchi & Saatchi, is David Cameron's closest adviser. Meanwhile public relations has soared in status, as recently evidenced by the presence of both David Cameron and Gordon Brown at the wedding of the financial PR tycoon Alan Parker. Similarly the Political Class highly esteems successful businessmen, rewards them, awards them patronage and looks to be rewarded with sinecure, consultancies and directorships on leaving office.

The table overleaf lists some of the major British institutions and commercial activities according to their compatibility with the Political Class and the now defunct Establishment.

Among Establishment institutions only the intelligence services have emerged strengthened from the emergence of the Political Class. The Secret Intelligence Service in particular has shown a willingness to evolve its methods to fit in with the demands of the Political Class, though at some cost to its integrity, reliability and the trust in which it is held.

In general, it is very striking how very little connection there is between the Establishment and the Political Class. While the

Monarchy	Aristocracy	Trade Unions	Armed Forces	Civil Service	Foreign Office
Political Class					
No	No	No	No	No	No
Establishment					
Yes	Yes	Yes	Yes	Yes	Yes

Intelligence	Judiciary	Big Business	Media	Advertising	PR agencies
Political Class					
Yes	No	Yes	Yes	Yes	Yes
Establishment					
Yes	Yes	No	No	No	No

Establishment governed through civil service and Parliament, the Political Class has sought as a matter of course to sideline institutions, only accepting them to the extent that they were ready to abandon their traditions, identities and codes of behaviour. Political Class operatives typically look to find allies inside a target institution who are ready to abandon the disciplines in which they were trained, and demonstrate loyalty to the Political Class.

General Sir Mike Jackson as Chief of the General Staff was induced to lend his authority to the brilliantly orchestrated Political Class attack on the 300-year-old British regimental tradition. In an analogous situation, the intelligence chiefs John Scarlett and Sir Richard Dearlove sacrificed the conservatism, scruple and hard-won integrity of the intelligence services in the run-up to the Iraq War, taking part in a process which converted the Secret Intelligence Service into a propaganda arm of the British government. A number of senior domestic civil servants have secured career advancement by making themselves operatives for the Political Class. Likewise Michael (now Lord) Jay allowed the Foreign Office, formerly one of the great institutions of the British state, to be consigned to irrelevance during his four years as Permanent Secretary, dating from 2002 to 2006. Very few public servants have refused to join in or at least tacitly accept this *trahison des clercs*. For those that have stood aside the consequences have sometimes been grave. Sir Alistair Graham, chairman of the Commission for Public Standards, was eased out of his job. The Ministry of Defence official Dr David Kelly, who expressed scepticism about the fabricated claim that Saddam Hussein could unleash chemical and biological weapons within forty-five minutes, was hounded to his death by a vengeful Political Class. These individuals were exceptional. Broadly speaking British institutions, or at least the most senior individuals inside them, have collaborated in their own destruction.

3

THE POLITICAL CLASS AND THE COLLAPSE OF PUBLIC STANDARDS

'The guide applies to civil servants, not ministers' – John Prescott's spokesman, after revelations that the Deputy Prime Minister had broken rules prohibiting officials from making 'improper use' of the workplace

Leading figures during the long period of Establishment rule conformed to a public doctrine that deprecated the importance of the individual. They believed that great national institutions embodied important truths that stretched beyond the comprehension of one man or woman alone, however eminent or personally brilliant. Those who held high office had been brought up to believe they were transient figures, temporary custodians of something of value that endured down generations.

This doctrine helped to make politicians more modest than they might have chosen to be. They saw themselves as serving Crown, Parliament, nation or political party, a doctrine that still survives in small corners of public life, most obviously among the voluntary sector, local activists from all political parties, the older members of the royal family, and above all the armed forces, where young men and women are still prepared to risk their lives and to endure desperate privations on behalf of their country.

However, this doctrine of service has been cast aside by the

Political Class. It does not look to serve great national institutions: on the contrary, it looks to those institutions to serve them. This shift has led, in a very short space of time, to a new pattern of behaviour among the governing elite. They have started to smash the boundaries not just between public and private, but also between party and state. This crumbling of institutional structures has had a disastrous effect on public standards and seen a return to a fundamentally pre-modern connection between the individual and the state based around exploitation and greed rather than public service and duty. This chapter shows how many individual members of the Political Class, including Cabinet ministers, now routinely bully, cheat and steal from the taxpayer. When they get caught out, they tend to lie to get out of trouble. And even when that tactic fails to work, fellow members of the Political Class expect to pay a lower penalty than ordinary people.

The Special Virtue of the Political Class

It is the special belief of the Political Class, constantly reiterated by its numerous influential supporters within the media and elsewhere, that it conducts itself in a far more virtuous and disinterested way than other sections of society. The most famous manifestation of this belief in recent years came from Tony Blair, when he told Labour MPs after the 1997 election victory that they should be 'servants of the people'. The new Prime Minister went on: 'You are not here to enjoy the trappings of power but to do a job and to uphold the highest standards in public life.' (This remark should be understood as an unconscious tribute to the system of public morality during the period of institutional dominance, because his conduct in office was to show that the Prime Minister cannot possibly have meant what he said.)

This supposedly high standard of personal behaviour is reinforced by the parliamentary convention which makes the explicit assumption that MPs are 'honourable' men and women of unassailable personal integrity. It is an offence against the rules of the Commons to suggest otherwise.

Members of the Political Class tend to assert that they perform an almost priestly function and that especially rigorous and exacting standards apply to them. The former Downing Street aide Geoff Mulgan, a New Labour intellectual whose recent work *Good and Bad Power* is an important articulation of Political Class values and beliefs, has made a formal statement of the claim as follows:

> We expect leaders to abide by far more demanding rules than the rest of us. So for example, we expect them to suspend personal considerations when exercising impersonal power: not to give special favours; not to treat people well just because they like them. We don't let them use their power to enrich themselves, or gain sexual favours.[1]

This is a fascinating passage, gaining special weight because Geoff Mulgan was head of policy inside Downing Street when he wrote it. The particular interest lies not in the series of assertions that Mulgan is making about politicians, but in the assumption he is making about wider society. He is not just saying that voters are making extraordinary demands on politicians when they insist that they do not show favouritism to friends or use their power in order to obtain sexual favours. He is also accepting that ordinary people – as Mulgan puts it, 'the rest of us' – do indeed behave in exactly the corrupt manner he describes.

Assumptions about the venality of the world outside politics form an important line of defence for the Political Class when accused of low standards or corruption. One Political Class apologist, John Lloyd of the Reuters Institute, attacked the media for highlighting the cases of Peter Mandelson and Stephen Byers, claiming that 'they were pursued not for large derelictions of duty, or crimes, or corruption – but essentially for being human'. It should, however, be remembered that Mandelson made a misleading declaration on a mortgage application form, then involved himself in the request for a passport made by one of the Hinduja brothers at the very moment when they had emerged as donors for the Millennium Dome. Byers lied repeatedly in an interview with the broadcaster Jonathan Dimbleby, by any standards unacceptable conduct from a Cabinet minister.*

This attitude amounts to a misunderstanding of normal, civilised conduct. The casual assertions made by Mulgan about ordinary people are false and insulting: they are nevertheless a symptom of the estrangement of the Political Class from civil society. It is emphatically not acceptable in everyday life to abuse power to enrich yourself or obtain sexual favours. To give two examples, it is a sackable offence for a company buyer to augment his salary by setting up side-deals for private benefit, or for the personnel director of a large company to use the status his position gives him to find a job for a friend or relation. It would probably be against the law as well. It would certainly be against the law if he abused his power to pressurise potential employees into consenting to sex. Any civil servant, member of the armed forces or employee of a private-sector company would be severely disciplined or worse for engaging in the kind of behaviour which Geoff Mulgan claims to regard as normal.

The reality is exactly the other way around. Members of the Political Class have exceptionally poor standards in comparison with ordinary people. They constantly conduct themselves in a way that would be unacceptable in any mainstream organisation, whether in the private sector or in a public body. A very telling example of this disparity of standards is the affair between the Deputy Prime Minister John Prescott and his secretary Tracey Temple, which became public knowledge in April 2006. Prescott would have been sacked on account of his conduct had he worked in practically any other walk of life, as the following report, written by the *Evening Standard* City editor Chris Blackhurst at the height of the storm over Tracey Temple, suggests:

---

* Lloyd's remark is taken from his 'Media Manifesto' in *Prospect* magazine, October 2002. The article merits reading in full as an insight into the special sensibility of the Political Class.

At a dinner party last week I was forcibly struck by the anger in the business community about John Prescott. Around the table were the chairman of one of our largest retailers, the chairman of a pubs group, the spokesman for a major broadcaster, and one of Prescott's Cabinet colleagues.

The latter said little about Prescott, although her view was obvious. She was forced to listen as one by one the other guests said that if anyone had behaved like that in their organisations – a man having an affair with a woman who directly worked for him, and having sex in the office – they would be instantly dismissed. No question. The retailer was able to recall cases where shop managers had been found out and fired. The pub company boss said the same of his staff. But they didn't just say the stricture applied to juniors – if anyone at the top, including themselves, was doing what Prescott did, they would be out.

It was the fact that Tracey Temple answered to Prescott that riled them – that no matter how willing she was, he held power over her. He could, if she'd refused, have made her life a misery; had her moved, blocked her promotion. It would be her word against his and he was John Prescott.[2]

The remarks cited in this commentary capture exquisitely the disconnection between members of the Political Class and civil society. John Prescott's conduct was not merely in flagrant contravention of prevalent norms in the private sector. In early 2006, just months before Prescott's transgression came to light, two policemen were convicted for the offence of having sex with members of the public while on duty. This precedent led Alistair Watson, a retired Glasgow police officer, to make a formal complaint to the Metropolitan Police, calling for an investigation into Prescott's conduct. Watson insisted that his motives were not malicious. 'If there are rules that apply to ordinary people, John Prescott should be treated the same, or more harshly.'[3]

John Prescott is in general a disappointing case because he is not really a member of the Political Class. The son of a railway signalman, Prescott served as a steward in the merchant navy before studying at Ruskin College, Oxford, and becoming a full-time union official. He never sought to change his natural accent or speech pattern, and his obvious authenticity was a massive strength in the fraudulent and manipulative world at Westminster. I was there when he made the wonderful speech that established his national reputation, defending John Smith's reforms to the Labour constitution at the 1993 party conference. His speech was especially powerful because he stood out as a man with strong instincts and values that connected him to a world of basic decency outside politics.

Yet once in power John Prescott succumbed to the hallmark Political Class perception that it is exempt from the rules that apply to ordinary people. His behaviour even flouted the rules for civil servants in his own department, the Office of the Deputy Prime Minister. Shortly after news of the affair broke, a newspaper article reported Tracey Temple's disclosure that she and the Deputy Prime Minister repeatedly had sex behind the open door to his office while his staff worked outside. Yet the 1,000-page guidebook for civil servants in Prescott's department instructed officials not to make 'improper use' of accommodation, furniture and workspace, especially during 'official time'. It also said that innuendo, leering, lewd comments and deliberate brushing against others were to be discouraged because they could lead to claims of sexual harassment, an injunction that was flagrantly broken by both Prescott and Temple, who later told the *Mail on Sunday* that 'things always started with us touching. It might have been me touching his arm, or him patting me on the back. We would kiss and things would go on from there.'[4]

When these rules were drawn to John Prescott's attention, his spokesman replied that the Deputy Prime Minister had not breached the rule-book. He said: 'The guide applies to civil servants, not ministers.' Here Prescott's spokesman was explicitly articulating the ethic of the Political Class, which tolerates one set of standards for politicians and a second, significantly higher standard, for those who work for them. This approach was endorsed by the Prime Minister's spokesman in 10 Downing Street, where Tony Blair gave Prescott his 'full support'.[5]

There is an even greater disjunction between the standards of the Political Class and ordinary voters. In January 2006, as a result of press enquiries, it emerged that the Deputy Prime Minister had failed to pay council tax on his grace-and-favour flat in Admiralty House. During much of this time he had actually been the minister responsible for council tax policy. He subsequently paid some £3,852 in back tax, explaining his omission as an 'inadvertent error based on a genuine misunderstanding'. Meanwhile ordinary taxpayers who failed or neglected to pay their council tax bills faced prosecution.*

This kind of disregard for ordinary rules of conduct or decency is duplicated again and again. David Blunkett, a successful Cabinet minister for the first eight years of the Blair government, was a multiple transgressive who displayed a fundamental inability to understand the distinction between the public and the private domain. His infractions occurred in a number of spheres, most famously in the case of his lover Kimberly Quinn. While Home Secretary he provided Mrs Quinn with first-class rail tickets, intended for MPs' spouses, even though she was actually married to somebody else. He made his official car available to Mrs Quinn for trips between London and his house in Derbyshire. When his affair with Mrs Quinn reached its crisis point two Home Office officials – John Toker, head of news and his private secretary Jonathan Sedgwick – attended a private meeting with her lawyers. This episode appeared to take the two civil servants beyond their proper public role, and deep into the private domain.[6]

---

* Prescott claimed there was no legal obligation to repay this tax. He seems to have considered his Admiralty House flat to be his main residence while regarding his Hull constituency address as his second home. Therefore he paid council tax at a discounted rate for his property in Hull, and was under the mistaken impression that council tax for Admiralty House was paid at the full rate and taken from the general payment he made for the use of the property. See Jon Ungoed-Thomas and Robert Winnett, 'Two Jags and his mystery council tax bill', *Sunday Times*, 18 December 2005.

Defenders of Blunkett maintained that the episodes with the rail tickets and the official car were trivial. However, if either offence had been carried out by an army officer it would have led to serious disciplinary action, potentially even court martial and dismissal. As with the case of the Deputy Prime Minister John Prescott, the Home Secretary was showing contempt for rules that were actually deadly serious for others. Mrs Quinn also made claims, which were denied by Blunkett, that he had ordered a policeman to stand guard outside her front door during the May Day riots in central London, and that he had passed on to her sensitive information about security.[7]

Political Class infractions manifest a constant pattern. On the one hand members of the Political Class are prepared to behave in a way that breaks well-established conventions of correct behaviour. On the other hand they abuse the power given them by their office for personal advantage. This dual transgression has become such a constant theme of British governance in the twenty-first century that the abuses committed by the new Political Class come and go without notice. In September 2006 Tony Blair smashed the tight guidelines concerning leaks of sensitive economic data while making a speech to the Trades Union Congress, telling them that 'tomorrow we will see a fall in unemployment, which is very welcome indeed'.

It was easy to see why Tony Blair issued the information. He was expecting a hostile reception from trade union delegates and it was politically very helpful indeed to deliver some cheerful economic news. Yet had an official inside the Office of National Statistics committed a similar indiscretion he would probably have been sacked. This is because the information was highly sensitive. Sterling rose at once on the Prime Minister's speech because the solid economic news was seen as boosting the chances of an interest rate rise. But there was no apology from Downing Street and a Number 10 spokesman brushed off the episode, saying that it was not a major breach.[8] In order to justify their own very low standards, frequently bordering on the criminal, members of the Political Class habitually seek to defend themselves by pretending that everyone else behaves just as badly, or even worse. Here is the Political Class apologist Polly Toynbee on David Blunkett. For Toynbee, Blunkett's infractions were minor compared to the business sector:

> What is the morality of politics to be judged against? Who do we compare it with? Certainly not the world of private business, the kleptocrats stealing unwarranted salaries from their shareholders and corrupting the values and pay structures of the nation.[9]

This claim that businessmen systematically steal from their shareholders shows an almost disarming naivety about how the world outside Westminster and Whitehall works, a fundamental ignorance which is highly characteristic of the Political Class and its allies. While Toynbee may well be right to claim that high executive salaries are unwarranted and damaging, it is nevertheless the case that they have always been approved by shareholders, and therefore legal. She is also wrong in her claim that senior executives of British companies abuse their private offices, or confuse their fiduciary responsibilities with their private interests, in the way that David Blunkett, John Prescott and other government ministers routinely did. This does, of course, sometimes happen – as it did when the press tycoon Conrad Black abused shareholders' money – but this kind of conduct opens up the likelihood of prosecution. Toynbee's claim that private business has lower standards than Westminster is ignorant and false but nevertheless characteristic of the Political Class. I once asked a well-known Labour minister, over the course of a private dinner, why Tony Blair's government had allowed itself to get caught up in so many sleaze scandals. He replied that the reason was very simple. New Labour had made the decision to distance itself from the unions, and get close to business instead. But he said that meant behaving in the same way that business people behaved and carrying on in a corrupt way. He listened with poorly concealed contempt and incredulity as I explained to him that standards in the British business world were reasonably high –

and certainly far more exacting than was generally the case among politicians.

What emerges here is a contempt for, or possibly an overwhelming ignorance of, the ordinary standards of civil society. In Britain, the great majority of occupations, professions, corporations, institutions and civil associations of one kind or another have evolved over time an exacting set of codes of morality and behaviour. They insist on high standards of honesty and integrity. Members of the Political Class, who have very little experience beyond the connected worlds of the media, politics and public relations, find it extremely hard to understand this. They have a tendency to believe that virtue only resides in the state, and that civil society is largely corrupt, and certainly not to be trusted. In fact, rather than observe a uniquely high set of standards, the Political Class often conducts itself in a way that would be utterly abhorrent to respectable British people.

Case Study 'A': Tory Sleaze in the 1990s

Evidence that sleaze and corruption was returning to Westminster as a systematic feature of British national life first came to light in the 1990s, when John Major's government was brought low by a series of sleaze scandals. These scandals, which at one stage seemed to break out on a weekly basis, can be divided into two categories. The first – and much the more numerous – concerned sexual behaviour. These revelations of homosexual conduct or adulterous affairs were breaches of the Establishment code of ethics, based ultimately on religious teaching, discussed in the last chapter. Today they would be regarded as carrying zero public significance.

The second kind of scandal concerned the abuse of power or public office for apparent financial gain. The most notorious of these cases concerned the Cabinet minister Jonathan Aitken, who perjured himself over his connection (which remains mysterious today) with a foreign businessman. In addition to the Aitken case a number of Conservative MPs were caught out accepting what were effectively cash bribes in return for asking parliamentary questions or lobbying on behalf of business interests. One of these MPs – David Tredinnick, who fell victim to a newspaper sting operation when he agreed with an undercover reporter to put down a parliamentary question in return for cash – remains a Member of Parliament today.

It was extremely tempting at the time to interpret these trans-gressions as a manifestation of the nepotism and corruption of the dying British Establishment. The Labour opposition, led by the dynamic young Tony Blair, very naturally sought to present the succession of Tory sleaze stories in exactly this way. Furthermore some of the sleaziest Tories – above all the languid and charming Jonathan Aitken, with his shadowy business life and rumoured links with British intelligence – seemed to fit precisely into this paradigm.

Yet the perspective of hindsight enables one to see that this was not the case. Far from being a symbol of old-fashioned corruption, the financial scandals of the Tory years signalled something new. They were the first indications of the arrival of a Political Class that was discarding the codes of conduct which had governed Britain during the era of Establishment dominance. This new elite did not see Parliament as a place to serve the public good. Rather they saw it as a promising vehicle for self-enrichment. As I will vividly show in the course of this book, New Labour's pledges to clean up British public life were wholly misleading and illusory. There is a horrifying continuity between the sleaze of the final years of the John Major administration, and the embedded abuses of New Labour in government.

Case Study 'B': Cherie Blair and the Collapse of Boundaries

The case of Cherie Blair, spouse of the Prime Minister for ten years from 1997, provides a grotesque illustration of the attitudes and practices of the new Political Class. The Prime Minister's wife manifested a new morality in the heart of government, namely that it was acceptable to use the highest office as a method of personal enrichment. With Cherie Blair, the boundaries between the public and private domain vanished. She treated public officials as if they were there for her personal use. This systematic failure to distinguish between the private and the public makes Mrs Blair an interestingly pre-modern figure. She would have been a familiar part of the landscape in the mid-eighteenth century, when the governing class made little secret that it sought public office as a vehicle for pursuing self-interest.

The arrival of Mrs Blair marked a break-point. Previous spouses at Number 10 had been relatively modest and unobtrusive, and had never sought to exploit their position financially. In the 1960s, officials warned Mary, wife of Harold Wilson and a talented poet, on no account to receive the sum of £33 for some verses she had published in a magazine.[10] They informed her that doing so could be seen as trading on her husband's position as Prime Minister. Mary Wilson complied without complaint. Cherie Blair's conduct could not have been more different. She blatantly made use of her position as the Prime Minister's wife – or Britain's 'First Lady', as she was unconstitutionally labelled in the American market that provided an important source of income – in order to earn hundreds of thousands of dollars for delivering lectures and speeches in the international marketplace.*

Mrs Blair placed herself on the books of the Harry Walker Agency, the New York-based company which represents clients as senior as Bill Clinton and Henry Kissinger. Though she formally marketed herself as Cherie Booth, her maiden name, Harry Walker nevertheless left no one in any doubt about her connection with Tony Blair. This connection proved profitable. In February 2006, for example, she reportedly earned some £150,000 in a tour of the

---

* Cherie Blair justified her conduct during the filming of the documentary *The Real Cherie*, when asked about it by the BBC journalist Fiona Bruce, saying, 'I probably make a hundred speeches a year. Of these ten are for payment. There is no way I have exploited my position.'

United States which involved at least five speaking engagements. The previous year she is thought to have earned at least £140,000 for eight days' work.[11] In June 2005 she was paid some £30,000 to be interviewed before an audience by the CNN anchorwoman Paula Zahn, given while Tony Blair was on an official visit to the White House. Sir David Manning, British ambassador to Washington and seemingly willing to stretch any point well beyond the cause of duty as far as Tony and Cherie Blair were concerned, made a warm-up speech. When questioned over the trip, Downing Street insisted that it was 'normal procedure' for the British ambassador to accompany or to introduce 'any prominent British citizen visiting Washington'.[12]

Mrs Blair's behaviour on this occasion nevertheless stretched the tolerance of the Prime Minister's civil service advisers past breaking point. She was strongly advised in advance not to take up this engagement by Cabinet Secretary Andrew Turnbull. Turnbull urged her not to embark on the undertaking at all adding that, if she did insist on going ahead, she should donate her fee to charity. Cherie ignored this advice, saying, 'Maybe we should not have done this, but we are in too deep.'[13]

At the start of 2006, the British embassy in Saudi Arabia complained after the Harry Walker Agency arranged for Cherie Blair to address the Jeddah Economic Forum for a speaking fee of £25,000. Embassy staff picked up Mrs Blair at 1am when she and her staff flew in for their twenty-four-hour stay. A Saudi government press release described her as 'Cherie Blair, wife of British Prime Minister Tony Blair'. She was listed on the programme under her professional name Cherie Booth QC, but an internet link added a profile beginning 'Cherie Blair QC is the wife of the British Prime Minister'.

Conference organisers say that it is not normal for speakers to get paid for the Jeddah Forum, although it sometimes does happen. It certainly marked a breach with custom for the wife of a serving Prime Minister to demand a fee for this kind of engagement. Downing Street, however, insisted that Cherie Blair was attending in a private capacity, adding that her appearance was not a breach of Whitehall's ministerial code which forbids ministers from exploiting their status to allow spouses to earn money. 'Mrs Blair is a leading international human-rights lawyer,' insisted a spokeswoman, 'and was in Jeddah in a private, professional capacity to lecture on human rights. She appeared in the conference programme as Cherie Booth. The ministerial code does not apply.'[14]

Cherie Blair's speaking tour of Australia at the start of 2005 was another notable infraction. She agreed to make a series of speeches, one to raise funds for the Children's Cancer Institute Australia (CCIA), a research charity. Rather than do the work for free – as would have been expected of a Prime Minister's wife – Cherie Blair shockingly agreed to accept money. She was billed as a 'writer, lawyer, human rights advocate'. According to the publicity literature a VIP table for ten to include 'pre-dinner cocktails' and a 'photo-opportunity' cost £4,100.[15] According to the provisional schedule of expenses agreed for the tour, Cherie Blair was to receive the prodigious sum of £102,600 for the tour, while the charity was booked to receive a 'minimum' fee of £99,900. Whether it did remains open to question. It later emerged that the CCIA breached fundraising laws in Victoria at Cherie Blair's function. An investigation carried out by Consumer Affairs Victoria, a state agency, found that 'the Victorian fundraising dinner raised gross appeal proceeds of $192,114. While the amount passed on to, or available to be passed on to beneficiaries was $15,800, or 8.22 per cent of gross appeal proceeds.' In other words the vast bulk of the earnings of the Victoria event went on the dinner itself and the guest speaker. Mrs Blair's fee is estimated to have been significantly larger than the sum raised for charity at this event.

The second way that Cherie Blair used her position in Downing Street to leverage personal financial advantage was the extraction of discounts and even giveaways from retailers. She was flagrant about this. One Christmas she rang Greg Dyke, in his capacity as a board director of Manchester United FC, to ask him if he could arrange a discount on a club shirt for her son Euan. 'Cherie Blair, whom I knew quite well, rang one Christmas to ask if I could get a discount on a Manchester United shirt. Her son, Euan, wanted David Beckham's number 7. I offered to give her the shirt for free, but she insisted on paying. For a while I was tempted to keep the cheque Cherie sent me for the shirt and frame it; in the end I decided the money was more important than the memento, so I cashed it.'[16] She reportedly used her lifestyle guru Carole Caplin to negotiate thousands of pounds' worth of discounts on designer clothes and other fashion accessories. Details of these arrangements are hard to obtain because those who entered into the deals were obliged to sign confidentiality agreements. Jewellery designer Sarah Jordon told the *Sunday Times*: 'I have signed a confidentiality agreement. I would not be able to make any comment because my neck's on the line.'[17] Once again, senior civil servants felt compelled to warn Cherie Blair about her conduct. The Cabinet Secretary Andrew Turnbull told Cherie Blair that she was receiving items so cheaply that they were effectively gifts. Senior Whitehall sources say that Turnbull compared these commercial arrangements to a 'firm sponsoring the Prime Minister's wife'. He concluded that Cherie Blair should either disclose these items as gifts or not accept them at all. Cherie Blair angrily rejected this advice, informing Britain's most senior civil servant: 'You are infringing my rights under the European Convention of Human Rights.' Mrs Blair, who is a leading human-rights lawyer at Matrix Chambers, insisted that the law gave her the right to 'enjoy her possessions' without the interference of the state.[18]

On overseas trips Cherie Blair was yet more demanding. In Melbourne in 2003 Mrs Blair and her children visited the designer store Globe International, where as a courtesy she was invited to help herself to a 'few items' as a gesture of 'hospitality to the wife of the second most powerful man in the world'. She responded by helping herself to sixty pieces or more. According to one witness: 'It was an invitation to pick out a few items and they walked out with seventy.' Downing Street later stated that Mrs Blair had repaid in full the £2,000 value of the goods taken.[19]

On one occasion, making a business trip to Istanbul, Mrs Blair arrived at Heathrow Airport to discover that she had left her passport behind. She summoned the full weight of the Downing Street machine to her rescue. A police motorcyclist, a member of Scotland Yard's elite Diplomatic Protection Group, was dispatched to retrieve the passport from Downing Street. He then hurtled through the London traffic – siren sounding and blue lights flashing – to deliver the passport. Meanwhile the plane was delayed until Cherie Blair could take her seat. When asked about this episode, Downing Street said: 'We have nothing to say on the matter. She was travelling in her capacity as a barrister.'[20]

During visits to China in 2003 and 2005 she spent lavishly on the freshwater pearls for which the country is famous. According to staff at Tongs Jewellers, in Beijing's Pearl Market, the Prime Minister's wife achieved discounts of 50 per cent or more on her jewel purchases. The staff said that while ordinary customers might achieve a 10 or 20 per cent discount 'for her we do 50 per cent'. They said that she had paid some 5,000 yuan, or around £335, for a three-string necklace but that 'normally the price is 5,000 yuan for one string'. During these bargain-hunting trips in China, Mrs Blair used British diplomats as her 'personal shoppers'. Consulate staff visited a Shanghai silk shop, and ordered made-to-measure dresses on behalf of Mrs Blair. According to the general manager of the Silk King store, Wan Hong Lam: 'Two foreigners came to our shop and chose three pieces of silk. I found out later that they were from the British consulate. They picked out materials and styles and asked us to make three items of silk clothing for a female customer. They gave me measurements but they did not tell me who the customer was.' Wan Hong Lam was instructed to take the finished items to the Westin Hotel, where the Blairs were staying. 'I was shown into a big, luxurious room. I was very surprised to find Tony and Cherie Blair in front of me. I was awe-struck and surprised to find we had been making clothes for the First Lady of Great Britain.'[21]

This aggressive pursuit of goods from shops and designers fitted into a pattern of behaviour also manifest in the Blairs' predatory search for holiday villas, where they were not expected to pay the bill, or at any rate not much of it. It was also consistent with the arrangements which surrounded her book about previous Downing Street spouses, *The Goldfish Bowl: Married to the Prime Minister*.* The work was heavily reliant on the testimony of previous occupants of Downing Street. However, Mrs Blair and her co-author Cate Haste were as happy to make use of the *ex gratia* contributions of these former Downing Street denizens as they were to take a reported £50,000 advance on their work from the publishers. Once again, Cherie Blair's conduct appalled Cabinet Secretary Andrew Turnbull, who was alarmed that she might be seen to be benefiting from the efforts of previous Downing Street spouses, including Norma Major, Mary Wilson and Clarissa Eden, who all contributed for free. But Downing Street argued that Mrs Blair was not breaking the rule prohibiting Prime Ministers' wives from talking about current life in Downing Street because the book was mainly about the experience of other spouses.

There were perhaps grounds for sympathy in the case of Mrs Blair. She was the first prime ministerial wife to be a career woman. The secondary, anonymous role which had been the lot of earlier Number 10 wives did not come easily for her. She did plenty of unsung and, for that matter, unpaid work for charities and others along the traditional model. To cite just one piece of testimony Nina Kapur of Breast Cancer Care, for which Cherie Blair was patron, has said her work was 'well beyond the call of duty. She puts herself out for us, gave us an evening at Chequers for our key donors, her idea.'[22] There is no law which would have forced Cherie Blair to have donated earnings from lectures to charity. Nevertheless Cherie Blair is one of a number of transgressive figures who have emerged at the top of British politics. Her failure to distinguish between the public and the private domain was characteristic of the new Political Class.

By the end of her stay in Downing Street Mrs Blair had become a leading member of what was in effect a British version of the

---

* The book was published by Random House, whose Chief Executive Gail Rebuck is married to the Downing Street adviser Philip Gould.

old Soviet *nomenklatura*, a member of a privileged elite who did not have to adhere to the rules and norms set down for the bulk of the population.

Case Study 'C': The Malign Influence of Charles and Jonathan Powell

Cherie Blair makes an especially interesting study in one special aspect of Political Class behaviour: a catastrophic confusion of private interest and public role. She is a frightening illustration of the way the collapse of the institutional structure of the state has opened up the path to a kind of predatory individualism which uses public life as a method of self-enrichment. We have already seen this confusion at work in Case Study 'A' above, where Tory MPs used their privileged position in Parliament not for serving the public good but for making money.

The career trajectories of Charles and Jonathan Powell also tell a story about the corruption of the Political Class. But it is a moral form of corruption, with no suggestion at all that either man used his position inside Downing Street as a vehicle for personal gain. Both men are nevertheless moral transgressives. First the elder brother Charles, then the younger brother Jonathan, smashed the dividing lines that used to separate the interests of political parties from the state.

These boundaries, painstakingly put in place by the Victorians and scrupulously maintained by the Whitehall mandarins of the first three-quarters of the twentieth century, have been wiped out by the Political Class. It has created instead a curious new borderland between public and private and between party and state. This is treacherous and to some extent lawless territory, and a new category of men and women has emerged to exploit it.

In some cases these creatures started out as members of the Political Class who moved across into the public sector, but without leaving behind their earlier political affiliations. In other cases they began life as public servants, but gradually allowed the neutrality of their public role to be elided into political partisanship. This heavily compromised group of men and women are now among the most emblematic figures in the British ruling elite, just as the dour but irreproachable figure of the permanent secretary was deemed to symbolise the governing ethic of the previous epoch.

Both Powells rose to occupy extremely influential roles inside Downing Street, Charles on behalf of Margaret Thatcher and his younger brother Jonathan for Tony Blair. The two men affect different personal styles. Charles (now ennobled as Lord Powell of Bayswater) claims to be Tory in his sympathies, while Jonathan is conventionally held to be Labour, though the extent of his loyalty to the Labour Party as a whole rather than to Tony Blair personally is by no means clear. When Charles Powell was informed about his brother's lifelong sympathy with the Labour Party he is reported to have replied: 'Well, it's news to me.'[23] In practice both brothers effectively acted as instruments of personal rule, and neither was in any meaningful sense a party man. Lord Powell pronounces their common family name as 'pole', with just one syllable. This was the same pronunciation that was preferred by the notoriously snobbish society novelist Anthony Powell, whose most memorable character Kenneth Widmerpool anticipated in a number of respects the kind of conduct that would today be associated with the Political Class. Jonathan Powell, by contrast, prefers the more commonplace two-syllable usage of 'pow-el', as in towel.

In essentials, however, the two brothers – sons of an air vice-marshal – are uncannily alike. They are both almost perfect manifestations of the new elite which has risen to prominence at the expense both of the old civil service mandarins and the traditional school of British politicians. Close study of their extraordinary joint success is extremely revealing about the way the machinery of the British state has evolved during the last twenty-five years. The key point about the Powells is that they are both apparatchiks rather than public servants. Though exercising considerable power, they are not accountable. Indeed both Charles

Powell and Jonathan Powell consistently turned down requests to give evidence before Parliament, claiming an exemption that is never available either to ministers or to civil servants. For instance, Charles Powell avoided giving evidence to the Foreign Affairs Select Committee in 1994 during their investigation of the Pergau Dam affair, in which he had been centrally involved. Jonathan Powell rebuffed attempts to bring him before committees.[24]

They both occupied a secretive role that was essentially anti-democratic. They are hauntingly reminiscent of the long period of Soviet communism in Eastern Europe rather than the high noon of representative democracy in Britain.

Charles Powell's considerable powers arose by chance. When he went to work as Private Secretary to Margaret Thatcher in 1984 he was an ordinary civil servant. His job, though offering constant access to the Prime Minister, was normally offered to high-flying officials destined for the very top of the Foreign Office. Powell's special task was to act as liaison between the Foreign Office and Downing Street, and to serve as the Prime Minister's adviser on foreign affairs and defence.

The singularity of Charles Powell was that he soon developed exceptionally strong personal links with the Prime Minister of the day that went far beyond his official role. Previous occupants of his post had spent two to four years at most before moving on. Not so Powell. He stayed for seven years, right up to and beyond the moment that Margaret Thatcher herself quit, helping John Major bed in to his role during his first year. Previous incumbents retained a strong loyalty and connection with the Foreign Office.[25] By the end, Powell appeared to be giving his loyalty exclusively to Margaret Thatcher. Previous occupants of the post understood from their rigorous Foreign Office training that they were fundamentally servants of the Crown. Powell transferred his allegiance from directly to the Crown and gave naked political support to the leader of a political party. The case was later put very bluntly by Nigel Lawson in his autobiography: 'He never saw it as his role to question her prejudices, merely to refine the language in which they were expressed. And like [Bernard] Ingham, he stayed at

Number 10 far too long.'[26] Powell actively involved himself in partisan lobbying, for example – as Alan Clark recorded – pressing the *Telegraph* proprietor Conrad Black to swing the newspaper behind Margaret Thatcher in 1990.[27]

By this stage of his career Charles Powell had effectively severed his links with the Foreign Office. Once again Alan Clark is illuminating about this transgression: take his account of a conversation with Charles Powell's wife Carla at a Lancaster House lunch in September 1988: 'Carla told me that Charles was *not* leaving immediately, but they were terribly short of money, having to borrow against the little house in Laghi which had been left to her by her father. He didn't want an Embassy, not unless a real cracker (by which I inferred Paris or Washington), would rather go straight into the City.'[28] Powell's career as a public servant effectively came to an end when Margaret Thatcher ceased to be Prime Minister. Thereafter he continued to pursue his business career, retaining connections with a group of powerful businessmen, many of whom were close admirers of Margaret Thatcher, the most important by far being the Syrian billionaire Wafiq Said. Powell's official CV now states that he is 'currently Chairman of Sagitta Asset Management Limited, and Chairman of LVMH, Louis Vuitton Moët-Hennessy in the UK. He is a board member of, among others, the Textron Corporation, Caterpillar Inc., LVMH, Mandarin Oriental Hotel Group, Schindler Corporation, Northern Trust Global Services, Yell Group, Matheson & Co., and British Mediterranean Airways. He also holds a number of other positions, in particular President of the China–Britain Business Council, Chairman of the Trustees of the Oxford Business School and a Trustee of the British Museum.'

Jonathan Powell enjoyed an equally powerful and shadowy role in Tony Blair's Downing Street, though with one very important difference. Jonathan Powell's position did not arise by accident, as was the case with Charles, but was deliberate to the extent of being worked out in advance. Like his brother, Jonathan Powell was a career diplomat. He first met Tony Blair while serving in the British embassy in Washington. Blair was then the leader of the opposition, and Powell was deputed to look after him on a visit. The two men got on well, and Powell was quickly offered the post of chief of staff in Blair's private office, a move that was deemed irregular inside the Foreign Office.[29]

This work involved some responsibility for the future Prime Minister's extremely controversial 'blind trust'. Thus right from the start a conflict of interest was embedded in Jonathan Powell's role. On the one hand he was involved in intricate New Labour funding arrangements, though Powell (like Tony Blair) denied being aware of the identity of individual donors. On the other hand he was one of a small group of men and women who advised the Prime Minister on access to his private office and the handling of policy issues.

Jonathan Powell's role was always likely to involve exactly the kind of conflict between private interests and the government machine which the creators of the modern British civil service had sought to eliminate. On the one hand it was Powell's job to help raise money for the Labour Party and Tony Blair personally. On the other he helped to make key decisions about policies and other matters that were important to those donors. While in opposition this conflict was mainly of concern to the Labour Party. However, it became a matter of relevance to the nation at large in the wake of the Labour election victory in 1997. This conflict, which manifested itself again and again in the Blair government, came to public attention very quickly indeed with the scandal surrounding relations between the Formula One tycoon Bernie Ecclestone and 10 Downing Street, which burst to the surface in the autumn of 1997.

According to Tony Blair's biographer Anthony Seldon, it was Powell who had first made the move to contact Ecclestone when Labour was in opposition.[30] It has been widely reported that it was Powell who set up the meeting on 16 October 1997 when Ecclestone and other figures from the industry made the case for a special exemption from the European directive banning tobacco sponsorship in sport.[31] Tony Blair accepted the Formula One case, and then announced that he was going to try to secure an exemption. Powell appears to have issued no warning about the wisdom of this course of action, which is perhaps surprising in view of the fact that Ecclestone had already donated £1 million to New Labour, and was coming under pressure from party fundraisers to give even more. Powell reportedly took no formal minute of the meeting, an omission that anticipates later Downing Street failures to take records of meetings at sensitive times.

It is exceptionally difficult to gain an accurate picture of Jonathan Powell's position in Downing Street since for the most part his role has remained opaque and he is not publicly account-able. Nevertheless he received unwelcome publicity in the large financial scandals which from time to time afflicted New Labour, owing to his function connecting private interests with the machin-ery of government. There seems little question that Jonathan Powell played a luminous role in the events leading up to the Hinduja passports scandal, which caused the second resignation of Peter Mandelson from the Cabinet at the start of 2001, and is described more fully in the next chapter. According to Andrew Rawnsley's extremely well-informed description of New Labour in power, *Servants of the People*:

> As with Bernie Ecclestone, the Prime Minister's chief of staff was the main linkman with these wealthy men. There was an exchange of warm correspondence with the brothers – either signed by Jonathan Powell or 'yours ever, Tony' ... According to Peter Mandelson's allies, it was actually No. 10 that first initiated the involvement of the Hindujas in the sponsorship of the Dome. Supporters of Mandelson say that Powell sent him an official minute suggesting to the then Dome Minister that they were offering money. Written in Powell's typically blunt style, the minute informed Mandelson that SP Hinduja had approached the Prime Minister with an offer to donate to the Dome. Powell told Mandelson that the Prime Minister wanted him to follow this up without delay.[32]

Jonathan and Charles Powell were both adroit operators. They both worked best behind closed doors. They were both post-democratic figures, masters of the quick fix and the backstairs deal. Though there is no evidence at all that either brother did anything illegal, they were party to a great deal that would in traditional terms be seen as highly irregular. It is no coincidence that their rise to power from the mid-1980s onwards coincided with the collapse of the public domain, a shocking fall in standards of British public life and the emergence of the Political Class.

4

THE FINANCIAL STRUCTURE OF THE POLITICAL CLASS

'Politics has now become a gainful profession, like advocacy, stockbroking, the dry goods trade, or the getting up of companies. People go into it to live by it, primarily for the sake of the salaries attached to the places they count on getting, secondarily in view of the opportunities it affords of making incidental and sometimes illegitimate gains' – James Bryce, *The American Commonwealth* (1888)

The Political Class has emerged out of the wreckage of the party system. The Labour and Conservative parties both collapsed in the sixty years that have passed since the end of the Second World War. The process of decomposition has been so rapid and profound that it is today misleading to assume that the main political parties have anything meaningful in common with the party system as it existed fifty years ago.

This assumption remains embedded, however, in a great deal of political reporting. The mistake is excusable because many of the most obvious characteristics of traditional political parties still exist and even appear to flourish: annual conferences at seaside resorts; election manifestos; party leaders; an approved list of candidates; constituency agents (though a sharply diminished number of these). However, their more substantial characteristics have changed beyond recognition. The central point to make is that the mainstream parties have lost the overwhelming majority of their members. The Conservatives peaked at 2.8 million members after the Second World War, while Labour also had well over 2 million members in the 1950s. Since then memberships have slumped to approximately 10 per cent of what they were, with the Tories claiming around 250,000 and Labour just under 200,000 members. Even these meagre figures are probably over-estimates. This dramatic change in numbers is very profound. It is as if the National Health Service, instead of employing 1 million people, as it does today, were to employ significantly less than 100,000. Such a change would not merely be quantitative. It would also mean a devastating and fundamental change in the nature and the function of the NHS. In many ways it would be true to say that the NHS no longer existed at all. Rather than the healthy mass-membership parties as they were through the first two-thirds of the twentieth century, the Conservatives and Labour are now husks.

Secondly, fifty years ago both parties definitely possessed sharply defined economic and social identities. Labour was exactly what it claimed to be: the party of the labouring man (though leavened by a handful of middle-class intellectuals). The Conservatives were less easy to define with precision, because they already possessed some of the diffuse and inchoate characteristics of the late-twentieth-century political party. Nevertheless, generally speaking the Tory party represented the professional and propertied classes. Nowadays it is impossible to make this distinction. Indeed many of the richest men and women in Britain support Labour – in a surprisingly large number of cases, going to the lengths of serving as ministers. Both parties, for reasons of electoral advantage, have sought to widen their base by turning their back on the people they once represented.

Thirdly, neither party any longer claims to press forward the kind of clear programme for action aimed at benefiting their mainstream supporters. They have become coalitions of interest groups. Their basic electoral proposition is the ability to provide a competence and integrity missing among their opponents, rather than any thoroughgoing attempt to address the concerns of their core voters. Political parties, now lacking an over-riding moral purpose or powerful membership base, have been turned into deracinated vehicles for the ambition of the Political Class. Going back fifty or one hundred years, Labour MPs were no more than manifestations of the collective will of the national membership, sent into Parliament to put into effect the will of the party conference. This relationship has been wholly put into reverse, and the residual function of Labour members has mainly become to legitimise the direct rule of the party leader. The Tory leader David Cameron is now attempting to impose the same type of relationship on his own party members.

These are all important changes, with far-reaching consequences for political debate and conduct, the most important of which will be carefully examined in the final chapter. The most urgent consequence, however, is financial. The collapse of the membership base has had a disastrous effect on the income of both the Labour and the Conservative Party. The mass parties of the mid-twentieth century were able to appeal for funds to their millions of members, as well as affiliated organisations such as trade unions. Furthermore, twentieth-century political organisations enjoyed ready access to a pool of volunteer workers. These no longer exist, forcing modern parties into capital-intensive methods of communicating with voters, such as phone banks, advertising and focus groups. The cost of running a political party has therefore risen very sharply, at precisely the same time that income from membership has fallen.

Modern political parties wishing to avoid bankruptcy and collapse have been forced to turn to the state for resources. There are two ways of doing this: first through direct subsidy and secondly by exploiting their privileged access to government in order to make decisions which have meaningful financial or other helpful implications for large corporations and private business. This kind of covert exchange between donors and politicians – whether expressed through distorted decisions on public policy, the exchange of honours for donations, the issue of visas and passports to foreign billionaires as well as other favours – has become a systemic part of mainstream British governance.

The purchase of access to senior politicians by the business elite has now become a normal function of British politics. Businessmen view friendly contact with leading politicians, particularly members of the governing party, as a core part of their job. They recognise that the only way this access can be reliably achieved is by paying for it.

This connection between the business elite and the leadership of the main political parties is extremely visible at annual party conferences. These events remain as a yearly point of connection when the party leadership makes itself accountable to the membership. In practice, however, the opportunity for rank-and-file party members to affect policy is extremely limited. Indeed, it has become common practice for the party political directorate ostentatiously to disregard the opinion of the membership.

A key modern function of party conferences is as a marketplace for business leaders to press their case with politicians. This change is especially obvious at the Labour conference, which now has the atmosphere of a corporate away-day, reflecting partial ownership of the political system by a newly enfranchised business elite. Paradoxically, recent Conservative conferences, despite the party's historic affinity with business, have exuded less of this corporate aura. The full measure of Conservative Party isolation after 1997 can be measured by the fact that for a number of years the most opulent social event at its annual conference was hosted by the Tobacco Manufacturers' Federation. This contradiction is readily explained. The overwhelming interest of big business is to influence specific government policies: property developers need planning consents; supermarkets out-of-town sites; consultancy firms are on the look-out for government contracts; airlines want slots for big hub airports. Opposition parties are in no position to deliver these tangible rewards.

However, opposition parties on the verge of winning power are always worth cultivating, as the essential case study of the accounting firm Arthur Andersen and New Labour illustrates. Arthur Andersen, though one of the world's great accountancy practices, was barred from doing business with the British government following the collapse of the John DeLorean car-manufacturing business in Northern Ireland. After DeLorean's failure, the Thatcher government sued Arthur Andersen for negligence, and placed the accountants on an unofficial Whitehall blacklist. Arthur Andersen's one hope seems to have been a change of administration. In the run-up to the 1997 General Election many of Andersen's best brains were placed at the disposal of New Labour. Its partners advised on the imposition of a windfall tax on privatised utilities, important tax reforms, the private finance initiative, and much more besides. After the 1997 election the reward was instant. Key Andersen personnel joined the Treasury on secondment, while once again government contracts flowed. The thirteen-year-old DeLorean court case was settled within months, at a fraction of the price the Conservative government had been demanding.*

Generally speaking, large business donors attach themselves opportunistically to successful political parties. This was demonstrably the case with New Labour in 1997, many of whose donors had shown no previous interest in the Labour Party and were encouraged for that very reason.

At these annual party conferences, there is an active market in access to Cabinet ministers, their advisers, and other prominent figures who have the ability to influence government policy. Typically these arrangements are brokered by corporate lobbyists. At the 2006 Labour conference Bell Pottinger Public Affairs, a well-connected firm founded by Margaret Thatcher's advertising guru Tim Bell, offered its clients a package of meetings with two Cabinet ministers, two ministers of state and three MPs, at an estimated cost of some £5,000.[1] This was just one tiny example among many. The Labour Party regularly sells access to the Prime Minister and

---

* Unfortunately the collapse of the US energy giant Enron amidst charges of financial malpractice once again brought Arthur Andersen into disrepute. On 15 June 2002, Andersen was convicted of obstruction of justice for shredding documents related to its audit of Enron. The firm agreed to surrender its licences and its right to practise before the Securities and Exchange Commission, a move which effectively ended the company's operations.

others. Senior businessmen are offered 'face time' with ministers and other special privileges on the day of the leader's speech. In addition, companies take stalls at conference. Though these are costly and almost never show tangible reward, companies are warned by the Labour Party that failing to take a stall will damage their relations. According to one corporate lobbyist, 'Labour always presses us into taking a stall, so we go. They charge a huge fee for the stalls, so this is our way of funding the party without appearing to do so.'[2] Numerous charities have stalls at party conferences. These charities are in general heavily dependent on government subventions, and their presence at party conferences is a discreet way of making a payback to their allies within the Political Class. Overall, Labour's annual party conference is viewed by party figures as an extremely important fundraising tool.

It is also normal for the Conservative Party to use access to the party leader as a saleable commodity. The Conservative Party has formed a so-called 'Leader's Club', which gives businessmen who pay up to £50,000 to party funds regular access to David Cameron by attending dinners and through private conversations. The club is based on the Labour Party's Thousand Club, set up in the late 1990s in order to get businessmen to exchange cash for access to senior party figures.[3]

There is no question that this type of access pays off in terms of favourable treatment in regulatory and other issues. We have already seen how New Labour granted the Formula One tycoon Bernie Ecclestone a special exemption from the overall ban on tobacco advertising after Ecclestone had donated £1 million to party coffers. Labour also received £1 million, ahead of the 1997 election, from the Political Animal lobby, a group which lobbied successfully for a hunting ban.

Tony Blair also lobbied on behalf of the international steel group LNM with his Romanian counterpart in order to help it acquire a local steel plant. The company was not – as Downing Street claimed – a 'British company'. The Prime Minister's readiness to involve himself in the affairs of a free-wheeling international enterprise is completely mysterious until one grasps that LNM was a major contributor to Labour Party funds.

An absorbing case, which casts an important light on the conduct of modern British government, concerns the passport acquired by Srichand Hinduja, the Indian billionaire, in 1998. The Hinduja family was swift to establish close relations with New Labour ministers after 1997, though stopped short of giving money to the Labour Party, perhaps because it would have been illegal for foreign nationals to do so. Nevertheless Hinduja family interests gave a large sum of money in 1998 to the Millennium Dome, then an urgent priority for New Labour, described by the BBC as something to be 'highlighted as a glittering New Labour achievement in the next election manifesto'.[4]

The report compiled by the former civil servant Sir Anthony Hammond into the Hinduja affair exonerated ministers and described the passport application as having been 'handled properly and within established criteria'.[5] However, the materials assembled within the report contradicted Sir Anthony's conclusion. He revealed that a special exception in the 1981 British Nationality Act had been invoked in order to facilitate Srichand Hinduja's passport application. The Act requires candidates for nationalisation to be absent from Britain for 'not more than 450 days'. Hinduja had been absent, according to figures provided by his own solicitors, for 819 days. Nevertheless, Hinduja received his passport within six months of applying, compared with the average twenty months taken for an application. No checks – either to the Inland Revenue or the Foreign Office – were made. If they had been, officials would have learned the disconcerting news that investigations by the Indian authorities into the Hinduja role in the Bofors arms scandal had intensified. In a departure from normal procedure Andrew Walmsley, director of the Immigration of Nationality Directorate, chose to handle the application personally rather than pass it on to staff.

An exceptionally interesting study is the influence of the so-called private equity business on government policy over the past decade or more. Ministers have proved extremely susceptible to lobbying by the British Venture Capital Association, the industry body. For example, in 2003 Gordon Brown dropped plans for a change in the way the venture capital funds were taxed. The year after, ministers abandoned proposals to toughen up their responsibilities for employee pension rights. Above all, Gordon Brown opened the way for private equity entrepreneurs to make massive fortunes when he slashed the rate of capital gains tax just after becoming Chancellor.* It should be noted that this support has come at the expense of Labour's traditional backers in the trade union movement and among ordinary Labour activists, who vigorously complain that the massive fortunes made by some private equity moguls has come at the expense of lost jobs and cynical asset-stripping.

At the same time, the private equity industry has injected millions of pounds' worth of donations not just into the governing Labour Party but into the Conservative opposition. Both parties give important public support to the very controversial private equity movement. There is no proof that there is the slightest connection between these large donations to the Labour Party (mainly from people who, like Sir Ronald Cohen, appear to have shown little interest in Labour until it was on the verge of power) and the generous tax treatments to the private equity industry. Nevertheless the coincidence between an extremely favourable tax treatment of an industry which has formed the basis of a number of massive fortunes, and substantial donations to political parties, is worthy of note.

For the first time since the eighteenth century, individuals are

---

* These so-called 'taper-relief' rules allowed executives at private equity firms to pay tax at a far lower rate than the great majority of the population, often as low as 10 per cent, so long as the private equity firm held on to its investment for more than two years before passing it on. This exemption staggered even some top figures within the private equity industry. For instance Nicholas Ferguson, chairman of SVG Capital, remarked in June 2007 that 'any common-sense person would say that a highly paid private equity executive paying less tax than a cleaning lady or other low-paid workers ... can't be right'. See Martin Arnold, 'Buy-out tax-rate is "lower than a cleaner's"', *Financial Times*, 4 June 2007.

beginning to purchase ministerial posts. There have been a number of examples of important donors entering the government, but the most remarkable concerns Lord Sainsbury of Turville, who received his peerage after Labour's 1997 General Election victory and then served as a minister in the Blair government for eight years until 2006. Sainsbury was chairman of the family supermarket chain for seven years until 1998, and only joined Labour at a late stage. He lacked many of the credentials that conventionally lead to ministerial preferment, and it is improbable that he would have become a peer – let alone a minister – but for his donations to the Labour Party. These were so substantial that for many years the most important financial props for the Labour government have been Lord Sainsbury (who turned out to be a decent and reasonably competent government minister) and the trade union movement.

Financing the Political Class

The emergence of a marketplace in influence and access has become the dominant fact of political life. Public trust in a democratic system of government can only be sustained if it is open to all. In Britain by the turn of the twenty-first century this was clearly not the case. The collapse of political parties as civic institutions had enabled them to be captured by financial interests, acting in alliance with the upstart Political Class.

Another example of a sustained attack on common values concerned the degradation of the honours system. The idea behind this system is easy to comprehend. Public honours are an important way that society can recognise those who have contributed to the common good. This contribution should never be monetary: honours acknowledge public service. That is why civil servants, charity workers, diplomats, educationalists and soldiers have always received a high preponderance of honours. According to the Cabinet Office website, the award of an honour 'reflects and pays tribute to outstanding achievement and service right across the community'. This residual function of the honours system still exists.

However, the Political Class responded to the collapse of party finances by removing the awarding of certain honours from the public domain, and aligning it instead with the market sector. Alongside recognising exemplary public service, honours began to be exchanged for cash donations or loans to party funds, or as a method of paying back favours and sometimes silencing party dissent. The purchase of honours had been made illegal by an Act of Parliament in 1925, a move which can be understood in retrospect as the final push in the great nineteenth-century surge of legislation aimed at cleaning up public life. As public standards fell precipitately over the final quarter of the twentieth century, the Political Class made a collective decision to smash the boundaries between public and private and once again exploit the honours system for financial gain.

By the early twenty-first century the sale of honours had once again become overt. A study of the system showed that a gift of £50,000 or more to the Labour Party increased the donor's chances of receiving an honour by more than 1,500 times. Large Labour donors were almost 7,000 times more likely to receive a peerage than non-donors.[6] The Conservative Party also awarded a disproportionate number of honours to donors, though on a smaller scale than Labour. This difference was accounted for by the purely contingent factor that they were not in government and therefore lacked powers of patronage, rather than any principled objection.

The scale of abuse was so great that in early 2006 the Metropolitan Police launched a criminal inquiry, led by Assistant Commissioner John Yates, into suspected breaches of the law relating to the sale of honours. Just as telling as the inquiry itself was the reaction by the Political Class. At first Yates was gently patronised. It seems to have hoped or expected that the police inquiry would turn out to be simply a formal exercise or apathetic.

However, it soon became clear that Yates was launching a diligent investigation into the circumstantial evidence that honours had effectively been sold. At this point a series of attempts were apparently made to discredit him and which could have brought his inquiry to an early halt. Three basic methods were deployed. First, the House of Commons Public Administration Committee put pressure on the Assistant Commissioner.

Theoretically, the purpose of the Public Administration Committee is to maintain the integrity of British public life. In this case it acted in a way that disrupted a police investigation. Early on – before the criminal investigation got under way – it launched its own investigation into the allegations, a move that would have hindered the police and possibly prejudiced any subsequent trial. Yates managed to dissuade the committee from this course of action. The committee continued to interfere, however.

In March 2007 the Public Administration Committee vociferously complained about the length of time the inquiry was taking. One member, the Labour MP Paul Flynn, announced that the committee 'was feeling irritated because this has gone on for a whole year'. Flynn's remarks appeared to reflect the widespread opinion among MPs, on all sides of the Commons, that accusations of law-breaking against politicians should be treated in a different way from similar accusations made against ordinary voters. 'This is a parliamentary mess,' he stated, 'and parliamentarians need to clear up the mess.'[7] Flynn's words partly reflected the comments made by committee chairman Tony Wright on the *Today* programme on 15 December 2006: 'I have taken the view that the investigation has been a kind of shock to the system,' said Wright, 'and on the whole, a good one. I am not sure that any further public benefit will be served by this going any further. I think the benefit from it has now been obtained.'

It is almost impossible to imagine a Commons committee acting in a similar way to engage with the police over any other criminal investigation. This meddling, though sanctioned by all the large political parties, was unprecedented, reflecting the Political Class orthodoxy that its own members were immune from the proper independent scrutiny that automatically attaches to the average person suspected of criminal conduct. This exploitation of the status and authority of a Commons committee gave every appearance of a technique modelled on the earlier use of the Commons Standards and Privileges Committee to protect members of the Political Class from investigation. I will give a very full description of this wretched business – and the mistreatment of the Parliamentary Commissioner for Standards, Elizabeth Filkin – in Chapter 10.

The second type of intervention came from government ministers and officials, who entered the public arena to denounce Yates. Some stayed anonymous, such as the Downing Street aide who told the *Observer* that the inquiry was a 'blight on all politics, not just the Labour Party'.[8] One unnamed 'senior minister' told the *Sunday Mirror* that the cash-for-peerages investigation was part of a 'politically motivated conspiracy' which had 'fundamentally damaged relations between the government and the police, which is dangerous for any democracy'. Others came into the open. Labour Party chairman Hazel Blears openly called for the police to bring their inquiry to an end, saying that 'the sooner we can get to a conclusion, the better'.[9] One Cabinet minister, Alan Johnson, pre-empted the Yates investigation by stating that no crime had been committed. 'They are comparing it to Watergate,' stated Johnson. 'At Watergate there was a crime. There was no crime near this shown at all.'[10] Nigel Griffiths, deputy leader of the House of Commons, also pre-empted the police's investigations with the announcement that the inquiry had failed to unearth criminal wrongdoing: 'I understand the Crown Prosecution Service, having looked at all the evidence in the cash-for-honours case, decided that there was no evidence to proceed with a conviction [*sic*] and I hope that that will lay to rest that issue.'[11]

As in the case of Elizabeth Filkin, the involvement of a Commons committee was accompanied by what amounted collectively to a smear campaign. As with Filkin, Yates was accused of being politically motivated, and set on discrediting British public life. This campaign against Yates was extremely effective, and the briefing by Downing Street officials and by ministers against the Assistant Commissioner was widely repeated by government allies in the press. The first journalist to make the invidious comparison between John Yates and Kenneth Starr, the Republican attorney who took over the Whitewater probe into the Clinton finances in 1994 and who came to be regarded with venomous hatred by the Washington Political Class, was Rachel Sylvester in the *Daily Telegraph*. She wrote: 'John Yates is starting to behave like a man on a mission – he seems to be following the lead of Kenneth Starr, the indefatigable pursuer of the Clintons.'[12] The *Guardian* agreed, claiming that 'the honours inquiry has grown into something far more like Starr's prurient investigation of Clinton than Watergate'.[13] *The Times* asserted that 'this would make the Gestapo proud'.[14] *The Times* also claimed that 'the media is ravenous for an Aitken moment'.[15] *Prospect* magazine accused the Metropolitan Police of a 'serious abuse of authority', adding for good measure that 'most of the cash-for-honours inquiry has been a media- and Met-driven farce fuelling political distrust'.[16] *The Economist*, meanwhile, attacked the police as being 'leak-happy' – a common charge which the police denied and for which no evidence was produced.[17] The *Observer* accused Yates of setting out to 'damage the standing of democratic institutions', adding that he was 'in danger of looking like a political provocateur'.[18] This accusation was repeated by Steve Richards in the *Independent*, who complained that the inquiry had 'become destabilising for the government and, more widely, for the reputation of British politics'.[19] In the *Sunday Mirror* the columnist Richard Stott accused Yates of ignoring justice and taking part in something 'perilously close to a witchhunt'.[20] The *Spectator* magazine ran an article that questioned Yates' professional competence.[21] In the *Financial Times* the columnist Philip Stephens ridiculed Yates, declaring that 'for all his talents as a self-publicist, Yates of the Yard may turn out to be more Clouseau than Poirot'.[22] Assistant Commissioner Yates always denied being the source of leaks about the inquiry.

The loudest attacks on Assistant Commissioner Yates tended to come from government or Labour Party sources. However, the attempt to undermine the commissioner should also be seen as a bipartisan effort between Labour and the Tories, with the Liberal

Democrats playing a passive but acquiescent role. It is exceptionally important here to note the collaboration of the Media Class in the smearing of Yates. The Media Class did not merely provide ample space for government-inspired attacks on the police investigation, but also internalised much of the Political Class hostility to the Metropolitan Police. This conduct sharply conflicted with normal models of media conduct, according to which reporters and journalists would have seen it as their duty to bring to light criminal conduct by people in positions of authority. This emergence of the media as an ancillary arm of the ruling elite is one of the special features of the emergence of the Political Class, explored much more fully in Chapter 11.

The behaviour of the opposition Conservative Party was also perplexing. Theoretically the main opposition party in a parliamentary democracy would seek to take advantage of a major criminal investigation involving senior government aides. Yet senior Tories readily briefed against Yates.[23] The opposition Conservatives, as in the case of Filkin, made little attempt to embarrass the government over cash-for-honours allegations. They, along with the Liberal Democrats and the supportive Media Class, were complicit in the use of the Public Administration Committee as a vehicle to scrutinise Yates. David Cameron reacted to the police investigation by seeking out a private meeting with the Prime Minister in his Commons office in early 2006. No other parties were invited, and the conversation between the two leaders was kept secret. According to conventional models of democratic behaviour, it would be normal for the main opposition to expose and disrupt the method of party financing adopted by New Labour. But the Conservatives in opposition chose to brush over, rather than rebel against, the endemic corruption of a Political Class government.

Only the minor parties and certain MPs who challenged the dominance of the Political Class broke from the main party machines and gave support to Yates. It is extremely significant that the original approach to the police came from a Scottish National Party MP, Angus McNeil. The SNP stood outside the cartel party system – indeed, they were victims of it – and had an interest in disrupting conventional techniques of political finance.

The Emergence of Cartel Politics

This failure of the political process to tackle the endemic sleaze and corruption described above demands an explanation. In theory an opposition should seize with relish on the transgressions of ministers and MPs from the governing party. Indeed, the constitutional textbooks would suggest that any self-respecting opposition had an over-riding public duty to do so. However, the Liberal Democrats and Conservatives showed little interest. On the contrary, again and again they worked alongside government to conceal, minimise and apologise for the transgressions of ministers and MPs. In the rare cases where MPs have sought to expose or bring misdemeanours to light, they have been marginalised or ostracised, even by their own parties.

The Conservative Party and the Liberal Democrats seem to have felt that their own interests, and not merely those of the British government, were threatened when the venality and greed of mainstream politicians was brought to public attention. Senior opposition politicians have concluded that the common identity they shared with fellow members of the Political Class was more important than the formal, and more superficial, party distinctions that divided them from the ruling New Labour faction. To put the matter another way: the Tories and Liberals considered that public scrutiny posed a more vital threat to their interests than New Labour did.

A new kind of politics has emerged in Britain, as the cross-party cartel over Commons expenses or loans for peerages clearly demonstrates. An important function of an opposition party is no longer to oppose, but to support and collude with the government of the day. No one should be surprised by this posture. As a result of the collapse of party structures, all mainstream parties share a common financial dependence on the state. It is this dependence that determines the fundamental allegiance of all three of the principal British political parties, and not their residual attachment to a depleted party membership.

This state of affairs illuminates with quite exceptional clarity one of the central themes of this book. The use of party labels like Tory and Labour as a terminology and method of thought continues to dominate most mainstream political discourse in Britain. In practice the method of analysis is out of date, misleading and a barrier to understanding.

Conventional accounts of British politics always assume that the Labour, Lib Dem and Tory parties are genuinely distinct, capable of offering alternative visions of society and the state. In practice the differences between the main parties are minor and for the most part technical. This contradiction between apparently bitter party competition on the political stage, and co-operation and collaboration behind the scenes, defines the contemporary political predicament. One consequence of this mystifying discrepancy between reality and perception is that most reporting on British politics, which continues to articulate out-of-date assumptions about party political competition, has become unintelligible and meaningless.

It is of course the case that all three main parties draw on sharply contrasting histories and intellectual traditions. However, they have all decisively abandoned these aspects of their past and in practice share an identical analysis. In practice it makes far more sense to talk of the New Labour, Conservative and Liberal Democrat parties as a homogeneous social and economic unit rather than as separate organisations with distinctive ideologies. In other words the real gulf in British politics is no longer between Tory and Labour. It is between a hegemonic Political Class and a population at large which is mainly disenfranchised and increasingly betrayed by what amounts to a conspiracy between the mainstream parties.

The crisis facing British democracy cannot be understood, let alone addressed, without a full understanding that the party system has collapsed, and been replaced by a provisional ruling elite which has become estranged from civil society. It is now time to take a step back and examine the key ideology of the Political Class that has conquered British politics over the past two decades: it is called *modernisation*.

5

THE IDEOLOGY OF THE POLITICAL CLASS

'And it is us, the new radicals, the Labour Party modernised, that must undertake this historic mission . . . To liberate Britain from the old class divisions, old structures, old prejudices, old ways of working and doing things that will not do in this world of change' – Tony Blair, speech to Labour conference, 1999

In the chapter above I have demonstrated how the Political Class has formed a protectionist club which crosses party boundaries, and deliberately sets out to repel outside scrutiny and interference. This type of cartel politics does not, however, solely manifest itself around issues of material subsistence and organisation. Cartel politics has also come to act as a parallel constraint in the arena of ideas.

Members of the Political Class are driven by a systemic hostility to large or challenging ideas, which in general they regard as dangerous and uncouth. Indeed the story of the rise of the Political Class is the story of how daring ideas have been ruthlessly eliminated from the approved menu of public debate.[1] This discrimination has taken place in various ways. Those who embody an ideological rather than pragmatic and worldly perspective have been systematically driven out of mainstream political life. This has been the fate, in recent years, of (for example) Frank Field,*

---

* Frank Field, Labour MP for Birkenhead, is an interesting case study because he explodes the fallacy that daring and unconventional thinkers can only be found

George Galloway and Ken Livingstone, the last two of whom were expelled from the Labour Party.* A very significant recent case concerns the failure of the Labour left to mount a challenge to Gordon Brown during Labour's leadership election in 2007. John McDonnell campaigned on a platform of opposition to nuclear weapons, withdrawal from Iraq and hostility to private-sector involvement in public services. His views accurately reflected the opinions of the great majority of Labour members, as well as great swathes of the electorate. They were not, however, acceptable within the Political Class, so he failed to muster the support of forty-five Labour MPs necessary to stand. As the Labour movement closed ranks against him, McDonnell wrote a telling article in the *Guardian* accusing Gordon Brown of what he labelled 'issue avoidance':

> How could any leading politician avoid addressing directly the bloodbath that is Iraq? How could Gordon fail to take on the concerns of not just the public-sector unions but communities across the country about the latest round of NHS cutbacks and privatisation in the health service? And at a Labour Party conference especially, how could he fail to mention the hottest issue causing controversy amongst even his own supporters, the spending of £76 billion on renewing Trident?[2]

There was no answer, on any of these questions, from the prospective Labour Prime Minister. The same hostility to ideas manifested itself on the right. William Hague and Iain Duncan Smith were both undermined as Tory leader because they were understood to be too closely connected to free-market thinking and other traditional Conservative Party belief systems. The expression of classic Conservative ideas, even conventional ones such as lower taxation or a smaller state, became a reason for severe disciplinary

---

on the fringes of politics. Field is an example of a radical thinker who occupies the ideological centre ground.

* Livingstone has since been readmitted, while Galloway is now an MP for Respect.

action. To give one example drawn from the 2005 General Election, the MP Howard Flight had the Conservative whip withdrawn and so was obliged to stand down as Tory candidate for Arundel and South Downs prior to the election following an incautious comment that a Conservative government would reduce public spending. Members of the Political Class are in general careful to disassociate themselves from politicians who in the past have been associated with strong beliefs or views – Margaret Thatcher and Tony Benn are two of the most potent recent examples.

Intellectuals can flourish at Westminster in the age of the Political Class only by adopting a stolid conservatism, staying loyal to conventional thinking, and by rigorously eschewing radical thought. The key to survival is to concentrate on complex details of administration or political tactics, rather than ambitious critiques of mainstream power structures. This strategy is pursued very effectively, for example, by the exemplary Political Class intellectual David Miliband. Anyone who doubts this proposition should read Miliband's blog on the DEFRA website, which provided almost daily examples of intellectual timidity.[3] The comparison between Miliband and the Conservative Party intellectual John Redwood is extremely instructive.* Redwood, a former fellow of the elite academic institution All Souls College, Oxford, has more powerful intellectual credentials than Miliband. His dogged insistence on putting forward daring and controversial intellectual propositions based on a rigorous training in free-market principles has, however, alienated him from the Political Class.

It is especially revealing to compare the records of David

---

* John Redwood is an exceptionally interesting figure on account of his refusal to conform to Political Class mannerisms and pieties. After a brilliant academic career Redwood worked at Rothschilds in the City. He retained this connection with private business even after entering politics, at one stage becoming chairman of the building firm Norcross. Later, as a Cabinet minister in the John Major government, he showed courage by rising to the occasion and picking up the gauntlet thrown down by the Prime Minister with his challenge for a leadership contest. Both these qualities – experience of the real world outside Westminster and raw political courage – are rarely to be found within the Political Class.

Miliband and John Redwood during their respective tenures as head of the Number 10 Policy Unit – Miliband in the early years of Tony Blair and Redwood under Thatcher. Redwood was a radical policy chief, engineering the flagship policies of privatisation and council house sales which today form the most enduring part of the Thatcher legacy. By contrast Miliband's four-year term of office was chiefly associated with the now discredited technique of target-setting, partially abandoned as a failure in Labour's second term. Miliband, however, is regarded as a rising figure within the Political Class, whereas Redwood is sometimes treated as an oddity and with contempt. One reason for Miliband's comparative failure as Downing Street policy chief was that the job had been downgraded from fifteen years earlier. Miliband was at all times expected to play second fiddle to Alastair Campbell, the Number 10 press secretary. Redwood as policy chief ranked much higher than the media chief Bernard Ingham in Thatcher's Downing Street hierarchy. This contrast in itself gives a telling insight into the special priorities in a Political Class government as evinced in Blair's Downing Street set-up.

This is not quite to say that the Political Class is uninterested in ideas: quite the contrary. As I have already shown, its membership possesses a specialist training in politics, including political thought, which far surpasses that possessed by any previous governing elite. Perhaps partly for that very reason, the Political Class tends to make a more playful use of ideas and techniques, a characteristic that distinguishes its members from politicians who were active in the era of mass parties.

For most of the twentieth century governing elites brought with them to Westminster a set of principles, tightly aligned to general party political thought and beliefs, which they sought to apply in government. When they felt the temptation to strike cross-party deals or renege on commitments, they were liable to be met with accusations of betrayal by the party membership. Today, political ideas no longer emerge from within party structures and belief systems. They are manufactured. Rather than referring inward to the party membership, politicians look outward to the general public. Instead of engaging with voters directly, however, marketing experts and political 'consultants' are employed to discern the popular will. Policies are constructed and later marketed in exactly the same way as consumer products, and very often by the same set of experts. The evolution of ideas becomes an essentially private form of activity, associated with a specialist elite whose primary purpose is not putting into practice any system of ideologies or beliefs but rather the shaping of policy for the mass market.

Ideas in the era of the Political Class are therefore converted into weapons or tools to be deployed or used for tactical convenience. Their key function is the denial of territory to opponents, the strategy of 'triangulation' first associated with the Democrat presidency of Bill Clinton and identified in particular with his consultant Dick Morris. This technique was first used, and with especially gratifying effect, in the presidential election of 1992, and involved a series of forays into Republican issues, above all law and order.

The over-riding purpose was the conquest of the central ground of politics, forcing political opponents to take up territory which could then be labelled extremist. The overwhelming aim of this form of tactical positioning was emphatically not to win the battle of ideas. Rather it lay in the ability to lay claim to a positional victory at the end of the day.[4] Derek Scott, for many years Downing Street economic adviser, has set out in detail how Tony Blair's European strategy was based on positioning rather than achieving substantial objectives:

One of the problems for the Blair government has been that in opposition Labour never worked out what being pro-European meant; it was simply part of rebranding and repositioning the party. This was made relatively easy by the chaos over Europe within the Tory party, which remains so scarred that it is still unable to speak with confidence on an issue of major national interest. In government the focus on positioning has continued. Tony Blair's tactics have been to caricature opponents into positions they do not hold: anyone who goes further than he does in criticising the European Union is accused not only of being eurosceptic, but of being anti-European or wanting to disengage from Europe – an isolationist![5]

The Clinton presidency was studied very carefully indeed by New Labour aides, who copied the tactic of triangulation with dazzling success in the British General Election of 1997. This proved also extremely successful as a governing methodology after 1997, and the tide of tactical victories was only halted when the Tories under David Cameron themselves adopted triangulation, embarking on their own set of forays into Labour territory, every bit as complex and dangerous a journey as one might expect.[6] By 2007 the wholesale embrace of triangulation as a strategy meant that it had become very difficult to make party distinctions in British politics. It was no longer possible to state with clarity whether Labour or the Conservatives were, in conventional terms, further to the 'left' or the 'right'. Labour had become tougher on law and order, and considerably more hostile to individual freedom than the Conservatives. The two parties broadly agreed about the level of taxation and the size of the state. By the time Chancellor Gordon Brown brought his 2007 Budget speech to an end with a 2p income-tax cut, a concession aimed directly at middle-income voters, it had become fair to say that the two parties were to all intents and purposes indistinguishable.

The manipulation of policies and ideas by experts has been one of the defining traits of the Political Class. While this insight has been electorally successful in the short term, it has converted politics into a specialised art or science, to be practised only by the adept. The art of politics has been taken out of the public domain and turned into the private activity of the Political Class. The term which defines, or at any rate attempts to make legitimate, this secretive and obscure form of politics is 'modernisation'.

The Cult of Modernisation

Just as Labour politicians used to describe themselves as 'socialist', and many Tories were happy enough to be called 'Thatcherites' or perhaps 'free marketeers', so members of the Political Class pride themselves on being modernisers. Modernisation is the common ideology of the Political Class.* The leaders of the Labour, Tory and Liberal Democrat parties all assert they are modernisers. Modernisation has become the creed which distinguishes members of the Political Class from less enlightened members of the parties to which they formally belong.

It means that they do not subscribe to the core beliefs that bind their organisations together. Modernising members of the Church of England, to take an example drawn from outside politics, do not accept the literal truth of the Resurrection, and quite often question the existence of God. In the case of the Labour Party, modernisers do not subscribe to the massive transfers of ownership to working people, the doctrine which still animates activists and with which the party has historically been associated. A Conservative politician who claims to be a moderniser is indicating that he has rejected the longstanding attitudes and beliefs of his party membership. These modernising Tories face an especially arduous task of intellectual self-justification. The Conservative Party, as its

---

* Thus Liberal Democrat leader Menzies Campbell at his first speech to his party at the 2006 spring conference on 5 March 2006: 'Liberal democracy cannot be a struggle between those who wish to modernise and those who do not. To be a Liberal Democrat is to be a moderniser.' Tory Chairman Francis Maude told the Conservative conference on 1 October 2006: 'Modernising is one of our party's great traditions. Back then in the Seventies we changed so we could win for Britain. Today we're doing the same.' The number of references by Tony Blair to modernisation, and affiliated words like modernity, new, change and modern, is beyond computation. Probably wisely, the Tory leader David Cameron only rarely uses the term. But there is no doubt that he is a moderniser. Gordon Brown used the word 'change' no fewer than eight times during his brief speech on the steps of Downing Street shortly after being appointed Prime Minister on 27 June 2007.

name uncompromisingly indicates, represents a tradition of entrenched scepticism bordering on hostility towards change and novelty. But these are the very things that modernisers believe in most strongly. Undeterred, modernisers have risen in a very short space of time to occupy the dominant positions inside the Conservative political directorate.

It is important to note that this determination to extract ideology from politics has been the foundation of enduring cross-party friendships. The Tory leader David Cameron, and the group of MPs and advisers who surround him, have long been very close to the modernising vanguard surrounding Tony Blair. Cameron himself, to give one example among many, is a personal friend of the former Downing Street strategy chief Benjamin Wegg-Prosser.* Cameron also enjoys a cheerful and well-documented acquaintance with Peter Mandelson,† Wegg-Prosser's former employer. In general, connections among core Tory and Labour modernisers are warm, and stretch far beyond the merely political. It is normal for them to form business and social partnerships. Rachel Whetstone, for example, a Tory moderniser and adviser to Michael Howard, worked for Portland, the lobbying concern founded by the former Downing Street aide Tim Allan, whose major client was Rupert Murdoch's News International. During the 2005 General Election, one of the figures whose views were most widely

---

* Wegg-Prosser is a core Political Class figure. He enjoyed spells as Researcher and Special Adviser to Peter Mandelson, as well as periods working for News International and the *Guardian* before entering Downing Street as Director of Strategic Communications. He reportedly gained his first Political Class employment after going to the trouble of sourcing Mandelson's pre-gym drink for him. See *Evening Standard*, 1 August 2005.

† Mandelson's appointment as Director of Campaigns and Communications for the Labour Party in 1985 was a transformative moment in the history of New Labour, and therefore modern politics. His historic achievement was to assert the dominant position of the print and broadcasting media in political struggle. He possessed one of the cleverest and most original British political minds of the late twentieth century. His career, however, ended in anticlimax at the European Commission, a regular bolt-hole for senior members of the Political Class. Nevertheless, he can boast an astonishing legacy as the inventor of both Tony Blair and David Cameron.

quoted in Conservative Party strategy meetings was Tim Allan.[7]

At the heart of the modernising project, party distinctions were over-ridden by a single-minded governing consensus. Members of the Cameron inner circle made no secret of their intense admiration for Tony Blair. At a private dinner given by *Daily Telegraph* executives at the 2005 Tory conference, Cameron confided that he saw himself as 'heir to Blair'. Modernising Tory MPs admitted that they would like to serve in a Blair Cabinet. One of Cameron's closest backers, the Conservative MP Michael Gove,* provided an awestruck endorsement for Tony Blair in *The Times*, stating:

> Blair's outbreak of courage deserves the respect of natural Conservatives. You could call it the Elizabeth Bennett moment. It's what Isolde felt when she fell into Tristan's arms. It's the point you reach when you give up fighting your feelings, abandon the antipathy bred into your bones, and admit that you were wrong about the man. By God, it's still hard to write this, but I'm afraid I've got to be honest. Tony Blair is proving an outstanding Prime Minister at the moment.[8]

This quote was merely a reflection of the very widespread admiration of the New Labour Prime Minister by Tory modernisers, many of them congregated with Gove on *The Times* newspaper. One Tory MP, Ed Vaizey, privately asserted that he might have voted for Tony Blair had he not been a Conservative candidate in 1997.† This warmth was very keenly reciprocated by Labour counterparts, who did not attempt to hide their admiration

---

* A *Times* reporter before becoming MP for Surrey Heath in 2005, Michael Gove is a classic second-generation Political Class member in his characteristic straddling of the media and political domains. In June 2007 Gove entered the shadow Cabinet.

† The son of a Labour peer who later defected to the Conservatives, Ed Vaizey has a background in journalism, public relations and the Conservative Research Department. His extensive media connections have secured him a higher reputation than he might otherwise have achieved – a common syndrome among the Political Class.

for David Cameron. Tory and Labour modernisers formed a politically androgynous zone at the heart of British public life. Their opponents were anyone awkward, obstructive and difficult: trade unionists, anti-Europeans, anyone who stood in the way of money-making or threatened orderly government.

In part they were united by a shared snobbish disdain for less sophisticated political activists. It was always possible to spot modernisers at a party conference. They were more smartly dressed, they were in a hurry, they had privileged access backstage and to the private hotel suites of the party leaders: they never had time to give their full attention to anything. They ate in the best restaurants, and they were extremely well connected with the media. Socially they were homogeneous: metropolitan, polished and well-educated. They belonged to the same clubs, laughed at the same things, and lived comfortable lives. They were the new British ruling class. Whichever party was in power, the modernisers would run the country.

Though it is easy to identify a moderniser at fifty paces, it is far harder to say what modernisation actually is. It is nevertheless essential to attempt this analysis, because modernisation has become Britain's governing ideology in the age of the Political Class.

Defining Modernisation

Modernisation is an abstract word, which has begun to acquire a menacing tone. Town centres get modernised, which often strips them of charm and originality. Industrial modernisation has become a euphemism for lost jobs. Modernisation brings the connotation of something unavoidable, unwelcome, and imposed from outside; something which people are powerless to prevent, administered by bureaucrats.

Modernisation as a concept originally belongs to sociology, an academic discipline which studies the evolution of backward communities into 'modern' nations based on exchange and manufacture. The American theorist Talcott Parsons categorised societies as primitive, archaic and modern. The more modern a society became, the more powerful and wealthy, the more open to change, and the more able to resist reactionary forces. For Talcott Parsons, the United States stood at the pinnacle of social evolution, and modernisation was a virtuous concept.[9]

In recent British political culture the concept of moderniser has a specific, though connected, application. It began as a collective description of the group of Labour politicians and strategists who, under the leadership of Neil Kinnock, sought to transform the party after the calamitous election defeat of 1983.* As far as this Kinnock cabal was concerned, the term 'modernisation' had important advantages. It moved the official language of the party away from socialism. It seemed an upbeat word, not only giving a sense of movement (badly lacking once traditional objectives had been abandoned) but also a direction of travel. It conveyed an impression of good sense and brisk efficiency. Just as helpful, it defined the landscape in a way which portrayed the opponents of modernisation – both Kinnock's internal Labour Party opponents, and the ruling Tories – as eccentric, out of date, and reactionary.

A copious literature now surrounds the rhetoric of modernisation, as applied by the Political Class in recent decades. The academic Norman Fairclough noted that the word 'new' appeared 609 times in 53 speeches made by Tony Blair between 1997 and 1999, a phenomenon now repeating itself in speeches by David Cameron. The word 'modern' appeared 89 times, 'modernise' or 'modernisation' 87 times, and 'reform' 143 times.[10] Fairclough

---

* Meg Russell, historian of New Labour, describes how the Labour Co-ordinating Committee (LCC) 'became ever more concerned with changing the party's image to make it more appealing to the electorate. As one former LCC activist put it, many came to believe that "any price was worth paying to get Labour into government". LCC members thus increasingly found common cause with those on the right of the party who were interested in embracing change. It was this grouping in the late 1980s and early 1990s that came to be known as the "modernisers" – opposed to the "traditionalists" to both their left and their right.' See Russell, *Building New Labour* (London: Palgrave Macmillan, 2005), p. 19.

drew attention to the wide application of the term: it could be applied to the Labour Party, Britain, the constitution, the health service, education, the welfare state, defence, and so on.*

Commentators also noted that the term 'modernisation' involved an enthusiastic acceptance of the market economy, and admiration for contemporary business practice. The political scientist Mark Neocleous stressed how the concept of modernity has tended to replace capitalism.[11] The sociologist Anthony Woodiwiss noted 'the rapid increase in the number of index references to "modernity" with the equally rapid decline in the number of such references to "capitalism"' over recent years.[12] Professor David Marquand remarked that the doctrine of modernisation demanded that

old habits, old practices, old traditions, old ways of life must be ruthlessly jettisoned if they conflict with the imperatives of modernisation, which in practice bear an uncanny resemblance to the imperatives of the global marketplace.[13]

For New Labour the concept of modernisation performed a crucial, though partly invisible, function. It worked as a device to shift the mainstream left towards a general acceptance of international markets and big business. It presented 'globalisation' and the power of capital as inevitable, unavoidable, and above all virtuous. It was no longer the task of the Labour Party to fight capitalism, but to engage with it: a shift of fundamental, historic importance.

Beyond the stern injunction to be modern and up to date, it has never been made clear what the term actually meant. This lack of specific definition caused the academic Alan Finlayson to note, in

---

* Fairclough observed, however, that the word 'reform' rather than 'modernisation' was more likely to be used in connection with Europe. 'A striking contrast between "modernisation" and "reform" is that the former is overwhelmingly used with reference to the UK, whereas the latter is roughly equally used with reference to the EU.' See Fairclough, *New Labour, New Language?*, p. 20.

his brilliant study of the term, that the concept of modernisation had some of the characteristics of a cult:

> This is not just an ideology. It is a kind of social and political theory, even a philosophy, but with a solipsistic conceptual structure that is almost theological or cultic in its capacity to encompass everything or anything the movement might choose to do, while rejecting criticism as a kind of nonsensical heresy.[14]

In this way the concept of modernisation provided the overwhelming moral and ideological affirmation all governing elites – especially new ones – need. It gave the emerging Political Class legitimacy, rectitude and urgency. As the Prime Minister proclaimed: 'modernise or die' – modernisation was nothing less than a matter of life and death.* Modernisation told its members that they were right. Better still, it informed them that their opponents were deluded, malicious and plain wrong. This hostility to those who failed to share the modernising vision was an article of faith, often articulated by the leadership and formally set out by Tony Blair at the 1999 Labour conference:

> Arrayed against us: the forces of conservatism, the cynics, the elites, the establishment. Those who will live with decline. Those who yearn for yesteryear. Those who just can't be bothered. Those who prefer to criticise rather than do. On our side, the forces of modernity and justice.

And, as quoted at the beginning of this chapter, the Prime Minister went on to describe those who possessed the modernising vision:

---

* Tony Blair first employed the phrase in a mission-setting speech on 6 June 1997 made to the Congress of European Socialists. Five years later, the exact same phrase, with no apparent irony, was reiterated by Francis Maude in his speech to the Conservative Party Conference: 'As Conservatives we believe in choice and we now have the starkest possible choice: we can retreat further into a reactionary redoubt and try to hold the modern world at bay, or we can rise up and embrace it. Stagnation and oblivion or radicalism and revival? Modernise or die?'

'It is us, the new radicals, the Labour Party modernised, that must undertake this historic mission . . . to liberate Britain.'

Admittedly the term 'modernisation' lacked any traction outside the elite. If anything it reinforced the estrangement of the Political Class because it meant nothing to voters. But that was part of its appeal. Modernisation was an ideology with special application for the governing class. It granted cohesion and moral uplift to the initiated. For them it explained the world.

It was also exclusive, creating a dividing line between the un-enlightened masses who were either too stupid or perverse to understand, and the privileged few who grasped the future and possessed the moral nobility and personal courage to make the 'tough choices' needed to put modernisation into practice. It provided a language for government. The modernisers believed they had a special insight: 'Today we have a better understanding of the foundations of human nature,' they proclaimed. 'We know more about how evolution shaped our drives, our instincts, as well as our capacity to co-operate.'[15]

At first modernisation provided a structure for domestic reform. But as time passed, it provided an explanatory framework for foreign policy as well. For earlier generations of leaders, the transatlantic alliance embodied the 'free world'. According to Tony Blair, it was modernisation that stood at the heart of the alliance with the United States of America. Arriving at the White House in 1998 the Prime Minister informed President Clinton: 'On so many issues we think alike. We are in politics for the same things: because we want to modernise our countries in preparation for the new millennium.'[16] Blair expressed his confidence that he and Clinton could build 'a new transatlantic relationship based on the successful modernisation of our two countries'. Modernisation was later used to justify the invasions of Iraq and Afghanistan. In March 2006 Tony Blair explained that 'the struggle in our world today therefore is not just about security, it is a struggle about values and about modernity – whether to be at ease with it or in rage at it'. Three months later he enlarged on this theme in a speech to executives at Rupert Murdoch's News Corporation:

However, the even deeper roots of the troubles in the Middle East reach right down into a more basic struggle: between those who want to embrace and those who resist the modern world. The fanatical reactionary elements of global terrorism, based on a false view of Islam, are in reality a revolt against the modern world.[17]

Modernisation started out as a strategic device to distance the Political Class from what it saw as out-of-date or antiquated ideologies. It was meant to appear sensible, managerial, pragmatic, in touch. But in due course it became a powerful ideology on its own. It presented the British ruling elite with a conceptual structure which was based on a dislike of the past, a contempt for traditional institutions, a unique insight into the future, and a guide to ethics.

It was a progressive ideology which embodied a profound belief in the ability of a benign ruling caste to make life better for ordinary people. The writings of the early modernisers radiate excitement, enjoyment of life and a certainty that they were in at the birth of something exciting and extraordinary. When the Political Class in the form of New Labour took over the task of governing Britain in the early summer of 1997, they had a mission: adapt, dismantle, change and above all *modernise*. This zeal brought the Political Class into sharp conflict with the long-standing institutions and ancient freedoms of the British people. It is now time to turn our attention to the battle between the modernisers and the institutional structures of the British state.

PART II

THE ATTACK ON BRITISH INSTITUTIONS

6

THE EMASCULATION OF
THE CIVIL SERVICE

'To apply the values of the private domain is, in a profound sense, to corrupt it. It is equally shocking, because equally corrupting, to apply market norms to the public domain. That is why it is a crime to buy or sell votes or honours or government policies or justice' – David Marquand, *Decline of the Public*

The most impressive individual manifestation of British government during the long period of institutional dominance was the Secretary to the Cabinet. He was the most senior civil servant in Whitehall and during the course of the twentieth century came to reflect in his person all of the qualities of the British method: impartiality, discretion, intellectual scruple; conservatism, lack of imagination, what critics saw as an obstinate reluctance to be convinced by fresh ideas. For several decades around the middle of the century the position of Cabinet Secretary was held by a series of outstanding figures. Though not one became a household name, they were massively influential and indeed legendary within Whitehall.

The title – Secretary to the Cabinet – fails to communicate the real power that these civil servants possessed. The company secretary in a large corporation occupies an important and in certain technical respects analogous position to the Cabinet Secretary inside British government. But his role in taking minutes of board meetings and ensuring that regulatory and other obligations are met, though necessary, is not the most essential part of the running of the business. This is because great entrepreneurial enterprises require the commanding presence of a dynamic chief executive, whose function it is to drive his firm ruthlessly forward by opening up new markets and fighting off the competition.

This is by no means the case in the British system of government, which operates in a different way and has no place for a chief executive on the corporate model. Instead it devolves real power to individual departments of state. In this collegiate system the co-ordinating role of the Cabinet Secretary takes on a central importance. Nor does the Cabinet Secretary merely administer the Cabinet system of government. He is also the voice of integrity. He zealously guards the distinction between party and state. At all times this policing as well as his administrative function have been sharply resented by the Political Class.

One of the most significant developments of the last twenty-five years has been the sharp decline in the influence and weight of the Cabinet Secretary. He no longer carries anything like the almost mythical power he once did in government. He is no longer the independent voice of integrity. He is no longer central to the running of government. The Cabinet Secretary has often become a debased and peripheral figure.

The collapse in authority, both practical and moral, has come about as a direct result of the rise of the Political Class. Over the last generation politicians have fought hard to regain a dominant role in the regulation and administration of government; a role which they have not possessed since the early nineteenth century, before the introduction of the Northcote/Trevelyan reforms which established the independence and neutrality of the civil service. As a direct consequence of this new pressure, Cabinet Secretaries have seen their role reduced to assistants and even at times apologists for the Political Class. Again and again they have been pressured into carrying out furtive political favours for the Prime Minister of the day, causing an enormous long-term loss of authority. The long, hidden story of how the new Political Class has achieved this breakthrough, and its unhappy effects for the integrity of British public life, lies at the heart of this book.

There have been only ten Cabinet Secretaries since the title was invented in 1916. Each one has therefore occupied his office on average for just short of ten years.* However, in very recent times the longevity of a Cabinet Secretary has started to fall sharply. Sir Richard Wilson endured for just four years from 1998 until 2002, while his successor Sir Andrew Turnbull was an even more ephemeral presence, replaced in 2005 by Sir Gus O'Donnell. Sir Gus, however, is not due to retire until he reaches the age of sixty in 2012, giving him a more substantial seven years in which to make a serious impact and, it is to be hoped, restore some of the dignity of the post which has been wiped away in recent years.

The office of Cabinet Secretary carried most weight around the middle of the twentieth century. The first occupant of the post was Sir Maurice Hankey, who was secretary to Lloyd George's War Cabinet. According to the Whitehall historian Peter Hennessy, 'The start of modern, bureaucratised Cabinet government can be timed precisely: 11.30am on Saturday, 9 September 1916, the moment when Lloyd George opened the first meeting of the War Cabinet. Hankey and Colonel Dolly Jones took the notes which became the first Cabinet minutes ever recorded.'[1] Hankey moved rapidly to assert his authority by circulating throughout Whitehall his 'Rules of Procedure for the War Cabinet'. This document insisted that decisions made in Cabinet 'would become operative decisions to be carried out by the relevant Departments as soon as they had been initialled by the Prime Minister'. This instruction established the dominance of the Cabinet Minute – and therefore the Cabinet Secretary – in the machinery of British government.[2]

Sir Maurice Hankey survived from 1916 until 1938, a prodigious span. Yet his starting point as an instrument of the Lloyd George

---

* The ten occupants of the post have been: 1916: Sir Maurice Hankey; 1938: Sir Edward Bridges; 1947: Sir Norman Brook; 1963: Sir Burke Trend; 1973: Sir John Hunt; 1979: Sir Robert Armstrong; 1988: Sir Robin Butler; 1998: Sir Richard Wilson; 2002: Sir Andrew Turnbull; 2005: Sir Augustine O'Donnell.

wartime administration, and his early training as a Royal Marine artillery officer – well away from the Oxbridge and Bloomsbury background which characterised so many of the Whitehall elite – meant that he always had the air of an outsider. The tone and the status of the job were not quite set in stone until the tenures of his three great mid-century successors: Sir Edward Bridges, Sir Norman Brook and Sir Burke Trend. Between them these three distinguished figures governed Whitehall for thirty-five years, a period when the domestic civil service was at its most capable and self-confident. It ran the home war effort and for several decades after 1945 its role in maintaining the equilibrium of the British state was axiomatic.

The Cabinet Secretary Weakened Under the Tories

This moral and intellectual dominance was first seriously questioned by Harold Wilson's governments of the 1960s and 1970s. The diaries of the Cabinet minister Richard Crossman paint the British civil service machine not as a vital instrument of change, but rather as an obstructive nuisance, thus anticipating later criticisms from Margaret Thatcher and Tony Blair. Crossman possessed an intellectual arrogance on a scale that far surpassed the most acidic official. Rather than being intimidated by the civil service elite, he was contemptuous. As early as 1963 Crossman was criticising the 1945 Attlee government for its 'uncritical reliance on Whitehall' and urging that a successful left-wing government required 'an influx of experts with special knowledge, new ideas and a sympathy for the government's domestic and foreign policies'.[3]

This view was not widely shared, and certainly not by Wilson. It nevertheless came to be hugely influential. Richard Crossman's caustic commentary on the British system of government, which anticipated views later to be associated with the Political Class, was given a much wider currency with the publication of his diaries in the 1970s. His views were made more lethal by the collapse of post-war economic stability. The first public indication that the Cabinet Secretary was losing his primacy did not come until 1985, when Margaret Thatcher's Cabinet Secretary Sir Robert Armstrong agreed to fly to Australia in an abortive attempt to block the publication of Peter Wright's book *Spycatcher*. It was a disastrous undertaking in any case, made worse by the way that Sir Robert was mocked during cross-examination by Wright's counsel Malcolm Turnbull. Sir Robert, who returned to London a diminished man, says today that 'someone had to do the job', adding that he only agreed with some reluctance after various Cabinet ministers had turned down the task.[4] The *Spycatcher* trial exposed the Cabinet Secretary to full public view and thus destroyed much of his mystique, rather as the prestige of the royal family was being weakened by press intrusion during the same period. More significantly still, the *Spycatcher* affair set a precedent for Cabinet Secretaries putting their own integrity on the line on behalf of politicians.

During the ten-year Cabinet Secretaryship of Armstrong's successor Sir Robin Butler, this became more of a pattern. In 1991 the Chancellor of the Exchequer Norman Lamont discovered to his dismay that his London flat had been leased out to a tenant carrying out her business under the trade name 'Miss Whiplash'. Though there seems no suggestion that Miss Whiplash was failing to pay her rent, or in breach of any contractual obligation, her existence was a severe public relations setback to the Chancellor, who was at the time fighting for his political life. He resolved to evict her, and used government funds in order to help him do so. Even at the time it seemed strange that the state should come to the aid of a politician in an entirely private matter of this sort. Nevertheless the Cabinet Secretary concluded, after a 'rigorous and conscientious examination', that this was the correct course of action.[5]

Sir Robin made another curious decision when he cleared the Treasury minister Jonathan Aitken of claims that he had stayed at the Ritz Hotel in Paris at the expense of a foreign businessman. This was hopeless. In due course Aitken was jailed after it emerged that his account of the Ritz visit was wholly false. Though the main culprit here was the wretched Aitken, Sir Robin was made to look a fool because of the half-hearted and perfunctory nature of his investigation.

There was not a great deal of evidence that he guarded the boundaries between party and state with the diligence that might have been expected. He was very slow to authorise the release of documents to the Scott Inquiry into the 'Arms to Iraq' affair, opening himself up to charges that he had delayed publication of the report by several months.*

When – no thanks to Sir Robin – the report was finally published, he permitted a vigorous, partial and distorted defence of the Cabinet minister William Waldegrave to be issued on Treasury notepaper. Sir Robin enjoyed attending Tory party social events, and was a fixture at the 'champagne and shepherd's pie' parties thrown by the Tory peer and conman Jeffrey Archer. To be fair to Sir Robin, numerous Establishment figures were extremely happy to accept Lord Archer's hospitality.

Sir Robin at last showed signs of a more rigorous attitude in the very final months of the Major administration, in particular when he issued a rebuke to Michael Heseltine after the Deputy Prime Minister had tried to draw civil servants into a scheme to compile a list of businessmen prepared to support government policy (Heseltine instantly withdrew his proposal). But once Tony Blair came to power with his massive parliamentary majority, Sir Robin was – despite efforts to do so – unable to resist the sustained attack on the integrity of the British civil service which was one of the most notable characteristics of New Labour in government.

---

* See, for example, Richard Norton-Taylor on the Scott Inquiry: 'Butler spoke of the "meticulous way in which records were kept and preserved" – a claim which did not prevent the judge from rebuking him for the failure of the Cabinet Office to release documents relating to meetings involving ... the Prime Minister and Alan Clark over allegations that Clark gave "a nod and a wink" to British firms selling equipment to Iraq's arms industry.' Norton-Taylor also describes how 'departments, notably Sir Robin Butler's Cabinet Office, delayed passing on documents'. See Norton-Taylor, *Truth is a Difficult Concept*, pp. 117, 209.

The Trials and Tribulations of Sir Richard Wilson

New Labour built on the Tory model, and endeavoured both to exploit and diminish the Cabinet Secretary. New Labour was not interested in the Cabinet Secretary as a voice of integrity, and sought to make no use of him as an administrative lever. Instead it made surprisingly effective use of the role as a kind of constitutional convenience. Sir Robin Butler, who was proud of the impartiality and discretion of the civil service, sought to do the same professional job for New Labour as he had for the Conservatives. Fundamentally he was distrusted and abused by the inner coterie which surrounded the Prime Minister. The same fate awaited Sir Robin's successor Sir Richard Wilson.

Sir Richard became the victim of an early manifestation of this uncalled-for contempt when Peter Mandelson resigned as Trade Secretary at the end of 1998 following the revelation that he had accepted an undisclosed loan from his ministerial colleague Geoffrey Robinson. In an attempt to give the impression that due process had been observed, Downing Street claimed that the Cabinet Secretary had 'investigated' the affair. In fact Sir Richard Wilson had carried out no investigation. He merely sent a one-line message to the Downing Street chief of staff Jonathan Powell, which included the opinion that from Sir Richard's point of view there had been 'no impropriety'. Downing Street, so far as one can tell, put out a misleading statement about the so-called investigation to justify its own conduct.

Something astonishingly similar occurred when Peter Mandelson resigned for a second time, barely twelve months later, this time as a result of confusion about whether he had exerted improper pressure to secure passports on behalf of the Hinduja brothers. Once Mandelson had reluctantly resigned, a series of reports appeared in the press to the effect that Sir Richard Wilson had been responsible for his decision to quit. These can only have come from Tony Blair's Downing Street advisers, who were probably eager to place the blame for the resignation fiasco elsewhere. Once again they were quite untrue. On this occasion Sir Richard had flatly refused to launch any kind of official investigation, deeming that the judgement about whether Mandelson should quit was a purely political decision. On this occasion he was so incensed about the way that his advice had been misrepresented that he formally complained to the Prime Minister, who promised to put the record straight, but never did so.[6]

Sir Richard was converted into a kind of constitutional alibi to help the Prime Minister and his political aides escape embarrassment after ministerial resignations. This was not the worst kind of abuse that he suffered. He was also used as an errand boy for the Political Class. Cabinet Secretaries had suffered this kind of mistreatment before, as we have already seen during the Conservative period in government, most famously in the sad case of Sir Robert Armstrong and the *Spycatcher* affair. This kind of abuse became systematic under New Labour. In July 1998, within months of his appointment as Cabinet Secretary, Sir Richard Wilson was employed by Tony Blair as hatchet man in a Cabinet reshuffle. The Prime Minister was eager to sack Geoffrey Robinson, the paymaster-general. Two motives lay behind the move. Robinson was a close ally of Gordon Brown, who was already a major thorn in the flesh for Downing Street. Second, Robinson's business affairs were under attack in the wake of an article – robustly denied by the minister – published in the magazine *Business Age* outlining his alleged dealings with Robert Maxwell.

First, Tony Blair attempted to do the job himself, calling Robinson in for a meeting in his office. Robinson, after consulting Gordon Brown, refused to attend. At this point Tony Blair abandoned hope of personally sacking Robinson and, disgracefully, called Sir Richard Wilson into play. First the Cabinet Secretary visited Gordon Brown. 'I heard subsequently that Gordon was requested to ask for my resignation to avoid any further awkwardness,' records Robinson in his autobiography. 'Gordon asked why and was told that the press campaign was an embarrassment to the government.'

Failing to convince the Chancellor that Robinson should go, the

Cabinet Secretary then visited Robinson in his Treasury office. Robinson records:

> He was all sweetness and light, very old-boyish. 'Rough old game, politics,' was his opening gambit, as he walked through the door. He went on to the Maxwell affair, and cited the *Business Age* article despite his conversation just a few minutes earlier with the Chancellor. Icily but as politely as I could, I told him it was a pack of lies. He replied blithely, 'But it is all out there.' 'Are they the grounds for my leaving the government?'
>
> 'Yes,' he replied. 'And it's rather more dignified to resign than to be sacked.'
>
> I thanked him and said I would think about it as I showed him to the door. He was visibly shaken as he left. In the doorway he turned to impart his final disarming shot: 'I like you.'[7]

This story is not isolated. In the same reshuffle that saw the failed attempt to dispatch Geoffrey Robinson, Tony Blair also used Sir Richard Wilson as an instrument to try to keep a minister. He dispatched him to try to persuade Frank Field to stay in the government even though he was to be moved from being Minister of State in the Department of Social Security, where Field had hoped to become the architect of a historic reform. Sir Richard's opening words as he entered Frank Field's office were: 'The Prime Minister believes you have solved welfare.' Field was not taken in by this piece of flattery. 'Nothing could be further from the truth,' he recorded, 'but the Prime Minister was evidently seeking a way of letting me down gently.'[8] Field insisted that he was interested in no other department, so Wilson's entreaties failed.

It is certainly the case that the Cabinet Secretary has a significant role involving himself in passing judgement on ethical problems involving ministers. But in the cases of both Geoffrey Robinson and Frank Field he was allowing himself to be used politically as an intermediary between the Prime Minister and a minister. Tony Blair should not have requested, and Wilson should never have agreed, to carry out these errands.

It was, nevertheless, very hard for Wilson to refuse, just as it had been before him for Sir Robert Armstrong and Sir Robin Butler. The British system makes a dual demand on any civil servant. On the one hand it insists that he should serve ministers of the Crown and carry out his or her instructions. On the other hand civil servants, and in particular the Cabinet Secretary, are expected to act as a guarantor of good process. No Cabinet Secretary can carry out his task without a close, trusting and confidential relationship with the Prime Minister. Wilson may well have felt that if he turned down the requests in the case of either Field or Robinson, it would have permanently damaged his relationship with Tony Blair. It was therefore extremely unfair of Blair to make the request, and it would have taken an heroic act on the part of Wilson to resist them. Wilson was a competent and dedicated official whose rise inside Whitehall had come during the long Conservative years. Like other Whitehall civil servants, he was extremely eager to show that he could work with New Labour as well, even if that meant blurring boundaries.

He showed this in a number of ways. During his early period as Cabinet Secretary, he was available to put himself forward as an apologist for the New Labour changes to the civil service. He told the House of Commons Administration Committee that the doubling of the number of special advisers had left the balance between government and Whitehall unaltered. 'I do not think the Senior Civil Service of 3,700 people is in danger of being swamped by 70 special advisers. That is not what is happening and I do not see it as creeping politicisation.'[9] This statement was highly questionable, and it is extremely unlikely that Sir Richard Wilson believed what he was saying even at the time. Likewise when interviewed about the New Labour system on BBC Radio by Romola Christopherson, a former government information officer, Sir Richard claimed that nothing had changed. 'The power is formally vested in secretaries of state, who run departments. You have a Cabinet at the top of the government who collectively reach decisions – with the Prime Minister as chairman of the Cabinet and the person who makes the key appointments.'[10]

This was an account of how government was supposed to have worked in the past, and perhaps Sir Richard's wish of how it still worked at the time he was speaking. It bore only a formal resemblance to the system that actually prevailed during the Blair years. At the stage when he uttered his remarks, the Cabinet Secretary was fighting a battle to maintain the role of the traditional civil service within the New Labour system, and was understandably unwilling to jeopardise relations with Downing Street.

The first half of the Wilson period as Cabinet Secretary was marked by a long, unavailing attempt to reach some kind of accommodation with the crony government imposed by Tony Blair from 1997 onwards. But at some stage the iron entered Sir Richard's soul. During the second half of his time as Cabinet Secretary Wilson came out fighting. Ill at ease with the ever greater debauchery of the civil service, Sir Richard started to press heavily for legislation which would give it full legal protection against political interference. At first this pressure seemed to be successful, and the Prime Minister gave Wilson an informal commitment that he could look forward to a Civil Service Act of some kind. Sir Richard publicly called for protections for the civil service, and new curbs on New Labour's rampant special advisers. In a speech given on 26 March 2002, he said:

Very often the issues are about boundaries: the boundaries between what is and what is not acceptable. The boundaries between government and party; grey areas where judgements are difficult and different people acting in good faith may properly come to different conclusions. There is a danger that if we continue to leave these issues unattended they will fester. They will increasingly become rubbing matters, matters of political controversy used to embarrass government, damaging the civil service and perversely making it more difficult to bring about the changes which are needed.[11]

Sir Richard also demanded that 'special advisers should not ask civil servants to do anything immoral or illegal', nor 'do anything to undermine the political impartiality of civil servants to give their best advice to ministers'. This was an astonishing lecture, in effect a withering attack on the way that New Labour had conducted itself in government. It was all the more extraordinary for the fact that at this stage Wilson was still in office, and therefore under heavy restraint in terms of his ability to speak out. It is likely that had Wilson remained Cabinet Secretary for much longer there would have been a major clash between the centralising, presiden-tial Blair system of government and the traditional civil service.

But the retirement of Wilson early in 2002 gave the Prime Minister an opportunity to change the job description. Wilson's successor was Sir Andrew Turnbull, permanent secretary at the Treasury, who made clear while being interviewed for the job that he shared the Prime Minister's impatience with the traditional structures of the civil service.

Right from the start he set about undermining Sir Richard Wilson's campaign for fresh protections for the civil service, indicating that he was relaxed about special advisers and dis-missive of alarms about process and impartiality. 'We have to be careful about fighting the battles of yesteryear,' he said in an early interview with the political commentator Peter Riddell. He said that the nineteenth-century reformers were 'worried about cronyism, the wrong people getting in, people with no merit or claim. We have a different problem ... to get the right people rather than the wrong people in.'[12]

The *Times* interview with Turnbull appeared on the same day as a House of Lords debate in which a group of former mandarins lined up to support Sir Richard Wilson's call for a Civil Service Act. Turnbull made it plain that he was unenthusiastic: 'We have lived without one for 150 years.' This was a brutal rebuke, and allies of Wilson felt certain that Downing Street had arranged the timing of the Turnbull interview in order to pull the rug from under him.

The essential point about Sir Andrew Turnbull was that he represented a new kind of Cabinet Secretary, one without the same moral weight. He did not, like his predecessors Sir Robin Butler and Sir Richard Wilson, speak out for the old system of Cabinet government. On the contrary, he seems to have collaborated in its destruction. He accepted that there should be a fundamental change. He appears to have ceased to be a co-ordinating figure, working smoothly at the interface between Number 10 Downing Street and the various Departments of State. He gave away many of the responsibilities that had traditionally fallen to the Cabinet Secretary.

Sir Andrew seems also to have abandoned the role of guardian of the independence of Whitehall. During his time in office many of the ordinary disciplines of government seem to have completely collapsed, and the Downing Street 'sofa culture' reached its peak. The process of administration became extremely sloppy. Minutes ceased to be taken at key meetings. When the Hutton Inquiry looked at the administration of Downing Street in the aftermath of the Iraq War in 2003, the Cabinet Secretary did not figure, a situation that would have been unimaginable in the twentieth century.

Sir Andrew Turnbull plugged away assiduously from the centre, driving through what Downing Street liked to call 'delivery'. Nothing in his experience at the Treasury had prepared him for the role he was given, and there is no special evidence that much progress was made in reform to British public services during the curious period during which Turnbull held office. Turnbull's role now became closer to managing director than to Cabinet Secretary. This turned him into an isolated figure, because he lacked most of the tools to drive the change he wanted in Whitehall. Sir Andrew Turnbull did not seek to exercise the role of Cabinet Secretary as understood during the bulk of the twentieth century. As a result the integrity of British government came close at times to total collapse. His short-lived incumbency coincided with a low point in the history of the modern British civil service. This, however, was the result of decisions made by the Prime Minister, and not the fault of Sir Andrew.

The Political Class and Ministerial Responsibility

The degradation of the Cabinet Secretary was only one part of a general recalibration of the relationship between ministers and civil servants that has taken place over the last twenty-five years. The Political Class also sought to weaken, and then to abolish altogether, the longstanding doctrine that ministers should be responsible for errors made within their departments, and in extreme cases be expected to resign.

Going back half a century to the immediate post-war period, well before the emergence of the Political Class, it is easy to see that Britain was defined by an exceptionally strong ethic of civic responsibility. It was understood to be axiomatic that ministers whose conduct fell below acceptable standards would resign. To give one example, the Labour Chancellor Hugh Dalton felt obliged to quit the government after he had incautiously told a journalist of a proposed measure in his 1947 Budget. This kind of conduct is unthinkable today. Indeed many recent Budgets have been systematically leaked in advance by spin-doctors, acting on behalf of the Chancellor of the Exchequer, and this has not generally been viewed as disreputable behaviour.

Two years after Dalton's embarrassment a junior Labour minister, John Belcher, was found to have accepted a suit, a holiday in Margate and a cigarette case, as well as accommodation at sporting events. His benefactor was Sidney Stanley, an un-discharged bankrupt who used his gifts to claim to business associates that he had influence in government. In the ensuing tribunal Belcher's conduct was not found to have been corrupt. Nevertheless the minister resigned his job and also stepped down as an MP, declaring that: 'I have not at any time in the course of my official duties been conscious of any deviation from the path of morality or rectitude.' He was praised by the Prime Minister, Clement Attlee, who declared: 'The whole House is conscious of the terrible tragedy which has overtaken him. He has spoken with dignity and courage.' Belcher had been a railway clerk before entering the Commons and returned to his old job, in due course rising to become an Assistant Goods Agent. However, it is said that he never personally recovered from his public humiliation and died at the relatively early age of fifty-nine.

The almost exact comparison here is with the conduct of John Prescott, Deputy Prime Minister under Tony Blair, who accepted hospitality and gifts from the American billionaire Philip Anschutz. Besides a weekend stay on the Anschutz ranch in Texas (not declared on the Commons register of interests), Prescott was given a pair of tooled leather cowboy boots, a Stetson and a silver-buckled belt reportedly bearing the letters 'JP'. At the time Anschutz was bidding to set up Britain's first super-casino on the site of the Millennium Dome. Prescott, though he denied it, had a key role to play in the process. His officials, for example, played a part in discouraging bidders who might stand in the way of the Anschutz bid. In this case the Prime Minister refused to set up an inquiry into Prescott's indiscretion, and he was allowed to stay in his post.

During the decades following the Second World War concepts of honour, duty and moral responsibility generally weighed high in the minds of politicians and counted for more than careerist considerations. This was partly because politicians were more closely connected with mainstream morality than has subsequently become the case. The most important code in this period was ministerial responsibility. It was held that ministers were accountable through Parliament to the wider public for the successes and failures of the departments they ran. This was a structure which fitted with a generally accepted and extremely widespread ethic which extended far beyond Westminster. For example, the directors of a public company were charged by shareholders with ensuring its good performance and might be expected to walk the plank if they failed to deliver. In the armed forces, officers who failed to sustain the morale and competence of the men under their command were demoted.

In the case of ministers an implicit deal was at work. They were the public face of their department, able to defend their actions in a way that the officials who worked for them were not. This doctrine was capable of straying into unfairness. Rather as the Admiralty decision to have Admiral Byng shot for cowardice in 1757 often strikes contemporary minds as an extreme and undeserved punishment, so many twenty-first-century observers now feel it unfair that the agriculture minister Sir Thomas Dugdale adhered so rigorously to the code of ministerial responsibility that he resigned over the so-called Crichel Down scandal of 1954.

This affair concerned government misappropriation of some private land, which had been used as a bombing range during the Second World War. In the ensuing inquiry civil servants were criticised for errors of judgement. Sir Thomas, following the precept that ministers should bear the responsibility for the errors of civil servants, handed in his resignation.*

This code continued to exist for at least a generation after Dugdale. In 1982 the then Foreign Secretary Lord Carrington (who by coincidence had been Dugdale's junior minister during the Crichel Down affair, and had himself attempted to step down, though his offer was rejected) resigned in the wake of the Argentinian invasion of the Falklands. In practice few people felt that Carrington was personally at fault for the capture of this remote British dependency, though some opposition critics affected to believe something of the sort. Carrington, however, who had a fine war record and was one of the last of the grandee politicians, could not be dissuaded from taking the responsibility. In the same year the Home Secretary Willie Whitelaw also sought to resign, only to be dissuaded by the Prime Minister, after an intruder broke into the Queen's bedroom at Buckingham Palace.

The Carrington resignation was the last of its kind, though Peter Brooke's offer to stand down as Northern Ireland Secretary in

---

* At any rate this is the version that persisted for some thirty years after the event. The later release of government papers related to the affair suggested, however, that Dugdale actually had known and approved the decisions taken by his officials, and had allowed them to take the public blame for decisions that were rightfully his.

1992, after he showed a lack of sensitivity in singing 'Clementine' on a TV chat show in the immediate aftermath of an IRA atrocity in which eight people were killed, bore some of the hallmarks of an earlier code of conduct. In general, however, the election year of 1992 marked a break-point. After it, ministers ceased to leave government as a result of policy or departmental failures. The first, and still the most shameless, example of this novel insouciance concerned the Conservative Chancellor Norman Lamont, who remained in office after the collapse of his economic policy with sterling's brutal departure from the Exchange Rate Mechanism in September 1992.

Lamont's conduct contrasted sharply with the fate of the Labour Chancellor of the Exchequer Jim Callaghan, who was shifted from the Treasury after sterling's devaluation in 1967. Lamont, however, reflected the mentality of the Political Class that was stealthily taking control of British government from the 1990s. Lamont's overwhelming loyalty seems to have been to his own survival in office. The system of sentiments and practices which governed conduct in civil society – honour, integrity, 'doing the right thing' – had provided a guide for politicians during the period when they felt an intrinsic connection with the wider British nation, but not beyond.

On 17 September, the day after the ERM débâcle, Lamont invited Max Hastings, editor of the Tory-supporting *Daily Telegraph*, into the Treasury. Hastings' account of the conversation captures the clash between the narrow Political Class outlook and normal expectations of proper conduct:

> We exchanged pleasantries. For years, Norman had been something more than an acquaintance, something less than a friend. 'I thought it would be helpful to have you in, Max,' he began smoothly, 'and to emphasise that our economic policy – monetary targets and so on – will remain unchanged as a result of yesterday's events.'
>
> 'Yes, Norman,' I said, 'but who's going to be in charge?'
>
> 'How do you mean – "in charge"?'

'Who's going to be Chancellor?'
'I am.'
'But you can't be.'
'Why not?'
'Because nobody's got any confidence in you any more.'
'The Prime Minister has expressed his full confidence in me.'
'But no one else will.'
'Nobody could have anticipated what happened yesterday.'[13]

In retrospect Lamont's decision can be seen to mark a turning-point. From the early 1990s onwards ministers were starting to evolve a distinction between their formal position as secretary of state and the policies and achievements of their department. They continued to claim the credit when matters went well, if anything grabbing any praise going with a greater shamelessness than ever before. But when errors occurred or their policies failed, they evolved a new doctrine. An important moment came in 1995, when three prisoners escaped from Parkhurst top-security prison. The Home Secretary, Michael Howard, faced calls to resign, and his predecessors might well have responded to them. But Howard refused to quit, and was swift to disavow the ancient convention that ministers should stand up and take the blame for mishaps within their own department. He insisted that the prison break was an 'operational' matter, and in due course it was Derek Lewis, director of prisons, who was forced to go instead.

That episode opened the way to a changed concept of ministerial responsibility, which was formalised after the arrival of New Labour in power in 1997. This event soon formally established a new orthodoxy: namely that ministers should never resign in any circumstances because to do so would be a defeat for the government. However mendacious or venal a minister might be, he must be allowed to stay in office. An early beneficiary of this disreputable doctrine was the Foreign Office minister Keith Vaz. Vaz was found to have misled the Parliamentary Commissioner for Standards over cash payments he had received from an individual he had recommended for an honour, and was accused of flatly refusing to co-operate with the Commissioner's inquiry into his affairs. However, Vaz was strongly protected by the Prime Minister.

Another early case in point was the Cabinet minister Stephen Byers, who faced calls for his resignation after he had lied repeatedly to the television presenter Jonathan Dimbleby about his treatment of a senior official. In response to calls that he should resign, a protective arm was thrown around him by the political and government machine. The same protective mantle was also thrown round the Home Secretary David Blunkett even after it became plain that he had abused his private office.

The effect of these – and many other – episodes was to stretch past breaking point the connection between the Political Class and ordinary voters. If Tony Blair had sacked lying or abusive ministers his policy would have sent out a message that the Political Class shared the ethical standards of mainstream society. Instead the decision to protect them created a dual reality. There was the world lived in by the Political Class, where men like Keith Vaz, Stephen Byers and David Blunkett were officially signed off as honest and decent by the Prime Minister of the day. Meanwhile there was an outside world, where they could be detected at once as liars or imposters. These alternate structures of perception and morality are beginning to tear British political society to shreds.*

Partly because of this ministerial refusal to resign, the connection between ministers and their officials changed yet again. Ministers not only made it clear they would take no responsibility for departmental errors. They also displayed a ruthless willingness to head

---

* This contradiction between official standards and wider morality has had another interesting effect. The Political Class determination never to admit to wrongdoing or transgression has led to resignations which officially take place for no reason at all. Both the formal resignation note from the outgoing minister, as well as the reply from the Prime Minister of the day, will stress that no wrongdoing has occurred and that there is therefore no *bona fide* reason to resign at all. These baffling cases are extremely common. Both Peter Mandelson's resignations, the second Blunkett resignation and the Byers resignation all fall into this approximate category.

off trouble by publicly blaming or scapegoating the civil servants. This again was an inversion of the norms of civil society, where men and women in senior positions expect as a matter of course to take the responsibility for the organisations under their command.

This tactic was used, for example, by the solicitor-general Harriet Harman after she had improperly passed private documents concerning family court matters to a ministerial colleague. Rather than take proper responsibility for the dereliction, Harman – herself a lawyer – passed the blame on to a government legal adviser for giving wrong advice.[14]

But this was a minor episode compared to the lethal and sustained attacks launched on civil servants by senior Cabinet ministers throughout the post-1997 era. The Home Secretaries David Blunkett and John Reid were especially brutal, and their political objective has been clear: to ensure that officials rather than the new Political Class got the blame for errors of policy and other mismanagement. They have set out quite deliberately to destroy the Victorian settlement which created a clear dividing line between politicians and Whitehall. This attitude has created a crisis of trust between ministers, the home civil service and the public at large, and it is now time to turn to this shocking and unpleasant subject.

The Capture of the Civil Service

The British system of government does not rely, like the American model, on a system of checks and balances in order to ensure integrity and root out wrongdoing. Instead it depends on a system of sharply defined dividing lines between the politician and the official. On the one side there is the politician: elected, visible and temporary. On the other side you have the official: anonymous, self-effacing and permanent. The official makes one massive act of renunciation. He or she is banned from taking part in political activity, and formally owes his allegiance to the Crown. The civil service, in the graceful words of the late *Guardian* columnist Hugo

Young, believes 'that it represents and personifies the seamless integrity of past, present and future government rolled indistinguishably into one'.[15]

The task of the official, nevertheless, is to carry out the orders of the elected politician. It is a matter of professional pride that civil servants should be able to serve, with equal competence and enthusiasm, all governments whether of right or left. Very strict rules, arising originally from the Northcote/Trevelyan reforms of the nineteenth century, insist on this neutrality.

These rules also define the exclusive domain of the bureaucrat. This clarification is essential, because ministers from a new administration must be able to trust the officials who report to them. They must know that their confidences will be kept, that their plans will not be leaked, and their policies will not be sabotaged. The machinery of state has to be neutral. British democratic government, which relies on five-yearly elections and frequent changes of government, cannot function without an efficient civil service which is prepared to serve all political parties and every political outlook.

But the prophylactic devices inspired by the great nineteenth-century civil service reformers were not merely necessary to save politicians from corrupt or motivated civil servants. They were yet more necessary to protect the civil servants from the politicians. Elected politicians, convinced of the justice of their cause and the urgent necessity of putting their ideas into practice, rapidly become impatient of the ingrained scepticism and experience of the lifelong bureaucrat. They always tend to confuse caution with hostility and interpret sensible preparation as obstruction.

Furthermore, politicians are constantly under pressure to reward their supporters. They therefore suffer an extreme temptation to use the machinery of government for political ends. Many politicians, for instance, interpret the state and its associated agencies as one vast pool of patronage. This is why elected politicians are barred from intervening in the career structure and employment arrangements of departments. Matters of promotion and discipline can be dealt with by the civil service alone.

During the thirty-five years between the end of the Second World War and the election of the Thatcher government, the model described above worked extremely well. There were two reasons for this. One was that governments turned over with great regularity during this period. New governments were elected to power in 1945, 1951, 1964, 1970, 1974 and 1979. This meant that the two-party system became embedded in the British administrative mentality. Individual civil servants rarely had enough time to transfer their loyalty from the British state to any of the political parties that temporarily held sway in Whitehall. In any case there was little or no personal advantage, and considerable career risk, in doing so, because the arrival of a fresh government was only a matter of time. This state of affairs was to change after the emergence of Margaret Thatcher. There has been only one change of government in the quarter-century and more that has followed her victory in 1979. During the last twenty-eight years civil servants have had far more opportunity, and also a keener motive, to breach the dividing line between party and state by transferring their allegiance to elected politicians.

There was a second reason why the model of a neutral civil service worked exceptionally well in the post-war years. During the first three post-war decades, the two governing parties – though different on ultimate aims – shared fundamental beliefs about how Britain should be governed. They both believed in a mixed economy and the Keynesian model of demand management, the two central doctrines of the post-war British governments, both of which gave the civil service a pivotal role. No Prime Minister seriously challenged this orthodoxy until the economic collapse of the 1970s and the arrival on the scene of Margaret Thatcher. In the early 1980s Thatcher collided with certain senior civil servants, who did not share her radical views of the British state. 'There was a genuine clash of cultures,' recorded Margaret Thatcher's biographer Hugo Young, 'between a political leadership fired by an almost Cromwellian impatience with the status quo, and the mandarin world of Whitehall in which scepticism and rumination were more highly rated habits of mind than zeal or blind conviction'.[16] An early victim of this collision was Sir Douglas Wass, the permanent secretary at the Treasury, an archetypal product of the Whitehall machine, and devout believer in the post-war consensus.* Wass found himself cut out of the decision-making process, and gradually replaced by figures who were better disposed to the monetarist policies of the new government. The most effective of these was an outsider, brought in from the London School of Economics as the new chief economic adviser at the Treasury, Terence (now Lord) Burns. A similar process went on elsewhere in Whitehall, though the clash of cultures was rarely as marked as at the Treasury.

By the time of the New Labour victory of 1997, civil servants had been reporting to Conservative ministers for eighteen years. During this long stretch of opposition, many Labour politicians had become convinced that one-party government had compromised the objectivity of officials, and that they had become cheerleaders for the Conservative Party. There was evidence that a handful of civil servants had indeed crossed the boundary between giving impartial advice and becoming the political instrument of the government of the day: Margaret Thatcher's foreign policy adviser Charles Powell was an unhappy case in point. But in general it would be a great exaggeration to conclude that the civil service at large had been converted into an extension of the Conservative Party. On the contrary, in 1997 the vast majority of officials welcomed the change of government, in part as a change of scenery and in part as a test of their professionalism.

Nevertheless, New Labour continued to cherish its suspicion of the British civil service. The new government, empowered by its massive parliamentary majority, launched a sustained and brutal attack on the influence of permanent officials in the years after it came to power. Within a short space of time this had led to a

---

* Hugo Young records that Sir Douglas once told him that 'the majority of Whitehall officials were natural social democrats: middle-of-the-road people who believed, as was only to be expected, in the benign role of government in the lives of the people'. See Young, *One of Us*, p. 156.

change in the structure of Whitehall, and the fundamental nature of British administration, which was far more dramatic than anything brought about by the Thatcher or Major regimes.

The first sign that Tony Blair meant business was a sharp turnover of personnel in key areas. In the twelve months that followed 1 May 1997 more than half of all Whitehall information chiefs and deputy chiefs had been replaced. By August 1999 all but two of Whitehall's seventeen directors of communication had gone.[17] This rate of turnover reflected the new priority attached to presentation and media work by New Labour. It was a completely unprecedented replacement rate: by Whitehall standards, nothing short of carnage. Some of these senior Whitehall figures went out of choice or because they were coming up to retirement. But a significant number went because Downing Street wanted to place information officers under sharper political control.

Much more significant, though at first much less obvious, were the changes to the machinery of government. The most telling of these was the reorganisation of the Downing Street operation. Until the arrival of Tony Blair, the most influential aides surrounding any Prime Minister had been civil servants. In particular two figures had been completely pivotal. First was the Principal Private Secretary (PPS) to the Prime Minister. This individual tended to be a youngish, high-flying civil servant, selected on the grounds of exceptional ability, and destined to rise to the very top of the civil service. His or her job was to keep minutes of meetings and to liaise on behalf of the Prime Minister with Whitehall. The second, and most powerful, figure in the Prime Minister's life in government was the Cabinet Secretary.

It is obvious in retrospect that New Labour from the very first concluded that it would govern without these two civil service figures. Tony Blair sought right from the start to move over to a presidential system. He chose not to make use of the civil service bureaucracy that lay ready to hand, but instead use a select group of political aides and enforcers as his executive tool. The effect was revolutionary. In 1997 the British Prime Minister sidelined the bureaucracy and gave a new Political Class control not merely over policy and decision-making but over execution and administration as well. In practice as well as in theory, this involved a reconfiguration of British administration which very swiftly led to a repudiation of the constitutional doctrine that civil servants owe their final allegiance not to the governing political party but to the Crown.

The Prime Minister had decided even before the 1997 election that he did not want a career civil servant, however talented or distinguished, to perform the crucial role of PPS. He was determined to impose Jonathan Powell, the so-called chief of staff in his private office when he had been leader of the Labour Party. This appointment was strongly resisted by Sir Robin Butler, then the Cabinet Secretary and head of the home civil service. Butler met Tony Blair at the future Prime Minister's Islington home during the 1997 election campaign to discuss the proposal.[18] Butler argued against the move on two grounds. He claimed first of all that it would be irregular and also disastrous to civil service morale for a political appointee such as Powell to be given such a senior job, particularly one that required such elaborate liaison with the rest of Whitehall. Secondly, Butler pointed out that there were a number of aspects of the PPS role – handling the honours system, dealing with the leader of the official opposition, receiving intelligence briefings – which demanded absolute neutrality and were incompatible with a political identity. Butler was successful in fighting off this incursion on the fiefdom of the civil service. His victory was, however, limited. Powell may have failed to get the title of PPS. But he came to occupy many of the functions, and was actually given a desk in the small Private Secretary's office adjacent to the Cabinet room. Well-informed civil servants insist that actually Tony Blair won the battle with Sir Robin Butler, even if nominally he did not.

In any case, Tony Blair did emerge the winner from an equally significant argument against Sir Robin Butler. He was determined that his key political aides should be given much fuller powers than previous advisers to the Prime Minister had ever been given before. This was important so that they could be integrated with the machinery of government, rather than float around, as was the case with the political aides who had operated inside Downing Street in previous regimes. But this proposal ran up against seemingly insoluble constitutional problems. Special advisers, under civil service rules imposing impartiality, have never been able to issue orders to civil servants and were formally impotent in Whitehall, finding themselves in the embarrassing position of eunuchs inside a harem. This position was intolerable for Tony Blair. He applied pressure. In due course Sir Robin gave in. In a transgression of the dividing line between the Political Class and the mandarin class, certain special advisers were granted executive powers over civil servants, a move that was to be fraught with consequence. The decision was such an infraction of existing constitutional arrangements that it needed to be ratified by special Orders in Council which were issued at the Privy Council. The two individuals granted this unprecedented status were Jonathan Powell and Alastair Campbell, the Downing Street press secretary.* This meant that Campbell, an unelected political operative, was able to give orders to career civil servants inside the Whitehall information machine. As for Jonathan Powell, he did not merely rank senior to the PPS in the Downing Street hierarchy: the PPS reported directly to him. This became clear when towards the end of the 1997–2001 Parliament the Cabinet Secretary Sir Richard Wilson issued a map of Downing Street functions. This showed Powell as Downing Street chief of staff at the apex of the Number 10 structure. The policy unit, the press office and the PPS Jeremy Heywood and the Prime Minister's private office were all shown reporting to the chief of staff. After the General Election of 2001 Powell's role was expanded to Head of Policy, one of three Number 10 departments, all of which were headed not by officials but by party figures.

Meanwhile New Labour had doubled the number of special advisers from thirty-five or so under John Major's Conservative

---

* A third was held in reserve. It was said to be intended for Charlie Whelan, Gordon Brown's press adviser, but never filled.

government to eighty or more under New Labour. The number of those operating inside Downing Street rose even more dramatically. Defenders of the new regime declared that none of this mattered, and contrasted the paltry number of special advisers with the enormous numbers of civil servants. These protestations were disingenuous. In practice these special advisers undertook much of the high-level administration and liaison work previously carried out by civil servants in a Cabinet minister's private office. The sheer number of special advisers now gave ministers an alternative communications network in Whitehall, which could allow ministers to deal with each other and make decisions without ever touching the formal civil service – a revolutionary and bracing moment.[19]

Sidelining the Treasury

The most audacious of all the attacks on the civil service was the assault on the Treasury carried out by the new Chancellor Gordon Brown and his tightly-knit inner team of advisers in the immediate months after the 1997 General Election. The Treasury had long been the most dominant and self-confident of all government departments: meritocratic, classless and intellectually robust. Within days of taking office, however, the new Chancellor – who today claims to be an admirer of traditional civil service methods – effectively closed down the official structures of government he had just inherited. The Permanent Secretary, Sir Terence Burns, was at once sidelined, a parallel process to the sidelining of the Cabinet Secretary inside 10 Downing Street. It instantly became apparent that Brown was refusing to work through the official systems that had been used by previous Chancellors.

Brown imposed a parallel system of command. The key decisions were made outside the Treasury – at first in the penthouse flat lived in by the paymaster-general Geoffrey Robinson at the top of the Grosvenor House hotel. According to one very senior official, Gordon Brown 'was really only prepared to work through a small circle of trusted officials who were not part of the official machine'.[20] Another well-placed source said: 'It became clear that Gordon Brown would not deal with the Treasury as a whole.' Gordon Brown smashed the normal structures of Cabinet government. For example, in a clear infraction of procedure, he brought his special advisers to Cabinet committee meetings. The Chancellor would snub Cabinet itself, ostentatiously bringing his own work with him into the Cabinet room and carrying on with that rather than engaging with the round-table discussion. According to one senior civil servant who witnessed this, Gordon Brown's behaviour was akin to a 'male dominance ritual' because he knew that only he could get away unrebuked with this kind of conduct.

Gordon Brown refused to engage with the paperwork that would normally be carried out by government ministers and officials. He refused to attach his name to documents. Treasury officials would send a letter to the Chancellor and expect a response within twenty-four hours. Weeks would pass without an answer. 'The normal ways of advice didn't happen,' says one official. According to Sir Stephen Wall, Tony Blair's European adviser in 10 Downing Street, one extremely senior Treasury official 'took to standing in the corridor outside the Chancellor's office and waylaying one of the private secretaries' in order to discover the way the Chancellor's mind was working.

At first Gordon Brown would only work with the team of three or four personal friends or advisers he had brought with him from outside government. The most important of these by far was Ed Balls, at first a special adviser, though later rewarded with the key Treasury post of Chief Economic Adviser and now an MP and member of the Brown Cabinet. Though outside the Treasury structure, one well-placed official told me: 'People very quickly learned that if they wanted the Chancellor, to get the Chancellor to agree with something, they had to get it cleared with Ed first.'

In due course this inner core of trusted personal friends widened to embrace a small number of civil servants who gained the full trust of the Chancellor. According to observers, this could only be achieved by giving unconditional personal loyalty to Gordon Brown. Those who failed to earn the Chancellor's trust, such as Gill Rutter, the press secretary he inherited from his Tory predecessor Ken Clarke, could be driven out of the Treasury. 'You differ with Gordon Brown at your peril,' remarked one Treasury civil servant.

This refusal to engage with the normal process of government, to take notes, and to consult with civil servants and others, can be seen in retrospect to be responsible for many of the most grievous policy failures of recent years, above all the fiasco and waste of money surrounding the introduction of tax credits. It has also made engagement with other government departments extremely complex and unwieldy, mainly because Treasury officials who attended meetings often had no idea of what the Chancellor's view really was of the issues under discussion. Gordon Brown's decision to govern through a small group of greatly empowered special advisers and some highly politicised civil servants changed the nature of government.

War Between Politicians and Officials

The doubling of the number of special advisers, along with a massive increase in their power and influence, inevitably led to tensions in Whitehall. Civil servants did their best to accommodate them, but some found it very hard to cope with the new culture of bullying and manipulation. In due course the tensions came to a head in an extremely dramatic way with the case of Jo Moore, the very influential Special Adviser to Transport Secretary Stephen Byers. The astonishing events surrounding the embarrassment and final departure of Jo Moore are worth addressing here in some detail because they show with great clarity the way the new methodology of administration worked. In addition, the final *dénouement* of the Jo Moore affair, which took place in Downing Street at a tense meeting of the full Cabinet in March 2002, graphically demonstrates the sheer scale of the collapse of relations between the New Labour political machine and the British civil service.

Jo Moore was one of the most gorgeous manifestations of the new Political Class. Attractive, conscientious and industrious, she had worked for Tony Blair in opposition and was one of the most trusted members of New Labour's inner core of special advisers. Away from this political machinery, however, Jo Moore was much less popular. She enjoyed a reputation for bullying civil servants and anyone who stood in her way. In 2001 she was involved in an extremely unpleasant clash with Alun Evans, the Director of Communications in her department. Moore ordered civil servants to brief against Bob Kiley, the London Transport Commissioner appointed by Ken Livingstone, who was causing political difficulties for the government. Evans complained about this order, and in due course he was moved from his post.

Jo Moore first hit the headlines when her infamous e-mail to members of the Department of Transport press office, announcing that 11 September 2001 was a 'good day to bury bad news', was leaked in the press. Though Jo Moore's instruction caused a storm, it never put her job seriously in danger. She was too important a member of the core New Labour team to be given up, so both Stephen Byers and in particular the Prime Minister fought to save her. Her position only came under real threat three months later, when a second e-mail came to light. This one suggested that Moore had by no means learned her lesson, and was eager to use Princess Margaret's funeral as a device to provide cover for a further barrage of difficult announcements. To this day it remains unclear whether Jo Moore really did want to pull off this stunt, and whether it would have worked in any case.

But there is no question that this second e-mail was leaked from inside the civil service with the intention of destroying Ms Moore. Two days of messy newspaper headlines followed, and then she was forced out, taking the head of information at the Department of Transport, Martin Sixsmith, with her. From this moment relations between ministers and the civil service became icy. Ministers sided with Jo Moore. They blamed the leaks of the two e-mails on civil servants, disregarding Moore's own arrogance, and remaining unperturbed by claims that she had acted improperly.

Three weeks after Moore's forced resignation, the Cabinet turned on the civil service. The scene for the attack was the routine Thursday morning Cabinet meeting. John Reid, always Tony Blair's closest ally in Cabinet, opened a bitter attack on officials which, in the view of some present, appeared co-ordinated. According to a source at the meeting, Reid revealed that he, like Stephen Byers, 'had never been able to trust his officials' while at the Department of Transport. Scottish Secretary Helen Liddell spoke next, declaring that she unequivocally agreed with Reid. But the longest and most powerful assault came from the Home Secretary David Blunkett. He launched into a series of scathing criticisms of the values and the attitudes of the British civil service, accusing it of incompetence and disloyalty. At the end of his speech he declared: 'There has been talk of a bill to protect civil servants from ministers. What we need is a bill to protect ministers from civil servants.'

Blunkett was referring to the proposed legislation being urgently pressed for by the Cabinet Secretary Sir Richard Wilson, and it was known that he had secured the half-hearted support of the Prime Minister. Blunkett's remarks – and indeed the entire Cabinet discussion – were directly aimed at Sir Richard, the head of the home civil service and therefore obliged to take the ultimate responsibility for all the transgressions alleged over the Cabinet table. Astonishingly Sir Richard was also at the Cabinet table on that very occasion. He was there in the traditional capacity of the Cabinet Secretary, taking minutes. He was bound to write down each of the caustic and brutal attacks made on his colleagues. With his head bowed, those in the room found it hard to discern his expression. Some wondered whether he would walk out. When the Home Secretary had finished his outburst, it was Tony Blair's turn to speak. He made a flippant remark: 'At least you know, Sir Richard, that you have the full support of the Home Office.' The Prime Minister made no attempt to defend the civil service, still less to rebuke Cabinet colleagues who criticised civil servants. It was quite clear that he agreed with their criticisms and wanted them aired.

This Downing Street model was not confined to the centre. It swiftly entrenched itself across every Whitehall department. All Cabinet ministers were expected to mirror the arrangement around the Prime Minister and surround themselves with a small coterie of politicised operatives or special advisers drawn from outside the civil service. At the Department of Health Joe McCrae was Frank Dobson's adviser. In an article in *Progress* magazine, the New Labour house journal, McCrae informed readers that he had told civil servants 'you can't win twenty-first-century political battles with techniques and technology from thirty years ago'. It clearly did not occur to McCrae that the winning of 'political battles' fell well outside the domain of the civil servant. At the Department of Social Security special advisers flexed their muscles by insisting that information officers rewrite press releases according to political orders – Steve Reardon at the DSS press office told the Commons Select Committee on Administration that, 'In particular the drafting of departmental press releases was closely scrutinised to the point of obsession by the special advisers, who frequently issued instructions about drafting and re-drafting directly to junior press office staff without my knowledge. There were frequent arguments about the proper language to be employed in a departmental draft and special advisers sought to reproduce the tone of the Labour manifesto and repeat its election commitments as emerging news.'[21]

Sofa Government and Its Consequences

Fundamentally New Labour had introduced a system of centralised government based on command and control. It was modelled on the way Tony Blair had used his private office to dominate the shadow Cabinet while in opposition, which in its turn had been inspired by a sketchy understanding of the US presidential system during the Clinton administration. It operated in flat contradiction of the system of government inherited from John Major in 1997, which had been in use – with short-lived exceptions during wartime – throughout the twentieth century.

There were two novel features. First, Tony Blair governed from the centre, directing government departments from inside Downing Street, with Cabinet ministers in outlying departments reduced to subordinate status, a method based on a misunderstanding of the British system of government. The Prime Minister at the best of times possesses very few actual powers. These for the most part are legally vested in secretaries of state. A Prime Minister has, of course, the power of patronage. He can dismiss, and appoint, individual Cabinet ministers. Other than that, he is really the chairman of the Cabinet, where decisions are reached collectively, after going through the wearisome and time-consuming Cabinet committee procedure. This system had, however, worked for the great reforming Cabinet ministers of the twentieth century: Neville Chamberlain at the Ministry of Health in the 1930s; Aneurin Bevan as Health Secretary in the immediate post-war period, and Roy Jenkins as Home Secretary in the second half of the 1960s. There was no room in the Blairite methodology for powerful Cabinet ministers of this type, people using their own initiative to effect great works or administrative reforms. Instead Tony Blair expected Cabinet ministers to report to him and above all obey orders.

This meant that under Blair the Cabinet system fundamentally went into abeyance. Cabinet meetings were greatly truncated, often lasting three-quarters of an hour or less. They very rarely dealt in any meaningful way with policy or the great issues of the day, such as Iraq. Instead, ministers were issued with instructions about the 'line to take'. For the first time political advisers were welcome as regular visitors in the Cabinet room, signalling the much greater weight they now carried in government. Crucially Alastair Campbell, Tony Blair's press secretary, was routinely present in Cabinet. Meanwhile the system of Cabinet committees which had previously driven government business became partly moribund, a situation which only came to light thanks to the parliamentary inquiries into the background to the Iraq invasion. It emerged that the Overseas and Defence Committee had not met even once before the Iraq War.

With civil servants thrust to one side, a tiny group of political aides, who were implicitly trusted by the Prime Minister, became the real decision-making centre. During the salad days of the Blair government – a period lasting from 1997 to the aftermath of the Iraq invasion in 2003, when the Prime Minister suddenly began to lose authority – this ramshackle group ran Britain. Besides the Prime Minister himself this heterogeneous collection included: Alastair Campbell, a former *Daily Mirror* journalist; Jonathan Powell; Anji Hunter, an old childhood friend of the Prime Minister who later became his Commons Secretary; and Sally Morgan, the Downing Street political secretary. Other occasional members included Cherie Blair, Peter Mandelson (during the longish periods when he was not a Cabinet minister), and Philip Gould, the Prime Minister's political consultant.

According to witnesses, this coterie was hostile to outsiders, and communicated with each other in what appeared to be a 'private language'. One witness said the group resembled a 'commune' or a 'cult'. It tended to meet around the sofa in Tony Blair's 'den'. Decisions, according to observers, were often reached without analysis, sometimes with scarcely a word being uttered. This group was just as interesting for whom it did not contain as for those that it did. In the early days, Tony Blair's first Cabinet Secretary Sir Robin Butler tried to break into the Prime Minister's inner circle, but was repulsed. Butler's successor Sir Richard Wilson was also kept at arm's length. Indeed he was so remote from the citadel of power in Downing Street that at times the Cabinet Secretary was forced to resort to using the Downing Street press secretary Alastair Campbell as a medium for reaching the Prime Minister. Only one civil servant was ever fully trusted. This was Jeremy Heywood, who was appointed Tony Blair's Principal Private Secretary in 1999. According to fellow civil servants, Heywood was at first suspected – as were all permanent officials –

by the Downing Street inner circle. But with the passage of time Heywood was fully accepted as a member of the group of allies around the Prime Minister. In the view of colleagues in the civil service, Heywood became part of the informal 'sofa culture' surrounding the Prime Minister, and as a consequence became laxer than he should have been about note-taking and administering the machinery of government.

This new method of government, with the civil service kept at arm's length and executive power exercised by an informal clique loosely attached to the Prime Minister, represented a stunning victory for the Political Class which had entrenched its power since the 1997 General Election. The boundaries between permanent officials and temporary politicians had been breached. This led to a number of important consequences for the nature of British government.

The first concerned an abrupt decline in elementary competence. As a general rule government is a dreary business. Administrative reform only happens thanks to endless attention to detail: long meetings, careful minute-taking, above all remorseless thoroughness. Top civil servants are trained precisely for this kind of meticulous, rigorous, unglamorous activity. With officials sidelined, these tasks fell to the Downing Street inner group, with unavoidable consequences. A large reason for the failure of the Blairite public service reforms must be put down to the lack of real attention to process implicit in the new system of government. Cabinet colleagues spoke of the 'garden look' that came over Tony Blair's face when detailed policy was discussed. The Prime Minister would look distracted and gaze out of the window at the Downing Street garden. The sloppiness of the new Downing Street machinery became clear for all to see in the summer of 2003, when the Hutton Inquiry into the death of Dr David Kelly sought to reconstruct the decision-making process that had led to the release of the name of the Ministry of Defence scientist in national newspapers. Lord Hutton learned that some four meetings, all involving senior officials and Cabinet ministers, each chaired by the Prime Minister, had taken place in Downing Street to discuss

Dr Kelly in the forty-eight hours before his name had been released.* In an amazing breach of usual Whitehall procedure, not one of these meetings had been minuted. Normally it would have been the job of Jeremy Heywood, then the Principal Private Secretary to the Prime Minister, to draw up these minutes. The failure to make a record of these urgent discussions – and presumably many others – is a reflection of the lack of attention to detail among the governing coterie inside Downing Street. In the event, a retrospective minute was drawn up for the benefit of Lord Hutton.

The second problem arising out of the new presidential system was a collapse in the old dividing line between party and state, which had been established as a fundamental principle of British government by the mid-nineteenth-century Victorian reformers. The Blairite clique inside Downing Street was unable to comprehend that such a distinction had meaning. Having obtained power, it set about using the machinery of state for party advantage.

Alastair Campbell was technically a civil servant and as such subject to the same heavy constraints which forbade other civil servants taking part in political activity. In practice Campbell and the rest of the Downing Street press office were partisan, and constantly flouted civil service procedures that insisted on integrity and impartiality. On one occasion it emerged that Campbell, along with another press officer, had played an extremely significant role in the intrigues that caused the Conservative MP Shaun Woodward to defect to the Labour Party. When Whitehall officials complained about this breach of protocol, Jonathan Powell leapt to Campbell's defence, asserting: 'Alastair Campbell may be a civil servant, but he works for the government and the government's job is to increase its majority in the House of Commons.' Not one of the civil servants at this meeting challenged Powell's flawed understanding of the role of a civil servant.[22] Tony Blair himself

---

* Lord Hutton nevertheless reached the startling conclusion that Tony Blair had not been responsible for releasing the name.

showed just as hopeless a grasp of the distinction between the new Political Class and the traditional civil service.

New Labour in government did not merely triumphantly challenge the principle of civil service neutrality. In a gigantic irony, it also constantly sought to undermine the Northcote/ Trevelyan principle of promotion by merit and open competition. Ministers endlessly intruded themselves into the procedure for the selection and promotion of civil servants. To give one example, Jack Straw as Foreign Secretary sat on the board which selected Sir Peter Ricketts as Permanent Under-Secretary at the Foreign Office. Jeremy Heywood was an interesting example of prime ministerial favour. The Prime Minister tried very hard to disregard the usual civil service career structure and rocket Heywood directly to permanent secretary rank. On this occasion, however, he was frustrated.

The collapse of civil service integrity, the ending of the old neutrality and the emergence of an invidious favouritism were all unhappy side-effects of Tony Blair's decision to turn his back on his civil service advisers. But this fatal strategy also had a larger importance. The Prime Minister was deprived of the precise levers of power that would enable him to govern Britain, and put into practice the kind of public service and other reforms that he promised in his election manifestos.

In previous governments the Cabinet system of government, overseen by a self-confident mandarin class, had repeatedly provided the mechanism for great transformations of British society. Tony Blair, however, refused to make use of the tools that naturally came to hand. Instead he preferred to operate through central command and control, what his adviser Jonathan Powell privately christened the 'Napoleonic' system. His Cabinet Secretaries, Sir Robin Butler and Sir Richard Wilson, tried to argue him away from this course of action. Sir Richard even went to the lengths of preparing a series of papers describing how the Cabinet system operated, what Cabinet ministers did, and the mechanisms they had to bring about change. He warned the Prime Minister not to expect instant results, and that it was a slow, wearisome job to turn around massive organisations like the National Health Service. In a series of minutes he urged Tony Blair to perceive himself as the chairman of the board, with his secretaries of state charged with implementation inside their various departments. Sources say that the Prime Minister took this as an affront, and insisted on being seen as an energetic chief executive driving through change.

Tony Blair converted the Downing Street Policy Unit from its original purpose as a hothouse for the generation of fresh ideas to an execution team. The Prime Minister, aided by David Miliband, the unit's young head, issued orders and imposed thousands of 'targets' that departments were expected to meet. In the summer of 1999, when this target culture was at its most rampant, during the happy intervening period after the thousands of targets had been issued but before they had failed to be met, Miliband and Alastair Campbell came into the *Daily Express*, where I then worked, to sell the government message. Miliband described with great pride how the Prime Minister would call Cabinet ministers and their permanent secretaries into his office once a month, and ask them about their plans. 'In the Department for Education there is a named official responsible for every target,' Miliband boasted. 'If we don't drive through these changes they will never get done.' I asked Miliband whether there was a place for Cabinet government in the face of all this central control. 'In the past,' answered Miliband, 'Cabinets were important when governments were factionalised and divided.' Alastair Campbell was yet more dismissive: 'When they had big Cabinet, they spent their day doing one of two things: tearing lumps out of each other or writing diaries.'[23]*

Neither the Prime Minister, David Miliband nor anyone else

---

* Ironically Campbell himself kept a diary, which was intended for publication, throughout his time as Press Secretary to Tony Blair. The first instalment was presented to the public as *The Blair Years* in July 2007. Publication of these diaries was a delicious case of special privileges claimed by the Political Class. Civil servants and other public officials would normally be barred from breaches of confidence of this type.

seems to have concerned themselves much with the mechanism through which the targets were going to be met. Furthermore they failed to anticipate the gross distortions they were bound to cause in large organisations, such as hospitals, where management had to deal with many competing priorities. By the end of New Labour's first term of government in 2001 it came to be recognised by those close to the Prime Minister that the attempt to drive through reform by setting targets from the centre had failed. Tony Blair did not respond to this failure by abandoning his experiment and returning to the old Cabinet system of government. His lack of faith in the civil service was by then as great as ever. Instead, the Prime Minister looked outside the civil service towards the private sector. He went to management consultancies, headhunting firms and investment banks. Having crossed the boundary between party and state, he set about smashing the dividing line between the public sector and the market sector. The attempt to use the disciplines of private business to remedy the alleged failings of the public sector was to be every bit as disastrous.

The Corporate Takeover of the British State

The British civil service, though its procedures were cumbersome and slow, had nevertheless been astonishingly effective for the bulk of the twentieth century. It administered the historic changes imposed by the Attlee government after 1945, including the National Health Service and the welfare state. After 1979 it put into effect the new Thatcher settlement as the scope of the state was narrowed.

The emergent Political Class, however, rejected the British civil service as slow, soporific and disloyal. Instead it sought to impose a method of administration which was deliberately modelled on the corporate sector. Large tranches of public administration were handed over to the management consultancy industry. Huge sums were spent bringing in management consultancy firms to carry out jobs traditionally done by the civil service. The result was a waste of public money, and a run of spectacular disasters. By 2006 a new IT system for magistrates' courts was some £200 million over budget; the intelligence monitoring service GCHQ was some £400 million over its original £21 million budget, while a system for benefit administration was scrapped after some £698 million had been wasted.[24] Meanwhile senior management consultants were brought into the heart of the public service. Former Accenture accountant Ian Watmore was appointed head of the Number 10 Delivery Unit, while David Bennett, a former partner of McKinsey, was appointed head of the Number 10 policy unit.

Ministers set about promoting a system of government that was explicitly based on the way they assumed that large business concerns worked. Both the Thatcher and the Major governments played a very important role in corrupting the idea of public service through the implementation of 'Compulsory Competitive Tendering', privatisation and the use of private business to advise government. The Conservative Party's assault on the allegedly inefficient civil service, and the creation of new units such as executive agencies, led to the dilution of accountability.[25] This view that Cabinet government was inefficient and amateurish was set out by New Labour strategists such as Peter Mandelson, who denounced Cabinet government in the following terms in 1996: 'It is impossible to imagine a commercial operation operating so inefficiently through such a large number of executive directors reporting to one chief executive.'[26] Home Secretary Jack Straw, careful to reflect the prevailing view, echoed this sentiment after the 1997 General Election: 'Changing a government is like sweeping away the entire senior management of a company. The Prime Minister is operating as chief executive of ... various subsidiary companies, and you are called into account for yourself.'[27]

This corporate model did not merely have ferocious implications for Whitehall structures. It also brought about a sweeping change in assumptions about the connection between the individual and the state. The traditional model of an organic relationship between government and citizen was junked for a new connection consciously modelled on the relationship between a private corporation and its consumers.

Senior officials openly repudiated the traditional doctrine of public duty. In November 2001 the Treasury mandarin Sir Steve Robson explicitly set out the new ethic when under questioning by Tony Wright, chairman of the Commons Public Administration Committee. Sir Steve told Wright that in his view 'the public-sector ethos is a bit of a fantasy. It is rather like middle-aged men who fantasise that beautiful young women find them very attractive.'* Voters and public service users began to be treated as if they were private consumers, to whom public services should be marketed and sold. Enormous attention was paid – and huge sums spent – on departmental branding. 'We have to move to a position,' remarked the head of communications at one city council, 'where the corporate communications department is thinking "customer".' One Department of Education official remarked: 'We see our work as being driven by our customers, who are young people.'[28] These officials were simply reflecting official thinking. As Tony Blair remarked in his 2001 party conference speech: 'This is a consumer age. People don't take what they're given. They demand more.'

These changes also embedded huge conflicts of interests of a kind that had been eliminated from the civil service after the reforms of the mid-nineteenth century. The distinction between private and public domain was smashed, opening the way for the first time in more than a hundred years for the routine exploitation of public-sector relationships and contracts for massive private gain.

---

* Quoted in Anthony Sampson, *Who Runs This Place?*, p. 124. Sir Steve Robson was a characteristic figure of the turn-of-the-century British civil service. He joined the Treasury in 1969, aged twenty-six, and rose to the elevated status of Second Permanent Secretary. Inside the Treasury he made his reputation as an expert on privatisation. On leaving government service in 2001, he was at once snapped up by the private sector. He now lists the Royal Bank of Scotland and JP Morgan (formerly Cazenove) among his directorships. JP Morgan, in common with other investment banks, chases hungrily after British government business.

7

THE FALL OF THE FOREIGN OFFICE – AND THE RISE OF MI6

'In reality the most common characteristic of political secret service at all times is its stupidity and the unconscionable waste of money which it entails. Where its task is to obtain "intelligence", it most frequently produces tales which could not stand five minutes' cross-examination in a law court, but which, by the presumed nature of the service, are secured against effective criticism, and are made credible by being framed to suit the bias of the employers' – Sir Lewis Namier, *The Structure of Politics at the Accession of George III* (1929)

The twenty-first-century Foreign Office (FO) is an almost perfect study in the moral and practical degradation of a British institution under determined attack by the Political Class. A generation ago the FO was one of the most respected departments of state, renowned for intellectual confidence, institutional strength and *esprit de corps*.

This integrity caused the Foreign Office to be disliked by some politicians and resented by domestic civil servants. Margaret Thatcher was suspicious, while Norman Tebbit dismissed the FO because he thought it 'represents foreigners'. These attacks mainly left it unscathed. Under the Conservatives the post of Foreign Secretary remained the most senior in the Cabinet except for the Chancellor of the Exchequer, Lord Chancellor and Prime Minister.

Under Margaret Thatcher and John Major there were a series of very distinguished Foreign Secretaries. From Lord Carrington to Douglas Hurd and Malcolm Rifkind, each Foreign Secretary enjoyed a high reputation and robustly defended the interests of his department. Paul Routledge, the *Daily Mirror* political columnist, once proposed that Douglas Hurd should be nationalised and put to use as a permanent Foreign Secretary, whichever government was in power.

The collapse – there is no other expression for it – of the Foreign Office since 1997 has taken place at a number of levels. The Blair government acted very fast to attack the integrity and the morale of the Foreign Office itself. Since the professionalisation of the foreign service at the start of the twentieth century, senior appointments had in all but a handful of cases been awarded on merit rather than political patronage. There were very few exceptions. In 1968 Harold Wilson appointed Christopher Soames, a former Conservative minister who was Winston Churchill's son-in-law, as British ambassador to France. Ten years later, in a very controversial appointment, Jim Callaghan made his brilliant son-in-law Peter Jay, an economics journalist, ambassador to the United States.

These kinds of appointments, which brought in outsiders and over-rode the conventional career structure of the Foreign Office, were very rare. But the Blair government, ironically enough, disliked the meritocratic career structure of the Foreign Office and brought back aspects of nineteenth-century nepotism, with jobs being handed out to placemen and political retainers. A very early incident in the early months after the 1997 General Election landslide provided an interesting example of this. The new Foreign Secretary, Robin Cook, disliked the arrangements in his private office. He resented the diary secretary he inherited from his predecessor Sir Malcolm Rifkind, Anne Bullen, and actively considered replacing her with his mistress Gaynor Regan, who had acted as his diary secretary when he was in opposition. A Foreign Office official spoke to Regan about the possibility of her taking the job before she was ruled out.

Soon Ambassadorships and High Commissionerships were being used as political tools. A comparatively innocent early case involved the Tory MP Alastair Goodlad. In 1997 Tony Blair promised his close friend (Blair had been Goodlad's House of Commons pair) the forthcoming vacancy as the British European Commissioner. When this news became known inside the Foreign Office there was consternation. Goodlad, though possessing over-whelming pro-European credentials, was not regarded within the Foreign Office as intellectually equipped to do the job.

In order to solve the Goodlad problem, senior Foreign Office officials realised that they needed to do two things. First, they must persuade Goodlad himself to reach the conclusion in his own way that the post of European Commissioner would be too onerous and demanding. Secondly, they needed to present Goodlad with an acceptable alternative. In due course, after a series of careful manoeuvres, and with the help of the Prime Minister, Goodlad was induced to change his mind and accept the post of High Commissioner to Australia (where, to be fair, he proved an outstanding figure), opening the way for Chris Patten to accept the now vacant commissionership.

This deployment of a stray diplomatic outpost to solve a tricky political problem worked well in connection with the Goodlad matter. Soon senior diplomatic posts were being scattered around. When Downing Street was working overtime to get Frank Dobson to step down as Labour candidate for Mayor of London, the Foreign Office was once again held to provide a potential solution. The diaries of the former Downing Street press officer Lance Price record how the prime ministerial aide Anji Hunter said, 'It was essential that we avoid the huge damage that Ken winning would do to TB and that Frank could have whatever he wanted if he agreed – the Lords, an ambassadorship, whatever.'[1] Though in the end Dobson remained in the House of Commons, these remarks show how Downing Street was coming to regard the Foreign Office as a useful source of outdoor relief for failed or passed-over politicians.

When Tony Blair wanted to sack Jack Cunningham from the

Cabinet, he offered to sweeten the pill by making him High Commissioner to Canada, though Cunningham turned the offer down. As the 2005 General Election approached, pressure mounted to move Paul Boateng away from his post of Chief Secretary to the Treasury, where he was felt to have failed. Sacking Boateng might have carried the risk of putting an embittered former Cabinet minister on the back-benches. Instead Boateng was offered, and readily accepted, the High Commissionership in South Africa. The same ruse was used when the time came to ditch Scottish Secretary Helen Liddell. She accepted the High Commissionership to Australia when Alastair Goodlad's term came to an end. This appropriation of diplomatic appointments as a method of political patronage is common practice in the United States, where senior posts such as the ambassadorship to London are understood to be part of the spoils system with which an incoming president rewards his supporters.* It is, however, alien to the traditional British system of government.

The use of Foreign Office positions as a source of political patronage showed the contempt in which professional diplomats were held by the new Political Class. It started to treat Foreign Office officials in some cases as personal retainers. In September 2000 one Foreign Office minister, Keith Vaz, hosted a meeting at the Foreign Office in order to solve a dispute between a restaurateur called Amin Ali and the Norwich Union. Amin Ali was making a claim for £175,000 after his Red Fort restaurant had been damaged by a fire. There was no conceivable British government interest in Amin Ali's argument with the Norwich

---

* In 1832 President Andrew Jackson appointed Martin Van Buren ambassador to Great Britain. The decision came under attack from Senator Henry Clay. Senator William Marcy sprang to the defence of the appointment in the following terms: 'It may be, sir, that the politicians of New York are not as fastidious as some gentlemen are as to disclosing the principles on which they act. They boldly preach what they practise. When they are not contending for victory, they avow their intention of enjoying the fruits of it ... If they are successful they claim, as a matter of right, the advantages of success. They see nothing wrong in the rule, that to the victor belong the spoils of the enemy.' Quoted in *Safire's Political Dictionary*, p. 679.

Union. The restaurateur was, however, a Labour donor and close to Vaz and a client of Vaz's wife. The episode showed a total failure to distinguish between private and public interest. It was nevertheless defended by the Foreign Office, which claimed that pressure of work was the reason. 'Time constraints occasionally require private meetings to be scheduled in the Foreign Office,' declared a spokesman.[2] The news department of the Foreign Office was no longer in the hands of career Foreign Office officials, as had previously been the case. Instead it was under the control of a former *Daily Mirror* journalist who, though highly competent, had political loyalties which lay outside the department.

Very soon after entering Downing Street the Blair family started to see the foreign service, with its access to large houses in desirable overseas locations, as a potential travel agent. The Blairs enjoyed holidays at the British ambassador's residence in Portugal while it was occupied by John Holmes, who had earlier worked inside 10 Downing Street. They spent several holiday breaks in the magnificent Government House in Bermuda.[3] On another occasion, in a clear abuse, the Blairs retained the British consular service to help them search for potential holiday homes. In the summer of 2002, the Blairs stayed at a château belonging to Arielle Auvergnat, the widow of a professor of medicine, in the small village of Le Vernet in southern France. The property was found for them by the British honorary consul in Toulouse, Roger Virnuls.

This repeated appropriation for private use of Foreign Office or consular officials by the Blair family was yet another manifestation of the familiar failure to understand the distinctions between the private interests of ministers and the public duties of politicians. There was an interesting paradox at work here. The Prime Minister and his entourage grasped very quickly that the Foreign Office might be a source of holiday homes, assistance on shopping expeditions and sources of patronage. But they were disdainful of the Foreign Office's professional knowledge of diplomacy or public affairs. There are numerous cases of this contemptuous neglect, but the most striking relates to the failure to take on board Foreign Office advice in the wake of the destruction of the Twin

Towers on 11 September 2001, and in the run-up to the invasion of Iraq.

The British Ambassador to the United States during much of this period was Sir Christopher Meyer, and he has provided abundant testimony about the catastrophic relationship between Downing Street and the Foreign Office. He records in his memoir, *DC Confidential*, that 'Between 9/11 and the day I retired at the end of February 2003, on the eve of war, I had not a single substantive policy discussion on the secure phone with the FO. This was in contrast to many contacts and discussions with Number 10.'[4] This revelation was astonishing. It has of course always been the case that British Prime Ministers have sought to build a relationship of personal trust with US Presidents. But they have always relied on the foreign policy experts inside the Foreign Office.

It soon emerged that Downing Street did not merely want to cut the Foreign Office out of the relationship with the White House, but the British ambassador in Washington as well. This became clear in the aftermath of 9/11, when Tony Blair and his Downing Street team travelled to the United States to meet President Bush. It is worth repeating here the exceptionally powerful testimony given by Meyer of the journey from New York, where Tony and Cherie Blair had attended the memorial service for victims of the 9/11 atrocities, to Washington where the British party were due to meet the US President for crisis talks. Meyer describes how the British Prime Minister tried to get him removed from the talks with the President and replaced by his press adviser Alastair Campbell.

> In the first-class cabin, all was fret and impatience. Blair was in a huddle with his advisers Jonathan Powell and Alastair Campbell. Powell came up to me: 'Tony would rather have Alastair at the supper with Bush than you. I'm sorry.'
>
> After all the tensions and fraught exertions of the last ten days, and on this day of all days, that was not a terribly well-judged thing to tell me. In fact Powell might as well have punched me in the solar plexus. For a moment I could not find the words to respond. When they came, they were furious and expletive-laden.

'If this happens you will cut me off at the fucking knees for the rest of my fucking time in Washington. Is that what you want?'

Meyer went on to explain that he did not expect to attend the one-on-one meetings between the President and the Prime Minister:

> But when the meeting broadens to include a small group of principal advisers, it should include the ambassador. I had to provide the continuity and carry the weight of the relationship between prime ministerial visits. It could not all be done by phone from London. If I had been absent from that meeting I would have lost all credibility in the eyes of the President and senior members of the US administration. They would have concluded that I did not enjoy the Prime Minister's confidence.
>
> If they had made that judgement then the effectiveness of the embassy would have been damaged at just the moment when the British government had rarely needed it more.[5]

On this occasion Meyer managed to insist on attending the supper. But in general the Foreign Office was completely excluded from the dealings with the US President. He concludes in his book: 'The Foreign Office never stood a chance. America belonged to Downing Street.' There were a number of ways in which Tony Blair and Downing Street sought to undermine the authority of the British Foreign Office.

The first was the creation of a powerful foreign affairs team inside 10 Downing Street. This well resourced central unit gave Tony Blair as Prime Minister an extremely powerful counterweight to the Foreign Office.* It meant that he had the ability, not

---

* Downing Street officials stressed that the Number 10 unit was mainly manned by trained diplomats. In practice, however, Foreign Office officials who made the move to Number 10 soon switched their allegiance to the faction around the Prime Minister. David Manning, foreign policy adviser to Tony Blair and later British ambassador in Washington, is a case in point.

possessed by previous Prime Ministers, to run a foreign policy independent both of Foreign Office advice and also of Parliament. This central unit was not enough, however, for the Prime Minister, who sought to reinforce his independence through freelancers who reported to him alone.

The most curious of these foreign affairs 'advisers' was Tony Blair's personal fundraiser Michael Levy. Levy's attraction to the Prime Minister lay in the precise fact that he transcended all recognised categories. He did not owe any allegiance to the diplomatic corps, to the Labour Party or even the government of the day. Levy's connection was purely personal. This meant that he could and did function simultaneously in the public and private arenas. Michael Levy was a transgressive who operated through secret influence and private understandings. These characteristics made him a perfect instrument for the Political Class as it set about undermining traditional structures of party and state.

The scale and ambition of his activity is astonishing. He was authorised to represent Tony Blair at the highest level, taking in kings and presidents and prime ministers in his numerous tours. It was deemed essential that Levy should work in the dark, and these trips were shrouded in secrecy. Some of his earliest journeys were to President Assad of Syria on a mission apparently connected with Tony Blair's longstanding objective of securing peace in the Middle East.* This exposure did not provide a hindrance to Levy's ambitions. During the course of his irregular career he visited Syria, Jordan, Egypt, Oman, Bahrain, Israel, Tunisia,

---

* News of this trip did not take long to surface in the British media, thanks to leaks from Damascus, but its significance was promptly dismissed by Downing Street. 'He was not doing anything on behalf of the Prime Minister,' said a spokesman. 'This was a personal matter.' Later, however, this version of events turned out to be incorrect. In due course Foreign Office minister Geoff Hoon was obliged to tell Parliament that Levy had 'delivered personal messages on behalf of the Prime Minister' as well as being provided with accommodation, cars, drivers and official support from the British embassy. See the illuminating account of Levy's role by Douglas Davis: 'The man behind Blair', *Jerusalem Post*, 24 September 1999.

Morocco, Palestine, the United States, Germany, France, Kazakhstan, Mexico, Peru, Venezuela, Panama, Switzerland and Brazil. Many of these countries were visited again and again. When travelling in the Middle East he tended to deal at head-of-state level.[6] These meetings went ahead despite the fact that, probably on account of his close links with the Israeli political establishment, he was not especially welcome in Arab countries, some of which sent private messages to the Foreign Office that they would rather not meet Levy and only did so out of courtesy to the British Prime Minister.

The most obvious manifestation of the contempt in which the Foreign Office had come to be held was not, however, the presence of Michael (now Lord) Levy as Tony Blair's overseas envoy. It was the Coalition Information Centre, a propaganda organisation. The CIC was set up during the 2001 Afghanistan invasion in order to counter Taliban media influence, and was given a new stimulus ahead of the Iraq invasion. Formally it seems to have been part of the Foreign Office, but in practice it was controlled by Downing Street. This small and carefully selected group of men and women operated at arm's length from traditional diplomats, most of whom did not know what the CIC was actually doing. It seems to have been subject to none of the rigorous empirical checks and disciplines that would be customary in a major Whitehall department and it remains surprising that Sir Michael (now Lord) Jay, the Permanent Under-Secretary at the Foreign Office, considered the presence of the CIC consistent with the orderly running of a great department of state. Foreign Secretary Jack Straw appears to have been too much in awe of the Downing Street machine to complain, at any rate until the public consequences of its amateurism became apparent.* The CIC was responsible for the so-called 'dodgy dossier', formally entitled 'Iraq: its Infrastructure of Concealment, Deception and Intimidation', which was issued

---

* The day after the 2001 General Election Tony Blair's press secretary boasted to a friendly journalist that Jack Straw had been appointed Foreign Secretary 'because Jack will do what we tell him to do'.

to Sunday newspaper journalists during Tony Blair's trip to Washington at the end of January 2003. This document turned out to be deceitful.

In general the morale, integrity and working practices of the Foreign Office have all suffered terribly in recent years. Some of the changes may seem quaint, such as the abandonment of the tradition of the valedictory telegram from retiring British ambassadors, reflecting on the lessons of a long career. Some may seem formal, such as the disregard of the Foreign Secretary's private office in favour of powerful political advisers. Most damaging of all is the failure of the Foreign Office voice to be heard when key decisions are made. British ambassadors based in the Middle East complain that their advice was not listened to ahead of the calamitous Iraq invasion, and more recently before the Israeli attack on the Lebanon.

A fundamental political drive lies behind the smashing of the prestige of what was until recent times a great department of state. However, some responsibility must lie on the shoulders of permanent officials. In a public lecture at the London School of Economics at the time of his retirement as Permanent Under-Secretary in 2006, Michael Jay showed surprisingly little awareness of the way in which the integrity, reputation, and above all the authority of the Foreign and Commonwealth Office had collapsed in a very short space of time.

The Rise of the Secret Intelligence Service

As the conventional Foreign Office went into sharp decline, so the Secret Intelligence Service, its sister organisation commonly known as MI6, rose in power and influence. The SIS was a small, intimate organisation, operating under the public umbrella of the Foreign Office, until the final years of the twentieth century. Its activity, though sometimes important, was discreet. Even its existence was long officially denied. Though it contained a very large number of patriotic and in some cases heroic individuals, they never sought publicity. The Secret Intelligence Service was fully at home with the value system of the British Establishment. It embraced duty, self-effacement and discretion to an almost fanatical extent. It frequently felt isolated and remote from the centre of power.

The rise in the public status of the Secret Intelligence Service has coincided with the rise of the Political Class. One of the most dazzling achievements of the Political Class has been the capture of some of the most senior personnel inside the SIS and their conversion to the less scrupulous methodologies of the new ruling elite. There is evidence, however, that the great majority of serving SIS officers retain the high standards of integrity and aversion to ostentation that formerly characterised the SIS as a whole.

This new alliance between the SIS and the Political Class is alarming. More than any other agency or department of the British state, the intelligent services have the power and the authority to intrude into the lives of ordinary people. They are able to tap phones, use deception, open letters and e-mails and inspect bank accounts in order to familiarise themselves with the private activities of citizens. Overseas intelligence agents are allowed to bribe, travel under false identities and use a wide variety of illegal techniques in order to gain information.

None of this activity is open to public inspection or even accountable to the British public except in an extremely indirect and oblique system of parliamentary committees. That is despite the fact that many of the actions routinely carried out by the SIS and the domestic intelligence service are an infringement or worse of the rights of the ordinary citizen. The only reason why the intelligence services are granted the extraordinary powers they enjoy is that they are deemed essential to national security. That is why it is important that the intelligence agencies only ever use their power in the national interest, and that they should never be abused or used for party or factional advantage.

The connection between New Labour and the intelligence services is extremely curious and revealing. In the early years after

1997 it was marked by suspicion on both sides, but in particular on the part of the government. Many Labour MPs had come under security surveillance at one time or another, mostly by MI5. This was because a large number of key figures in the new government had been members of the Communist Party or other hard-left organisations dedicated to the destruction of the British state, and in a number of cases their membership had only lapsed relatively recently.

Once in office, as we have seen, ministers tended either to laugh off or dismiss as unimportant their involvement with the CP and other extreme organisations. Nevertheless, it is worth remembering that until the fall of the Berlin Wall in 1989 the Communist Party of Great Britain had been dedicated to the overthrow of the democratic British state, and its replacement by a client government run from Moscow.

As well as John Reid and Peter Mandelson (a Young Communist in the late 1970s, at one stage attending a youth conference in Fidel Castro's Cuba, an event that was heavily documented by the intelligence services and on which a large file is still said to exist), key Labour advisers such as the Chancellor's press secretary Charlie Whelan are former CP members, and policy advisers Geoff Mulgan and Charlie Leadbeater both wrote for the journal *Marxism Today* (though it should be stressed that Mulgan and Leadbeater were both on the anti-Moscow euro-communist wing). I once took Whelan to lunch at the Savoy Grill. At the next table John Reid, then a junior minister, arrived and sat down with some businessmen. He acknowledged Whelan. 'We was [*sic*] in the CP together in the Seventies,' remarked Whelan.

Many ministers who had not been communists had nevertheless, like the future Home Secretary Charles Clarke, been communist allies in the furious student politics of the 1970s. Another category – the former Cabinet ministers Alan Milburn and Stephen Byers are examples – had been connected, at any rate loosely, with the Trotskyite groups that flourished at the time. The emergence of the New Labour government in 1997, so full of these former subversives, caused a certain amount of strain or bafflement as far as the more primitive type of MI5 officer was concerned.*

All this meant that New Labour brought an atavistic hostility towards the security services into government. This would periodically emerge publicly from time to time, for instance during John Reid's outburst against 'rogue elements' inside the intelligence services in the summer of 2003. During the early years in office this hostility may be one reason why New Labour consistently abused the information it received from the intelligence agencies. A very early case concerned the activities of a British intelligence 'asset' who worked inside the German Bundesbank. The existence of the source, who is thought mainly to have supplied information about German monetary policy, and whose presence the SIS had carefully (though deceitfully) denied, had been a well-kept secret for some years. Nevertheless, New Labour took steps to make this agent public very shortly after winning power.

The motive seems purely to have been spite against political opponents and point-scoring in connection with the Black Wednesday débâcle that had seen sterling ejected from the Exchange Rate Mechanism five years earlier. Treasury ministers learned from officials that the Tories had seen SIS intelligence about the Bundesbank negotiating position in advance of the disastrous meeting of central bankers and finance ministers at Bath in early September 1992. They had nevertheless pursued a doomed strategy of browbeating the Bundesbank chairman Helmut Schlesinger into making a declaration that he would not raise interest rates. The fact that the Tory government had failed to make use of this advance briefing thus made them even more culpable than it had previously appeared for the ERM fiasco. This story was quite widely put about by Gordon Brown's allies in briefings to the press, a casual indiscretion about intelligence

---

* Some MI5 figures were also interested by the private lives of senior Cabinet ministers, which would have been a matter for prurient monitoring only a few years earlier, but were now out in the open.

sources that was extremely damaging and ran contrary to established practice.*

Another example of the abusive relationship between Labour ministers and the SIS dates from the start of August 1997, over the weekend when the Foreign Secretary Robin Cook's affair with his secretary Gaynor Regan became public knowledge. In a bid to distract attention from this potentially damaging story, government spin-doctors rang up contacts in the press and told them that the former Tory chairman Chris Patten was under investigation by the SIS for breach of the Official Secrets Act. This story had no truth to it. It was fabricated inside Downing Street, which showed a willingness to bring the intelligence services publicly into play in order to solve a short-term media-handling problem.[7]

This atmosphere of casual indiscretion was fostered by Tony Blair. He made a habit of using intelligence information for political purposes without clearing it with spy chiefs. An example of this came just after the Afghanistan invasion in the winter of 2001, when the Prime Minister publicly blew the gaff on secret plans to eliminate poppy growing. This revelation came on a tour of the north of England by the Prime Minister, mainly aimed at Labour audiences sceptical about the so-called 'war on terror'. The Prime Minister sought to win these activists over by claiming that Britain would eliminate poppy growing, with benign knock-on effects for the reduction of heroin sales on British streets.

This might not have mattered but for the fact that the *Sunday Mirror* columnist Richard Stott was among the audience. Stott insisted on running the story, at which point, according to one reliable source, 'the phones went crazy between Downing Street and the spooks'. Plans for the poppy-eradication programme were at a very early stage at that point. It had not been agreed either with the interim Afghanistan government or – more crucially – with the Americans, or gained the support of the United Nations. In the end a sanitised form of words was agreed between Downing

---

* I was surprised to be told about this secret intelligence in a briefing from a New Labour source. The information was clearly intended for use.

Street and the newspaper. Tony Blair was quoted saying that the scheme 'is about persuading the local population with incentives to grow other things. With a relatively small commitment from us we can hopefully curb the flow of hard drugs into Europe and on to our streets.' The British initiative was a fiasco, not helped by Tony Blair's decision to blurt it out prematurely in public.

This behaviour was highly characteristic. The Prime Minister would talk publicly about intelligence briefings in a way that no Prime Minister had before, making lurid claims about what he was being told by the security services that were unsubstantiated and appeared to have little or no basis in fact. For instance, in February 2005 he coolly informed listeners to *Woman's Hour* that 'there are several hundred of them [terrorists] in this country who we believe are engaged in plotting or trying to commit terrorist acts'. The Prime Minister was trying to make the case for control orders, and listening to his remarks one could only have felt that, within days of the Prevention of Terrorism Act being passed, these 'several hundred' individuals would have been under lock and key. Yet this did not happen, and the Prime Minister's claims were quietly dismissed later by the Home Office and the security services.[8]

On the face of things, this repeated indiscretion and reckless abuse should have led to a coldness and distrust between intelligence chiefs and politicians. The oddity is that it did not. Indeed, Tony Blair's time in office ended up coinciding with an unusually intimate relationship between the intelligence services and Downing Street. Intelligence sources say that it has been far warmer than under previous governments, where they felt 'unloved' and 'out in the cold'. This new intimacy between politicians and senior intelligence officers is one of the most important and sinister new developments in British public life, and requires explanation.[9]

The first point is that the intelligence services have been granted far more access to 10 Downing Street than they had before, part of a massive change in power, range and status enjoyed by both the foreign and domestic intelligence services since 1997. In the 1990s and before, intelligence chiefs always had the possibility of a direct connection with the Prime Minister, but in practice this route was very rarely used. SIS chiefs dealt with 10 Downing Street either through Foreign Office channels, or through the Joint Intelligence Committee, the intelligence assessment machinery based inside the Cabinet Office.

These two channels of communication continued to exist but the situation changed. SIS chiefs in particular were encouraged to deal direct with 10 Downing Street, often simply ignoring the formal Cabinet Office and Foreign Office routes. This is not all. Senior intelligence figures started to become part of the Downing Street furniture, members of the Prime Minister's inner team, in a way that was unprecedented. To a striking extent they replaced mainstream diplomats as the primary source of foreign policy advice. This massively increased status has not simply manifested itself in terms of access to the Prime Minister, but also resources. As the funds available to the SIS have increased, so those available to the conventional Foreign Office have gone down. The Foreign Office today has become the poor relation of the foreign intelligence services, and in many embassies overseas conventional officials are now matched or even outnumbered by spies.

The effect of this change in circumstances was felt in a number of areas, but has been most obvious in connection with the invasion of Iraq. The conventional Foreign Office, despite the awesome weight of its Arabist tradition, knowledge and experience, made little meaningful contribution to planning or even advice ahead of the March 2003 invasion. By contrast the Secret Intelligence Service was given a massive pre-invasion role. With FO officials rigorously excluded, senior SIS men were brought into the heart of the Downing Street preparations, smashing through conventional communications. In addition to its usual operational role, it was offered and embraced the opportunity to take part in the super-charged Downing Street propaganda campaign designed to soften up the very sceptical British public opinion ahead of the invasion.

This was a critical moment: the capture of the British intelligence establishment by the Political Class. As war approached, the role of politician and intelligence chief merged and became indistinguishable. This led to a change in the nature of intelligence-gathering. The intelligence services had been cautious and above all discreet. Though some of their methods of obtaining information were daring, their analysis of information had always been exceptionally careful. This now changed, and gave way to soaring leaps of the imagination. The intelligence-gathering operation ahead of Iraq was inept in the extreme and utterly catastrophic. But this ineptitude did not matter, was even perhaps welcome inside the Political Class: the British and American governments did not want truthful and accurate information. They needed propaganda material to support their case for war. This meant a repudiation of traditional intelligence methods, which require the careful assembling and scrutiny of evidence before reaching a conclusion. The new technique was set out in an astonishing leaked briefing given by Sir Richard Dearlove, head of the SIS, at Downing Street on 23 July 2002. According to the official minute, Dearlove gave an account of his recent visit to the United States:

> Bush wanted to remove Saddam, through military action, justified by the conjunction of terrorism and WMD [weapons of mass destruction]. But the intelligence and facts were being fixed around the policy.[10]

This new approach, an out-and-out betrayal of ordinary procedures, seems to have been embraced with equal enthusiasm on both sides of the Atlantic. The intelligence services had by now entered into a conspiracy with the governing elite, a collusion which went deeper than has been realised. British intelligence did not merely assemble false and inadequately verified information for propaganda use by the politicians. It also allowed Tony Blair to make a number of wholly misleading statements about the position of the intelligence services in the House of Commons and in the media. There were a large number of examples of this abuse in the run-up to the Iraq War, when Tony Blair repeatedly laid claim to knowledge about Saddam Hussein's stockpiles of chemical and biological weapons that were simply not justified by what was known by the intelligence services.[11]

The Prime Minister did not merely misreport in the media what he was being told by the intelligence services. He also did so in the House of Commons, telling MPs that the September 2002 dossier was 'extensive, detailed and authoritative' when intelligence experts were well aware it was nothing of the sort. There was no complaint from spy chiefs on any of these occasions that their judgements were being misrepresented. This failure of intelligence chiefs when the Prime Minister gave false information to Parliament meant that they were entering into a tacit conspiracy to deceive MPs and, through them, the British people.

In a parliamentary statement the following February, Tony Blair told MPs about the second Iraqi dossier. He declared that 'we issued further information over the weekend about the infrastructure of concealment [in Iraq]. It is obviously difficult when we publish intelligence reports, but I hope people have some sense of the integrity of our security services. They are not publishing this, or giving us this information and making it up. It is the intelligence that they are receiving and we are passing on to people.'

This Commons statement was, once again, completely misleading. Though the second dossier did contain a very small amount of allegedly fresh information, it had not been seen in advance by British intelligence, let alone published by it. It had been placed in the public domain without consultation with intelligence chiefs, a shocking breach of procedure. Once again there was no protest at the misrepresentation to MPs from either Sir Richard Dearlove or from John Scarlett, chairman of the Joint Intelligence Committee. Only when a Cambridge academic, Glen Rangwala, revealed to the world that the second dossier was in key respects a fabrication did intelligence chiefs receive a private apology from Alastair Campbell. The original lie uttered by the Prime Minister remains uncorrected on the Commons record.

By February 2003 an unmistakable pattern of collusion had developed between the SIS and the New Labour government. As

I have shown, it dated right back to Tony Blair's early days in power when Downing Street falsely linked the Tory grandee Chris Patten to an SIS investigation or when Treasury sources let slip hints about the existence of a British agent inside the Bundesbank. There was something in this arrangement for everybody. On the one hand New Labour in power was able to rely on the Secret Intelligence Service as an uncomplaining propaganda tool. On the other hand Downing Street constantly pumped fresh money into the intelligence services and gave a new status to spy chiefs, ending their formerly semi-independent role and putting them at the heart of the Whitehall bureaucratic machine.

This collaboration continued after the Iraq War with the crisis that blew up over what was to become the David Kelly affair in late May 2003. Once again Downing Street, confronted by a first-rate political furore, put out a series of misleading statements concerning its relations with the SIS. These included the blatant falsehood that 'not one word of the dossier was not entirely the work of the intelligence agencies'. Once again the SIS played along with the Downing Street deception of the British public. John Scarlett must have known this statement was complete nonsense, as he had personally changed the wording of the dossier in order to comply with requests from both Jonathan Powell, the Downing Street chief of staff, and from Alastair Campbell, director of communications.

Scarlett protected Tony Blair throughout the Kelly affair, providing helpful cover during the most serious political crisis to hit the Blair government. In order to save its skin, Downing Street lied repeatedly about the way the September dossier had been prepared (and other issues). On 4 June 2003 the Prime Minister cited Scarlett personally in his attempt to dismiss claims that there had been alarm within the intelligence community about the Downing Street claim that Saddam Hussein could launch an attack involving chemical and biological weapons within forty-five minutes. The Prime Minister told Members of Parliament that 'the allegation that the forty-five-minute claim provoked disquiet among the intelligence community, which disagreed with its inclusion in the dossier – I have discussed it, as I said, with the chairman of the Joint Intelligence Committee – is also completely and totally untrue'.

Actually – as later emerged during the Hutton Inquiry – there was extreme disquiet within the intelligence community, with one senior member of the defence intelligence staff, Dr Brian Jones, head of the nuclear, biological, chemical, technical intelligence branch, taking the memorable step of writing to management to express his alarm. Tony Blair was invoking the name of John Scarlett, chairman of the Joint Intelligence Committee, to give official authority to his false version of events. Admittedly, Scarlett was later to inform the Hutton Inquiry that he was unaware of Brian Jones's concerns. It remains very hard, however, to reconcile Scarlett's professed ignorance with his duties as official intelligence co-ordinator. His failure to correct repeated falsehoods coming from Downing Street amounted to an intervention in British politics. It has always been understood that an element of deception was an important part of the craft of spying. But to take that deception out of the secret world and into the democratic arena was a terrible breach of the trust in which the Secret Intelligence Service has been held.

The Hutton Inquiry revealed the extent of the collusion between Scarlett and Downing Street officials. It showed how on 9 September 2002, in an unprecedented breach with protocol, Scarlett attended a meeting chaired by Alastair Campbell. Scarlett was in direct e-mail contact with Campbell's assistant, the press officer Tom Kelly. Very junior members of the Downing Street media team, such as the press officer Daniel Pruce, were invited to comment on Scarlett's dossier. Pruce referred to Scarlett familiarly as 'John'.

This intimate association between the Downing Street media operation and intelligence chiefs opened the way to a different kind of settlement between the Political Class and the British state. Until the Iraq fiasco, intelligence information, in all its uncertainty and confusion, had been far outside the reach of press manipulation. But ahead of the Iraq War it became malleable, something to be shaped by spin-doctors to suit the exigencies of daily political combat.

A fascinating transmutation took place. As the Iraq War approached, the disciplines of spin-doctor and spy merged. Spin-doctors gained access to intelligence material, while one spy chief, John Scarlett, started to take on the role of press agent. By the summer of 2003, when the Kelly crisis erupted, Scarlett had become a trusted and essential member of Tony Blair's core media operation. Documents issued to the Hutton Inquiry show that Scarlett was one of a number of Downing Street aides clustered round the word-processor of the press spokesman Godric Smith, drawing up the press release which led to the scientist David Kelly's name becoming public. This was a hopelessly inappropriate and undignified position for the chairman of the Joint Intelligence Committee.

In the parlance of his profession, Scarlett has been captured and turned into an agent for the Political Class. This emergence of a political 'asset' in the intelligence world was a momentous occurrence. Scarlett abandoned the objectivity and fastidiousness expected of a Whitehall civil servant and became a factional instrument. This is always a danger with spies: they are empowered in any case to ignore the ordinary restraints which bind their fellow citizens. Both Scarlett and his friend Alastair Campbell, the Downing Street media boss, were postmodern figures, straying beyond their proper categories. Scarlett had crossed the dividing line between intelligence chief and politician while Campbell's infractions were multiple: smashing the boundaries between party and state, and between journalist and politician. The following year John Scarlett was promoted to head of the Secret Intelligence Service. This kind of intimate collaboration between the intelligence services and the Political Class is characteristic of totalitarian and not, on the whole, democratic states, and raises a threat to the freedoms of ordinary citizens, the subject of the next chapter.

8

THE POLITICAL CLASS AND
THE RULE OF LAW

ALICE: Arrest him.

MORE: Why, what has he done?

MARGARET: He's bad!

MORE: There is no law against that.

ROPER: There is! God's law!

MORE: Then God can arrest him.

ROPER: Sophistication upon sophistication.

MORE: No, sheer simplicity. The law, Roper, the law. I know what's legal, not what's right. And I'll stick to what's legal.

ROPER: Then you set man's law above God's!

MORE: No, far below; but let me draw your attention to a fact – I'm not God. The currents and eddies of right and wrong, which you find such plain sailing, I can't navigate. I'm no voyager. But in the thickets of the law, oh, there I'm a forester. I doubt if there's a man alive who could follow me there, thank God.

ALICE: While you talk, he's gone!

MORE: And go he should, if he was the Devil himself, until he broke the law!

ROPER: So now you'd give the Devil benefit of law!

MORE: Yes. What would you do? Cut a great road through the law to get after the Devil?

ROPER: I'd cut down every law in England to do that!

MORE: Oh? And when the last law was down, and the Devil turned round on you, where would you hide, Roper, the laws all being flat? This country's planted thick with laws from coast to coast – man's laws, not God's – and if you cut them down – and you're just the man to do it – do you really think you could stand upright in the winds that would blow then? Yes, I'd give the Devil benefit of law, for my own safety's sake.

– Robert Bolt, *A Man for All Seasons*

175

Perhaps the most powerful and striking characteristic of the Political Class is its profound hostility to individual freedom and the rule of law. Its emergence has coincided with some of the most bitter and ferocious attacks by the executive upon the judiciary since the battles of the 1620s which established the modern basis of English common law.

The seeds of the conflict were sown under the populist Tory Home Secretary Michael Howard. Howard's attempts to take aggressive control of the criminal justice system, along with the rising importance of the mechanism of judicial review as a means of challenging administrative decisions, led to a period of open conflict between politicians and the courts. He set a pattern which led to the break-point in relations between the executive and the judiciary after the election of New Labour in 1997 on the back of a massive popular vote. The incoming government actively sought to form an alliance with the media against judges. Their intention and effect was the destruction of public respect for judges and the judicial system.

Until 1997, ministerial attacks on judges were extremely unusual. Writing in 1997, the constitutional historian Rodney Brazier could cite only one example of a government minister attacking the judiciary outside Parliament. This was a relatively obscure instance when Michael Foot, as Lord President of the Council, criticised the role of judges. Foot's criticisms were, however, aimed at their historical actions rather than the contemporary role of the judges. Brazier also cited a scathing attack by Margaret Thatcher on a sentence passed in a rape case in 1982, adding that 'perhaps having reflected on the propriety of what she said, she was subsequently more circumspect'.[1]

This restraint – adopted by ministers from all parties when confronted by judicial decisions that embarrassed the government – reflected an over-riding respect for the rule of law, allied to an awareness that attacking judges would undermine public consent in the judicial system. According to Rodney Brazier, 'as a matter of comity, each branch of government should show respect for the other branches and should be slow to attack them in public. Each should respect the others as equally important parts of the constitution. It would rarely be right for a minister to comment adversely about the judiciary outside Parliament.'[2]

Ministers abandoned this respectful attitude towards the judiciary soon after 1997. The new relationship manifested itself in various ways. First, ministers smashed convention by launching a sustained series of public attacks on judges. Behind a flurry of apparent outbursts by ministers lay a very carefully constructed government narrative that the judicial bench was weak, 'liberal', and disastrously out of touch with 'ordinary people'. These attacks were made with the complicity and approbation of large sections of the British media. The second tactic was the use of private influence to undermine the judiciary by drawing it into the political process. This pressure took various forms, but its primary thrust was to undermine the separation of powers between the executive and the judiciary which had existed since the modern British constitution took shape at the end of the seventeenth century.

Instead of upholding respect for the law, ministers took a brutal and thuggish view of their duties, an attitude typified by David Blunkett's announcement that he wanted to 'open a bottle' after hearing about the suicide of mass murderer Harold Shipman.* In April 2004 David Blunkett licensed the use of the term 'bonkers' in connection with the Chair of the Special Immigration Appeals Commission, Mr Justice Collins' decision to release on bail an Algerian suspect held without charge under anti-terrorist legislation. Blunkett went on: 'Allowing someone like this out on bail is an extraordinary decision, which puts massive pressure on our anti-terror and security services, and sends a very different signal

---

* Blunkett told a lunch for regional journalists: 'You wake up and you receive a phone call telling you that Shipman has topped himself. And you think, is it too early to open a bottle? Then you discover that everybody's ... upset that he's done it. So you have to be very cautious in this job, very careful.' See David Charter and others, 'Blunkett's early joy on Shipman suicide', *The Times*, 17 January 2004.

to the one we have been sending ... I have not called it bonkers, but no doubt other people will.'[3]

These remarks were fully approved by Downing Street. The Prime Minister also attacked judicial decisions. For instance, in May 2006 Tony Blair branded a case in which Mr Justice Sullivan permitted nine Afghan hijackers to stay in Britain 'an abuse of common sense'.[4] The Downing Street attack was echoed by the Home Secretary, John Reid, who remarked: 'When decisions are taken which appear inexplicable or bizarre to the general public, it only reinforces the perception that the system is not working to protect, or in favour of, the vast majority of ordinary, decent, hard-working citizens.'[5]

At the same time, Tony Blair unleashed John Reid to pick a fight with judges, ordering him to 'look again at whether primary legislation is needed to address the issue of court rulings that over-rule the government in a way that is inconsistent with other EU countries' interpretation of the European convention on human rights'.[6] These remarks, though full of political weight, showed a lack of legal, intellectual or moral grasp. It is the function of the British courts to interpret the law, not other countries. Many of these attacks on the judges gave the appearance of being carefully choreographed to ensure generous media coverage. Thus Home Secretary John Reid's virulent attack on a Cardiff recorder for giving an inadequate sentence to a paedophile came as the *Sun* launched a 'name and shame' campaign against liberal judges.[7]

On this occasion Reid received a very rare rebuke from the Lord Chancellor Charles Falconer, amidst fears that Lord Philips, the head of the judiciary, was preparing to respond in kind, something that would have prompted a constitutional crisis. However, Downing Street immediately extended a protective arm around the Home Secretary rather than the Lord Chancellor, stating that he was 'rightly articulating the public concern that there was a disconnect between the public's view of the offences and the sentences that were being handed out to deal with the offence'.[8] As the *Sun* reported: 'Tony Blair backed John Reid yesterday in a row with Attorney-General Lord Goldsmith over soft sentencing.

The PM said it was RIGHT for Mr Reid to demand a tougher sentence.'[9]

Again and again ministers lashed out at judicial decisions. When the High Court ruled that the black American Muslim leader Louis Farrakhan posed no threat to public order, Home Secretary David Blunkett sounded off that he was 'frankly astonished'.[10] When a judge ruled that the detention of asylum-seekers at the Oakington immigration centre was an abuse of human rights, Blunkett said that he was 'deeply disturbed' by the ruling.[11] The constant public flow of remarks of this kind by ministers had the effect of sending out a public message that there were two contradictory codes of justice at work in Britain. On the one hand there was the official code as denounced by ministers, but unfortunately practised in the law courts. According to the government this code, which seemed largely to be applied to minority groups such as asylum-seekers or alleged terrorist suspects, had no popular or moral legitimacy.

On the other hand there was the unofficial code of justice, as expounded by ministers and by certain newspapers. Unfortunately, this more common-sense code of justice, which reflected the popular will, was not the law of the land. Ministers who promoted this version of events were therefore making a statement that the British system of law was invalid, and effectively sanctioning vigilantism. This was not merely dangerous populism but was also profoundly dishonest. In the majority of cases, the judges who came under venomous attack from the Political Class were doing no more than applying the letter of legislation which had been introduced to Parliament by the very same ministers who lashed out at them. For example, the judge attacked by John Reid in the Welsh paedophile case was actually giving the toughest sentence he could under the sentencing system imposed on him by ministers. Many other of the controversial decisions attacked by ministers were applications of the Human Rights Act. Ministers were cynically diverting the blame for unpopular laws they had themselves introduced on to the judges, thus further fuelling resentment against the rule of law.[12]

On occasion politicians, in a shocking breach, came very close to sabotaging the chances of a fair trial for criminal suspects. Within hours of the arrest in November 2003 of Sajid Badat, Blunkett cheerfully declared that Badat posed 'a very real threat to the life and liberty of our country', adding that the security services believed that he had connections with al-Qaeda.[13] Shortly afterwards, the Attorney-General ironically issued a warning to the media over contempt of court. Likewise ministers made ruthless use of the arrests made in Wood Green, north London, in early 2003 in connection with an alleged conspiracy to launch a chemical attack in Britain using the deadly ricin poison. The Prime Minister, the Home Secretary and others all used the so-called Ricin Plot as a publicity resource ahead of the Iraq War. It is extremely unusual, and highly prejudicial, for ministers to comment on upcoming court cases. Eventually the trial judge was provoked into warning the Home Secretary to curb his public remarks for fear of prejudicing the case.[14] Finally, of course, it emerged that the official claims had been false and there was no ricin in the Wood Green flat.

Where they could, ministers intervened in the course of justice for nakedly political reasons. David Blunkett took the unusual step of changing the procedures concerning electronic tagging in order to keep Maxine Carr, the former fiancée of the Soham murderer Ian Huntley, in jail after she had been recommended for release.[15] Carr was a model prisoner, who presented no danger to the public and was put forward for release by the governor of the women's prison where she was held.[16]

The Political Class Attack on Liberty

A key dynamic of the modernising movement was a drive towards the aggregation and entrenchment of power at the centre, at the expense both of institutional independence and individual liberty. The Political Class, dependent as it is on the state for status and material subsistence, felt little of the alarm of earlier governing elites at the arbitrary power of the executive. On the contrary, most members of the Political Class regarded the state as benign, and as a consequence viewed institutions that hampered the power of the executive with suspicion, bafflement and sometimes fury. The Political Class believed itself to be the true reflection of the popular will,* and tended to see the judiciary as an antiquated, anti-democratic phenomenon which stood in the way of efficient government. It did not see the ancient British notion of freedom under law as an absolute value, rather as an irritant that could and should be subordinated to the greater public good.

This position was informally set out on the numerous occasions when Downing Street and the Home Office denounced the judges as out of touch with ordinary people. At the 2001 Labour Party conference the Political Class doctrine (or at least, in its progressive form) was officially stated by the then Home Secretary David Blunkett, who told delegates:

> It wasn't lawyers and judges who secured democracy and freedom for our people. It was political action by those who sought to bring about change to liberate those who didn't have power, wealth, privilege, for whom the law did not provide protection in years gone by.

David Blunkett was here confusing two things: social and economic emancipation brought about by political struggles, and the protections offered to British citizens by the courts. In fact freedom under law dates back to the Middle Ages if not before, and has certainly existed in Britain for centuries before the arrival of mass suffrage. Blunkett's analysis was extremely close to the Marxist proposition that the protections offered by the courts are simply 'bourgeois freedoms' which represent propertied interests, but not working people. Blunkett was making the dangerous claim that because politicians articulate the needs and desires of ordinary voters, they are entitled to break the law. This is a fundamentally illiberal and totalitarian argument, which historically

---

* For instance, see the remarkable statement in the 1997 Labour Party manifesto, which laid claim to be the 'political arm of the British people'.

has been used to open the way to the oppression of minorities and in extreme cases to barbarism.

David Blunkett and a succession of Home Secretaries, urged on by Downing Street, used this basic analysis of the political illegitimacy of judges to launch a series of attacks on longstanding British freedoms. Each of the central principles which underlie British law was targeted: free speech, trial by jury, *habeas corpus* and the central principle that there should be a separation of powers between the judiciary and the executive. As ministers grew more confident they started to look towards finding alternatives to the justice system altogether, always a preferred method for governments with totalitarian tendencies. This involved a move away from formal justice to an improvised method of executive justice, thus sidestepping the due process of law that has always been one of the defining features of the British system.

This form of casual justice was introduced for a variety of offences, for instance hooliganism, shoplifting and certain motoring offences. The resultant move to fixed penalty notices meant that suspects could buy their way out of the formal process of punishment by paying a fine. This new approach has started to mean that some kinds of offence, such as shoplifting, are effectively now subject to taxation rather than criminal punishment.

This new form of justice was accompanied by a massive increase in the intrusive power of the state. An example of the way in which the protection afforded to the citizen by longstanding legal principles has been undermined in recent decades is the accelerating growth in powers of entry: the legal provisions that allow state officials to enter a citizen's home without their consent. This development provides a clear contrast between the insistence on the rule of law cherished by traditional English political culture, and the contemporary Political Class's deprecation of the concept.

In a judgement of 1765* the courts struck down a late attempt by the executive to assert arbitrary authority in matters it regarded

---

* *Entick v. Carrington* (1765), 19 Howell's State Trials 1030.

as falling within its competence; a concept that was increasingly at odds with developing notions of due process and the limited state. The principle was laid down that the state could enter a private home only when it could rely upon positive law to authorise its actions, enjoying no inherent power to do so.

The protection this clear principle afforded to the citizen has lost a great deal of its meaning over the past few decades, due to the huge proliferation in the number of laws that set it aside by conferring entry powers. A recent study identified no fewer than 266 statutory provisions and ministerial orders that allow entry to private dwellings, often with the option to use force.[17] The great number of these laws, and the bewildering inconsistency of their procedural provisions, leaves the citizen at a loss to understand his rights.

Governments of all political persuasions have contributed to this multiplication, awarding entry powers as enforcement mechanisms for newly created agencies without any systematic consideration of the cumulative effect on traditional liberties. The instinctive priority of the Political Class has been to expand the role and powers of the executive and its proxies, sacrificing civil liberties if necessary.

It was inevitable that the modernisers should seek to undermine the system of trial by jury, which had lain at the heart of the justice system since at least 1215, when the revolt of the barons forced King John to agree to the principle by signing the Magna Carta. Jury trial defended the citizen against arbitrary interference with its insistence that he or she should not be judged by a state official but by 'twelve good men and true'. The 2006 Queen's Speech contained provisions in the Fraud (Trials Without a Jury) Bill to remove the jury from fraud cases. Supporters cited the collapse in 2005 of the Jubilee Line fraud trial as evidence that juries found difficulty in understanding the detail of complex cases. This was based on arguments that the elite enjoyed a superior vision and understanding, that justice could be equated with administrative efficiency, and on deceit. In fact claims that the Jubilee Line fraud trial had collapsed because the jury had been unable to keep up were false. The report for the Inspector for the Crown Prosecution Service later concluded that 'the size and nature of the case was not such as to make it intrinsically unmanageable before a jury', adding that 'this outcome was not a systematic failure of the criminal justice system or the nature of jury trial'. In fact the government can boast a conviction rate of more then 70 per cent in serious fraud cases, with half of those prosecuted ending up in prison.*

Most significant of all was the attack on *habeas corpus*. Once again this principle can be traced back at least as far as Magna Carta, which states that the sovereign cannot lock up his subject without putting them through the process of law.

Getting Rid of Habeas Corpus

The effect of *habeas corpus* – the inability of the executive to detain citizens for more than a very short time without sufficient evidence to proceed to trial – has been compromised by a succession of anti-terrorist legislation. Although Parliament had previously authorised internment on a specific, temporary basis to deal with particularly acute security crises such as the World Wars and the most violent phase of the Troubles in Northern Ireland, this had always been a strictly limited last resort, and had never been proposed as a general or permanent measure.

The first sign of an intention to moderate the protective effect of *habeas corpus* in the long term came with the Terrorism Act 2000,

---

* In March 2007 moves to get rid of fraud trials met with a massive setback when the House of Lords voted to delay further debate by some six months. The debate bears further reading. Speaking for the government, Lord Brooke made the Political Class case against the judiciary: 'We have here a totally unelected House, which is flying in the face of what the elected people in the Commons have perceived to be the correct way forward.' Replying for the opposition the Conservative spokesman Lord Kingsland replied that: 'Jury trial has been the central component in the conduct of all serious criminal trials for about the last 700 years.'

which allowed detention without charge for up to forty-eight hours in the case of those persons who were designated as terror suspects by the police. In so doing it adopted one of the core provisions of the Prevention of Terrorism (Temporary Provisions) Act 1989, but removed the original requirement for an annual renewal by parliamentary vote, thus making it a permanent legal fixture rather than a time-limited response to a particularly heightened security risk. Indeed, the Act was passed at a time between the signing of the Good Friday Agreement and 9/11, when the known terrorist threat was as low as it had been for decades, further indicating the abandonment of the linkage between weakening of *habeas corpus* and great national emergency.

The purpose of the *habeas corpus* principle is to prevent citizens being deprived of their freedom when they cannot be proved to have broken the law. It is therefore not surprising that when it is undermined, the result is that individuals increasingly find themselves detained in just such circumstances. In evidence to the Select Committee on Home Affairs in 2005, then Home Secretary Charles Clarke acknowledged that of 750 people arrested under the Act, only 22 had been convicted of terrorist offences, attributing the poor success rate to the difficulty of gathering evidence in complex cases.[18] The time limit for holding suspects in custody was doubled to fourteen days by the Criminal Justice Act 2003.

In the aftermath of 9/11, Parliament passed the Anti-Terrorism, Crime and Security Act 2001. Part 4 of the Act allowed the Secretary of State to designate foreign nationals resident in the United Kingdom as terrorist suspects, who could then be detained indefinitely until such time as they could be deported. Because some of these suspects could not be deported due to the poor human-rights records of their countries of origin, the provisions could amount to permanent imprisonment without trial. Although it was possible to appeal to a special judicial tribunal against the Home Secretary's decision to detain, hearings could exclude the detainee and his lawyers, amounting to a near total withdrawal of the protection of *habeas corpus* in the case of non-UK citizens.

In December 2004, the House of Lords ruled that the provisions of Part 4 of the 2001 Act were incompatible with the European Convention on Human Rights, being unduly discriminatory and a disproportionate reaction to the threat faced by the UK. In reaction, the government put forward a system of control orders. Established by the Prevention of Terrorism Act 2005, these orders are made by the Home Secretary and impose a number of restraints upon the behaviour of the subject, the cumulative effect of which can be so restrictive as to amount to a deprivation of liberty. In such cases, the Home Secretary is obliged to apply to a court for authority to derogate from the European Convention on Human Rights, something which is legally possible only in a state of war or grave national emergency.

Despite this safeguard, control orders allow the freedom of subjects to be substantially compromised, such as by prohibiting the holding of particular forms of employment, preventing communication with specific persons, and requiring electronic and photographic surveillance to be carried out. The state is able to impose such restrictions without having to put forward evidence to the criminal standard, with members of the government pointing to the desire to keep such evidence secret as a justification for the existence of control orders.[19]

In October 2005, the government introduced the Bill that would become the Terrorism Act 2006, which once again doubled the time limit for detention without charge in terrorist cases from fourteen to twenty-eight days. Later Gordon Brown would stake the credibility of his government on a push for a forty-two day limit. Even this large increase was a substantially shorter term than that originally proposed by the government, which argued for a ninety-day limit. This would have led to subjects being detained for a period equivalent to that normally served under a six-month prison sentence, but without any criminal charge or trial.

Trying to Nobble the Judicial Bench

Frustrated by a variety of setbacks at the hands of the judiciary, ministers started to look to other methods of restraining it. During battles with other institutions, a routine Political Class tactic has constantly been to try to win over key figures as collaborators or apologists. On this occasion there seems to have been an approach to the head of the judiciary, Lord Bingham. The approach was made in early 2005, very shortly after the Law Lords ruled in the Belmarsh case that detaining suspected foreign terrorists without trial was incompatible with their human rights. This decision plunged government policy into crisis. With existing anti-terrorism laws due to run out in March, ministers faced the urgent problem of whether or not to seek the renewal of the detention powers that had been ruled incompatible with human rights.

We know about this approach because it was revealed by Lord Bingham himself at an interview in Gray's Inn, one of the four Inns of Court, in front of an audience drawn from members of the Inn. Bingham's testimony about the extraordinary private approach from government deserves to be quoted in some detail:

> So far as I am aware, only once in the history of the world has there ever been a suggestion that the Law Lords should meet with a group including the Home Secretary.
>
> There was such a suggestion earlier this year, although the suggestion didn't come from the Home Secretary himself.
>
> It came at a stage when the judgement had been given by the Law Lords in the Belmarsh case and the government had not announced what its response was going to be.
>
> I said: 'What is the purpose of the meeting?' because it is quite clear that there are some matters it would be quite inappropriate for the Law Lords to discuss. 'I can't believe,' I said, 'that this is intended to be a purely social meeting.'
>
> The answer I was given was that it was to be a purely social meeting. One was, perhaps, a little sceptical. Whether sceptical or

not, I took the view, having discussed it with at least one of my colleagues, that it was very unwise for such a meeting to take place, for the first time ever, at that juncture.[20]

Lord Bingham's rejection of the approach from Charles Clarke showed a detachment from political pressure that was admirable. In general, judges stood up to the unprecedented level of Political Class attack over the last decade extremely well, and have maintained the integrity of the judicial system in Britain. Their robustness and attachment to principle compares extremely favourably to the civil servants, spy chiefs and others who have capitulated to the Political Class.

9

THE MONARCHY AND THE POLITICAL CLASS

'The strength of the monarchy does not lie in the power that it has, but in the power that it denies to others' – Sir Anthony Jay

The monarchy posed a special kind of problem for the Political Class. Parliament, the judiciary, the civil service, the intelligence services and Foreign Office were all institutions which exerted genuine power and influence. This was not strictly true of the British monarchy, which had not been a meaningful player in power politics since the nineteenth century.

Furthermore, the monarch was independent of party. The political views of the Queen have remained a mystery. It has been confidently stated that she enjoyed her warmest relationships with the Labour Prime Ministers Jim Callaghan and Harold Wilson. It has also been alleged that she was least at ease during Margaret Thatcher's time in office, and that she was agitated in particular by the miners' strike and by Mrs Thatcher's failure to attach enough significance to the British Commonwealth. But these assertions have never gone beyond informed speculation.

The British monarchy occupied a wholly symbolic situation at the apex of the British state, a state of affairs that was elegantly summarised by the masterly dissector of British public life Anthony Sampson in the following way:

By the twentieth century the political power of the monarchy had become vestigial, but it retained its popular appeal and charisma, quite separate from the power of politicians. The head of state could represent the nation with all its traditional pomp and splendour, while the head of government appeared in a more workaday role. It was this separation of pomp from politics which persuaded even some radical critics of the merits of the monarchy. 'It is at any rate possible,' wrote George Orwell when Churchill was wartime Prime Minister in 1944, 'that while this division of functions exists, a Hitler or a Stalin cannot come to power' (though President Von Hindenburg could not prevent Hitler setting up a dictatorship when he became chancellor of Germany in 1933).[1]

The vestigial symbolic role occupied by the monarchy was, however, an affront to the Political Class and in particular the New Labour government which came to power in 1997. New Labour swiftly sought to occupy for itself the public space that had long been the proper preserve of the British monarchy.

The challenge started almost at once, with the State Opening of Parliament only a few days after the 1997 election. Tony and Cherie Blair sought to capture the event for themselves, making the unprecedented decision to walk from Downing Street to Parliament while the Queen arrived in her royal coach. This decision mattered because the drama of the state opening is all about the Queen: her departure by stagecoach from Buckingham Palace, her arrival in Parliament through the Sovereign's Entrance under the Royal Tower, the putting on of the crown and robes of state before the final entrance to the House of Lords chamber. Although this famous ritual theoretically celebrates the authority of the Queen in Parliament, in practice it is about something else. When the monarch reads the Queen's Speech before all parties and both Houses of Parliament she is showing that the power of the British state has been thrown behind the ruling party. She is demonstrating that it is far more than a factional programme and has a national legitimacy. In the words of Anthony Sampson,

'The Queen remains the most effective symbol of the impartiality of the state, especially when she opens Parliament and ministers walk alongside their political opponents.'

By making their journey from Downing Street to Parliament, soaking in the cheers of the crowds as they went, Tony and Cherie Blair were doing a great deal more than challenging the public role of the Crown. They were converting the state opening of Parliament into a partisan political occasion. The incident upset and disturbed the Queen, and in a rare and potentially dangerous rebuke the Prime Minister was asked not to do it again, an injunction he reluctantly obeyed.[2] Later, friends of the Prime Minister were to present the walk to Parliament as a purely chance decision made on the spur of the moment.

This kind of attempt to intrude on the territory of the monarch was to become a repeated feature of the Blair period in office. The death of Diana, Princess of Wales in August 1997 gave a massive opportunity for the Prime Minister. The words he uttered on the morning after the tragedy, in which he expressed his devastation at the death of Princess Diana, were brilliantly chosen and widely praised at the time for expressing the mood of the nation as a whole.

Members of the royal family, from the Queen downwards, had been trained from birth to suppress their emotions, exert restraint and show dignity. The political philosopher David Marquand noted that when Diana died 'the royals behaved as they had been taught to do: as symbols of the state, quintessential inhabitants of the public domain, with all its emotional austerity and self-control'.[3] Previous generations of mainstream politicians, from all political parties, had shown comparable restraint (and the Tory leader William Hague was criticised for an inadequate expression of grief when he made his statement about the Princess's death). Tony Blair, in his perfectly presented articulation of his personal devastation at the loss of the Princess, was at his most formidable as a politician. By showing open grief, and by using the inflammatory phrase 'people's princess', he was opening up new ground and massively extending the territory of the Political Class. He was placing emotions which had until that moment been regarded as private into the public domain. This was profoundly dangerous to a royal family which could only express itself through formality and restraint.

New Labour brilliantly captured the death of Princess Diana and turned it into a political occasion. Commentators at the time detected this, and recorded the death of Diana as a turning point for Tony Blair. Once he had secured mastery over the royal family by putting himself at the head of the national display of public grief, Tony Blair then made sure that he was then on hand to 'save' the monarchy. New Labour spin-doctors were dispatched to Buckingham Palace to advise the Queen on how to react to the mood of public devastation that followed the Princess's death. Their advice – or, to be more accurate, the Downing Street version of it – was soon leaked to the press.

Five years later, following the death of the Queen Mother, the Prime Minister sought to intrude once again into the public domain occupied by the British royal family. Within twenty-four hours of the Queen Mother's death on 30 March 2002, Tony Blair was seeking to enlarge his public role in the funeral. An official from Downing Street rang Lt-General Sir Michael Willcocks, known as 'Black Rod', the official in charge of the ceremony. 'The substance of this call,' recorded Sir Michael later, 'was to query the role of the Prime Minister in the coming ceremonials. Phrases such as "Doesn't the PM meet the Queen?", "Doesn't he meet the coffin?" and finally, "Well, what is his role?" were used. I answered all such questions by pointing out firmly, there being no latitude in the planning, that the PM had no such roles but would merely lead the tributes of the House of Commons and if possible be present with the House in Westminster Hall for the arrival of the coffin on Friday 5 April.'

Willcocks went on to record that

after this initial contact, and throughout the next five days, my staff and myself were telephoned, at times it seemed constantly, by staff at Number 10 repeating these questions on the role of the

PM, but also exerting rather more pressure along the lines of: 'Don't you think the PM ought to be at the north door?' [of Westminster Hall] ... 'He must have more of a role, surely' ... 'Don't you think that he ought to be given a role?', etc. The records show at least half a dozen or so of such calls, all of which followed the pattern above.[4]

This pressure continued right up to the last moment. Even after the Queen Mother's coffin was being moved along the Mall to its lying-in-state, Downing Street dispatched a message to Black Rod informing him that the Prime Minister planned to walk from Downing Street to Westminster Hall, entering through the north door, where the royal family was gathering to meet the coffin. As Black Rod – described in the diaries of Alastair Campbell as a 'little fucker' – recorded: 'I received an urgent message from Number 10, via the Co-ordinating Officer for the Police Protection Officers, saying that the PM intended to walk to the Palace from Downing Street and wished to know if he could enter through the north door. I had a fairly public discussion on the merits of such a walk, with among others the Lord Chancellor, and sent back a message that I didn't advise it.'*

The problem for Tony Blair and New Labour is simple to explain. The ten-day remembrance period for the Queen Mother left him without a central role. At state events like the Queen Mother's funeral, the Prime Minister of the day ranked lower than politically far less significant figures such as the Lord Chancellor and the Speaker of the House of Commons. This was not, of course, a threat to the government. Indeed it could not present such a threat, because the funeral of the Queen Mother had nothing at all to do with politics as it had conventionally been practised. But it was a challenge specifically to New Labour, because the commemoration period for the Queen Mother claimed back a part of British public

---

* Downing Street put pressure on Lt-General Willcocks to give a false account. He refused to do so. Campbell's diaries record that 'David Manning was genuinely shocked by Black Rod's behaviour'. See Campbell, *The Blair Years*, p. 624.

life, normally outside politics, that New Labour has asserted as its own. This meant that the queues for the lying-in-state were almost as disconcerting for New Labour as the grief for Princess Diana had been for the royal family five years previously. The great celebration of the Queen Mother's life was an affront to the Political Class because it was a reminder of the existence of a Britain whose loyalties and allegiances went far deeper than party, but had everything to do with the love of Queen, country, village, school, town and family. These allegiances were wholly compatible with voting Labour, Liberal Democrat, Tory or any number of other political parties. They are not, however, compatible with total-itarian politics, which lays claim to space that lies well outside party politics as it has always been practised in Britain.[5]

These major collisions between the political might of the Prime Minister and the formalised restraint of the monarchy were only a part of the picture, however. In private the Blairs and their official entourage showed a startling lack of respect for the royal family. For the first time since the Queen acceded to the throne in 1952, relations between the royal family and the Prime Minister became unpleasant. This reflected a new attitude from the Prime Minister and those around him. His aides were capable of great impatience with royal procedures, often going beyond rudeness. In 1998, during a visit to Highgrove, the Prince of Wales and the Prime Minister were settling down to a meeting to discuss the handling of the Princess Diana memorial fund when the two men were interrupted by Prince Charles' butler Tony Rabey. 'I have just had a call from some of the Prime Minister's entourage who are on their way,' said Rabey. 'They would like to know would it be possible for them to use the swimming pool.'

This was a tiny example of lack of courtesy. It caused offence to Prince Charles, but arguably the Prince was being much too stiff and formal. A much more aggressive episode occurred in February 1999 when the Prince of Wales and the Prime Minister flew to Jordan to attend the funeral of King Hussein. Tony Blair and the Prince were obliged to share a small meeting room, with just one chair in it, as they waited for the ceremony to begin. The Prince of

Wales entered the room to find Tony Blair and his press secretary Alastair Campbell already established. Blair, who was already standing, greeted the Prince warmly. But Campbell, who was sitting slumped in his chair making calls on his mobile, simply ignored the Prince.

Cherie Blair's manners were also bad. She would refuse to curtsey when she met the Queen, and was capable of blanking out senior members of the royal family when she encountered them. She made no pretence at all that she enjoyed royal occasions, and often, through physical and other signals, made it unambiguously clear that she would rather be elsewhere. This private lack of respect towards the royal family came to be reciprocated. Once Cherie Blair told Princess Anne to 'call me Cherie'. 'Mrs Blair will do,' replied the Princess Royal.

This widespread private discourtesy was matched by a public failure to acknowledge the role and duties of the monarch. Shortly after he was appointed Foreign Secretary in 2002 Jack Straw gave an interview to the *Guardian* in which he referred twice to Tony Blair as 'head of state'.[6] At one stage the Downing Street website described how the Queen enjoyed audiences with Tony Blair, and not the other way around. The Treasury was soon proposing the removal of the royal coat of arms from its logo and dropping the initials HM from its official title. The change was said to 'reflect a modern image under Gordon Brown's stewardship', but was never in the event implemented.[7] During a visit to Kosovo Tony Blair referred to 'my' armed forces, oblivious to the important constitutional fact that British troops owe their allegiance to the monarch as head of state.

Meanwhile the incoming government set out to write the monarchy out of British public life, an audacious task involving the unravelling of 1,000 years of history. The most important example of this was the very serious attempt by the Labour government to create a new national identity. This involved disregarding the institutions of the state that had historically been at the heart of Britain, and replacing them by others, such as a new national day. In a series of speeches Gordon Brown argued that

Britain should be defined by abstract values such as fairness and decency, while failing to explain how these values distinguish us from other countries such as France or Sweden, which are presumably regarded by Brown as also being repositories of these values. Britain, he declared, 'would not be a place defined by race or institutions'. The key characteristics, he insisted, would be values such as 'liberty, civil duty, fairness and internationalism'. This series of speeches by Gordon Brown about 'Britishness' – an ugly and artificial word – systematically excluded the British monarchy, even though the Queen is head of state and the monarchy encapsulated Britain's long history better than any other institution, including Parliament.[8] In June 2007 a pamphlet by the ministers Ruth Kelly and Liam Byrne explored ways of creating a new British identity. The pamphlet cited local branches of the Sure Start initiative as important institutional statements of Britishness, but made little mention of the monarchy, even though for most people it played an organic role in symbolising what Britain is about.[9] And in July 2007 the new Prime Minister broke with convention by announcing the contents of the Queen's Speech to Parliament some months ahead of the usual timetable.

An air of understated but definite menace at all times lay behind New Labour's dealing with the monarchy. In 1997 the New Labour manifesto gave an assurance that 'we have no plans to replace the monarchy'. This undertaking would not have been made had an attack on the British monarchy not been on the agenda. Plans to get rid of the Royal Yacht were put at the heart of the election campaign, sending out a subliminal message to the republican left that the party was opposed to the royal family. In private briefings New Labour in government was hostile to the monarchy. In the run-up to the 2001 election the Queen was reported to have urged Tony Blair to delay polling day because of the Foot and Mouth epidemic. A leader in the *Sun*, always very attuned to the mood inside Number 10, declared, 'The Queen has no business warning Blair, even in private, about the timing of the election. The fact that she has any role at all in our democracy is, to be frank, an international embarrassment. There are those in Downing Street who support our argument in private. After the election we will want them to speak out.'[10] There is little doubt that New Labour in power yearned to make a full-frontal and lethal attack on the British monarchy. There is little doubt that only the sustained popularity of the Queen prevented it from doing so. Had Prince Charles become king ten years ago, New Labour and the Political Class would have taken advantage of any weakness to strip the royal family of its remaining public role, and given a much fuller expression to its private republicanism.

10

THE ATTACK ON PARLIAMENT

'Parliament has safeguarded freedom and limited government for hundreds of years – many of our liberties stem from parliamentary tussles with successive governments. Parliament is probably less well-equipped to engage in these battles now than ever before in peace-time' – Andrew Tyrie MP[1]

There is a massive paradox concerning the House of Commons at the start of the twenty-first century. It has rarely been weaker or less influential in public debate. It exercises less influence over the way that Britain is governed than at any stage since the power of the monarchy was restrained, and the sovereignty of Parliament established, by the Glorious Revolution of 1688.

Yet parliamentarians themselves have never been better organised, or more professional. They have never had such plush offices, such high salaries or such generous allowances.

These two novel phenomena – the powerlessness of Parliament and the bourgeois comforts enjoyed by modern MPs – are closely linked. They are both a consequence of the emergence of the Political Class. By turning politics into a specialised profession, with its own rules and language, it has cut the House of Commons off from the British people.

This is new and extremely dangerous. All explanations of why Britain, almost uniquely among European countries, does not owe its constitutional arrangements to a violent revolution quickly come down to Parliament. In the nineteenth century it gave a method of political expression to the rising middle classes. In the twentieth century it provided an instrument for the aspirations of the working man. For the last two hundred years Parliament has been the central focus for the legitimate aspirations of the British nation as a whole. In the twenty-first century it is no longer obvious who or what Parliament represents, beyond the factional ambition of the new Political Class.

There is no longer any serious question of its irrelevance. When I became a lobby correspondent sixteen years ago I used to stay after my daily duties for the *Evening Standard*, and linger for the great debates. They happened often. At that stage Gordon Brown, now quite deliberately leaden and dull, was the most wonderful Commons performer. He was witty, brilliant, and possessed almost every oratorical gift. I remember watching entranced as Brown confronted Michael Heseltine, President of the Board of Trade, in several great set-piece debates.

John Smith, shadow Chancellor when I arrived at the Commons, was another massive Commons figure who took part in huge struggles with the Chancellor Norman Lamont over the conduct of economic policy, cheered on by massed supporters on either side. These epic battles seem not to take place any more. The typical afternoon scene inside the Commons chamber today is a minister standing up to read a prepared speech, with maybe three or four MPs on the government benches behind him, and half a dozen opposite.

In the early evening, if there was no important debate that day, I might well use my rights as a lobby correspondent to linger for hours around the Members' Lobby at the entrance to the Commons chamber. I hardly knew any MPs at first, and would normally have to ask the policemen on the door for their names. After a while I gained confidence and would tentatively approach some of them to seek their opinions on the great issues of the day. In due course I started to understand what was going on. It was a fabulous place to stand and watch opposition MPs hatching plans to defeat the government, or to observe government whips working out how to wrong-foot the opposition. I learned much of what I know as a political journalist just standing in that lobby as a bystander and engaging with MPs and ministers as they wandered through. Occasionally I stand there now out of nostalgia, but there's no point any more. The policemen are still on duty, but most of the time the Members' Lobby is just as empty as the Commons chamber.

The reason for the emptiness of the Members' Lobby is the explosion of new offices for MPs in the vicinity of Westminster. A generation ago many MPs either did not have offices at all, or (like the young Tony Blair and Gordon Brown, when they entered Parliament together after the 1983 General Election) were obliged to share squalid and cramped accommodation. You'd often see an MP sitting in a committee corridor with his secretary, signing letters and dealing with correspondence. Now each has not just his own comfortable office but also ample space for researcher and secretary. The most desirable of these buildings is probably Portcullis House, across the road from the House of Commons, with its air of a large corporate headquarters rather than a cockpit of political controversy and legislation.

Many ministers now pay little attention to the House of Commons. Tony Blair as Prime Minister never showed himself there if he could avoid it. Thanks to a succession of large majorities, he could ignore it most of the time, voting in fewer than 10 per cent of all divisions while he was Prime Minister. Margaret Thatcher, who was also accused of neglecting the Commons, and often enjoyed fairly generous parliamentary majorities, averaged around 30 per cent. Blair's record, so far as I can tell, is by far the worst of any Prime Minister since records began.

Just as important, the government no longer treats the House of Commons with respect. MPs, and normally ministers, do not matter very much, and certainly not as much as the senior aides who run government and the party machines. When Peter Mandelson gave up being Labour Party Director of Communications to become a back-bench MP, he spoke of going 'into exile'.[2] The former Downing Street policy chief Matthew Taylor said that special advisers 'speak of a culture in which the approval of advisers in Number 10 or Number 11 is more important than the opinion of the ministers they serve'.[3]

Parliament has completely lost, for example, its role as the dominant source of information about the activities of the executive arm of the state. Until recently it was normal for the British government to come to Parliament first with important announcements. There were meaningful moral sanctions – and on occasion exemplary punishment – for ministers who infringed this convention. This is no longer the case. All important announcements are now made through the media, and only as an afterthought through the Commons.

This new procedure has been the case for a number of years. Just days after the 1997 General Election the then Chancellor Gordon Brown used a press conference rather than the customary statement to Parliament to announce the independence of the Bank of England, an important constitutional change. For years afterwards the Speaker of the House of Commons regularly protested about this ruthless and systematic ministerial contempt for the House of Commons.[4]

These protests were routinely ignored. To give a contemporary example, the historic announcement of the withdrawal of the first tranche of British troops from Iraq was made first through Rupert Murdoch's News International newspapers and the pro-government *Financial Times*, secondly through the broadcasting media, and only thirdly in Parliament.[5] These papers had been strong supporters of the original invasion. The final announcement to Parliament was made only as an afterthought, rather in the same way that a corporate predator might inform the stockmarket of a takeover bid only once the consent of large shareholders has been secured.

The second function Parliament now fails to perform in anything resembling a satisfactory way is the scrutiny of legislation. As the Tory MP Andrew Tyrie has demonstrated in an extremely informative pamphlet, the government is able to control the timetable of the Commons, as well as key committees, to ensure that laws get passed with a pathetic amount of inspection. The use of guillotine motions – drastic measures to bring debate on the floor of the House of Commons to a halt and therefore allow the government to take its business forward – began in the 1880s as a method of stopping Irish political parties from using wrecking tactics to curtail debate. Over the last two decades, and in particular the past ten years, it has become commonplace to use guillotines. Only sixty-seven bills were guillotined during the whole of the period from 1946 to 1997. Some ninety-four bills were subjected to guillotine over the course of the following six years. As Tyrie remarks: 'The whole legislative process could have been invented – indeed, to a large extent it was – by people determined to ensure that the executive got its laws with a minimum of effective scrutiny.'[6]

Many Commons committees are little more than arms of the executive, rendered impotent or worse because they are controlled by government business managers. Standards of integrity have fallen extremely sharply. The requirement in the ministerial code that ministers and others who mislead the House of Commons should correct infringements themselves 'at the earliest opportunity' has partly fallen into disuse. For example, Tony Blair has left uncorrected numerous misleading statements he made to the House of Commons in the run-up to the Iraq War – his confident but false assertion to MPs on 24 September 2002 that intelligence concerning the existence of weapons of mass destruction in Iraq was 'extensive, detailed and authoritative' being just one example. There are numerous others.

Parliament has become so marginal as a forum for public debate that even resignation statements now take place outside the Commons. As recently as 1990 Sir Geoffrey Howe used the forum of the Commons to launch his bitter attack on Margaret Thatcher, a speech that played an important part in bringing about her downfall. By contrast in the spring of 2006 the dismissed Home Secretary Charles Clarke, who also felt abused, used a series of media interviews as his instrument.

How the Political Class Seized the House of Lords

This Political Class attack on the House of Commons was accompanied by an even more thoroughgoing assault on the House of Lords. This assault provides a particularly clear example of collision between the old and new ruling elites, and therefore enables a close appreciation of the characteristics, disciplines and methods of the new Political Class in action. Essentially it is the story of the replacement of the old ruling class by a new and equally self-referential governing cadre.

According to the caricature constructed by the Political Class and its media allies, the House of Lords as it existed at the end of the twentieth century had become a defunct and anachronistic institution serving no democratic purpose. This picture ignored the fact that the Lords remained one of the two chambers of the British Parliament, with great latent strength to make and break law, endowed with powers that in many respects are equal to those of the House of Commons, except in the field of finance. By convention, most notably the so-called Salisbury Convention that it did not reject bills which had been foreshadowed in party manifestos, the old House of Lords did not exercise its full power. Instead, it evolved a role as a scrupulous and careful revising chamber, examining and amending draft legislation in a way the Commons, controlled by party machines and shackled by timetabling and guillotines, often did not. It therefore acted as a complement to the more muscular but far shallower House of Commons. At its best it stood for an independence of mind, clear-sighted scrutiny and readiness to support minority or unpopular causes. All these characteristics aroused hostility among the Political Class.

Claims that the presence of hereditary peers gave the House of Lords a Conservative bias were partially true. However, the Lords had not spared Conservative governments, chewing up John Major's rail privatisation legislation and rejecting Margaret Thatcher's War Crimes Bill, for example. Furthermore, the presence of hereditary peers in the Lords provided rich links into civil society which were in the process of being mislaid by the professional House of Commons. Out with the old House of Lords went the Duke of Buccleuch, a leading world expert on forestry and supporter of disability causes; the young Lord Iveagh, targeted by Labour because of an inclusive Bill to give citizenship to the people of St Helena; Viscount Montgomery of Alamein, most knowledgeable of all parliamentarians on Latin America; and scores of lesser-known figures who had given many years to service in Parliament, without ever seeking any limelight. Anthony Sampson noted: 'Many of the aristocrats, with all their eccentricities, were deeply rooted in rural areas. Territorial grandees like the earls of Derby from Lancashire or the dukes of Devonshire from Derbyshire, however protected by their great estates, could speak for interests and activities outside London, and provide some kind of voice from the Midlands.'[7]

The hereditary peerage has been replaced by an equally anti-democratic political elite, nourished by a cascade of quango appointments. Whereas the hereditary peerage enjoyed strong regional links, the new peerage – which included a founder of the Groucho Club, Lord Evans of Temple Guiting – was significantly metropolitan in background and attitude. The new peers came from the same professions – law, media, the corporate elite and above all professional politics – which had captured the House of Commons. It was possible to uncover extensive social networks, just as nepotistic as the family connections which had distinguished the ancient aristocracy at its most pervasive. For example, Lord Goldsmith shared legal chambers with Lord Falconer, who shared a flat with the young Tony Blair. Lady Ashton, once a professional Campaign for Nuclear Disarmament administrator, is wife of the Blair-favoured pundit Peter Kellner. Lord Alli, who made a fortune from the cultural triumph of *The Big Breakfast* television show, was a youth adviser to Mr Blair.

The acid and condescending Baroness Jay, daughter and daughter-in-law of peers, was Blair's chosen instrument to remove the hereditary peers. She gave a perfect demonstration of the

Political Class hostility to the wider institutions of civil society as she announced the Bill removing the hereditary peerage from the Lords: 'The time has come to wish them well and to say "Thank you and goodbye".' She spoke to the Lords in terms that revealed the Political Class detestation of the Establishment and much of non-metropolitan Britain. Some 60 per cent of hereditary peers claimed a rural, farming background; 42 per cent had served in the Armed Forces, she said; 37 per cent had been educated at Oxbridge; and 'only 1.4 per cent describe themselves as workers'. Regrettably no one rose to ask how many of the new peerage could meaningfully be designated as 'workers' or to challenge Margaret Jay to display her mangle-reddened hands to the House.[8]

An attempt was made to redress the balance of membership of the Lords towards ordinary people through the creation of so-called 'people's peers', who were to be nominated by members of the public. Lord Stevenson, a friend of the Prime Minister, was put in charge of approving these appointments. His first and, as it turned out, final list contained such demotic names as the BP chief executive John Browne; the merchant banker Sir Claus Moser; the diplomat David Hannay and Lady Howe, wife of the former Tory Foreign Secretary.[9]

This new elite immediately showed itself to be significantly more entranced by the trappings of power than the hereditary peerage it replaced. During the debate on Lords reform Lord Ferrers, who had served in the Lords for over forty years, suggested that the title 'Lord' be removed. Peers were instructed by government to vote the proposal down. Meanwhile the Lord Chancellor, Lord Falconer, made a nonsense of government proposals to turn the Lords into an elected chamber by giving peers private assurances they could stay for life.[10]

Above all, the Political Class disliked the constitutional role of the Upper House. While happy to accept the privileges and title of the peerage, it resented the sacrifice of time and energy involved in the traditional scrutiny of the actions of the executive. Lord Browne, in common with many other peers, scarcely turned up to vote. One new peer, Lord Warner, expressed this Political Class hostility to the democratic role of the House of Lords in examining legislation. Calling for the Lords to 're-engineer our working practices', Warner complained about 'taking the great majority of Bills in the Committee on the Floor of the House. That simply ties up a large number of people unnecessarily in the House in order to keep the government on edge by playing the *voting game* [my italics].'[11]

Many peerages were for sale. The Downing Street policy chief Geoff Mulgan recorded in his book *Good and Bad Power* that 'in later years the scarcely concealed sale of peerages to wealthy party donors, and the appointment of the party's top donor – Lord Sainsbury – to ministerial office, did little to restore the British public's confidence'.[12] The rate of peerage creation soared following the 1997 General Election. By May 2007 no fewer than 359 out of the 735 members of the House of Lords – some 48.8 per cent – had been appointed by Tony Blair. Some 153 out of the 211 Labour peers owed their position to their Prime Minister. Tony Blair created peers at a rate unknown among any previous Prime Minister, and matched only during Harold Wilson's final two years in office, notorious for the 'lavender list'. Blair appointed 376 peers, or 37 for each of his ten years in office. That compared with 25 peers each year under John Major and 18 a year under Margaret Thatcher.* Many of these peerages went to big businessmen, with Labour observers noting that almost a third of Blair peers lacked anything in the way of Labour track records. They were not justified by a need to replenish the Lords: even after the loss of the hereditaries its membership is still considerably higher than the Commons. In any case many of the new peerages were all but inactive. In the 2005/6 session of Parliament 51 Blair peers appointed to the Labour benches failed to vote in more than 50 per

---

* The record of Prime Ministers since the introduction of life peerages in the 1950s has been as follows: Harold Macmillan: 90, or 16 per year; Sir Alex Douglas-Home: 29, or 26 per year; Harold Wilson (1964–66): 143, or 25 per year; Edward Heath: 48, or 12 per year; Harold Wilson (1974–76): 83, or 38 per year; Jim Callaghan: 60, or 19 per year; Margaret Thatcher: 216, or 18 per year; John Major: 171, or 25 per year; Tony Blair: 376, or 37 per year. Source: Lords Library.

cent of divisions. Lord Renwick of Clifton made only 3 of 192 divisions, Lord Grabiner just 37; Lord Levy 32; Lord Puttnam, 43. By comparison the 91-year-old Labour hereditary peer Lord Strabolgi voted 97 times.

Blair's business appointments were curious – Lord Simon of Highbury, former BP chief, who was made a minister, but was soon disillusioned and has since left active political life; Lord Stone of Blackheath, joint Managing Director of Marks & Spencer in one of its least successful periods; and Lord Simpson of Dunkeld, who presided over the demise of GEC, one of Britain's greatest old companies. After years of scarcely voting at all, Simpson permanently removed himself by taking Leave of Absence, as did Lord Simon. Fundamentally one unaccountable elite was being exchanged for another. As the late Robin Cook observed in 2004, the House of Lords had moved 'from the fifteenth-century principle of heredity to the eighteenth-century principle of patronage'.[13] Nevertheless, the House retained its theoretical powers, some of its independent procedures, and the tradition of standing for ancient liberties remains alive. It is thanks to the House of Lords that the government has not succeeded in restricting the right to jury trial; in overthrowing *habeas corpus* so as to allow detention without charge for ninety days; restricting freedom of speech about religion; taking powers to survey every private e-mail; or imposing compulsory ID cards. It also thwarted government plans for the legalisation of sex in public lavatories, preserved live music in pubs and protected church choirs from licensing bureaucracy. The House of Lords squashed a Commons Bill designed to exempt MPs from the provisions of the Freedom of Information Act, thereby enabling them to conceal their expenses claims. The next few years will determine if it subsides into becoming a club for the new Political Class, or retains a role as a powerful complement, and stimulus, to the Commons in holding the executive to account.

MPs' Pay and Conditions

The sudden and very noticeable drop in the national importance of Parliament has coincided with the rise of a professional Political Class. The low salaries and poor accommodation formerly enjoyed by MPs perhaps deterred aspiring politicians from seeking a living from politics. In 1954 a select committee observed that 'few would support the idea of a House of Commons composed principally of full-time politicians in the sense of men and women cut off from any practical share in the work of the nation'.[14] This notion that MPs should enjoy outside forms of engagement with civil society has not survived. By 1993 the political commentator Peter Riddell devoted a book to the emergence of the professional MP, *Honest Opportunism: The Rise of the Career Politician.* Riddell noted that British politics was becoming a closed world, 'confined to those who have made a youthful commitment to seeking a parliamentary career. It is like a religious order which requires an early vocation, or perhaps a post-entry closed shop.'[15] Andrew Adonis (then a journalist, now a minister) noted in 1997 that the consequence of a professional political elite was 'the modern democratic paradox, a Parliament and political system less representative of society than at any time since Britain became a democracy'.[16] Anthony Sampson observed shortly before his death that reforms to the working hours of the Commons meant that 'the Palace of Westminster is more like an office-block, with bureaucrats leaving at six every evening'. This conversion of politics into a profession meant that MPs soon began to develop the preoccupations of any profession: status, self-interest and – most important of all – money. The section below shows how MPs used their ability to set the law of the land to assure extremely comfortable lifestyles for themselves.

In order to understand Parliament in the era of the Political Class, there is no avoiding a study of the pay and conditions of MPs. This is a story of steadily rising affluence and financial security. As the employment conditions of the average worker or private-sector executive have grown ever more precarious, so MPs have become ever more secure. As the pension schemes in the private sector have been closed down and collapsed, so the schemes for MPs have become more generous and more ring-fenced. As the Treasury has clamped down ever harder on the perks and allowances of ordinary taxpayers, so the allowances and perks available to MPs have become ever more generous. These changes have created a new collegiality and awareness of their common status.

The modern position of MPs, with their salaries, pensions and (increasingly) career structure, is novel. During the nineteenth century ministers received a generous salary, but parliamentarians got no pay at all. The practice, not uncommon in medieval times, of MPs receiving an allowance from their constituents had died out. MPs were expected to have independent means, either because they were self-made, had inherited wealth, or possessed other sources of income. For example the future Prime Minister H. H. Asquith funded his early career through advocacy while Winston Churchill relied on journalism to pay his bills.

At the start of the twentieth century the rise of the Labour Party, and the arrival of working men in Parliament, led to calls for a living allowance for MPs. It is still interesting today to read the 1911 debate in which the issue was discussed. Those who spoke for the motion stressed the urgent need to give assistance to public-spirited men who had no resources of their own, and struggled to survive financially in London. Arthur Lee, speaking for the opposition Conservative Party, warned that payment for MPs would 'sound the death-knell of the system of voluntary service which has been the chief and unique glory of British public life'.[17]

At the end of the debate MPs were awarded an annual stipend of some £400 a year. David Lloyd George, then Chancellor of the Exchequer, expressed the mood of the House when he insisted that this sum was designed as an allowance to cover expenses and would not be a 'recognition of the magnitude of the service'.[18] This sense that the job of MP contained its own reward, measured in honour, was to persist for a further fifty years.

The break-point did not come till 1970, when it was announced that MPs' salaries would be referred to the Top Salaries Review Board (TSRB), the body which decided on the scale of remuneration for senior civil servants and other public-sector employees. The TSRB at once put paid to the notion that serving as a Member of Parliament was a special occupation, expressing the view that MPs should be paid the 'proper rate for the job'.[19] In a second radical departure from past practice, it recommended that MPs' expenses should be treated as a separate matter from salary. This ruling was the start of parliamentary allowances. Though MPs are now formally paid some £61,820 per annum (approximately two and a half times the average wage), many of them also benefit hugely from the complicated, poorly policed and widely abused system of expenses.

The most important of these is the Additional Costs Allowance (ACA). When the ACA was introduced in 1971 it had a single purpose: to meet costs incurred by MPs outside London who needed to stay in the capital in order to attend Parliament. The TSRB urged that this allowance should be paid as a daily subsistence allowance, as permitted to assistant secretaries in the civil service. It also recommended that MPs would be expected to account for this expenditure in the same careful and rigorous way as civil servants.[20] In a move pregnant with consequence for the future, this second recommendation was rejected by Willie Whitelaw, then Leader of the House.[21]

In 1985 there was another significant departure. John Biffen, by now Leader of the House (though under attack from Downing Street for being a 'semi-detached' member of the Cabinet), confirmed that the allowance could be used to pay mortgage payments.[22] This move opened the way for MPs to make massive windfall gains on the property market, funded by the ACA. It needs to be stressed that this significant financial benefit is not available in any other profession. Many people in government service, as well as personnel working for international corporations, need financial help from employers while on secondment from home. But they are never allowed to make capital gains as a result of this concession.

Sixteen years later, in a highly irregular move, MPs defied pay guidelines to increase the ACA limit by 42 per cent. MPs are now able to claim some £22,110 a year – roughly equivalent to the national average wage and, furthermore, tax-free – to help with the costs of staying away from their main residence.

By this stage the ACA allowance had incrementally evolved a very long way from its modest original purpose. MPs began to use the ACA as a secondary form of income. A very good example concerned Cabinet ministers benefiting from grace-and-favour accommodation in London. When these ministers have their own constituency home as well as a free London residence, they cannot be truthfully regarded as incurring extra expense from their overnight stays in the capital. However, they have continued to claim ACA for properties they did not use, arguing the need to keep these properties as a safeguard in the event of their dismissal from office.[23]

The ACA can now be used to pay for renovations on a second home. In October 2004 it emerged that the Prime Minister had obtained £43,000 from the ACA for carrying out maintenance work on his constituency home, Myrobella. It was far from clear – and not disclosed – how the Prime Minister had paid such a huge sum on repairs to a house that had originally cost some £20,000.[24] Once again, this payment showed how far the ACA had stretched beyond the original intention of paying the overnight costs of MPs attending Parliament.

A further case in point is that of the former Home Secretary David Blunkett, who in 2005 claimed more than £20,000 from the ACA to cover the cost of renting a cottage on the Duke of Devonshire's 35,000-acre Chatsworth estate. The cottage lies just fifteen miles from his Sheffield constituency, where he already owned a home. It was estimated that the total of mortgage repayments, council tax and utilities bills related to this property would have amounted to less than £2,800 a year, so that if Blunkett had claimed the ACA for his Sheffield house instead of the nearby Chatsworth cottage, he could have saved the taxpayer more than £17,000 per year. Mr Blunkett disputed this figure, but did not provide an alternative.[25]

Mr Blunkett's claim was an abuse of the ACA because the expense of the rented cottage was patently not 'wholly and necessarily' incurred in the performance of his parliamentary duties. He already owned a home in his constituency from which all his legitimate functions in the area could have been performed, but by choosing to claim the ACA for the Chatsworth cottage, he was able to fund a more luxurious lifestyle at the public's expense.

There are numerous other examples of abuses of this kind, all of them approved by the House of Commons Fees Office, which administers the system. MPs have created for themselves what amounted to an extremely generous, though legal (after all, they made the laws), slush fund. Its formal purpose remains the payment of necessary overnight expenses, but in practice it has become a pool of cash that can be ransacked more or less at will. Along with other parliamentary benefits, the ACA means that while a formal MP's salary stood at £60,000 a year, in practice many MPs are being paid the equivalent of around £100,000. In private, some parliamentarians are candid about this. They state casually that they are badly underpaid, but there was little they could do about this because of the public outcry provoked by dis-cussion of salary increases. This means that they feel it is legitimate to use the ACA (and other methods) to lift their salary to what they regard as a reasonable standard. As one MP confided to me:

> The ACA is to all intents and purposes a salary add-on. We don't have the courage to award ourselves a salary increase. It isn't taxed – that's the amazing thing. If I was the chief executive of a company and got paid expenses, that would be seen as a benefit in kind and I would get taxed on it.

I asked the MP if he would go on the record and make his statement publicly. He refused to do so, giving as his reason: 'We spend a lot of time here. Who wants to be a non-person?' As an example of what he meant, he cited the Liberal Democrat MP Norman Baker, who has worked hard to publicise expenses scandals concerning MPs from all parties: 'You see Norman all alone in the [Commons] tea-room, in solitary confinement.'[26] Norman Baker is one of the heroes of this book.

Another generous form of benefit involves travel expenses. MPs are able to claim travel costs incurred 'wholly and necessarily on parliamentary duties'. In February 2007, the House of Commons was forced to reveal a breakdown of members' travel expense claims, after fighting a bitter two-year battle against a Freedom of Information Act request. The figures highlighted some eye-catching claims. The Labour MP Janet Anderson received some £16,612 in mileage allowance, reportedly enough to have driven her twice around the world. The statistics showed that Ms Anderson drove the equivalent of 222 miles to her Lancashire constituency and back every day that the Commons sat last year. The Tory MP for Beckenham, Jacqui Lait, pocketed £6,716 for some 20,000 miles' worth of car journeys, even though her constituency is just ten miles from Westminster. Another Labour MP, Diane Abbott, spent £2,235 on taxis, though her Hackney constituency is only five and a half miles from Westminster.[27]

The ever-increasing allowances are not merely a covert way of increasing the earnings of many MPs. They are also of enormous political benefit, giving massive advantage to sitting MPs over challengers from rival parties. For example in early 2007 MPs awarded themselves a 'communications allowance', ostensibly to inform their constituents better about the work they do in Parliament. In practice this amounts to £10,000 a year extra cash, equivalent to £50,000 during a full term of Parliament, for MPs to promote their work to voters. Challenging candidates cannot hope to compete with this kind of expenditure.*

---

* Sitting MPs benefit from a large number of carefully contrived 'incumbency factors', which provide a bias in favour of existing parties and a barrier to change. Besides the communications allowance discussed above, these incumbency

This extremely generous system of expenses was certainly legal. But it did not readily bear public investigation. It amounted to a payment system on a scale and laxity that was available to no one else in the country, whether in the private or the public sector, where civil servants were notoriously forced to account for every last penny in expenses. This special arrangement for Parliament emphasised the privileged and separate status of the Political Class. It also played a large part in forming a common consciousness and mutual understanding among MPs that crossed party boundaries. MPs were uneasily aware that the generosity of their expenses system would never bear public scrutiny, and so went to great lengths to keep them secret. In the process they became all too aware that, while formally they might be opposed to each other, their real enemy was the British public. In May 2007 MPs of all parties combined to vote themselves a special exemption from the requirements of the Freedom of Information Act, so that their expense claims could be kept secret. They only changed their minds after a huge public outcry.

This sordid little episode was a further reminder of what a very long distance the Political Class had come from ordinary standards of wider society. The greatest proof of this tragic abyss which divides MPs from mainstream standards of honesty, decency and propriety remains, however, the removal of Elizabeth Filkin, the Parliamentary Commissioner for Standards.

The readiness of ministers and MPs to sit idly by while Mrs Filkin was pilloried and driven from her job is one of the most morally disgusting episodes I have witnessed as a journalist and as a human being. I tried to expose it at the time, but no one wanted to listen.[28] It has lingered in my mind ever since, and every so often I have learned fresh and ever more disquieting facts about it. It is essentially the story of how MPs destroyed the reputation of a

---

factors also include staffing, constituency office and 'incidental expenses' allowances; sitting MPs also continue to draw their salaries during election campaigns. In addition, there are a large number of incumbency factors benefiting political parties with large representation in the House of Commons.

woman emphatically not because she had done anything wrong, but because she was too assiduous in doing her duty. The revolting spectacle of how all three main political parties colluded in the use of Parliament to destroy the reputation of a decent woman was my main spur for writing this book. The full story is only being told now, for the first time.

The Hounding of the Parliamentary Commissioner for Standards

The story is important in three separate ways. First, there are Mrs Filkin's investigations themselves. During the relatively short period they were permitted to last, the Parliamentary Commissioner exposed a shocking pattern of arrogance, corruption, greed, bullying and deception among ministers, ordinary MPs and leading figures from the Conservative opposition.

Second, there is the Political Class reaction to her investigations. Senior MPs and ministers – primarily using the mechanism of the House of Commons Standards and Privileges Committee, but also using personal threats, press smears and other methods – acted in concert to block, overturn and discredit Mrs Filkin's investigations. Confronted with compelling evidence that leading politicians were corrupt, liars or cheats, the Political Class did not respond in the way that one would hope and expect: by cleaning up its act and punishing wrongdoers. Instead it turned its fire on the person who investigated the misdemeanours, and tried (very successfully) to cover up their own wrongdoing.

The third important point is that all three major political parties – not just the governing New Labour party but also the Conservative and Liberal Democrat opposition parties – joined in the conspiracy against Mrs Filkin and sought to discredit her. The story of Elizabeth Filkin therefore demonstrates a profound sickness at the heart of British democracy.

Elizabeth Filkin was appointed Parliamentary Commissioner for Standards in 1999, replacing Sir Gordon Downey, the original

Commissioner. The post had been created three years before, on the recommendation of the Nolan Commission, which was set up in the wake of a series of corruption scandals involving mainly Conservative politicians. Filkin was exceptionally well-qualified for the post. Having worked as adjudicator for the Inland Revenue and for Customs and Excise, she was well accustomed to fending off powerful institutions and individuals.

The terms of her appointment demanded that Filkin should sift through all allegations made against MPs, whether from members of the public, journalists or parliamentarians themselves. She dismissed the majority of these as trivial or mischievous, and dealt only with the more substantial claims. After she had carried out a report she would make her personal recommendation whether the complaint should be upheld or not, and submit it to the House of Commons Standards and Privileges Committee. This body was composed of MPs from all parties, though the governing New Labour party had the majority.

Soon a sinister pattern became apparent. When the Commissioner produced a report on a member of the government, her critical comments were – without exception – watered down or rejected. By contrast, the Standards and Privileges Committee actually revelled in reports about rebellious MPs and those who for whatever reason threatened the interests of the main political parties. Far from being rejected, these reports about dissident individuals, or those who could not rely on the protection of the big party machines, were given extra billing and emphasis.

This dual standard became apparent very early indeed, as a comparison between the complaints against the then Cabinet minister Mo Mowlam and the back-bencher Bob Wareing demonstrates. Wareing and Mowlam were very different politicians. Mowlam, at that stage of her career, was Northern Ireland secretary and a rising New Labour star. Wareing was a rebellious Labour MP, member of the Socialist Campaign group, and frequent rebel against the government who was later to march against the Iraq War. Though they could hardly be more unlike in terms of profile, they were both found guilty of almost identical offences. They both failed to declare an outside interest and then, when the Parliamentary Commissioner moved in to investigate, provided the inquiry with false information.*

The Standards and Privileges Committee set about dealing with these two cases in glaringly different ways. It showed no real concern about Mowlam's infraction. While the Committee had effectively no choice but to uphold Elizabeth Filkin's finding that Mowlam had broken parliamentary rules, it took the minimum necessary disciplinary action, and did not ask Mowlam to apologise. This was a flagrant instance of the Political Class going out of its way to protect a senior figure who was a member of the Cabinet and a valued part of the government. But the Committee set out to victimise Wareing, inflicting the savage penalty of suspension from the Commons.

The identical double standard was on display when the rebel Conservative back-bencher Teresa Gorman and the Labour minister Geoffrey Robinson both came under investigation for failure to register an interest in an offshore trust. The Standards and Privileges Committee was vindictive towards Gorman, and imposed the strongest punishment ever given, a Commons suspension of a full month. Once again there was a blatant inequity between the treatment of an errant back-bencher and the justice meted out to a front-bench politician. Geoffrey Robinson was cleared (he was later to be punished for misleading MPs, but not on this occasion).[29]

This same unfairness manifests itself in the contrasting treatment of Ken Livingstone and John Major. Livingstone was investigated by the Parliamentary Commissioner after a complaint that he had failed to register details of speeches made outside Parliament. The complaint was not merely upheld but exploited by the Standards and Privileges Committee. According to the political scientist Dr Robert Kaye in his forthcoming book *Regulating Westminster*:

---

* Filkin ruled that Mowlam had failed to register a donation of £5,000 to her research fund, and then aggravated the offence by failing to disclose the payment when she was investigated.

What is significant about the Committee's response is not that it concurred with the Commissioner, nor that it recommended that Livingstone should apologise to the House. Rather, the Committee's report is unusually descriptive and verbose. In former cases, the Committee's short response had played down negative findings. In *Livingstone* it revelled in them.

Given the length of the Commissioner's report (twenty-two paragraphs), one would expect the Committee's report to be between four and eight paragraphs long. The figure for the Livingstone Report is fourteen, over twice as long as one would expect. Whereas in previous cases the Committee would simply note that the Member had amended his Register entry as required, in *Livingstone* it printed his new entry in full. It also notes – which Filkin's report does not – that he had received, in just under two years, £220,992, of which £158,599 was subject to the requirement to disclose remuneration.[30]

Shortly after this Livingstone case, Elizabeth Filkin was invited to investigate claims that John Major had committed the identical misdemeanour by failing to disclose his earnings from speeches. She found that Major ought to have registered his speeches. But on this occasion the Standards and Privileges Committee made nothing of the offence.*

Major was a senior member of the Tory hierarchy, and a former Prime Minister. It is not surprising that a mainstream Commons committee looked to protect him. Livingstone was another matter entirely. He was running a one-man revolt against the Labour Party leadership by planning to stand as an independent in the elections for Mayor of London against Frank Dobson, the approved party candidate. He also posed a threat to Tory and Lib Dem aspirations of winning London. It therefore suited the interests of both the Labour and Conservative party machines to use

---

* I have simplified the issues at stake here for the sake of brevity. For a clearer and lengthier explanation of this complicated story see Kaye's forthcoming work *Regulating Westminster*, or the committee report itself.

Mrs Filkin's report to inflict as much damage as they could on Livingstone. All the established political parties had a vested interest in the destruction of Ken Livingstone, and there is no strong reason to doubt that is exactly what they were setting out to achieve by strengthening Mrs Filkin's criticisms of Livingstone in their report.

But they only sought to make the most of Mrs Filkin's findings when dealing with party rebels. The Parliamentary Commissioner was snubbed again and again when she reported adversely on ministers. The Standards and Privileges Committee overturned her judgement when she ruled that John Prescott, the Deputy Prime Minister, should have registered the flat he received at a cheap rent from the Rail, Maritime and Transport Union.[31] A famous case concerned Peter Mandelson. During the period of Mrs Filkin's investigation in early 1999 Mandelson was in a lull between Cabinet jobs, having been forced to resign as Trade Secretary and still tremulously awaiting clearance to return to government. Filkin was asked to investigate the loan from his ministerial colleague Geoffrey Robinson that had caused his resignation. Disastrously for Mandelson and the Blair government, as we have seen, she found that as minister he had misled the Britannia Building Society by failing to declare the loan on his mortgage application form. The Standards and Privileges Committee acted swiftly to overturn this Filkin ruling, a landmark decision as far as Mandelson was concerned because it cleared the decks for his return to the Cabinet later the same year.

By now Filkin was becoming a very serious irritant to the Political Class. It was not long before she found herself under personal attack. Mrs Filkin herself believes that it was the investigation into the rising ministerial star John Reid that led to her downfall.

Filkin was asked to investigate an allegation that John Reid was abusing his Commons office costs allowance for party political purposes. This was a classical Political Class transgression – the diversion of the resources of the state for party benefit – but was illegal under strict House of Commons rules. The allegation concerned Reid's son Kevin who, ostensibly employed as a parliamentary researcher, was accused of actually working full-time for the Labour Party. Later, when Kevin Reid went to work formally for Labour, his father allegedly employed another Labour researcher, Suzanne Hillard, on the same shadowy basis. It was also claimed that a third activist was working for the Labour Party while signed up as parliamentary researcher for John Maxton, a neighbour of Reid.

Unfortunately for John Reid, Filkin considered that the evidence was very strong. Three former senior Labour Party officials corroborated the story. More damaging still, it emerged that Reid and Maxton had pressurised these witnesses not to give evidence to the Parliamentary Commissioner. Mrs Filkin duly reported that Reid had diverted taxpayers' money for party political purposes, and sought to interfere with witnesses. But her report was thrown out in its entirety by the committee. There is no question that the basis for the decision was political. Even the timing of the committee report was highly suspicious. It was published on 21 December, as Westminster prepared to close down for Christmas.*

It was during the inquiry into Reid that the Blair government made a decision to discredit Elizabeth Filkin and drive her from office. The attack was sanctioned by the Prime Minister, and orchestrated from within the government Whips' Office. But this was not just a New Labour-inspired operation. The Conservative and Lib Dem opposition parties were both active in the campaign to oust Filkin.

There are three different kinds of evidence for this. Government sources encouraged a campaign of vilification. I was a member of the parliamentary lobby at the time and can remember being encouraged to 'take a look at Filkin' by one Labour MP close to the Whips' Office. This kind of negative briefing was widespread.

---

* Dr Kaye has established beyond reasonable doubt that the decision to overturn *Reid* was made on political grounds, rather than on the basis of the evidence gathered by Filkin and put before the Committee.

One political reporter was told by Labour MPs that 'she was a mad alcoholic. People I didn't expect were coming up to me. MPs had obviously been authorised to brief against her.'[32] Attacks from ministers and other senior members of the Political Class were vicious. Betty Boothroyd, the retired Commons speaker, referred to Mrs Filkin as a 'witch-hunter' and called for her replacement. 'The House would be better served by somebody who knew it well,' declared Boothroyd, 'working quietly in the background.'[33]

The social security minister Jeff Rooker went on the attack in the *Independent* newspaper to warn Elizabeth Filkin that 'unlike her, Members of Parliament are elected and judged by their constituents at the ballot box. She should stick to what she is extremely well-paid and has been appointed to do, which is to police the Register of Members' Interests.'[34] It was put about that Cabinet ministers were 'deeply annoyed' by Filkin and doubted her competence.[35] According to Robert Kaye, 'by early 2000 government ministers had tacit permission to discredit the Commissioner'. Tory MPs joined in the briefing against the Commissioner. One, unnamed, Tory told the *Independent*'s deputy political editor Colin Brown that 'there is a problem over the rules governing her job. She has to investigate complaints, and it appears that there is a scandal surrounding MPs before they are cleared.'[36] John Major attacked the Commissioner's demand that he should reveal details of his lecture work as 'untenable'.

But the government did not merely use the press to menace Mrs Filkin. They also threatened her in person. According to Mrs Filkin herself, Peter Mandelson first used 'smarm and charm' in order to evade criticism during his investigation. When that failed Mrs Filkin records that he 'went cold and hinted that it wouldn't be good for me if the finding went badly for him. In several phone calls he gave me the impression that all would not be well from my point of view if I did not do what he wanted.'[37] When neither charm nor bullying worked, Mandelson attacked Filkin publicly, accusing her of lacking 'logic and consistency'.[38] The pressure soon intensified. As the John Reid investigation got under way Mrs Filkin was approached directly by a number of Labour MPs and members of the Standards and Privileges Committee urging her to soften her style. Lord Cocks, a Labour fixer who had been a notoriously thuggish chief whip in the dying days of the Jim Callaghan government in the late 1970s – and rewarded with a peerage – invited himself to visit Mrs Filkin. He knew Filkin professionally, which was probably why he had been given this particular task.

'I've been sent to see you,' he snarled on arrival.

'Who sent you?' replied Filkin.

'I can't tell. I'm here to tell you that you have been upsetting a large number of powerful people. You are jeopardising your seat in the House of Lords, and they just won't put up with it.'

Filkin stood firm. She told him that she had a job to do, and was going to get on with it.

Cocks indicated displeasure. 'Well, Elizabeth,' he grunted, 'I've always thought very highly of you. I have to warn you that this may turn out badly for you.'[39]

Journalists rang Filkin, who had recently gone through a divorce, asking loaded questions about her private life. Press articles attacked her. Certain journalists – she remembers one *Times* reporter being especially unreliable – misrepresented what she said or did.

The trigger for all-out attack was the decision by the Standards and Privileges Committee to overturn the Filkin decision on John Reid. Allies of John Reid launched a powerful campaign in the Scottish press to destabilise the Commissioner. They claimed that the Committee decision to reject Filkin placed a fatal question-mark over Mrs Filkin's judgement. In a malicious leader article the pro-government Glasgow *Herald* labelled Mrs Filkin 'witch-finder general', adding that 'the original [witch-finder general] hunted down witches who were guilty until (very rarely, if ever) proved innocent. It is a damaging nickname to acquire.' The *Herald* asserted that 'Ms Filkin has been badly damaged by the latest committee finding,' adding, 'If she truly wants to be the necessary champion of Westminster probity, she needs to prove that she can conduct a fair investigation and reach a conclusion objectively.'[40]

The *Herald* piece was followed by an article by Paul Sinclair, then political editor of the *Daily Record*.* Sinclair accused Filkin of using 'selective evidence' and creating a 'damning impression ... What is becoming obvious is that the inquiries which Filkin leads are not working.' Both the *Herald* and *Daily Record* articles give an invaluable insight into the kind of arguments that were used by the Political Class to undermine Mrs Filkin.

There is also important evidence, brought to light by Dr Robert Kaye, that the government Whips' Office placed pressure on members of the Standards and Privileges Committee. Though purely circumstantial, it is nevertheless compelling. Again and again, at a crucial point in the committee investigation, key MPs on the committee were suddenly promoted to parliamentary private secretary (PPS). These PPS posts are extremely junior, and represent no more than the first intangible indication that the holder may be singled out one day for ministerial preferment. Those who hold them are never on the government payroll. They are, however, obliged to abide by all the disciplines imposed on front-bench spokesmen. The ministerial code states that parliamentary private secretaries 'are not precluded from serving on select committees'. But it adds that they 'should avoid associating themselves with recommendations critical of or embarrassing to the government'.[41] So these appointments had the treble effect of sweetening MPs with the hope of future promotion and preventing them from criticising ministers, all while allowing them to keep their place on the Standards and Privileges Committee.

Disquiet about such appointments arose during the investigation into Peter Mandelson. On 20 May 1999, before the committee met to deliberate, the Labour MP Michael Foster was appointed PPS to the Attorney-General. As Dr Kaye remarks: 'If Foster's appointment was not an exercise in jury-nobbling, it at least had the potential to be seen as such.' Foster was later criticised by the Labour MP Alan Williams, who said that MPs 'should either be a

---

* Paul Sinclair, cadet member of the Scottish Political Class. Sinclair was later to leave the *Daily Record* to go and work for the Cabinet minister Douglas Alexander. He now works for Gordon Brown as a press handler.

Parliamentary Private Secretary and not be on the committee, or vice-versa'.[42]

Soon after the Mandelson investigation the MP Tom Levitt was appointed PPS. Coincidentally this appointment came shortly before the committee assessed Mrs Filkin's report into the Cabinet ministers Mo Mowlam and Jack Cunningham. Dr Kaye notes that 'Levitt's appointment was part of a wider reshuffle', but adds: 'It is notable, however, that for a second time a committee member was appointed PPS, and once again, it was immediately before a report on a Cabinet minister.'

The step of appointing PPSs – and therefore making the committee subject to front-bench discipline – was most notable in the case of John Reid. Just five days before the committee made its report, the MP Shona McIsaac was made PPS to Northern Ireland minister Adam Ingram, a move which meant that *all three* of the newly elected members of the Standards and Privileges Committee were PPSs and therefore bound by collective responsibility. According to Dr Kaye:

> While Tom Levitt's appointment as a PPS may have been utterly unrelated to his position on the Standards Committee, the timing of the appointments of Michael Foster and McIsaac, both in the middle of deliberation of findings against key Blair loyalists, and both in cases where the Commissioner's verdict was overturned, stretches credulity. In McIsaac's case, suspicion is heightened by the circumstances of the appointment. Foster and Levitt were both appointed in the course of wider reshuffles, prompted by the departures of Donald Dewar and George Robertson respectively. The vacancy for McIsaac, however, was created when Des Browne, PPS to Ingram, and a close friend of John Reid, stood down. (Browne, Ingram and Maxton share adjoining constituencies, with Reid's only a few miles away.) It was a straight swap between Reid's friend and his judge. No explanation was given for Browne's return to the back-benches. Only six months later, however, he returned to the Northern Ireland Office, under Mandelson's successor, Dr John Reid.[43]

The circumstances surrounding Des Browne's decision to step down as PPS for six months are unusual. At the very least it was unsatisfactory that the Labour MPs who received these promotions remained on the committee, given that their independence was then compromised. Fresh questions about the use of government patronage emerged later when the more senior members of the committee received peerages in the wake of the 2001 General Election.

Eventually, in October 2001, the House of Commons Commissioner Archie Kirkwood announced that Mrs Filkin's job was being put out to public appointment. Simultaneously it was made known that the post was being downgraded from four to three days a week. It was briefed out that the downgrading in the number of days available to the commission was to prevent the examination of 'trivial' cases, while Robin Cook as Leader of the Commons insisted that Mrs Filkin was free to reapply, saying that 'she has done a good job, that is why she is a candidate, and if she is the best candidate she will be offered a further contract'.[44] There is every reason to be sceptical of all these claims. Mrs Filkin's predecessor Gordon Downey had been asked to stay on as Commissioner without going through the trouble of a reappointment process – and the advertisement for Mrs Filkin's successor indicated that he or she would be at liberty to seek an extension of the initial contract. Mrs Filkin decided not to reapply. In her letter to the Commons Speaker she explained her decision:

I knew, when taking on this job, that pressure would be applied by some members when facing an investigation and by their supporters. I knew well from my previous post that this faces an impartial investigator on occasion.

However, the degree of pressure applied has been quite remarkable. In some cases this has been applied directly by members, some holding high office. In other cases, it has been applied indirectly by unchecked whispering campaigns and hostile press briefings, some, I have regret to have been informed, executed by named civil servants.

Her replacement, Sir Philip Mawer, came from deep within the Whitehall establishment and has proved a less controversial figure.

The case of Elizabeth Filkin is wholly shameful. The three most junior members of the Standards and Privileges Committee were hobbled by being appointed to quasi-governmental positions at sensitive times. The only cases where the committee over-ruled Elizabeth Filkin involved criticism of government ministers – Peter Mandelson, John Reid, John Prescott and Nigel Griffiths. The only cases where the Committee went further than Filkin in its criticisms involved party dissidents. The allegations made by pro-government MPs and their supporters in the press against Mrs Filkin were false. It was spread about she made much of 'trivial' cases. This was untrue. She was privately accused of leaking material to the press. The truth was that leaks only occurred after Mrs Filkin's reports had been passed to the committee.[45]

It is extremely notable that all three major parties played a part in dislodging Mrs Filkin. The Conservative MP Eric Forth, shadow Leader of the Commons, was complicit. He had been an extremely supportive and senior member of the Standards and Privileges Committee as it overturned repeated Filkin rulings against Peter Mandelson, John Reid and others.* The Liberal Democrat MP Archie Kirkwood (raised to Baron Kirkwood of Kirkhope in the 2005 honours list) was the House of Commons Commissioner responsible for Filkin's removal and subsequent replacement – though he absented himself from the interview process as he was subject to a pending complaint – by a figure who would be more congenial for MPs generally. Kirkwood's Liberal Democrat colleague Malcolm Bruce seems to have been a key ally of Labour in overturning committee decisions.

---

* He confirmed this point to the author in a series of contemporary conversations. Eric Forth was perhaps animated by the old-fashioned view, associated with the late Enoch Powell, that the House of Commons was a sovereign body and therefore external regulation of the kind supplied by Mrs Filkin was wrong and illegitimate.

It is all too easy to understand why the ruling New Labour party should have wished to dislodge an independent figure who saw her job as bringing ministerial sleaze and various kinds of abuse by Members of Parliament to public attention. But it is hard to comprehend why the Liberal Democrat and Conservative oppositions should have supported the government in its mission to squash an irritant. In theory, the Conservatives and the Liberal Democrats should have sought to embarrass the Labour government by coming to the defence of a figure of obvious public probity who was actively engaged in uncovering government sleaze and corruption. Their decision not to do so – and actually to join the assault on Mrs Filkin – is therefore at first sight paradoxical.

The explanation produced by MPs themselves is unconvincing. As we have already seen, the accusation that Mrs Filkin was 'over-zealous' and made too much of 'trivial' misdemeanours was simply not justified.* The real explanation seems to be that all parties have taken the attitude that the Political Class should be exempt from the kind of rigorous examination of their conduct that ordinary members of the public expect to face as they go about their daily lives.

The transcript of Peter Mandelson's appearance before the Standards and Privileges Committee in the wake of Mrs Filkin's report into his home loan strongly suggests that this was the case. Eric Forth, the senior Tory on the committee, actually apologised to Mandelson for taking up his time. This interview with Mandelson, which makes extremely sorry reading today,

---

* The one independent member of the Commission, Martin Bell MP, stated: 'I think it sends a very dispiriting signal about Parliament's willingness to police itself thoroughly. I think a lot of senior MPs were not happy with her thoroughness, but that is the whole point of having an independent Commissioner.' Bell's fellow Commission member Peter Bottomley, Conservative MP, added: 'My belief is that she has done the job perfectly impartially and fairly and she should have been offered a second term. I think that some people in senior positions clearly don't like the results of her work.' See 'Second term snub for MPs' anti-sleaze watchdog', *Guardian*, 19 October 2001.

came after Filkin had established beyond any dispute that the former Cabinet minister had lied to the Britannia Building Society, and furthermore failed to meet his obligation to Parliament to register the Robinson loan. The committee showed no interest at all in holding Peter Mandelson to account for this transgression.

It was not just Cabinet ministers who had secrets they would rather not see entering the public domain. Conservative and Liberal Democrat MPs also had dirty linen they would rather not wash in public. It is true that there would have been a political advantage for both the Liberal Democrats and the Conservatives in using the Filkin investigations to embarrass the government. But both opposition parties seem to have decided that this course of action would have brought only a short-term benefit. Their over-riding concern was to protect the political elite from prurient or demeaning inspection by outsiders. Mainstream politicians showed no signs of grasping that the Commons Standards and Privileges Committee is part of an elaborate system of con-stitutional machinery which is designed to maintain integrity in British public life. On the contrary they used the Committee as a way of protecting their own corruptions and abuses.

It is extremely significant that the only cases where the Committee showed real vigour and actually exerted its authority were where rebel MPs threatened the happy tripartite collabor-ation between Liberal Democrats, Conservatives and Labour. The Committee worked hand in hand with party machines in a mission to slur or damage rebel MPs or those, like Ken Livingstone and George Galloway, who threatened the cartel structure of British politics. This pattern of conduct is profoundly contrary to the model found in traditional politics textbooks. These envisage an adversarial system of democracy, where the opposition parties ruthlessly hold the government of the day to account. Seen from within such a theoretical context, the conduct of opposition parties in recent years is baffling. Filkin and other contemporary cases show that modern British politics no longer works in the way that the textbooks suggest, and that a new model needs to be found capable of delivering a more adequate description of twenty-first-century government. It is now time to tell the story of how the Political Class has captured the British media, and turned it into a tool.

PART III

THE CAPTURE OF THE MEDIA

11

CLIENT JOURNALISM

'Indeed, it is above all the successful journalists who find themselves having to face particularly onerous inner challenges. It is no small thing to consort with the most powerful people of this earth in their drawing rooms, apparently on the basis of equality, to be flattered because you are feared, while all the time knowing that no sooner has the door closed behind you than your host may have to defend himself to his guests for having invited the "scoundrels of the press". In the same way, it is no small thing to deliver prompt and yet convincing judgments on anything and everything that the "market" happens to call for, on every conceivable problem of life, without succumbing to absolute superficiality, or what is even worse, to the humiliation of self-exposure with its inexorable consequences. We should not find it astonishing that so many journalists have gone off the rails or have otherwise lost their value as human beings'
– Max Weber, *Politics as a Vocation*

I have shown in the preceding chapters how the Political Class set out to sideline, to replace or to capture the main institutions of the state and civil society which had governed Britain in the twentieth century. There were various motives for this. One of them was impatience. Britain is not an elective dictatorship, mainly because Parliament and the judiciary provide mechanisms for holding the executive to account between elections. The Political Class disliked this restraint. It consciously set out to weaken representative democracy and replace it with a novel system of government offering direct engagement between the governing elite and the British people.

Political Class apologists have consistently protested that the press has tried to take on the role of formal opposition under this new method of government. This is a false diagnosis. The Political Class, thanks to its complicity in the debasement of Parliament and its intolerance of the judiciary, had set out to achieve something new and remarkable. It sought to give an almost constitutional role to the British media by building it up as an alternative to existing state institutions.

This methodology became especially clear with the emergence of New Labour, though there had earlier been powerful intimations. The incoming government set out to empower the media in a number of ways. It ended the convention, which had been weakening in any case, that government announcements must be made through Parliament. They were issued through the media instead, often through leaks to favoured newspapers. The House of Commons was downgraded and the judiciary placed under constant attack. Meanwhile, the new government deliberately awarded a massive new importance to the media. It obsessively cultivated journalists. A disproportionate amount of Tony Blair's time was devoted to talking to reporters and editors, either privately or in small groups.*

Proprietors were treated with the same care and attention that was extended to trade union barons in the 1970s. They were given special favours, handed unique privileges, handled with near-total deference by the new administration. Editors were cultivated on a scale never before approached by any serving Prime Minister. Piers Morgan, editor of the *Daily Mirror*, boasted in his diaries that he had enjoyed 'twenty-two lunches, six dinners, six interviews, twenty-four further one-to-one chats over tea and biscuits plus

---

* Tony Blair now admits this: 'In the analysis I am about to make, I first acknowledge my own complicity. We paid inordinate attention in the early days of New Labour to courting, assuaging, and persuading the media. In our own defence, after eighteen years of opposition and the, at times, ferocious hostility of parts of the media, it was hard to see any alternative.' Speech on 'Public Life' given by the then Prime Minister at Reuters, 12 June 2007.

numerous phone calls' with the Prime Minister in under ten years.[1] It should be borne in mind that Morgan's top-level access, though extraordinary, was derisory compared to his red-top competitor Rebekah Wade, editor of the *News of the World* and then the *Sun*. This intensive face-to-face cultivation of tabloid editors was something completely new in British public life, and had not occurred before during either Labour or Conservative governments.* Again and again civil servants, military leaders and others who glimpsed Tony Blair's government from the inside expressed amazement at the extent that decision-making was dominated by the press.[2]

The structure of administration was fundamentally altered in order to generate this new dynamic. Under all previous governments, whether left or right, the role of press secretary had been relatively unimportant in the Downing Street hierarchy. He tended to be a relatively lowly civil servant, with the choice of individual mainly delegated by the Prime Minister to others.† Suddenly, with the arrival of Alastair Campbell in 1997, the press secretary was elevated into one of the two or three most powerful figures in government.

In a parallel but closely connected development, the post of chief whip was downgraded. This was a seismic moment and needs explanation. The chief whip had been one of the notable and powerful figures in both Labour and Conservative governments: keeper of secrets, enforcer of rules, the crucial link between Downing Street and the parliamentary party, sometimes the Prime Minister's closest confidant. (For example, the job done by Alastair Goodlad for John Major. The choice of an unsympathetic chief whip, Tim Renton, is often held to be one of the reasons behind Margaret Thatcher's fall from power in 1990.‡ By contrast chief

---

* While it was the case that Margaret Thatcher's Conservative Party devoted great care in cultivating the *Sun* from the 1970s onwards, Thatcher herself met the paper's editors Larry Lamb and Kelvin Mackenzie relatively rarely.
† This was even the case with Bernard Ingham, who only met Margaret Thatcher for a few minutes before he was given the job.
‡ See for instance Bruce Anderson: 'Tim Renton never crossed the chemistry threshold; he probably never could have.' Anderson, *John Major*, p. 177.

whip Michael Cocks and his deputy Walter Harrison held together the 1976–79 Callaghan minority government.) But after 1997 the power and status of the chief whip sank sharply, and the role was converted into little more than harmless drudge. The position of enforcer which had previously belonged to the chief whip was grabbed by the Prime Minister's press adviser.

It was understood that control was exercised through the media. The press machine ensured that only favoured ministers or MPs were allowed on the airwaves while others were frozen out and found themselves subject to hostile briefing behind the scenes. Cabinet ministers who suffered this fate included Mo Mowlam, Clare Short, David Clark and – intermittently – Gordon Brown. The characteristic method of attack used against errant or unpopular ministers by the Downing Street machine was to privately brief that they were mentally unstable and on the verge of cracking up, though other charges concerning sexual profligacy or drinking problems were also used to undermine the public standing of targeted individuals.

The demise of the chief whip and the rise of the press secretary was swiftly captured through popular portraits of the workings of government. In Michael Dobbs' highly successful television drama *House of Cards*, first broadcast in 1990, the most menacing and potent figure was Francis Urquhart, the fictional chief whip and arch-manipulator. More recent accounts of Downing Street, for instance the reality-based film *The Queen* and the television drama *The Deal* (both written by Peter Morgan), have laid comparable stress on the role of the press secretary Alastair Campbell.

This change accurately reflected a transformation in the organisation of government. The chief whip was no longer involved in many major decisions. Instead of seeking to rule through Parliament the incoming New Labour government successfully ruled through the media. It was natural that the press secretary should acquire the status that had previously been occupied by the chief whip. This arrangement was formalised after the 2001 General Election. In a highly symbolic move the chief whip Hilary

Armstrong and her team were moved out of 12 Downing Street, the magnificent Georgian building which had been occupied by the whips since the nineteenth century. As the whips searched for accommodation elsewhere, they were obliged to make way for the greatly strengthened Downing Street press team, which had previously occupied a cramped set of rooms on the ground floor of Number 10.

The essential objective of this new and supercharged Downing Street media machinery was to capture the now enfranchised press and media, and to turn it into the instrument of the new governing elite. Just as the capacious offices at 12 Downing Street had been used for years to whip in MPs, now they were deployed to whip in the press. A number of techniques were brought into play to ensure this outcome, but the most important was control of the government publicity machine. In a startling and confident coup, New Labour privatised state information, putting it to use for a narrow, partisan advantage. Downing Street used its monopoly control of political news to create a client press. For a number of years this strategy was astonishingly successful.

Every kind of government information was selectively placed into the media. Even the date of the 2001 General Election was given exclusively to the *Sun*, as a senior member of the Downing Street media team was later to admit.[3] We have seen above how honours were used as a method of inducing potential donors into giving cash to political parties. The honours list, besides boosting party finances, proved a rich source of media patronage, as newsworthy names on forthcoming lists, especially sportsmen, actors and pop-stars, were systematically leaked to friendly newspapers.[4] This conversion of state information into a tradeable commodity was extremely widespread and has been described in detail by the former BBC reporter Nicholas Jones in a series of diligently assembled and ground-breaking books.[5]

All journalists need to secure scoops and obtain exclusive information in order to maintain their reputation as cutting-edge operators. It was therefore natural that many political reporters swiftly found themselves in a state of dependence on government sources. Furthermore, there was a damaging price to pay for writing hostile copy about the government. It was at all times open to Downing Street spin-doctors to punish unco-operative journalists by freezing them out of the information-supply process, by personal intimidation, or – a tactic which proved successful in the case of some media organisations – to go behind their backs and complain to their bosses. For example, government spin-doctors would endlessly complain to BBC management about broadcasts by reporters, and Gordon Brown's spin-doctor at one stage agitated for the political editor of the *Sun* to be dismissed.

It was not long before a strong sense of dependence was created inside newspapers. They did not just seek information but also access for interviews and sometimes other kinds of help. I witnessed this at first hand in the aftermath of New Labour's General Election victory when I was a political writer for the *Daily* and *Sunday Express*, both of them historically Conservative-supporting newspapers. Downing Street was permitted to interfere with and even to veto or try to inspire appointments. Early on during her period as editor, Rosie Boycott sought to appoint the journalist Paul Routledge as political editor of the *Daily Express*. This move came to the attention of Downing Street, which always kept an extremely close eye on the comings and goings in political journalism. Number 10 viewed Routledge, who had written a hostile biography of Tony Blair's close ally Peter Mandelson and held old-fashioned left-wing sympathies, with disdain. (Perhaps most potent of all, Routledge was accurately perceived as an ally of Gordon Brown.) Influence was used to block the Routledge appointment. The political journalist Tony Bevins was given the job instead. Bevins enjoyed a reputation as a fiercely independent journalist, but this was by no means always the case. He was often uncritically supportive of his friend Alastair Campbell. Here is a description by Campbell himself of Bevins' reaction after he handed him a story concerning the defection of the Tory MP Alan Howarth to the Labour Party: 'I told him what it was, and I saw tears welling up in his eyes. Are you serious? I said I was. I love you, he said, and I love him. I want to kiss you.'[6]

After this experience Boycott changed her method of staff allocation. When an education correspondent was needed, Bevins was dispatched to seek the guidance of Stephen Byers, then an ardently Blairite education minister, for advice about who the *Daily Express* should hire (the author witnessed Bevins announce the result of his mission). Boycott became notably co-operative with the government in other ways. *Express* readers – long famous for their truculent hostility to the European Union and all its works – were baffled when the paper became a supporter of Tony Blair's European Movement. A series of stories started to appear in the paper emphasising the economic benefits of membership of the European Union. One startling front-page splash announced that withdrawal from Europe would bring about mass unemployment and cost Britain some 8 million jobs.[7]

The Downing Street press secretary made regular visits to the *Express*, sometimes in company with the Prime Minister, sometimes with the head of the policy unit, occasionally on his own. At these meetings the Number 10 team set out the government line. In return they were berated by specialist *Express* reporters who complained that the paper was not being rewarded for its loyalty with the giveaway exclusives enjoyed by the *Sun* and the *Mirror*. It was always made clear, however, that *Express* support for the government was not in question. In one particularly embarrassing meeting I recall Rosie Boycott looking across the table at Tony Blair and asking, 'What can we do to help?'* This offer appeared to embrace all areas of government activity. In general, Downing Street spin-doctors were keen that the *Express* should 'make the case' for the euro, something that it of course did.

---

* I have confirmed this recollection with the journalist Martin Samuel, now of *The Times*, who was also present at these meetings.

The Moral Consequences of Client Journalism

This new methodology of journalism formed the general pattern in the years following 1997. Lobby correspondents became ever more reverential of power, and of government sources. This was obvious from the body language of all present at the famous briefings given by Alastair Campbell from his office in Downing Street.* Campbell is a clever man and an accomplished mimic, characteristics which meant that these briefings were exceptionally good entertainment. A group of trusty political editors and reporters would assemble at the front of the room, laughing subserviently as Campbell cracked his jokes. They were so good that one political editor would typically double up in mirth as he cackled away. These jokes were usually made at the expense of reporters who asked difficult or confrontational questions. Campbell would, for instance, delight in apeing the nervous mannerisms of the independent-minded political editor of the *Financial Times*, Robert Peston (now the BBC's business editor). Peston's *FT* colleague Liam Halligan was another rebellious figure. When Halligan asked awkward questions Campbell would try to publicly humiliate him. The fawning laughter demonstrated that the press power-brokers took the side of the government spokesman against reporters who questioned the ruling orthodoxy or caused trouble.

It soon became clear that the key dividing line in British political journalism was between those reporters whose general line came from the government and those who stood outside the official machinery. Some journalists went way beyond that line and converted into licensed operatives for the Downing Street press machine, though masquerading to the outside world as independent men or women of integrity. One vivid example of the complicity between political journalists and their political

---

* Later the briefings were moved to the foreign press centre, but by then Campbell had ceased to give these daily briefings in person.

taskmasters concerns the *Observer* newspaper. In the summer of 1998, when reporters were researching the lobbying scandal that became known as the 'Dollygate' affair, steps were taken to keep the political editor ignorant of the investigation owing to the – completely unfounded – fear that he would inform his Downing Street friends what was going on.*

Another example concerns the leaking of the details concerning the loan made by the Labour MP and millionaire Geoffrey Robinson to the Cabinet minister Peter Mandelson. The story had been obtained by Paul Routledge – his source was Charlie Whelan, Special Adviser to Gordon Brown – and included in his unauthorised biography of Mandelson. As publication date drew near, the publishers sent a proof copy of the book to Routledge at his office in the House of Commons. Owing to an unlucky mix-up, the book and its bombshell contents arrived in the hands of lobby rivals who spoke to Peter Mandelson's special adviser, Benjamin Wegg-Prosser, but did not actually write the story.

This was an extraordinary manifestation of the new client journalism, which became the dominant mode of political reporting around the turn of the twentieth century. Routledge's rivals, once the package had been opened in error and the revelation about the Mandelson loan discovered, had three possible courses of action. They could have quietly closed the manuscript, pretended not to have seen it, and returned it to Routledge, and forgotten all about the affair. That would have been the action of gentlemen. Alternatively they could have taken advantage of the error to make use of the story themselves. This would have

---

* The subsequent experience of Greg Palast, the investigative journalist who uncovered the 'Dollygate' scandal, is extremely revealing. Palast complained that his powerful revelations about the purchase by large corporations of access to government departments were systematically played down, not just by the *Observer* newspaper but by the British media in general. He wrote: 'Where were my fellow journalists? These little puppies yapped at the *Observer's* evidence, but none demanded that the government open its records.' He also attacked the lack of will shown by opposition parties. See Palast, 'Whatever happened to my scandal?', *New Statesman*, 25 September 1998.

been entirely legitimate, opportunistic behaviour: the action of journalists. The failure to publish, while effectively alerting the Mandelson camp, hinted at the possibility of a different pattern of allegiance.*

To put the matter at its simplest, journalists became instruments of government. Reporters and government joined a conspiracy against the public to create a semi-fictitious political world whose most striking features were media events and fabricated stories. This was the stage when the phrase 'spin-doctor' took firm hold in British public life. The term was imported by New Labour from the United States in the early 1990s, and well communicated the element of menace, subterfuge and mystique which had suddenly attached itself to the formerly drab and unpropitious post of public relations officer. During this period, whose long apotheosis lasted from 1997 until the disaster of the Iraq War became manifest in 2004, yet lingered beyond that, political reporting was almost wholly removed from reality.

Numerous examples of the genre of what one might call 'virtual' political journalism are given in the chapter on Iraq that follows. However, the new system became evident immediately on New Labour taking office, with the events surrounding its muddled and painful decision not to affiliate sterling to the European single currency ahead of its launch in January 1999. Lack of any government policy gave rise to chaos as decision day approached. Eventually the shambles was brought to an end when Chancellor Gordon Brown gave what was billed by *The Times* newspaper as an 'interview' setting out the British attitude on the euro. As an 'interview' it had the distinctly odd feature of the essential quotation being faxed over from the Treasury. The characteristic ingredient of this story was backstage collaboration between reporters and

---

* Details of this story remain complex and obscure. The most generous explanation of the behaviour of the reporters involved is that they were simply trying to check the story with the Mandelson camp. In that case, it remains puzzling that they failed to run the story, though there may be a legitimate explanation for this. It is also striking that the editor of the newspaper at the heart of this intrigue was kept in ignorance, but not the Mandelson camp.

the British government on how to present policy. Here is Alastair Campbell's account of this fabricated media event, deceitfully passed on to the readers of *The Times* as a genuine interview:

> It was not really an interview so much as a form of words which would be given to Phil Webster [political editor of *The Times*]. The Treasury drafted the words and I made a couple of changes to tone down the pro-Europeanism in a couple of places. I spoke to Webster and agreed that the intro was that he was effectively ruling it out for this Parliament while saying it would be folly to close options ... The words went to Webster, the spin was applied, and away we went.[8]

This form of systematic collaboration between newspaper reporters and senior ministers and their advisers represented a novel development in political journalism. Reporters no longer looked at a speech and reported strictly what was said. Instead they took briefing from backstairs staff who explained the meaning of the speech. This post-speech huddle became one of the most characteristic sights of British political journalism in the late 1990s and early twenty-first century.

Minutes after the Prime Minister's annual oration to Labour Conference his press secretary would stroll back into the press room. A group would form around Campbell, formally to ask questions but in practice to be told the main points of the speech. I once inadvertently walked into this huddle just as it was starting to assemble and found myself opposite Campbell. 'Anything to ask?' said Campbell. I asked whether an apparently spontaneous passage not to be found in the draft of the speech circulated to reporters had been pre-scripted. 'We don't answer process questions,' said Campbell abruptly, turning to the *Daily Express* political editor Anthony Bevins, who muttered two or three words I failed to catch. Whatever they were, they caused Campbell at once to reel off what he judged to be the 'big points' of the Prime Minister's speech, as the leading political editors took dictation.

It was the same story with Budget speeches made by the Chancellor of the Exchequer. Reporters would watch the Chancellor from their eyrie in the Commons chamber. The moment he sat down they would dash out of their seats and assemble around the Chancellor's point man to be told about the speech. In the early years of New Labour the Chancellor's backstairs briefing would start as the Leader of the Opposition stood up to deliver his reply. The reporters would ignore the opposition response, and nevertheless listen to the Chancellor's spokesman – a decision that demonstrated how the media had supplanted Parliament as the important forum of political debate.

This was effectively a move to a kind of secondary reporting. Journalists no longer concentrated on reporting the primary or raw event – the political speech, government announcement or whatever. Instead they focused on the speech or announcement as mediated and interpreted by the community of ministerial aides and spin-doctors. This method converted political reporting into an esoteric art. This was very attractive to a certain type of political reporter. It meant that their business – fundamentally wholly accessible to outsiders – suddenly became shrouded in a kind of glamour. The production of political news came to resemble a form of divination, accessible only to the adept and those who understood how Westminster worked. To put this state of affairs in another way, news stories effectively emerged as some kind of private deal between government and reporter. It meant that there was dual reality in British politics – the reality of what actually happened, and the reality of what was reported. By a classic postmodern inversion, the real became false and the false became true.

The best way of illustrating this is to give examples. An excellent case in point is Gordon Brown's spending review of summer 1998. The reality about this financial package is that it was incredibly stingy. Having committed himself in advance to the spending limits set by the last Conservative Party Chancellor Kenneth Clarke, it was impossible for Gordon Brown to loosen the purse-strings without losing face. However, it was politically undesirable for the Chancellor to present his first great spending announcement in that way. So instead Gordon Brown engaged in sleight of hand that made it appear that he was actually giving away a great deal of money. His aides told political reporters who were gathered round to be given their line after his speech that this was a give-away spending package. Instead of reporting what was actually contained in the spending review, the journalists wrote what they were told. The *Daily Mirror* trumpeted: 'The Gord giveth £56 billion', even though the Chancellor had done nothing of the sort. Even the *Daily Mail*, frequently alleged to be hostile to government, claimed that 'Brown goes on a summer spree'.

So there were two realities. There was the real, hairshirt spending package. And there was the give-away Budget trumpeted by a credulous, client press in collaboration with Gordon Brown's spin-doctors. The true story that public spending was under heavy restraint could easily be found inside official documents. The false story, as retailed by Treasury ministers and their aides, was passed on to the British public.

This collaboration between government – above all, Tony Blair's Downing Street and Gordon Brown's Treasury – and media in a systematic deception of the British public can be found in almost every area of government. We have already noted above how the reporting of government policy on the euro in the late 1990s was in part a fabrication. This conspiracy between the Political and Media Classes was extremely thoroughgoing. It meant, for example, that the government was able simultaneously to have two contrary policies on the euro. This process is well described by the journalist James Naughtie:

The 2001 General Election campaign provided a delicious example. Two weeks before polling day Blair captured the lead story in the *Financial Times* with an interview for the paper in which he sounded enthusiastic about the prospect of euro membership when the circumstances were right. A stream of soothing balm was directed at the City. On the same day the *Sun* carried an article under Blair's name which was carefully crafted to sit happily with the government's formula but to invite the interpretation that this was a Prime Minister who would never bounce his country into some foreign currency, an assurance which duly appeared on the front page in a form which made it sound like a sigh of relief from Wapping.[9]

Readers of the *Financial Times* were given to believe that the Prime Minister was pro-euro, while *Sun* readers were given to understand the opposite. One set of readers – if not both – were being misled. The Prime Minister and his aides could never have constructed, let alone sustained, this push-me-pull-you version of events without the eager help provided by client journalists. The Political and Media Classes entered into a conspiracy against the ordinary reader.

Again and again journalists were pleased to publish fictions produced by Downing Street. A nice exhibit concerns the press reporting of the story of Peter Mandelson's first resignation from the Cabinet on 23 December 1998. The truth of this event was very painful, as we now know from the published diaries of the Downing Street spin-doctor and close Mandelson ally Lance Price.[10] Mandelson fought to stay right up to the very last moment, and was still pleading with Tony Blair to keep his job on the morning of the 23rd. But that is not the account that appeared in the newspapers. They all reported, relying on heavy Downing Street briefing, a sanitised account to the effect that the decision was made the night before. This, for example, is from *The Times* on Christmas Eve:

The minister telephoned Mr Blair at about 10pm and, in an emotional exchange, said he was angry with himself for landing the government in trouble. He then told the Prime Minister that he intended to resign. In another conversation at around 10am he confirmed his decision and the Prime Minister did not attempt to dissuade him.[11]

Thanks to Lance Price we now know how this highly misleading version of events appeared in the press. This is what he recorded in his diary for 23 December 1998:

> The story hit the airwaves at twelve-thirty on ITN. We said (quite falsely) that Peter had rung TB last night and said that he wanted to resign; that TB had urged him to reflect on it overnight; that Peter had spoken to him again at ten this morning to say he was determined to go for the good of the government and the party.[12]

It is worth dwelling on this episode because it is extremely rare for the process of collaboration between the Political Class and Media Class to be well documented, or for that matter documented at all. As a general rule the most meaningful transactions between political journalists and spin-doctors take place well away from the public eye. They are furtive affairs, and both sides would typically be ready to obscure what really took place. However the diaries of Lance Price, for several years a senior member of the Downing Street and Labour Party press machines, enable comparisons to be made between the official narrative of events as published in the client political press and the reality of what actually happened.

The Times – and the rest of Fleet Street – were willing dupes. After the Lance Price diaries were published in 2005 neither *The Times* nor any other newspaper showed any interest in complaining to Downing Street that they had been misled, nor can I find any evidence that they qualified in their own newspaper the falsehoods they had passed on to readers.* This reluctance to publicly correct their original account of events after it had been shown to be false meant, whatever their original role, that they became part of a conspiracy of deception.

Newspapers were not merely happy to publish falsehoods and

---

* After an extensive search, the only references I have found which drew readers' attention to the contradictory accounts of the Mandelson resignation revealed by Price's book were in the *Guardian* of 19 September 2005 and by John Lloyd in the *Financial Times* on 30 December 2005.

fabricated material on behalf of their Downing Street patrons. They were also happy, again unknown to their readers, to collude with Downing Street. In the vast majority of cases these episodes or stunts were arranged in private between ministers or government information experts and political editors, and therefore did not come to light. However, the leaking of the so-called Downing Street Grid for the high summer of 2003 gives a sharp glimpse of the kind of collaboration between newspapers and Downing Street. The Grid mapped out for several days in advance the anticipated news schedule, and is particularly interesting for the week starting 18 August.

This third week of August marked the start of a week in which the *Sun* alarmed its readers with a series of hair-raising stories about the threat posed by asylum-seekers. On 18 August it warned: 'Halt the asylum tide now'. That day's leader thundered: 'The flood of shirkers, scroungers and criminals has to be stopped.' The following day it followed up with the warning: 'Our heritage is crumbling'. On 20 August it focused on a health scare.

The interesting thing is that Downing Street knew all about this campaign in advance, as the daily Grid entry under 'Main news: during the week' shows. It is listed there: '*Sun* asylum week'. Furthermore, the government had been able to plan its response before the *Sun* campaign even began. The advance Grid for Thursday states: 'Blunkett asylum interview in *Sun*'. This was duly delivered. The Home Secretary took an emollient line with the paper: 'I am not in dispute with the *Sun* on this week's coverage,' he announced, promising 'draconian' measures to address the problem.[13]

The Practical Consequences of Client Journalism

The story above brings out with great clarity one of the themes of this book: the collaboration or pact between the Political and Media Classes. Journalists and politicians have each abandoned their proper function. Politicians have ceased to regard government, or for that matter opposition, as their primary activity. Meanwhile journalists no longer report political events in a detached and fastidious way. The effect of this transgression of boundaries has been to force both politics and journalism towards methodologies that can most plausibly be described as postmodern. Both pursuits are concerned with a common objective: the careful construction of narratives whose building blocks bear only an exiguous connection with reality as it can be externally measured, and are in practice pure manifestations of power.

One of the effects of this novel political discourse is that journalism and politics have effectively ceased to be discrete disciplines. Instead they have merged, and each has acquired characteristics of the other. This fusion can be examined in various distinct aspects. One of them is the arrival of the new category of client journalist, who although representing themselves to readers as an independent or sometimes even fearless figure, in practice owes his or her first loyalty to factions within the Political Class, as well as sharing the assumptions and prejudices of the Political Class as a whole. The novelty here is not political allegiance, an enlivening characteristic of a great deal of political reporting for hundreds of years. What is new and remarkable is the fact that this partisanship is hidden from readers, and in some cases even from colleagues. Such lack of transparency is of course one hallmark of the Political Class.

It is important to add here that the forms of transgression described above are by no means unique to political reporting and can indeed be found in even more extreme form in other areas. Showbiz journalism is the most notorious example. Access to pop-stars or to famous actors can solely be obtained by means of hugely powerful publicists who determine in advance the exact terms and nature of the questions to be asked. Any attempt by an enterprising reporter to diverge from a prearranged trajectory leads instantly to blackballing and the termination of all access: in short, career destruction. As a result of this kind of arrangement, the majority of articles about Hollywood stars are partly fabrication and in any case almost wholly misleading. The technology of client journalism, which hands over power and editorial discretion to producer interests, was established as a respectable procedure by *Vanity Fair* magazine and other outlets in the 1990s.[14]

The same kind of cartel exists in a great deal of sports reporting, and especially in football, where access and exclusive stories are routinely gifted to reporters who can be trusted not to stray into difficult territory, one of the main reasons why the endemic financial corruption which is a hallmark of professional football in Britain is almost never exposed by those who report on it. It needed a reporter from outside the game to expose the systematic abuse of the transfer market.[15]

The press coverage of Sir Alex Ferguson and his club Manchester United would furnish the materials for a compelling Media Studies Ph.D. on press control. Ferguson is so powerful that he is able to exclude sceptics and operate through a court of sycophants. Manchester United even possesses its own TV channel, on which its players are interviewed with the results then disseminated to other outlets, giving the football club total control at source. A great deal of financial journalism operates along the same lines. A long tradition of City editors has understood that ingratiation with powerful corporate figures is the secret of career advancement. The *locus classicus* of this phenomenon is the disclosure by Ivan Fallon, when City editor of the *Sunday Times*, that Guinness boss Ernest Saunders had broken his promise to keep the Scottish banker Sir Thomas Risk as chairman of the drinks firm Distillers and retain the headquarters in Scotland. Fallon accompanied the news of this betrayal with a soothing column praising Saunders for his sound judgement.[16] The insight that access to senior business figures or exclusive information could secure glowing press notices was the inspiration for the debased trade of financial public relations, an activity which became the foundation of several significant personal fortunes around the turn of the twenty-first century. In travel writing this kind of arrangement enters the realm of financial degradation, with free holidays on offer in return for alluring copy. As a general rule these deals are artfully concealed from all but the most sophisticated readers.

Some of the arrangements which prevail in Hollywood and the sports, travel or financial sections of British newspapers also occur as a matter of course in British political reporting. Certain dominant ministers, including Gordon Brown when Chancellor, often demanded assurances in advance of interviews about what line of questioning would be taken. The same kind of blackball that exists in Hollywood is also exercised at Westminster. When the presenter of BBC Radio's *The World at One*, Nick Clarke, died of cancer, Tony Blair issued a moving tribute, declaring: 'Nick was an outstanding presenter who over many years represented the best elements of public service broadcasting in this country. A true professional, he will be deeply missed.' However, Downing Street had at all times sought to undermine the independent-minded Clarke, trashing his programme, while Tony Blair never once gave an interview to *The World at One* because it made a consistent habit of asking awkward or demanding questions.[17]

Likewise it is very easy for a government to take advantage of the mass media's urgent requirement for a flow of information to meet the daily or hourly demand for news. Except in a rare number of stand-out exceptions, a strong reciprocity of interest unites government and the media organisations that depend on its services. Political journalists collectively suffer from exactly the same mental and moral subservience as the kind which embedded reporters attached to fighting units in the field are famously prone, only with much less excuse. They lose the capacity for independent judgement and criticism, while starting to see the world through the lenses of the politicians they report.

Nark Journalism

This dependence leads to a profound ideological and intellectual sympathy with the producer interest, combined with a reliance on government or other sources. In certain circumstances a client journalist may mutate into a nark journalist. When this condition occurs, the reporter abandons all journalistic integrity and becomes a secret activist or conspirator on behalf of a commercial, intelligence or political organisation or very often the government of the day. A nark journalist will use the privileged access he or she is granted as the representative of an accredited news organisation in order to obtain sensitive information about the private views, thinking and preparations of rivals. The nark journalist may also be used as a specially trusted conduit, enabling political machines to put out misinformation, and often to smear their opponents. Fundamentally a nark journalist does not feel an overriding loyalty to readers, colleagues or even his own newspaper. His public function – reporting – operates as cover for another purpose. A nark journalist may be ready to withhold information from his readers, and on occasion to pass on false information, if it proves helpful to the wider cause.

To a large extent the nark journalist is acting under cover in the same way that an intelligence operative works on behalf of a government agency or private detective organisation. Indeed intelligence agencies have long exploited the unique access which journalists are granted by national government or by business organisations as a means of gathering information. 'Press attaché' at an overseas embassy was for many years a euphemism for KGB operative, while the notorious spy Kim Philby used his cover as a *Times* reporter with the nationalist side during the Spanish Civil War to act on behalf of his real employers, the Soviet Comintern. Similarly, industrial espionage organisations habitually attempt to make use of journalistic cover.

Even though this kind of activity is utterly contrary to every known code of reporting, it is surprisingly common, and indeed wholly taken for granted, inside British political journalism. This transgression of boundaries, as we have seen, was pioneered by Alastair Campbell, later to formally cross the dividing line between journalism and political activism as the Downing Street press secretary. In the early 1990s Campbell was privately engaged in giving advice to Labour politicians, writing articles and speeches, and furthering their cause in numerous other ways. But at the time Campbell repeatedly and angrily insisted on the integrity of his reporter status, threatening those who claimed he was other than he seemed.[18]

During the final years of opposition in the mid-1990s, a large number of journalists privately put themselves at the disposal of New Labour, in many cases because they felt an ideological sympathy, in not a few cases because of a self-interested desire to ingratiate themselves with an incoming government. Often self-interest and ideological convenience coincided. Right-wing journalists who for many years had celebrated Margaret Thatcher while demonising the Labour Party, and therefore may have felt they had a great deal to prove if they were not to be starved of access by the incoming Blair regime, provide an interesting study. One Tory political commentator purchased entry to the Blair circle by handing over wholesale the contents of personal briefings from Cabinet ministers to the New Labour machine.[19] This was why in the final, dying months of the Major regime New Labour press officers were able to achieve the puzzling feat of providing political journalists with much more comprehensive and colourful descriptions of Cabinet meetings than the official Downing Street machine.

In some cases newspapers and political magazines colluded in this kind of transgressive activity, as the following memoir by the former Labour Party official and Downing Street speechwriter Andrew Neather shows:

> I was sent with five attack unit staff to the 1996 Conservative conference in Bournemouth. The two most senior members of the team – one of whom went on to a career as a ministerial special adviser – had conference passes as journalists, wangled on spurious grounds in the name of a friendly magazine.[20]

The most senior figure of this deputation was Adrian McMenamin, himself an extremely interesting study in aggressive Political Class behaviour. A protégé of Peter Mandelson, McMenamin was given the high responsibility of heading the New Labour Attack Unit ahead of the 1997 General Election. This body was formally charged with rebutting attacks on Labour Party personnel and policies. But, according to a study by the *Sunday Times* Insight team, it also 'involved spying, amassing secret files, and digging dirt'. The victims of the activity were politically indeterminate, including rebellious Labour MPs as well as political opponents. McMenamin evidently performed his duties in a satisfactory manner, for he was rewarded with promotion to the sought-after job of special adviser.[21]

McMenamin now recalls that he 'or maybe a colleague' attended one Conservative party conference under the accreditation of New Statesman Databases. He says that, despite carrying the name of the famous left-wing weekly, New Statesman Databases was actually a subsidiary of the Labour Party. It is likely, however, that this distinction may have been lost on the Tory party press office.

This collusion between the Political Class and the Media Class described above is a manifestation of a much larger and more powerful cultural phenomenon. Journalists and politicians do not simply collaborate professionally in secretive and illicit ways. It is now time to consider how the two professions have merged, becoming twin manifestations of a single phenomenon, rather than the two warring parties they are traditionally understood to be.

The Merger of the Political and Media Classes

Historically the House of Commons enforced a system of social apartheid between politicians and reporters. Large sections of Westminster were – and indeed remain – barred to journalists while the average reporter very rarely met politicians, and never on equal terms. Partly this separation reflected class distinctions. Right up to the 1960s, many Conservative and even some Labour politicians came from the ruling caste. Reporters were socially deferential and far less well-educated. Until the 1960s it was extremely unusual for any newspaper reporter to have attended university, whereas a large number of MPs would have done so.

According to Anthony Howard, later to become editor of the *New Statesman*, there were only two other graduates in the Press Gallery when he first set foot in it as a young reporter in 1958 – Bernard Levin of the *Spectator* and T. F. Lindsay, parliamentary sketch-writer of the *Daily Telegraph*. Reporters would stand up at press conferences when ministers entered the room. Very rarely did they lunch privately with ministers – an ubiquitous occurrence today. Indeed one of the primary requirements of the lobby man was to arrange, though not to attend, lunches on behalf of his proprietor.[22]

This social distinction started to disintegrate in the 1960s. The Labour Prime Minister Harold Wilson brought to a close the atmosphere of master and servants that had characterised the connection between politicians and journalists in the 1950s. The arrival of television played a role, as did the rapid breakdown of ancient class strata during the post-war period. The Media Class suddenly became a new Westminster elite. Journalists, now for the most part graduates, were better educated, more assured, far better paid and more influential than most of the politicians they wrote about. Celebrity journalists started to find themselves courted by up-and-coming politicians, not the other way around. Socially they felt themselves equal, sometimes superior. Political journalism, as much as politics itself, became a desirable occupation for the traditional ruling caste. At least four senior lobby correspondents over the last decade have been educated at Eton.*

Meanwhile the media became the primary forging ground for aspirant members of the Political Class. Almost overnight it replaced the law, which had been the main Political Class seminary in the age of representative democracy, enabling ambitious young men to hone the debating and forensic skills that were necessary in Parliament, for centuries the cockpit of political ambition. Far-sighted people perceived that media know-how

---

* They are Roland Watson, political editor of the *Daily Express*, now *The Times'* head of news; Patrick Hennessy, political editor of the *Sunday Telegraph*; Boris Johnson, former editor of the *Spectator*; and James Landale, chief political correspondent for BBC News.

provided the ideal preparation for a political career under the emergent system of manipulative populism.

This was a very dramatic development. Media provided the most significant 'real world' career experience in the case of every single one of the members of the talented faction which guided Tony Blair to power in the 1997 election – Peter Mandelson and Gordon Brown in television, Alastair Campbell in print journalism and Philip Gould in advertising. Tony Blair, as so often a conservative figure, was the exception. He had taken the traditional route and practised at the Bar. Likewise the two key advisers around Chancellor Gordon Brown, Ed Balls and Ed Miliband, are both former journalists. It is extremely important to note that exactly the same analysis can be applied to the inner group that surrounds the Conservative Party leader David Cameron. Cameron's lieutenant, George Osborne's only experience outside politics was a brief spell in print journalism with the *Sunday Telegraph*. Steve Hilton, the Cameron strategist, is an advertising professional. Cameron's own experience of life beyond Westminster, as we have seen, amounted to a period as an executive for the television company Carlton Communications. In addition, as we have seen, many of the more prominent members of Cameron's outer circle – for example the Mayor of London Boris Johnson, and the MPs Michael Gove and Ed Vaizey – were successful journalists.

There was also traffic in the opposite direction. The media has become the primary default mode of earning a living for failed or passed-over politicians. Michael Portillo and David Mellor, rising Cabinet stars under Margaret Thatcher and John Major, re-emerged as talented Media Class figures, readily mastering the techniques of a jobbing newspaper columnist as well as TV and radio presenters respectively. The former Labour Party deputy leader Roy Hattersley is a prolific columnist and author, while newspapers, books and television spin-offs provided massive financial compensation for William Hague after his disastrous period as Tory leader and for David Blunkett after he was ousted from the Blair Cabinet. Indeed, the roll-call of names who have migrated from one calling to another is too long to list exhaustively.

By the 1990s it was noticeable that the two activities had become to a significant extent interchangeable. It had become natural for the Political Class and the Media Class to go out together, dine together, holiday together, flirt together, sleep together. The two professions lived mainly on expenses, with the exception of their most successful members they had ample spare time, they were never required to do productive work, their jobs mainly involved talking. They were fascinated with each other. BBC journalists began to acquire the same mannerisms and verbal tics as those they reported. The corporation's political correspondent John Pienaar, with his blokeish style and lapses into the demotic, could easily have been a modernising front-bench spokesman from any mainstream party. As they professionalised and grew more homogeneous the Political and Media Classes began to restrict membership to the middle classes, and increasingly to each other's sons and daughters. This was in large part because of the special pay structure of the Media/Political Class. Though stars in both arenas were capable of making very large sums of money indeed, new graduates are impoverished. A young researcher reporting to an MP, or a television producer starting out, are both extremely poorly paid. They are, however, expected to work in central London, which is prohibitively expensive and only possible with subsidy from well-heeled parents.*

Go to any Westminster restaurant on a weekday lunchtime or evening and you will find journalists and politicians at play. You will find them in August at the choice Political Class holiday locations – Cape Cod for the best connected, Tuscany for the socially grand, the Dordogne for the relatively impoverished. The annual season is punctuated with social occasions for the Political/Media Class. The marriage between Adam Boulton, the

---

* The Prime Minister's son Euan Blair is a classic manifestation of this trend, spending time as an unpaid intern in Washington, first with the Republicans and then a Democrat politician in the House of Representatives, and back in London undertook work experience with the financial PR group Finsbury. In May 2006 it was revealed that Euan had been awarded a full scholarship to study an MA in International Relations at Yale in the United States.

political editor of Sky TV, and Anji Hunter, longstanding aide to Tony Blair, provided an opportunity for close inspection of this elite. And as we have seen, both Gordon Brown and David Cameron attended the marriage of Alan Parker, the financial PR tycoon worth an estimated £100 million. At the reception afterwards members of the Political and Media Classes mingled with international business leaders.

These private occasions are a kind of conspiracy. For the politician a warm personal friendship with a journalist is a form of self-protection. He gives the reporter access, inside information, special insights, odd pieces of gossip. In return he expects to be looked after by the journalists or by the newspaper concerned. In the case of an ambitious young politician, this may mean that he wants to be singled out for special praise or tipped for promotion. A Cabinet minister may hope to be supported in a major policy battle, or to be repaid when the moment comes that he runs for the leadership of his party.

This means that there is a structural dishonesty about a great deal of political reporting. If a financial adviser tells his clients to buy a certain share without disclosing that he is receiving favours in return he lays himself open to prosecution, may well go to jail, and will in any case be professionally destroyed. Yet the vast bulk of political information passed on to the British public by lobby reporters is compromised in this way. Instances can be found almost every day in the newspapers. An innocent example concerns the attempt by the Conservative MP Alan Duncan to run for the Tory leadership in the summer of 2005. Duncan never stood a chance of winning, and was eventually forced to drop out of the contest without achieving the support of a single Tory MP. Yet for several weeks Duncan was written up in the national press as a live candidate, and the subject of several glowing profiles.[23] Duncan is a cheerful fellow who lives in Westminster, regularly attends media parties, and is available at most times of day and night for media appearances, lunches, dinners and so forth. He mingles assiduously with the Media Class, who mistook availability for leadership potential. Duncan reaped his reward in terms of coverage when it mattered, but newspaper readers who were led to believe Duncan stood a chance were misled.

The Media Class and Political Class share identical assumptions about life and politics. They are affluent, progressive, middle- and upper-middle-class. This triumphant metropolitan elite has completely lost its links with a wider civil society – farming, the professions, small business, trade unions, the shop floor – which characterised British public culture throughout the most confident period of parliamentary government during the nineteenth and twentieth centuries. It is obvious that the politicians and the media have far more in common with each other than they do with voters, readers and the public.

In rare cases individual politicians or journalists stand out against this system. The Tory MP Douglas Hogg, for instance, will not talk privately to reporters, grasping the delicate point that friendship is transgressive because it leads to an improper sense of obligation. In general, however, the collapse of Media Class deference has been accompanied by a rise in familiarity. It has made journalists more dependent on government and political machines, not less. It is essential for both parties to assert, and even perhaps to believe, that they have different interests and roles. In truth they are only distinct in the sense that a stockbroker and fund manager have conflicting interests when they transact business in the City of London. Fundamentally they believe in the same system and they are engaged in a conspiracy against the voter, thereby creating the necessary conditions for a political culture dominated by fabricated 'media events', artifice and deceit. This is one reason so much reporting of politics now amounts to an elaborate fraud perpetrated upon the British public.

The Influence of Rupert Murdoch

This kind of collaboration operates at all levels of the media, from national proprietors down to the most junior political reporter. In politics it starts with the Prime Minister and extends to the lowest level of MP and special adviser. The dominant figure in this shadowy and secretive world is the media tycoon Rupert Murdoch. Murdoch has long been a figure of overwhelming significance in British public life. This phenomenal individual owes this unique position to his control over wide swathes of the British media, which he has exercised over more than three decades through News Corporation (the global holding company whose UK newspaper subsidiary is News International). Now in his late seventies, he remains a remarkable man, spoken of by employees with awe. They love to describe how the tycoon will fly into London by private plane after just three or four hours' sleep, go to the gym, host a series of high-level meetings, and jet off again. He is still the dynamic and masterful head of his business. It is only twelve years since he founded Fox News with such spectacular success that it has reshaped the nature of news coverage in the United States.

In Britain, News International owns two daily papers, the *Sun* and *The Times*, which between them account for some 35 per cent of the British daily newspaper market. It has two Sunday papers, the *News of the World* and the *Sunday Times*, which have a market share of approximately 40 per cent of Sunday papers. Finally it controls the non-terrestrial channel BSkyB, as well as a massive range of worldwide media interests. British Prime Ministers may come and go, but Murdoch seems to have been around for ever, spanning both the decades and the continents. All political leaders, whether they come from the right or the left, pay regular dues to Murdoch.

His power, though perfectly understood by everybody who operates at the top level of British politics or journalism, goes unreported to a massive extent. It has never been in the interests of Downing Street or its allies and apologists to draw attention to the existence, let alone profundity, of the relationship between the British government and the Murdoch papers. The depth and intimacy of the connection has become so strong that Downing Street now treats its dealings with News International as if they were a high-level state secret.

One example of this sensitivity was the publication by Hodder & Stoughton of the Downing Street press official Lance Price's account of his experiences, *The Spin Doctor's Diary*. When Price submitted his manuscript to the Cabinet Office for clearance, he says that 'the government requested some changes, as is its right. When the first batch came through, it was no surprise that Tony Blair's staff were deeply unhappy. The real surprise was that no fewer than a third of their objections related to one man – not Tony Blair or even Gordon Brown, as I might have expected, but Rupert Murdoch.'[24]

Meanwhile, attempts to use the Freedom of Information Act to gain details about the level of access have invariably been turned down or stalled, on the suggestive basis that discussion between Downing Street and newspaper groups is confidential.[25] This assertion that newspaper groups are entitled to have private conversations with government that it is illegitimate for the public to see is exceptionally revealing of the collusive nature of the connection between the Murdoch press and the British government.*

For the last ten years Rupert Murdoch has been one of a handful of defining figures in the New Labour administration. According to Lance Price:

> I have never met Mr Murdoch, but at times when I worked at Downing Street he seemed like the twenty-fourth member of the Cabinet. His voice was rarely heard (but, then, the same could be

---

* Partly because of secrecy, chroniclers of the New Labour government as well as biographers of the Prime Minister have effectively ignored Rupert Murdoch. The media tycoon gained no mention at all in the first biography of Tony Blair, written by Jon Sopel and published in 1995. Andrew Rawnsley's 550-page early history of New Labour, *Servants of the People*, mentioned Murdoch just three times. Murdoch gets just ten brief mentions in John Rentoul's 600-page study of Tony Blair, three references in Philip Stephens' 380-page volume and just four references in Anthony Seldon's massive 700-page biography of the Prime Minister. This lacuna is also true of the Margaret Thatcher years, where Rupert Murdoch was almost as crucial. Hugo Young's much-praised book on Margaret Thatcher, *One of Us*, reserves one minor, passing reference to Murdoch.

said of many of the other twenty-three) but his presence was always felt.

No big decision could ever be made inside Number 10 without taking account of the likely reaction of three men – Gordon Brown, John Prescott and Rupert Murdoch. On all the really big decisions, anybody else could safely be ignored.[26]

Twice during his career as Labour leader Tony Blair has flown around the world in order to address the annual conference of News Corporation executives. In 1995 Tony Blair made the forty-eight-hour round trip to Hayman Island, just off the Queensland coast, to perform this duty. More striking still, he repeated this act of homage twelve years later when the annual NewsCorp meeting was held in California. These journeys were demeaning for an elected leader of a great political party and Prime Minister of Great Britain. They were, however, an extremely revealing statement about the distribution of power in modern Britain.

In practice there were moments when to all intents and purposes News International and Downing Street merged. News International, almost as a matter of course, provided a home for key members of Tony Blair's close inner circle when they moved out of government. It found a column for Alastair Campbell when he was forced to resign in the wake of the suicide of David Kelly. Campbell's deputy Tim Allan went on to become Director of Corporate Communications at Murdoch's BSkyB, and then Murdoch became a major client when Allan set up his public affairs and lobbying business Portland. The Home Secretary David Blunkett was found a column on the *Sun* newspaper after he was obliged to leave office. Blunkett's writing was regarded as at best moderate by professional journalists, but he was nevertheless paid a spectacular £150,000 a year, or £2.50 a word.[27] And Benjamin Wegg-Prosser, special adviser to Peter Mandelson, was hired by the *Sun* after Mandelson resigned from the Cabinet at Christmas 1998, though this appointment proved short-lived.

Meanwhile, Downing Street gives lavish access to Rupert Murdoch and his intermediaries. This operates at every level.

Murdoch himself can see the Prime Minister whenever he is in London. But he leaves most of the day-to-day negotiation with government to deputies. The key link-man in London is his son James Murdoch, the Executive Chairman of News Corporation, Europe and Asia. Another is the American economist Irwin Stelzer. There is no question that Tony Blair saw a direct connection between the political support handed out to New Labour by News International newspapers and his own treatment of Murdoch's business. When opposition leader, he confided to the former News International executive Andrew Neill that 'how we treat Rupert Murdoch's media interests when in power will depend on how his newspapers treat the Labour Party in the run-up to the election and after we are in government'.[28]

There is important evidence that the Prime Minister and his ministers are ready to act as the media tycoon's personal leg-men on business deals. In March 1998 Tony Blair raised the subject of Rupert Murdoch during a conversation with the Italian Prime Minister Romano Prodi. He asked in particular about Murdoch's £4 billion bid for Mediaset, the television, newspaper and publishing company owned by Silvio Berlusconi. The British Prime Minister then passed Prodi's reply that he would prefer Mediaset to be acquired by an Italian company back to Murdoch.[29] Downing Street will go out of its way to help out Murdoch newspapers in other ways. Before George W. Bush's visit to Britain in 2003, Tony Blair helped arrange an interview with the American President and the *Sun* newspaper.[30] Unusually Downing Street owned up to this connection, stating that 'the *Sun* approached us with a request for an interview with the President and we forwarded it to the White House with our support'.[31] This readiness to help out News Corporation in its private dealings is startling. Successive British Prime Ministers have used their access to the resources of the British state, and compromised the integrity of the public domain, in order to do a favour for the Rupert Murdoch media empire and secure partisan political advantage.

Tony Blair would probably have been able to realise his ambition and win his battle to join the euro but for Murdoch's opposition. And as I will describe in the next chapter, the evidence suggests that he would have found it hard to lead Britain to war against Saddam Hussein's Iraq but for the enthusiastic support of the Murdoch empire.

The Myth of a Hostile Media

At this point it should be acknowledged that the thesis set out in this chapter flatly contradicts the orthodox view, now accepted in academia, high journalism, and especially in official circles, that the British press is a destructive force constantly seeking to thwart and to damage the Political Class. (This is the thesis which has been forcefully propounded by Tony Blair, Professor Geoff Mulgan, adopted by Dame Onora O'Neill, vigorously reiterated by Tony Blair's former press secretary Alastair Campbell, and proselytised by virtually all government ministers.) It is a theme to which Tony Blair constantly returns, and has set the parameters for political coverage in the BBC and the British broadsheet newspapers. This notion of an ugly struggle between essentially benign politicians and a vermin press also underlies the popular US television programme *The West Wing*, the reason it is cult viewing among the British Political Class.

The first point to note is that none of these critics of the media has ever offered more than extremely meagre evidence in support of their proposition. The hostility of the press is simply taken as axiomatic. Normal standards of empirical proof, let alone more complex structural points, are left unexamined. Critics of the media from within the ruling elite repeatedly fail to address the alliances between successive British governments and the major corporate interests, above all News International. This omission is a phenomenon which started with Conservative Party denunciations of the press in the 1980s. In practice Margaret Thatcher, like Tony Blair, enjoyed a mainly client press. However, Thatcher's allies always denounced what they claimed to be the cynicism and rancid triviality of an overwhelmingly hostile media. These critics never turned their attention to Murdoch, even though he was beyond question more guilty of cynicism and triviality than any other media organisation. The reason was simple: the Thatcher clique did not want to annoy its friends at News International.

Official critics of the press have made no attempt to address the always interesting and frequently very powerful arguments from the left by Edward S. Herman, Noam Chomsky and others, summed up elegantly at the start of their joint work *Manufacturing Consent*:

> It is our view that, among their other functions, the media serve, and propagandise on behalf of, the powerful societal interests that control and finance them. The representatives of these interests have important agendas and principles that they want to advance, and they are well positioned to shape and constrain media policy. This is normally not accomplished by crude intervention, but by the selection of right-thinking personnel and by the editors' and working journalists' internalisation of priorities and definitions of newsworthiness that conform to the institution's policy.
>
> Structural factors are those such as ownership and control, dependence on other major funding sources (notably, advertisers), and mutual interests and relationships between the media and those who make the news, and have the power to define it and explain what it means.[32]

This emphasis on the links between government, major corporate interests and a supposedly free and independent media raises extremely awkward questions and carries weight. Most British journalists, if they are honest, will recognise the above as a fairly accurate description of the moral, social and intellectual environment in which they work.

The influential polemic by John Lloyd *What the Media Are Doing to Our Politics* sets out the official view. His book revolves around a single piece of evidence concerning alleged media destructiveness: the 6.07am *Today* programme interview given by the reporter Andrew Gilligan on 29 May 2003. No other British example is cited in the book, and indeed the Gilligan example is itself problematic. While there were inaccuracies, most of what Gilligan stated in his ground-breaking report into the flawed assessment of Iraq's alleged weapons of mass destruction programme was later proved to be remarkably accurate.

In his book Lloyd fails to inform his reader that he has been a friend and ally of Tony Blair, dating back to the early 1980s when they were both members of the Hackney South Labour Party. Indeed Lloyd played a minor role in helping Tony Blair secure his Sedgefield seat.[33] Lloyd's book contains as an appendix a long, four-page interview with an unnamed Cabinet minister. That anonymous figure – his identity concealed from the reader – is almost certainly Tony Blair.[34] Though Lloyd's book does contain insights and moral weight, a more balanced account by Lloyd would have made these extremely relevant personal interests clearer to his readers.

Lloyd's book appeared as the British government launched a campaign to demonise the media. This political project began in 1999 with a speech by Alastair Campbell at a Fabian Society seminar. Campbell accused the press of creating 'cynicism about politics, about politicians, about people who work in public life'. Campbell's immediate motive in the speech was to disaggregate the broadcasting and the print media, an objective which the BBC swiftly internalised. The distinction between an aggressive, illegitimate press and a well-meaning government has formed the template of a great deal of BBC reporting over the last decade. It became automatic for BBC reporters and commentators to portray any government crisis as a contest between press and government, just as Campbell had suggested. This narrative automatically favoured any democratically elected government over a corporately owned media elite.

Reporting within these carefully structured parameters led to repeated failures of diagnosis. To give one prominent example, BBC reporters systematically failed to give an accurate or even an intelligible account of the various tribulations of the Cabinet minister David Blunkett as he struggled to cling on to office. This was the case during the run-up to both Blunkett resignations. This failure occurred because the corporation repeatedly asserted the proposition pushed out by Blunkett and his allies in Downing Street that the Cabinet minister was an embattled figure hounded by a venal press in search of a 'scalp'. During the run-up to David Blunkett's first resignation at the end of 2004 this analysis led the BBC political staff to conclude that the 'battle' would lead to victory to one side or the other. Its staff predicted, right up to the end, that Blunkett would survive. This was presumably because it judged that in any struggle between an elected Cabinet minister and a rascally press, the government was entitled to win.

But the concentration on a contest that was not actually taking place (in fact Blunkett enjoyed a great deal of very significant press support, including News International and the allegedly anti-government *Daily Mail*) caused the BBC to give insufficient weight to the real issues that were at stake. As we have already seen, Blunkett was a transgressive politician who repeatedly confused the public and the private interest. He ordered civil servants to perform personal tasks, used his influence as Home Secretary to provide special favours for friends, failed to declare to Parliament financial interests which potentially conflicted with his ministerial role, abused his official car, breached public trust by making a series of misleading statements, and so on. The media was fulfilling its proper social and political function insofar as it investigated these numerous breaches. The claim that it was involved in some vendetta against Blunkett, made at the time by his numerous allies and subsequently repeated in the former Home Secretary's self-justifying diaries, is demonstrably untrue.

Nevertheless, many political correspondents supported this proposition. Here is the BBC chief political correspondent John Pienaar reporting on the state of affairs at Westminster on the eve of David Blunkett's second resignation, which came following the revelation that he had broken rules surrounding ministerial share-dealing. Pienaar told the BBC presenter Simon Mayo that Blunkett would not be forced from office, adding:

But I think when that time comes, if it comes, it will have more to do with the dynamic of the pack and the hound than anything else. The pack, and this has a lot to do with it – the media frankly, the pack has tasted David Blunkett's blood and they want more. They're not going to let off. I think he's going to survive this latest flurry. But the next one or the one after that will probably claim him, probably claim his tail or his scalp and it will probably have more to do with the fact that if you've got to choose who survives between the pack or the fox, well you're probably better off betting on the pack ... But I think that there is a recognition of how cruel politics can be and *actually*, how absolutely savage the media can be when in the political arena. These are almost forces of nature. And when a minister or any other politician falls foul of the wrong side of those forces they don't tend to stay on their feet very long. A test of wills is going on here I think. You know *another* test of wills, frankly, Simon. This may be a case where, you know, inside Number 10 they'd like to say that if we can get through this we'll end up stronger. 'Why should the media? Why should our opponents claim a scalp just because they're yelling for it?' But it's an enormous test of strength and when that's been tried in the past – and it has been time after time after time – it's been the minister's scalp that's gone and Downing Street loses the argument.

The following day, when counter to his prediction Blunkett did actually resign, Pienaar again stressed that 'media frenzy' was the culprit:

Maybe ... there's something wrong with a situation like that where someone is driven out of office for arguably, by him or his boss, for arguably doing absolutely nothing. But it's explicable. It's easily explicable in the world in which we live. You know, in a political culture where, look, when there's a chase of this kind, when there's blood in the water, when the sharks are circling, you know, the victim tends not to survive. That's not how it works.

Pienaar had the option of informing BBC listeners in a detached way that David Blunkett and his allies were claiming that the embattled Cabinet minister was the victim of media assassination. He failed to take it. It is fascinating to note here how one of the BBC's senior correspondents had thoroughly internalised the Downing Street-constructed narrative of events, cleverly designed to confuse two separate phenomena: media reporting and Blunkett's transgressions. Pienaar did not merely present the Downing Street line very faithfully – it was almost as if Tony Blair or Alastair Campbell were speaking. The mere fact that journalists were bringing these transgressions to light was projected as an act of hostility, rather than legitimate disclosure.

These diversionary attacks on the media were used again and again as a defence strategy. They provide an instant and automatic protective tool whenever a member of the Political Class is caught out doing anything venal, greedy or hypocritical. As the case of John Pienaar cited above demonstrates, the story ceased to focus on Political Class transgression, and instead shifted to Media Class legitimacy.* The government attack on the BBC which led to the Hutton Inquiry may well have been partly inspired by a desire to take attention away from the failure to discover weapons of mass destruction in *post-bellum* Iraq. The narrative of events was turned away from the deadly revelation that the government justification for war, that Saddam Hussein possessed weapons of mass destruction, was false. Instead the story became a conflict between government and media. These attacks on the media were almost always made with the consent and approbation of large sections of the client

---

* See for example 'Cheriegate', the Mittal and Black Rod affairs, the Stephen Byers fiasco, the second Mandelson resignation, the Tessa Jowell mortgage, and so on. In each case attention was diverted from transgressive behaviour by the Political Class into mainly false allegations about a dramatic confrontation between the media and Downing Street. The anti-media strategy only came into full use after the 2001 General Election, when it was used to defend Stephen Byers after he had lied on the Dimbleby show, during the so-called Mittal affair, and repeatedly thereafter.

media itself.* Journalists were recruited as an essential part of the apparatus of government control. In the next chapter I will use the case study of the invasion of Iraq in 2003 to demonstrate in much greater detail how British media organisations have assimilated the moral and intellectual assumptions of the Political Class.

---

* Not only the BBC bought into this analysis. So did Sky TV and other TV news channels. The broadsheet newspapers – the *Guardian, Financial Times* and *The Times* especially – shared it. So did the *Sun* and the *Daily Mirror*.

12

THE MEDIA CLASS AND
THE IRAQ WAR

'The man who never looks into a newspaper is better informed than
he who reads them; inasmuch as he who knows nothing is nearer
to the truth than he whose mind is filled with falsehoods and errors'
– Thomas Jefferson, 3rd President of the United States

In the run-up to the invasion of Iraq the British people were on the
whole opposed to war. With a few exceptions, however, the British
media did not reflect the popular mood. On the contrary, the
majority of newspapers and broadcasting organisations became
an enthusiastic part of the state propaganda machine. Coverage of
the preliminaries to war was determined by what amounted to a
collaboration between the Media and the Political Class to create a
fiction: that Saddam Hussein presented a threat to British interests.
Rather than coolly examine the series of false statements issued
by the Political Class ahead of the Iraq War, the media for the
most part endorsed them and added fresh colour of its own. This
remains a troubling period in British history, raising deep and
perplexing questions about democracy and the true allegiance of
parts of the British media.

The extent to which the British media became an instrument of
the Political Class is still not appreciated. This is partly because the
coverage of the war was subsequently converted into an important
piece of evidence in the now well-rehearsed argument that the
British media is biased against and opposed to the Political Class.

However, taken as a whole, the experience of the Iraq invasion, its long preliminary and its gruesome aftermath, emphatically shows the exact opposite. It demonstrates that the mainstream British media, far from cynically opposing the Political Class, is actually an extremely important instrument.

I arranged an extensive survey of the British media coverage of the Iraq invasion.* This is the first time, as far as I know, that a major examination of this kind has been published on the British press and the Iraq War, though there have been studies of reporting by the broadcast media. Studies by both the Cardiff School of Journalism and the Glasgow University Media Group showed broadcasting bias toward the pro-war case made by the British government and others. The United States press has launched several agonising investigations into how it came about that US newspapers reported so many falsehoods as fact.[1] Our research took into account not merely coverage of the long disinformation campaign conducted by Downing Street and other government departments in the run-up to the war itself, but also the coverage given in the immediate aftermath of the war.

This survey does not bear out any hypothesis that the British press and wider broadcasting media were unhelpful, let alone generally hostile, to the British politicians who made the case for war (the great majority). On the contrary, the research indicated a pro-war bias among British media organisations. Far from being destructive of government claims and assertions, many media organisations were extremely agile and creative on behalf of the pro-war case, seeking out fresh and ever more sensational

---

* This survey was largely carried out by Natalie Whitty of Trinity Hall, Cambridge. I am also grateful to Glen Rangwala, lecturer in politics at Cambridge University, for his advice and observations. I have found the Media Lens website – often unfair but sometimes highly perceptive – extremely useful. See also Piers Robinson, Peter Goddard, Robin Brown and Philip Taylor's 'Media Wars: News Media Performance and Media Management During the 2003 Iraq War'. The headline findings of this Economic and Social Research Council (ESRC)-funded study, yet to be published in full, can be obtained at http://ics.leeds.ac.uk/papers/pmt/exhibits/2758/iraqmedia.rtf.

angles to demonstrate Saddam Hussein's actual and alleged malevolence. Much of the information provided to readers was wrong or fabricated, and all of this invented material was helpful to the pro-war case. A substantial majority of the British press strongly supported the government position over the war. The *Daily Telegraph*, *The Times*, the *Daily Mail*, the *Daily Express* and the *Sun* backed the war. So did the *Sunday Times*, the *Sunday Telegraph*, the *Observer*, the *Mail on Sunday*, the *Sunday Express* and the *News of the World*. Of the papers we examined, only the *Independent** and *Independent on Sunday*, the *Daily* and *Sunday Mirror*, and the *Guardian* (weakly) opposed the war.

Not merely that, British newspapers and broadcasters failed to challenge various assertions and claims made by the Prime Minister and others which were capable, even at the time and without the advantage of hindsight, of being shown to be untrue. Many British newspapers peddled falsehoods that were extremely useful to the government position. There is every reason to speculate that 10 Downing Street and possibly Foreign Office sources used crony journalists and newspaper organisations to float sensationalist but insubstantial reports, thus inflaming the mood of public alarm on the eve of war.

On news pages there was a sharp disproportion between the amount of space given to the case for war as presented by the British government and the space given to the case for not invading Iraq. Articles covering anti-war issues tended to be smaller and appear further back in the newspapers. The government's own, partial account of Iraqi misdemeanours almost always grabbed the headlines.

Critics of the war were often marginalised in news reports. Their legitimate objections were frequently ignored altogether and when reported at all, they were lumped with other miscellaneous objectors in the main news story. For instance, the Labour MP John McDonnell (later to challenge Gordon Brown for the Labour

---

* The newspaper singled out, to the exclusion of all others, in Tony Blair's 'feral media' speech to Reuters on 12 June 2007.

leadership) asked a lethal question: how had the weapons inspectors been able to produce a report on the inspection of 'presidential palaces' in April 1998 if – as the dossier claimed – they had been denied access? Yet there was barely any mention of McDonnell's doubts.

The most interesting example of this selective neglect is Scott Ritter, the United Nations weapons inspector who provided eloquent testimony against the proposed invasion, and repeatedly questioned US and British claims about Saddam Hussein's plans to make so-called weapons of mass destruction (WMD). Scott Ritter's well-informed scepticism about Saddam Hussein's WMD programmes has been amply justified by subsequent events.

A search of the computerised newspaper archives for mentions of Scott Ritter in the six and a half months between September 2002 and the invasion the following March returns only ninety-four 'hits'. Of this, roughly half can be accounted for as references to a book written by Ritter, passing citations, or mentions in the communist paper the *Morning Star*. Of the remainder (thirty-six are described by the media database Lexis Nexis as 'major mentions'), most merely indicate his presence at the September 2002 peace rally in London and three focus on his arrest in 2001 on charges of trying to meet a young girl. The *Sun* newspaper showed particular enthusiasm for this story, describing Scott Ritter in one headline as 'a TRAITOR ... and now a PAEDOPHILE'.[2] This sensational line indicates how eager were elements of the pro-war press to follow the American lead in attempting to damage Scott Ritter's general reputation.

The most important observation to make, however, is that only a small proportion of stories concerning Ritter detail and quote the content of his critique of the Bush administration's approach to Iraq. All but one of these were given in the *Daily Mirror*, the *Guardian*, the *Independent*, the newspapers which most vigorously opposed the war. Other newspapers seem to have found his position as a hate figure in America as or more interesting than the unique perspective he could offer and the questions he was asking about the US and UK's case for war. He was not only undermined by smear stories, but barely allowed to elaborate his arguments against the war to the public.

How the British Government Captured the Media

The media did not just hype up and sensationalise government claims. Many reporters lost their objectivity and allowed government attitudes and value statements to intrude into their own reporting. This was not just true in the obvious cases of tabloid reporters on pro-war papers, but also with supposedly objective political editors of broadsheet papers and national TV stations. Here is a piece of reporting by Nick Robinson, then the political editor of ITN, talking on ITV to the lunchtime news anchor Nicholas Owen in January 2003, two months before the outbreak of war. Owen suggested to Robinson that the British public still needed to be convinced of the case for war. Robinson replied:

> However, Nick, they look at these things in a slightly different way in Downing Street. Yes, almost two-thirds of the public say they're not convinced of the case for war, that it hasn't yet been made, but Tony Blair would probably say the same. He would say we're not yet making the case for war, we're making the case that you have to be ready for war otherwise Saddam Hussein won't back down. The difficulty, as one Downing Street insider put it to me, is we're more in a parallel with 1930 than with 1939. In other words, this isn't a dictator who's already attacked another country: it's a dictator who might do something, who's got potential.[3]

Important here is Robinson's merging of the role of independent commentator and spokesman for the government position. He moves subtly from presenting the Downing Street view that Saddam's Iraq was the equivalent of Germany in 1930 to presenting it as his own opinion as well. By doing this, and perhaps without being fully aware of it, Robinson is granting Downing

Street's extremely specious and doubtful claims a certain independent status.* Still more significant, Robinson appeared to be giving an independent validity to the neo-conservative and Downing Street proposition – widely expressed as war drew near but surely needing to be passed on with great scepticism – that the threat from Saddam Hussein was analogous to the threat posed by Adolf Hitler.

Robinson is in general an extremely scrupulous and independent reporter, by no means unwilling to ask difficult questions and cause trouble for powerful people. He was dealing with a problem which confronts all journalists who wish to be well-informed. Their desire to establish an independent line is gravely compromised by their need to cultivate official sources in return for information.

Other commentators faithfully adjusted their version of events as the Prime Minister's line changed. The *Observer* columnist Andrew Rawnsley is a case in point. In February 2002, just as the machinery to take the world to war was hotting up, Rawnsley told his readers:

> The intelligence material that the Prime Minister sees makes him genuinely disturbed – it would not be going too far to say petrified – about Saddam Hussein's potential ability to use weapons of mass destruction.[4]

In September 2002, just ahead of the publication of the dossier, Rawnsley was yet more bloodcurdling:

---

* Robinson was just one of a very large number of reporters in the print and broadcasting media who joined Downing Street in comparing the invasion of Iraq to the situation confronting Great Britain in the late 1930s with the emergent threat of Nazi Germany. See, for example, the *Daily Mail* reporter Graeme Wilson, 'Blair and a day of destiny', *Daily Mail*, 19 March 2003. Wilson's opening paragraph claimed that Tony Blair's 18 March Commons speech 'was a scene that evoked other memories of other historic moments when Britain had stood on the brink of war'.

In Mr Blair's mind, the person whose judgment matters most is already totally convinced that Saddam is a lethal menace, and has been so for a long time. According to Paddy Ashdown's diaries, Saddam was gnawing at the Prime Minister as long ago as November 1997. The former Lib Dem leader quotes Blair saying: 'I have seen some of the stuff on this. It really is pretty scary. He is very close to some appalling weapons of mass destruction. I don't understand why the French and others don't understand this. We cannot let him get away with it. The world thinks this is just gamesmanship. But it's deadly serious.'[5]

However, in the aftermath of the war, when WMD failed to materialise, Rawnsley went out of his way to make plain the fact that WMD had never been much of an issue for the government in the first place, writing in the *Observer* on 13 April 2003 that

in the mind of Tony Blair, I don't think this war was ever wholly, or even mainly, about any threat posed by Saddam. These were arguments designed to make the conflict accord with international law. The Prime Minister was never very convincing that Saddam was a real and present danger ... For Mr Blair, getting rid of Saddam is legitimacy enough.[6]

Andrew Rawnsley is known for his excellent contacts with Downing Street. They have often given him unique insights into the mind of the Prime Minister. When dealing with the Iraq invasion, however, Rawnsley seems to have crossed the line between an independently minded columnist and Number 10 insider. As time went on, Tony Blair himself altered his own public account of his motivation, from alarm about the threat posed by Saddam to regime-change and the urgent necessity of removing an evil dictator. Rawnsley, abandoning the proper scepticism of a newspaper columnist, appeared to follow suit. He gave a series of carefully constructed accounts of what Tony Blair was thinking about Iraq which seemed to draw on the favoured Downing Street narrative of the internal workings of Tony Blair's mind at any given moment. In the run-up to the war, when the only legal justification for war was the alleged menace posed by Saddam's WMD, it was important for Number 10 to put it about that the Prime Minister believed that Saddam was a 'lethal menace'. After the war, when it turned out that WMD did not exist, it became important for Number 10 to put it about that regime-change had always been the primary preoccupation of the Prime Minister. In each case Andrew Rawnsley was on hand to give his sanction as an independent and well-informed columnist to Downing Street's preferred version of events as it changed over time.

It would be wrong to give the impression, however, that all the British press and broadcasting media followed and absorbed the government line. The *Daily Mirror* and the *Independent* were both hostile to the war, and campaigned vigorously against it. Both papers awarded ample space to critics of the war. And even those broadsheet papers which supported the invasion of Iraq tended to remain true to the pluralist tradition of the British press by giving generous opportunities to individual anti-war columnists. Simon Jenkins, for example, was allowed free range in *The Times* to explode government claims about the need for an invasion. And the *Independent* presented all sides of the argument to its readers, and allowed plenty of scope to pro-war columnists such as David Aaronovitch. Broadsheet newspapers were sometimes careful to present arguments for and against the war. For instance on 25 September 2002 the *Independent* and the *Guardian* both had 'debate' pages in which a range of experts commented on the government's intelligence dossier, approximately half of them critical.

It is noteworthy that even papers that differed from the government line devoted relatively little attention to examining the substantive case for war, and less still to the meticulous examination of dubious government claims. Instead they tended to focus on Tony Blair's dramatic battle to win over the doubters. The *Daily Mirror*, which in general took a stringently anti-government line, perhaps failed to make the most of its case as a result.

How the British Media Distorted the Truth about Iraq

On the whole, however, the British media did not cover the run-up to the war dispassionately. In a significant number of cases they went far beyond merely reporting government claims about the allegedly deadly threat posed by the Saddam Hussein regime. There were many distortions and fabrications in the tabloid press, but the supposedly more balanced and respectable broadsheet papers were also gravely at fault. The section that follows will show how the mainstream British press invented and exaggerated material in order to press the case for war.

This was pre-eminently the case with the coverage of the government dossier of September 2002. Rather than soberly report British government claims about Saddam Hussein's transgressions, British newspapers used material from the dossier as a starting point for the construction of lurid narratives of their own. The dossier's controversial claim that Saddam Hussein was seeking to obtain uranium from Africa proved especially fertile territory.*

The day after publication of the dossier, the splash story in *The Times* made the dramatic claim – which went far beyond anything asserted in the dossier – that agents for Saddam Hussein had been searching throughout Africa for uranium. The story gave prominence to the government assertion that 'Saddam's agents are trying to buy African uranium to make a nuclear bomb'. It added that '*The Times* has further discovered that Saddam's agents have been on a secret shopping spree in thirteen African countries in a so-far unsuccessful attempt to acquire uranium for nuclear

---

* The dossier stated on page 17 that: 'Uranium has been sought from Africa that has no civil nuclear application in Iraq.' This claim about African uranium was withdrawn by the United States after it was found to have been based on forged documents. The envoy responsible for checking the intelligence, Joseph Wilson, claimed to have told the White House that the allegation was highly unlikely to be true back in February 2002. British intelligence, however, continues to this day to assert that the uranium/Africa link was genuine.

weapons'.[7] In a second, more detailed story inside, a team of *Times* journalists hardened up a series of speculative claims made in the dossier about Saddam Hussein's attempts to buy equipment for his nuclear programme.[8]

These terrifying claims were both unfounded and misleading. The real source for the *Times* story seems to have been the September dossier. The paper asserted categorically that Iraq was seeking to obtain uranium from thirteen countries. It appears likely that figure was obtained by taking the dossier's infamous reference to 'uranium from Africa', and discovering that there were thirteen African countries with uranium deposits.

The article also exaggerated the dossier's claims about equipment purchases. The dossier listed six sets of equipment that it claimed Iraq was attempting to purchase. But in each case it specified that the equipment *could* be used as part of a nuclear programme, not that it *would* be used in this way. *The Times* underplayed the element of speculation.*

The *Guardian* also took the uranium story – later to be discredited in any case – much further than the dossier. Reporters were given prominent space to promote startling claims that members of Congolese gangs had been negotiating to sell uranium to Iraqi agents. Under the headline: 'Iraq dossier: African gangs offer route to uranium – Nuclear suspicion falls on Congo and South Africa', the *Guardian* boasted it had seen secret documents that proved contacts between Baghdad and militia groups. There was a certain amount of critical questioning of these assertions lower down in the article, but not before the story had been sold to *Guardian* readers as providing vital evidence of potential uranium deals.[9]

Generally speaking, the reporting of the dossier in the *Guardian* was loose. Its summary of the document contained a series of minor exaggerations. The dossier claimed that Iraq had 'up to

---

* Thus: 'The dossier reveals that for its secret nuclear project Iraq has, since 1998, tried to buy a range of equipment for converting uranium into bomb-grade quality. Equipment included "vacuum pumps which could be used to create and maintain pressures in a gas centrifuge cascade needed to enrich uranium".'

twenty' al-Hussein missiles capable of carrying conventional, biological or chemical warheads. The *Guardian* piece improved on this conservative estimate, saying that 'Iraq is believed to have twenty of them'. Likewise, *Guardian* claims on al-Abbas medium-range ballistic missiles went much further than the dossier. The *Guardian* stated that they 'are believed to be under development after satellite imagery showed a new engine-testing facility under construction'.[10] The text in the dossier did not directly claim that the engine-testing facilities were evidence for the development of these missiles.

The reporting in the *Guardian*'s sister newspaper, the pro-war *Observer*, was even more sensational. The *Observer* was sceptical of anti-war testimony, while granting space to various suspect witnesses who bolstered the case for invasion. The newspaper's security correspondent David Rose launched a scathing attack on the former weapons inspector Scott Ritter on 15 September 2002, just over a week before the publication of the government dossier. Rose left few stones unturned in uncovering inconsistencies in Scott Ritter's case. Rose unfavourably contrasted Ritter's (as it turned out accurate) claim that Saddam Hussein had given up on his weapons programmes with evidence provided by Adnan Saeed al-Haideri, an Iraqi building contractor who had defected to the US at the end of 2001. According to Rose, Haideri 'brought with him hard copies of more than twenty contracts between his firm and the government, showing that old proscribed weapons sites which had been bombed were being rebuilt, and new ones constructed'.[11] Rose's article, however, failed to raise the numerous reasons to be cautious about Haideri's testimony. Rose attacked Ritter for changing his story, but Haideri had done just the same thing. His claims about Saddam Hussein's weapons development became more definite and more alarming as time went on. The article should surely have mentioned that Haideri was given a three-week 'debriefing' by an Iraqi opposition group, and a further debriefing by US intelligence before being unleashed on the press. Nowhere in his piece did Rose cite any of these substantial problems with Haideri's testimony.

The previous week had produced an even more grievous example of double standards. The *Observer* reporter ran a spectacular 1,560-word interview with a woman who claimed to have been a lover of Saddam's before escaping Iraq 'to tell a story of rape and humiliation'.[12] She told how she and her family were destroyed by the Iraqi dictator. The woman, Parisoula Lampsos, gave thirteen hours of videotaped interviews to the Iraqi opposition group, the Iraqi National Congress, as well as an interview to ABC TV in September 2002, in which she provided lurid information about Saddam and his entourage. She claimed, among other assertions, that she had been with Osama bin Laden as a guest at Saddam's palace, and that Saddam had funded Bin Laden. David Rose did not question the credibility of the woman even though, towards the end of his long piece, he stated that her salvation only came when she was 'picked up by agents of the INC's so-called "information collection programme"'. The Iraqi National Congress (INC), fronted by Ahmad Chalabi, was responsible for much of the worst and most inaccurate reporting ahead of the Iraqi invasion. To be fair to David Rose, he is one of the very few British journalists to have had the decency to publicly recant, saying that he looks back with 'shame and disbelief' on his support for the invasion.[13]

Another example of inflammatory *Observer* reporting concerned the carnage caused by Saddam Hussein. A central part of Tony Blair's justification for war involved the proposition that, however many people might be killed in an invasion of Iraq, the number involved would turn out to be far lower than those killed by Saddam. For example Tony Blair told MPs on 19 March 2003 that Saddam Hussein 'will be responsible for many, many more deaths even in one year than we will be in any conflict'. This false claim was often reiterated by supporters of the Prime Minister. For instance it was echoed after the conflict by the *Observer* columnist Andrew Rawnsley in a piece that offered a strong vindication of Tony Blair's decision to go to war: 'Thousands have died in this war; millions have died at the hands of Saddam.'[14] Murderous though Saddam was, he killed nowhere near the numbers claimed by Tony Blair and his Fleet Street apologists. According to Amnesty International he killed 'scores' of people in 2001 and 2002, the two years immediately preceding his fall, a minute percentage of the casualties actually caused by the invasion.

The *Sunday Telegraph* was particularly credulous, both in the run-up to war and in the aftermath of conflict when the coalition failure to discover weapons of mass destruction called the original war aim into question. The most misguided member of the *Telegraph* staff was the newspaper's correspondent Con Coughlin. Coughlin is a colourful reporter, with a reputation for being close to the intelligence services. On occasion these appear to have let him down.

On 19 January 2003 Coughlin produced the following exclusive on the *Sunday Telegraph* front page:

> United Nations weapons inspectors have uncovered evidence that proves Saddam Hussein is trying to develop an arsenal of nuclear weapons, the *Sunday Telegraph* can reveal.
>
> The discovery was made following spot checks last week on the homes of two Iraqi nuclear physicists in Baghdad.
>
> Acting on information provided by Western intelligence, the UN inspection teams discovered 3,000 documents proving that Saddam is continuing with his attempts to develop nuclear weapons, contrary to his public declarations that Iraq is no longer interested in producing weapons of mass destruction.[15]

This piece, like many others at the time, picked up early reports of 3,000 nuclear-related documents and reached the premature conclusion that these were evidence of Iraqi nuclear programmes. However, the verdict of the inspectors, which came a few days later, showed that he had drawn the wrong conclusions. The inspectors found that there was significant material in these documents that had already been shown to inspectors, and that the rest were personal files belonging to one of the scientists. Coughlin's claim that these documents showed that Saddam was continuing to develop nuclear weapons was unfounded. The International Atomic Energy Agency had already announced earlier that week in a press release that they dated from the early 1980s.* Even on the day that Coughlin's story was published, the head of the IAEA was casting doubt on the significance of the documents.[16] I can find no evidence that the *Sunday Telegraph* came back to acknowledge its errors.

Once the invasion finished, Coughlin left few stones unturned in order to bring readers of the *Sunday Telegraph* reassurance that Saddam Hussein really had been set on threatening the rest of the world with his weapons of mass destruction, just as the British and American governments and their intelligence services had claimed. In May 2003 Coughlin brought this apparently electrifying news:

> British military officers have uncovered an attempt by Saddam Hussein to build a missile capable of hitting targets throughout the Middle East, including Israel, the *Sunday Telegraph* can reveal.
>
> Plans for the surface-to-surface missile were one of the regime's most closely-guarded secrets and were unknown to United Nations weapons inspectors. Its range of 600 miles would have been far greater than that of the al-Samoud rocket – which already breached the 93-mile limit imposed by the UN on any Iraqi missiles.
>
> Saddam's masterplan for the new missile, which was being developed by Iraq's Military Industrialisation Commission (MIC), the body responsible for weapons procurement, constitutes the most serious breach uncovered so far of the tight restrictions imposed on Iraq's military capability after the 1991 Gulf War. The range of Saddam's missiles was restricted to prevent him from using them as a delivery system for weapons of mass destruction.[17]

---

* The head of the IAEA, Mohamed El Baradei, insisted the documents dated from the 1980s, saying that Iraq was not advanced enough at the time to have produced such technology: 'We know they have not gone that far.' See http://news.bbc.co.uk/1/hi/world/middle_east/2672825.stm.

There was some basis to the claims made in this piece, sourced to 'British military officers'. The Iraq Survey Group would indeed go on to report that an Iraqi official had claimed that a committee had been convened in 2000 to look at producing a missile with a 600-kilometre range (though not 600 miles, as Coughlin asserted). The ISG reported that there had been some attempts to test this technology over the eighteen months that followed. However, it largely failed and in any case all of it was destroyed in advance of the arrival of UN inspectors in 2002. In his article Coughlin failed to mention that this programme had been abandoned before the arrival of the inspectors.

Coughlin was soon providing fresh and devastating evidence of Saddam Hussein's chemical and biological weapons programme. In August, in a story which had the side-effect of distracting attention from the row over the David Kelly affair back in London, Coughlin brought readers of the *Daily Telegraph* a sensational piece of news: Saddam Hussein ordered his soldiers to fire chemical weapons at the invading coalition army.

Thousands of miles from the febrile atmosphere of Court 73 of the Royal Courts of Justice in London, where Lord Hutton is conducting his inquiry into the death of Dr David Kelly, one of the British scientist's former colleagues was last week making yet another highly significant discovery in the hunt for Saddam Hussein's weapons of mass destruction arsenal.

Dr David Kay, the American weapons expert who heads the 1,400-strong Iraq Survey Team that is conducting an extensive search for Saddam's biological, chemical and nuclear programmes in Iraq, made the startling revelation that the Iraqi dictator had ordered his commanders to fire chemical shells at invading coalition troops during the recent conflict.

Dr Kay's discovery, which will be contained in a Congressional report to be published in Washington next month, is just the latest of a number of telling breakthroughs that have been made in Iraq by the survey team but which, because of the furore that has gripped the British media over the Kelly case, have gone largely unreported.

And if Dr Kay's recent predictions about uncovering the secrets of Saddam's various weapons of mass destruction programmes prove to be correct, then the painstaking investigation being undertaken by Lord Hutton into whether the British government exaggerated the threat posed by Saddam would be rendered irrelevant.[18]

This story can generously be described as doubtful. Kay's report to Congress which Coughlin claimed to be reporting on in advance was delivered on 2 October 2003. It never said that Saddam gave the order to fire chemical shells at coalition troops. Indeed, the October report indicated that there was no hard evidence for weaponised chemical or biological agents in Iraq. When Kay resigned in January 2004, he admitted that there had been no chemical or biological weapons in Iraq since the early 1990s. Coughlin's long report also asserted that David Kelly had worked 'as a member of Dr Kay's United Nations weapons teams in Iraq in the 1990s'. This was false. Kay led some individual inspections teams for the IAEA, not the UN, in 1991, but left to work in the private sector in 1992.

Tabloid reporting of the threat posed by Saddam was just as troublesome. The *Sun* front-page report, headlined 'Brits 45 mins from doom', was the *pièce de résistance*. This story conflated the dossier claim that missiles could reach Cyprus with a second claim that chemical or biological weapons could be deployed within forty-five minutes to produce an exaggerated story. The *Sun* account contained plenty of other errors. It claimed that Saddam had 'publicly vowed to develop an A-bomb', when this was not the case. It reiterated the assertion that Saddam had been attempting to purchase uranium from 'rogue arms dealers in Africa', and it repeated the claim – widely made by propagandists for war ahead of the invasion – that 'weapons inspectors were kicked out of Iraq four years ago'.[19]

Reporting of Tony Blair's Speech to Parliament on 18 March 2003

A glaring example of the almost wilful failure to examine the facts presented by the government in a sceptical fashion can be found in the press reporting of the speech made by Tony Blair to Parliament on 18 March 2003, right on the eve of war. This speech was widely praised, and not just by the pro-war lobby. It was also greeted with acclaim by the handful of anti-war newspapers. The *Independent*, for example, saluted Tony Blair for delivering the 'most persuasive case yet made by the man who has emerged as the most formidable persuader for war on either side of the Atlantic. The case against President Saddam's twelve-year history of obstructing the United Nations attempts at disarmament has never been better made.'[20]

In fact the speech contained a number of falsehoods and facts taken out of context which could easily have been identified by journalists at the time. For example Tony Blair claimed that Saddam Hussein had been playing the 'same old games' with weapons inspectors. This statement contrasted sharply with the statement made by the chief UN weapons inspector Hans Blix to the Security Council on 7 March, just ten days earlier. This statement – by a man with a good claim to be a major authority on the subject of Saddam Hussein's weapons – made it clear that the Iraqi regime was being remarkably co-operative. Likewise Tony Blair's claim that Iraq 'had far-reaching plans to weaponise VX', the deadly nerve agent, was hopelessly misleading.* Yet British newspapers almost without exception let these falsehoods go unchallenged.

---

* Indeed since the start of March the Iraqis had complied with the inspectors to the extent of destroying 72 out of 120 medium-range missiles, and were actually ahead of the timetable to destroy the entire stock. This information was available at the time. See Glen Rangwala, 'Misled into War', *Labour Left Briefing*, April 2003.

On the contrary, Fleet Street reports gave credibility to fallacious claims made by the Prime Minister, in some cases building on them to make them even more lurid and dramatic. An example is the threat posed by Saddam's chemical weapons. In his front-page article for the *Daily Mail*, political editor David Hughes reported that 'Frontline British forces prepare for action amid growing fears that Saddam would unleash chemical weapons'.[21] The *Sun* went much further, claiming that Saddam was already moving chemical weapons in readiness for war. An article headlined 'Fiend to unleash poisons' informed readers that

> British soldiers stepped up chemical warfare drills on the Iraqi border yesterday – as Saddam deployed the doomsday weapons he claimed he never had.
>
> The tyrant has started moving unidentified warheads – feared to contain deadly nerve agents – to frontline troops south of Baghdad.
>
> The artillery shells are under the control of Saddam's vile cousin 'Chemical Ali' who masterminded the notorious poison gas attacks on Iraqi Kurds.[22]

In a subheading the *Sun* boldly told readers that chemicals were being 'handed to Iraqis on [*sic*] front line'. The *Daily Express* made the same fallacious assertions. Under the powerful headline 'Deadly gas threat to our soldiers on the battlefield: Iraq plots chemical blitz', the paper told readers that 'Saddam Hussein is arming his troops with chemical weapons in time for a doomsday last stand around Baghdad'.[23] All these stories were complete rubbish. Neither the *Sun* nor the *Express* drew readers' attention to the fact that although Tony Blair had made a great deal of the chemicals threat in his speech, experts judged that Blair's claims were invalid. And while papers were ready to give front-page prominence to Tony Blair's claims that Saddam could unleash chemical weapons, they mainly ignored or gave very little prominence to remarks by the chief UN weapons inspector Hans Blix on

18 March that he doubted such weapons would be used, even if the capability did actually exist.*

The headlines and prominent articles focused on the content of the case for war. They did little to explore, though they did award some cursory acknowledgement to, the opposite side of the debate. There was none of the creative invention that helped the government case for war. Dissenting voices were acknowledged as part of the narrative of unfolding events, but their arguments were very rarely outlined or engaged with critically.† Arguments in favour of the war got a far more detailed airing. It is extremely striking that we in the press and broadcasting media concentrated on the style of the Prime Minister's speech – recording it as 'impassioned', 'powerful' or 'spell-binding', to give a few examples of the heroic epithets we attached to Blair's oration. We showed far less interest in peering beyond the rhetoric and examining the content. For us the predicament of Tony Blair provided the dramatic focus around which all the arguments both for and against the war were presented. This method of reporting led to a highly misleading account of events in the run-up to war. It meant that arguments were very rarely engaged with critically, but instead reported on their impact on the personal fortunes of the Prime Minister.‡

In conjunction with Downing Street the British press and

---

* The *Guardian* did examine the debate ('Saddam's track record raises fears of chemical and biological attack: experts divided on Iraq's ability to use nerve agents', 19 March 2003), but the report was not prioritised, appearing only on page 8.

† To give one example among many, the *Independent* presented the rebellion of back-bench MPs as an 'embarrassing setback for Mr Blair to fail to command half of the Labour MPs not on the "payroll" vote': 'Rebels fail to halt march to war', 19 March 2003. Likewise the *Times* front-page story reported ministerial resignations but failed to explore the anti-war arguments.

‡ Very few British journalists – and not the author – emerged with great credit from this passage of history. Among those who did can be included Simon Jenkins, Robert Fisk, Matthew Parris, Polly Toynbee, Simon Kelner (editor of the *Independent*) and Piers Morgan (former editor of the *Daily Mirror*).

broadcasting media constructed a dramatic narrative that Tony Blair was fighting a gallant and resolute battle against the odds. This applied even to papers commonly held to oppose the government. Under the front-page headline 'No retreat', the political editor of the *Daily Mail*, David Hughes, announced that

> Tony Blair launched a thunderous call to arms yesterday telling MPs he would rather quit than back down to Saddam Hussein.
> With an attack on Iraq expected within hours, Mr Blair confronted his anti-war rebels head-on.[24]

The Hughes article, spread over pages one and two of the *Mail*, gave very generous coverage to the quotations from the Prime Minister and his supporters. By contrast only one anti-war voice, the former minister John Denham, was quoted at the very end of this thousand-word article. The *Daily Telegraph* also emphasised the exemplary courage of the Prime Minister, with political editor George Jones's front-page article stating that the Prime Minister had 'staked his personal future on gaining the support of MPs to topple Saddam Hussein'.[25] The *Guardian* presented the same drama. Its front page on 19 March 2003 described how the Prime Minister was 'fighting for his own political life as well as what he called a twenty-first century of stability and order'. This formulation mixed reporting and comment, and gave a tacit editorial endorsement to Tony Blair's claim that the invasion of Iraq would produce 'stability and order'.[26] The *Guardian* piece, like most other reports of its kind, downplayed the protests of rebel MPs and resigning ministers. It failed to explore their reasoning, whereas the Prime Minister's own arguments were given generous space. It is striking that the *Guardian* published a piece of advocacy by the Prime Minister on the news pages, while the anti-war advocacy by Polly Toynbee appeared on the comment page. The *Guardian* front page contrasted sharply with the *Independent* front-page coverage by Andrew Grice. Grice presented all sides of the argument, and gave a balanced account of events. In most cases arguments against the war were absorbed into larger bodies of text, where the major pro-war speeches (by Tony Blair, William Hague and Iain Duncan Smith) tended to be granted their own autonomous body of text.[27]

The Loving Creation of Tony Blair the War Hero

In the immediate aftermath of the invasion, the Downing Street press machine appears to have orchestrated a powerful move to exploit the apparent success of the war for political purposes. The objective of the Prime Minister and his allies seems to have been the creation of a myth of Tony Blair the war leader, just as the Falklands campaign twenty-one years earlier created a myth for Margaret Thatcher. There were three major manifestations of this. First the Prime Minister gave an interview to the *Sun* in which he confided how he had gathered his three eldest children around him to tell them he might lose his job as a result of the Commons vote on the war.[28] It remains hard to see how or when the Prime Minister would have resigned, given that he was never likely to lose his Commons majority. This article was also published in the following day's *Daily Telegraph*. The Prime Minister authorised personal friends to give special interviews to the *Financial Times* political editor James Blitz casting light on his state of mind around the time the decision was apparently made to go to war. The result was a long profile, based on privileged access to members of Tony Blair's inner circle not usually available for interview by journalists, which portrayed the Prime Minister as an heroic figure driven by religious conviction.[29] The *FT* piece was accompanied by a series of rare posed photographs of the Prime Minister, by the celebrity photographer Rankin, casting him as a wizened statesman who had been to hell and back. Third, it emerged that Downing Street had taken the extraordinary and unprecedented step of allowing Sir Peter Stothard, the former editor of *The Times* who had been knighted on the advice of Tony Blair, to be embedded inside Downing

Street for the duration of the war writing a narrative of events.*

Once again the British media were happy to substantiate this image of Tony Blair the war victor. The BBC's then political editor Andrew Marr recorded how Tony Blair 'stands as a larger man and a stronger Prime Minister as a result' of the Iraq invasion.[30] Marr told BBC viewers that the victory in Iraq had enabled Tony Blair to put behind him the political difficulties he had been facing before the war. 'Well, I think this does one thing,' declared Marr. 'It draws a line under what, before the war, had been a period of . . . well, a faint air of pointlessness, almost, was hanging over Downing Street. There were all these slightly tawdry arguments and scandals. That is now history.'[31] Here Marr, like his ITN rival Nick Robinson in the run-up to war, was getting too close to his subject matter. There seems little question that Downing Street was hoping to be able to use the apparent success of the invasion as the opportunity for a major relaunch. But Marr gave this hope – in the event to be unfulfilled – the imprimatur of objective comment.† The great majority of political reporters during this period were guilty of the same kind of mistake. Far from playing the role of sceptical observers of the Iraq conflict and its aftermath, the British press and broadcasting media were astonishingly credulous of government claims, and some became engaged participants. Far from fulfilling their task of telling the British public the truth about this terrible conflict, for the most part the British press and broadcasting media lent an air of respectability to the numerous falsehoods and misleading statements put out by the British government. There is an interesting parallel between the journalists reporting on the Iraq War and the British and American intelligence officers who were ordered to

---

* Later published as *Thirty Days: An Inside Account of Tony Blair at War* by HarperCollins, the publishing company owned by Stothard's former employer Rupert Murdoch.

† To be fair to Marr, he came close to expressing sheepish regret about this report in his 2007 television series *A History of Modern Britain*.

gather information about Iraqi weapons of mass destruction ahead of the war. Both groups were subject to pressure from above, and in the end both became the creatures of their sources.

PART IV

A NEW SYSTEM OF GOVERNMENT

13

MANIPULATIVE POPULISM

'Politicians struggled for the first part of the twentieth century to find means of addressing the new mass public. For a period it seemed that only men like Hitler, Mussolini and Stalin had discovered the secret of power through mass communication. Democratic politicians were placed on roughly equal discursive terms with their electorates through the clumsiness of their attempts at mass speech. Then the US advertising industry began to develop its skills, with a particular boost coming from the development of commercial television. The persuasion business was born as a profession. By far the dominant part of this remained devoted to the art of selling goods and services, but politics and other users of persuasion tagged along eagerly behind, extrapolating from the innovations of the advertising industry, and making themselves as analogous as possible to the business of selling products so that they could reap maximum advantage from the new techniques'
– Colin Crouch, *Coping With Post-Democracy*

I have demonstrated in the chapters above that a hubristic Political Class has chosen to govern in alliance with the media rather than through Parliament. This new system is the direct result of a massive, sustained and partly successful assault on the system of representative democracy, which was the dominant mode in Britain through the nineteenth and twentieth centuries. It has produced a method of government which can most helpfully be described as manipulative populism.

This phrase becomes meaningful when the simultaneous weakening of traditional authority and collapse of deference towards existing institutions and structures causes the ruling elite to engage directly with the voters. This stimulates the Political Class to form an alliance with the media, which is itself subject to the identical need to sell product to a mass audience. This alliance forces government to respond much more directly than before to popular clamours. Human emotions against which wise governments have traditionally sought to guard – greed, fear, sentimentality – are converted into mechanisms for elite rule. Manipulative populism as practised in post-democratic countries like Britain and to an extent in the United States has certain important similiarities with the alliance between ruling class and the mob that is characteristic of some pre-modern societies, manifested in carefully monitored and controlled outbreaks such as pogroms in Czarist Russia or the Gordon Riots in eighteenth-century London. Under skilful direction from above, class resentment was diverted away from propertied interests on to vulnerable and comparatively defenceless targets such as Jews and foreigners.[1] Recent populist agitations in Britain, such as the so-called 'Sarah's Law' campaign against paedophiles led by the *News of the World*, with covert government collaboration, the propaganda put out ahead of the Iraq War, and the repeated press campaigns against Muslims ahead of terrorist trials, have numerous pre-modern characteristics.

Manipulative populism as a political methodology has many characteristics in common with totalitarianism, in particular a systemic hostility to institutions which represent values which are distinct from those held by the governing elite. As the historian Max Beloff hinted in a prescient article in 1997, written just months after the General Election, it is a governing system which can mutate extremely easily into fascism.[2] As a method of government it is dangerously susceptible to the vagaries of human nature, and is wholly dependent upon a virtuous governing class in order to function without causing terrible damage. This is because the system of manipulative populism lacks the institutional protections against malign actions enjoyed by representative democracies, with strong parliaments, a free press, an autonomous civil service, powerful judiciaries and so on. It is noteworthy that the process of political intrusion upon an independent civil service, combined with attacks on the judiciary and the sidelining of Parliament, was a feature of 1930s Germany.

The collaboration with a satellite media upon which manipulative populism thrives is inherently deceitful because the real objectives of the governing class diverge sharply from the popular sentiment it pretends to share. In a pure system of manipulative populism all of the agencies and institutions of representative democracy become meaningless: Parliament, political parties, the judiciary and eventually even General Elections. The Political Class negotiates with the voters through television and searches out their opinions through mechanisms such as focus groups and techniques based on market research or borrowed from the advertising industry. The role of the voter is no longer engaged and involved. Instead he or she is reduced to the role of inert spectator, though he or she may periodically be roused from passivity to take part in carefully controlled clamours of one kind or another.

In Britain this constitutional arrangement has already brought about profound changes to official priorities and the nature of decision-making. The least obvious of these extremely dramatic effects is the creation of a conspiratorial style of government. Paradoxical though this sounds, the broadcasting and newspaper media – which talk so often of transparency – are institutionally more opaque than Parliament. Media organisations are fundamentally secretive, and their over-riding commercial relationship is with shareholders and not the general public. Individual journalists have a duty to protect sources, a moral obligation which while admirable in itself can sometimes be converted into a licence either for mischievous invention or more often collaboration with elite interests. Announcements made in the House of Commons or the Lords are made on the record, subject to scrutiny, open to challenge, and subject to rules (some of which have been deliberately meddled with by the Political Class in order to stop them working) which attempt to ensure integrity.

Communications issued through the media are not like that. Ministers and other government representatives have massive power to influence the nature and the tone of the coverage because it is normal for them to enter into private deals of various kinds with media outlets. As I have already shown, ministers and their assistants prefer to operate through client journalists over whom they can exercise editorial and other forms of control. This is why government in co-operation with the media increases the power of the executive to set the parameters of public discourse and evade legitimate scrutiny.

A second change of style involves speed of reaction. Even in the House of Commons, let alone the Lords, there is relatively little opportunity to debate the immediate issues of the day. Though this posture is often ridiculed by journalists and others, it is actually a deliberate constraint, placed there so that intermittent populist clamours can be more readily resisted. Even at times of great crisis, such as the outbreak of war, parliamentarians judge that it is normally better to wait until the immediate heat of controversy is over before engaging seriously, let alone taking action on the matter at stake. The legislative process, with at least three separate stages of debate in the Commons, each stage set apart by several weeks, and the additional need for consideration in the House of Lords, can seem very cumbersome and slow.

This procrastination is one of the reasons why the Political Class has taken such firm action to weaken Parliament over the past twenty-five years. But the system has many advantages. It ensures that all voices can be heard. It allows losers from proposed legislation to put their case, and sets in place a large raft of protections against the victimisation of minority groups, so vulnerable under manipulative populism.

By contrast, government by media forces immediate reaction. A high premium is put on swift response, and far less weight is attached to the merits of delay. Due process, which is welcomed as a prophylactic against populist agitation in a representative democracy, is regarded as an irritant or a hindrance within a system of manipulative populism.

An exceptionally good example of governing-class surrender to media-class values is the response to the threat of domestic terrorism in recent years. It is tragically easy to demonstrate that the British government's policy has been driven very much more by the desire to generate favourable newspaper coverage than by the desire to combat or minimise the danger of terror. The over-riding desire of government ministers was to demonstrate to newspaper executives and readers that they were being 'tough on terror'. The evolution of a long-term strategy to deal with the problem appears at best to have been a secondary objective. Terror has repeatedly been used as a convenient political tool by the Political Class, as I will now demonstrate.

Tony Blair, the *Sun* Newspaper, and Government by Headline

In the immediate aftermath of the London bomb outrages of 7 July 2005, Tony Blair reacted in a statesmanlike way. He called for a measured rather than an alarmist response to the tragedy. He went to the House of Commons where, as one would traditionally expect at a moment of national crisis, he promised to co-operate with the main opposition parties. Steps were then taken to follow through this commitment. Lines of communication were developed between the government, the Tories and the Liberal Democrats to secure a non-partisan response to the tragedy. The Home Secretary Charles Clarke met shadow Home Secretary David Davis and Liberal Democrat spokesman Mark Oaten. The three men agreed a common way forward and prepared the way for the passing of an anti-terrorism act with cross-party support. This was scheduled for the autumn season. At the start of August Oaten, Clarke and Davis all went off on summer holiday.

Up to this point the Prime Minister had dealt with the crisis in the way that one would expect in a representative democracy. He had engaged with Parliament. He had operated through the Cabinet system of government, leaving the Home Secretary in charge of events at an operational level. The major political parties were brought in as partners, while the civil service was heavily engaged in the planning and co-ordination of legislation. There was no panic or alarmism. It is what took place at the start of August that shockingly demonstrates the effects of the shift to a novel system of government at the start of the twenty-first century.

On 5 August Prime Minister Tony Blair suddenly changed direction, and called a press conference. The Tories and the Liberal Democrats were given perfunctory notice. Both Oaten and Davis were misled into believing that the press conference was of no special significance. Although they were informed about it the day before, they were told there was nothing significant to worry about, and Tony Blair would not contradict or go beyond what had already been agreed between the main parties. Both Oaten and David Davis were rung up on the afternoon of 4 August by Hazel Blears, the junior Home Office minister who had taken charge while Charles Clarke was on holiday. Both opposition spokesmen now say that Blears gave them the impression the press conference was little more than a formality. Oaten told me later that 'the basis of the conversation led me to believe that what the Prime Minister was going to announce was of very little significance, that this was not a big shift, and that the consensus that we had would continue'.[3]

This advance guidance turned out to be completely wrong. What the Prime Minister actually announced on the day had massive consequences for the anti-terror strategy. He unveiled a so-called 'twelve-point plan', which would 'set a comprehensive framework for action in dealing with the terrorist threat in Britain'. Some of the measures had not even been discussed with the other political parties, and Blair therefore smashed the carefully constructed consensus between government and opposition. Tony Blair did not merely cut links with opposition parties. There is evidence that civil servants were not informed of the new Downing Street policy on terror either. Home Office officials stated privately afterwards that their 'jaws dropped' as they watched the Prime Minister's press conference on television. It is also very important to note that Parliament was cut out of the equation. Traditionally any major announcement claiming to set out the framework for the future conduct of government policy would be made as a matter of course in the House of Commons. The decision to make the announcement early in August, with the Home Secretary on holiday in the United States, also broke sharply with the principle of Cabinet government.

Since the Prime Minister's 'twelve points' had not been discussed with the opposition parties or with civil servants (there are suggestions that they were not even discussed with his own ministers), it is no surprise that they were specious and poorly thought-out. Though they did indeed receive a rapturous reception in much of the following day's media, in the long term it was a different story. Some of the 'twelve points' had to be dropped when later they turned out to be impractical, illegal, or suffer from other insuperable defects. It emerged that others were already law. Far from being the 'comprehensive framework for action' that he claimed, the Prime Minister's plan's long-term effect was the creation of fresh anger, disillusion, distrust and the further alienation of the Muslim community.

The evidence suggests that Tony Blair's decision to sideline the civil service and Cabinet, ignore Parliament and deceive the two main opposition parties over its handling of anti-terror legislation was media-driven. In the days before the plan was announced, the Prime Minister came under heavy pressure from a campaign in tabloid newspapers, led by the *Sun*, for strong measures against terrorism. In particular the *Sun* attacked MPs for going on holiday at a time of national crisis. On 3 August the paper raged: 'Let's hope the bombers are on holiday too'. On 5 August the *Sun*'s political editor Trevor Kavanagh wrote an open letter to MPs headlined: 'Dear MPs, six weeks holiday is enough for anyone'. On 6 August, as Tony Blair and his family flew to the West Indies and the holiday home of pop-star Cliff Richard, the *Sun* headline was altogether more reassuring: 'Victory for *Sun* over new terror laws'.[4]

The anti-terror plan unveiled in August 2005 was a classic Political Class manoeuvre. It was long on style and lacking in substance. It had the short-term merit of generating newspaper coverage, and thereafter inevitably collapsed. The Media Class and the Political Class collaborated in the creation of the illusion of action. However, with the exception of a few Whitehall and legal experts, nobody much noticed when the scheme started to unravel a few months later.

This methodology of fighting terror was to continue. In November 2006 the Home Secretary John Reid made a controversial speech urging Muslim parents to inform on their children if they believed they were involved in terrorism. The day that he made his speech he trailed his views in the *Sun*. This newspaper had been one of the strongest supporters of the Iraq War and was viewed with suspicion by many Muslims. The Home Secretary's curious decision to float his ideas in the *Sun* suggests that his primary interest cannot have been a positive engagement with Muslims. The Home Secretary's motive can only have been the familiar one: present himself to *Sun* readers as a 'tough' politician fighting a war against terror rather than trying to engage thoughtfully with an intractable problem.

The tragedy is that government in the age of manipulative populism is functionally unable to try to stand against the demotic style and urgent imperatives of the Media Class. On the contrary, it accepts them and incorporates populist discourse into the heart of government. An arresting example of this systemic subordination to media values concerns the imprisonment of the Iraqi dictator Saddam Hussein. In September 2005 the *Sun* splashed pictures of Saddam in his prison cell. These photographs – particularly insulting to Islamic eyes because he was shown stripped to his underwear – were displayed in clear breach of Geneva Convention guidelines, as the International Committee of the Red Cross immediately made clear, and even US military spokesmen later appeared to concede. Publication of the photographs was, in a small way, an act of barbarism and illegality. Yet British government ministers refused to condemn the *Sun* for this breach of international law and of Saddam Hussein's rights. On the contrary they defended the *Sun* newspaper. Hazel

Blears, always one of the most 'on-message' members of the Blair government, said, 'I know the *Sun* feels that they almost have a responsibility to publish them.'* This refusal to condemn the *Sun* conflicted sharply with the self-proclaimed concern for decent values which ministers claimed gave legitimacy to their invasion of Iraq.

The same style of collaboration with an especially noxious populism was on display when the *News of the World*, sister paper to the *Sun*, ran its 'Sarah's Law' campaign against child molesters. The *News of the World* launched this enterprise on 23 July 2000. Photographs and location summaries of forty-nine released sex offenders were published with the stated, though unfeasible, intent that the paper would not stop until all '110,000 were named and shamed'.[5] (Had the *News of the World* carried on at the rate of forty-nine released offenders a week, it would have taken the newspaper more than forty years to complete its mission.)

Publication unleashed a spate of vigilante attacks, with fire bombings on the Paulsgrove estate in Portsmouth. At least six innocent people with the same names as those 'named and shamed' were attacked. Rather than intervening in a responsible way, no government minister criticised the paper for provoking violence. The Home Secretary, Jack Straw, remained silent. The nearest any minister came to condemnation was the remark made by Paul Boateng, a junior Home Office minister, to the effect that the Sarah's Law campaign was 'unhelpful'. When the *News of the World* halted its campaign weeks later, the newspaper boasted that 'our critics are a tiny minority. An unknown Labour MP, a judge ... and two newspaper editors, Simon Kelner of the *Independent* and Charles Moore of the *Daily Telegraph*.'[6]

---

* It is not clear how Blears 'knew' about the *Sun*'s sense of responsibility. Graham Dudman, managing editor of the *Sun*, was unrepentant: 'This is a man who breached the Geneva Convention more times than you've had hot dinners, so please don't talk to us about the Geneva Convention.' See 'Bidding war for Sun's Saddam pics', *Guardian*, 20 May 2005. In the *Sun*'s defence it should be noted that most other media outlets, including the BBC, went on to publish the pictures.

The Labour MP was Robin Corbett, chair of the Commons Home Affairs Committee, who unavailingly asked the Home Office 'whether they will consider prosecution for incitement to public order offences'. Government silence lent the *News of the World* claim that its critics were in a 'tiny minority' a fig-leaf of respectability, but it was false. A spokesman for the Association of Police Superintendents said that the newspaper had created 'an atmosphere of fear among members of the public, among parents and among sex offenders'.[7]

In June 2006 a new Home Secretary, John Reid, doubtless discerning the opportunity to make political capital, commissioned an investigation into 'Megan's Law' in the United States, the inspiration for the original 'Sarah's Law' campaign. Rather than announcing this decision in the usual way, the news was given in the form of an expression of approval by 10 Downing Street, which claimed that it was right to 'take account' of public concern on the issue.[8]

Ministers under both Margaret Thatcher and later – to a far greater extent – Tony Blair always understood that News International was a key constituency. Government was tailored towards the production of cheap effects, the creation of headlines, and media appeasement. Though News International was the most powerful driver of this kind of politics, most other papers operated within the same system.

More than anything else the conduct of successive Home Secretaries demonstrates exactly how it works. All of them sought to form an alliance with tabloid newspapers. The *Daily Mail*, for example, was assiduously fostered by David Blunkett from 2001 to 2004. The objective was to join forces with the media against the judges and also against Parliament. The tone for this arrangement was set by Jack Straw, Home Secretary from 1997 to 2001. An entry in the diary of the *Daily Mirror* editor Piers Morgan, made on 28 September 1997, shows how the connection between the Political and the Media Classes worked:

Dinner with the new Home Secretary, Jack Straw, in Brighton to kick off the first Labour Party conference since they swept to power. He was in ebullient form, as they all are at the moment while the honeymoon lingers long.

I like Straw because he's got a sense of humour, and a shrewd legal brain and doesn't seem to take press criticism too seriously. As the wine flowed, I asked him what he plans to do about Myra Hindley, as he has to make a formal decision soon about whether she will ever be released from prison.

He smirked. 'Well, officially I fully intend to afford her the same rights as any other prisoner in Britain ... but unofficially if you think I'm going down as the Home Secretary that released Myra Hindley, then you must be fucking joking.'[9]

Two months later Straw announced that Hindley would end her life behind bars. The conversation between the Home Secretary and the editor of a mass-circulation newspaper is sinister. Straw was showing negligence in performing his duties as Home Secretary, namely to reach a decision about Myra Hindley objectively and without pre-judging the issue. Had this story come to light before Myra Hindley's death, Straw's remarks might have left him open to judicial review.

I have shown above how the modern collaboration between ministers and the media has changed the priorities of government. Government accepted the embedded media preference for the dramatic over the mundane, the sensational over the prosaic, sentimentality rather than compassion, and the short-term solution. These values have become the defining part of the government machine. Sometimes this attitude was merely farcical. It is worth pausing here on the case of 'Phoenix the Calf', an almost perfect illustration of crisis management within the moral parameters instilled by manipulative populism.

Phoenix was born on Good Friday, 13 April 2000, at the height of the Foot and Mouth crisis. She was a pure white Charolais calf, bred at a small fifty-acre Devon smallholding owned by part-time farmer Philip Board. The day after her birth all the cattle on the

Board farm were condemned under the government's 'contiguous culling' policy. The slaughtermen arrived, herded up the cattle, put them in a barn, administered lethal injections and left the animals to die. Six days later, when the barn was opened up so the rotting bodies could be disinfected, little Phoenix – 'blinking in the light and mooing softly' – was found still to be alive.

The animal quickly dubbed Phoenix became a media phenomenon. First she made the local Devon papers, then she was picked up by Fleet Street and by television. Very soon, Sky TV, GMTV, and dozens of photographers were camped outside the Boards' farm. The *Daily Mirror* launched a campaign to 'Save Phoenix from the ashes', while a senior official from the National Farmers' Union pronounced that killing Phoenix 'would make King Herod look like a humanitarian'.

None of this struck Agriculture minister Nick Brown or his officials as important. 'Poor old Phoenix was not at the front of my mind,' he said later. 'I assumed it was the latest human interest story.' Brown spent the day in a series of meetings dealing with the day-to-day problems raised by the Foot and Mouth crisis. Unknown to him, the Downing Street press office started briefing political correspondents that Phoenix had been reprieved. Papers whose front-page stories for the first editions had led on 'If Phoenix dies her death will haunt PM', or 'Phoenix fights on', were hastily changed to 'PM gives life to calf', 'Phoenix shows Blair listens', or 'Phoenix reprieved'. The Prime Minister was portrayed as compassionate, and in touch with public opinion. Downing Street had pulled off a public relations triumph. Many of the papers, relying on Number 10 briefing, stated that the reprieve for Phoenix the Calf was part of a much larger change of policy.

It was nothing of the sort. A further 4 million animals were to be slaughtered before the Foot and Mouth tragedy ended. The case of Phoenix was an episode in virtual politics. The decision was made by the Downing Street press office. All the key figures involved – the Agriculture minister, government scientists, civil servants, the chief vet – were not even consulted. The official Downing Street briefing states that 'the final decision to widen the discretion had been taken yesterday following meetings between Mr Brown, Professor King and Mr Scudamore, followed by a meeting with Mr Brown and the Prime Minister yesterday afternoon'. Brown now says that he did not go to Downing Street.[10] The decision, rather than being announced in Parliament, was fed out in irregular fashion to the news media.

From an administrative point of view, manipulative populism has made government more short-termist and reckless and less likely to press ahead with intractable issues – like public service reform – which require a long-term commitment and do not generate immediate results. Discourse through the media is largely faked. The effect of this is to prevent government from examining let alone solving underlying problems, while simultaneously creating the illusion of immediate action. As a system of government it has been a calamity for British democracy, as I shall demonstrate in the next, and final, chapter.

14

THE TRIUMPH OF THE POLITICAL CLASS

'As party programmes become more similar, and as campaigns are in any case oriented more towards agreed goals rather than contentious means, there is a shrinkage in the degree to which electoral outcomes can determine government actions. Moreover, as the distinction between parties in office and those out of office becomes more blurred, the degree to which voters can punish parties even on the basis of generalised dissatisfaction is reduced. At the same time, participation in the electoral process implicates the voter and, by casting elections as the legitimate channel for political activity, other, potentially more effective, channels are made less legitimate. Democracy becomes a means of achieving social stability rather than social change, and elections become "dignified" parts of the constitution' – Richard S. Katz and Peter Mair, *How Parties Organize*

The Political Class has won its battle to control Britain. The civil service, Parliament, the political parties, the judiciary, the intelligence services and the media have all been captured or compromised. In an unannounced takeover of power, the public domain has been seized by the Political Class.

The victory is recent. It is certainly the case that key Political Class attitudes and techniques had become prevalent by the 1980s, and to some extent even before. Margaret Thatcher's government contained hints of what was to come, especially in its methods of press management, warm relations with big business and centralised command structure. But the defining moment was the arrival of Tony Blair and the General Election landslide of 1997. This event produced the first Political Class government, and it is essential to explain how this was engineered.

New Labour arose out of the debris of the traditional Labour Party. It won by wrenching Labour away from its deep roots within civil society and turning the party instead into a means of advancement for a deracinated political clique. This faction weakened or broke links with the trade unions. It stripped away the powers of the National Executive Committee. Fraudulent new organisations – above all the so-called 'national policy forum' – were set up in its place. These gave party members the illusion, but never the reality, of determining policy.

This reshaping of the Labour Party, as we have seen, was achieved by a tight-knit group of men and women – the so-called 'modernisers' – who slowly emerged after the landslide defeat of 1983, and became New Labour after the election of Tony Blair as leader in 1994. Their key weapon was the media. Peter Mandelson used the media methodology of ridicule, smear and leak to dazzling effect in order to isolate and destroy internal opposition within the Labour movement. 'Of course we want to use the media,' he noted in an unguarded moment, 'but the media will be our tools, our servants; we are no longer content to let them be our persecutors.' Far from being its enemy, as New Labour has always misleadingly claimed, the media was an accomplice right from the start.

The modernisers encountered a setback following Labour's election defeat in 1992. John Smith, who assumed the leadership after Neil Kinnock, was hostile to the Political Class. He felt that clear-cut ideological and moral distinctions lay at the heart of politics, and believed in socialist principles such as redistribution of wealth. This point of view caused the modernisers to undermine his leadership by constructing a narrative that John Smith's 1992 shadow Budget, which proposed higher taxes for the middle class, was responsible for the loss of the General Election. John Smith, who has since been written out of the official version of Labour

Party history, believed in Parliament and the power of the political rank and file as the mechanisms for effecting change. During John Smith's two-year period at the summit of the Labour Party, Peter Mandelson was frozen out, and Tony Blair for a while contemplated abandoning politics altogether.[1]

The sudden death of John Smith – a disaster for British public life – allowed the modernisers to strike. As ever, the media was the primary tool. With Tony Blair now in charge, and Peter Mandelson his primary adviser, they were able to target the media as an ally not just against internal opponents (though the smearing of awkward Cabinet ministers and back-benchers of course continued) but also in due course against representatives of civil society – civil servants, leaders of difficult pressure groups, critics of government policy, and so on.

There was some feeble resistance to the Political Class election triumph of 1997. A minority of Labour back-benchers articulated grass-roots alarm at the new governing methodology. They were mainly silenced by the New Labour machine. The most interesting by far of these insurgents was the left-winger Ken Livingstone. He successfully defied the centralised Labour Party apparatus of control to force himself into power as Mayor of London. Livingstone is the most fascinating contemporary politician: his achievements are as yet imperfectly understood, and cry out for fuller appreciation and study. He is an extremely important model of how to resist the hegemony of the Political Class.

Residual elements within the Conservative Party also sought to confront the Political Class, but they lacked Livingstone's adroitness and popular ease. William Hague, chosen as leader to succeed John Major after the 1997 landslide, was a paradoxical figure. On the one hand he possessed a number of hallmark Political Class attributes. He had been a political activist at university, was selected by the party machine to carry out duties as a special adviser, and was elected an MP at the young age of twenty-seven, becoming a Cabinet minister in his early thirties. Once elected party leader he followed through the Political Class project of stripping power from local constituencies. These attributes may have beguiled modernising Conservatives into supporting Hague after their chosen leadership candidate, the former Defence Secretary Michael Portillo, lost his Enfield seat at the General Election.

Yet Hague swiftly emerged as an anti-Political Class Tory leader. His key characteristics – outstanding public speaking and parliamentary debating skills, combined with a low emotional intelligence – were poorly attuned to the new era of post-democratic politics. Hague treated the London media elite with a shocking indifference, trying instead to appeal to Tory activists and party members. This meant that he drew ideological dividing lines between the Labour and Conservative parties, highlighting issues such as Europe, taxation and fears about mass immigration. His decision to award a high salience to these issues soon led to a sharp split inside his own Conservatives.

This argument that opened up inside the Tories after the 1997 election defeat was comparable in certain respects to the Labour divisions after 1983. On the one hand the elected leader, William Hague, sought to use traditional political methods (party conference, public oratory, distinctive policies) in order to address the anxieties of the Conservative Party rank and file. Against him stood the Political Class or – as they labelled themselves in emulation of the faction that had grabbed control of Labour – the Tory 'modernisers'. These argued that the Conservative Party could only survive if it turned its back on its own core supporters, while simultaneously embracing the insights and methodologies of New Labour. To begin with the most prominent member of this group was the shadow Chancellor Francis Maude. However, when Michael Portillo returned to Parliament after winning the Kensington and Chelsea by-election in November 1999, he instantly assumed leadership of the modernisers and started to make headway.*

---

* There were paradoxes in the Portillo position. He had been a rebel inside John Major's government, championing the Tory grass roots against the centre over Europe. The logic of the modernising posture he adopted after 1997 forced him to

The immediate result of Portillo's return was a vicious, low-intensity Conservative Party civil war. His modernising supporters copied the techniques patented by Peter Mandelson. Just as Mandelson had used assassination by media as a means of destroying trade union leaders and Labour MPs, so Michael Portillo's allies meticulously undermined William Hague as leader through a series of carefully planted leaks, many of them to *The Times*, the modernisers' newspaper.*

After William Hague's resignation in the wake of the 2001 General Election rout, the modernisers were expected to win the ensuing leadership election. Their candidate, Michael Portillo, was defeated against all the odds by an outsider, Iain Duncan Smith. Unlike William Hague, Duncan Smith had no Political Class characteristics of any kind. After a sketchy university career, he had joined the army as a career soldier, followed by a short spell in private industry. When he entered Parliament in 1992, he remarked that he knew almost nobody in the building, let alone possessed the large network of connections that former special advisers and political careerists always enjoy. Once in Parliament, Duncan Smith did not rise through the traditional route. He scorned job offers, instead leading the campaign against the Maastricht Treaty, which can be retrospectively understood as an anti-Political Class insurgency. In this he was strongly supported by many Tory activists.

The wholly unexpected arrival of Duncan Smith was viewed as a catastrophe by the modernisers, who at once resolved to remove him. As was the case with William Hague, their chief instrument

---

champion the centre against the grass roots. The intricacies of the Tory battle post-1997 lie outside the scope of this book, but are described in scrupulous detail by the political journalist Simon Walters in his *Tory Wars* (London: Politico's, 2001).

* For example, Tory official Michael Simmonds was sacked after being proved to have leaked to *The Times* a draft copy of a speech by William Hague's deputy Peter Lilley. Simmonds was in certain respects unfortunate, for he was not the most prolific leaker, and in this case other motives may have been at work.

was the media plot. A succession of stories appeared in the modernisers' preferred vehicle, *The Times*. However, the spur for Duncan Smith's assassination was a series of leaked allegations, which Tory modernisers put into the public domain through the BBC, though subsequently found to be false, that the Conservative leader had been fiddling his expenses. The destruction of Duncan Smith was a massive victory for the modernisers, and in retrospect can be seen to have put an end once and for all to Conservative Party efforts to resist capture by the Political Class.

In the short term, however, the modernisers had a problem. Despite their cleverly choreographed destruction of Duncan Smith, they could offer no candidate of sufficient calibre. Duncan Smith's successor Michael Howard was understood by many commentators to mark yet another reversion to traditional politics. A shallow reading of Michael Howard's brief period as Tory leader, which saw the Conservatives revert to concentration on issues such as immigration and law and order, would suggest they were right.

Yet this was not quite the case. It is true that Michael Howard, a vital transitional figure, was unable for personal reasons – age, image, circumstance, an unhelpful back story – to put his modernising insights fully into practice. But he left behind two legacies after his brief spell in office. First, he understood from the start that his crucial role was to prepare the ground for a successor. Howard prepared the way for the succession by David Cameron, the candidate the Tory modernisers had been searching for ever since the election disaster of 1997. In effect Cameron was a continuation of Michael Portillo by other means. The capture of the Tory leadership by David Cameron meant that the modernising tendency was at last in control not just of the governing party, but also of the principal opposition. His arrival as Tory leader marked the triumph of the Political Class. It appeared to guarantee its survival, no matter which political party was technically in power.

Howard's second achievement was also important. Intellectually he understood the revolution brought about by New Labour:

explicitly, that politics was a matter of technique, pursued by experts, adopted as a separate calling. This approach led straight to the shattering insight: *in post-democratic politics the great majority of voters do not matter at all.*

How the Political Class Won the 2005 General Election

This insight was put into effect by both main parties at the 2005 General Election. They had learned it from the American political consultant Karl Rove, supreme architect of George W. Bush's electoral triumphs, and acknowledged as the high priest of modern campaign management. In the 2004 presidential election Rove and his acolytes used a highly sophisticated piece of computer software named 'Voter Vault' to sift out the tiny minority of voters who would determine the result.

Some 120 million people went to the polls in the United States. All voters in states where the result was a foregone conclusion, and all voters with a fixed preference, were instantly eliminated from the calculations. As far as Rove was concerned only a handful of voters in the swing states of Florida, Ohio and a few others mattered. And long before election day came, Voter Vault knew every relevant piece of information about these highly desirable people: their type of car, their social class, the size of their house and their likely religious and sexual preference. It used a mass of information about ordinary citizens, which most people wrongly assume is private: our credit card details, our shopping habits, what magazines we read, what restaurants we eat at, how far we are in debt.

This information enabled analysts to sift out those who were likely to vote Republican, vote Democrat or – the category to which Rove paid fullest attention – were swing voters and torn between the two. In the final weeks of the campaign the Voter Vault machinery enabled campaign managers to guide their voters to the polls with the precision of cruise missiles turning a street corner in central Baghdad.* Voter Vault told them who to ring, which questions to ask and what information to convey. In this sense the American presidential election of 2004 was the first ever 'designer' election in history, with policies tailored not for the country at large, but for a small number of individual voters.

As George W. Bush's 2004 victory reverberated, both the main British political parties were eager to learn the lesson. The Conservative Party paid a huge sum to acquire this Voter Vault technology. Tory co-chairman Maurice Saatchi proudly told me: 'We have a much more scientific weapon than anything we have seen before. We like to think that we are well ahead of the other parties.' Saatchi added that 'millions of pounds' would be spent on it.[2]

In America, Voter Vault's probing intelligence focused on the few million people who determined the result. In Britain it had an even narrower focus. Its all-seeing eye did not engage with retired colonels in Tunbridge Wells. Safe Tory voters were simply taken for granted. Likewise Voter Vault excluded from consideration unemployed shipworkers in Glasgow.

Liam Fox, the Conservative Party chairman, told me that Voter Vault was dedicated to just 900,000 people, or 2 per cent of Britain's 45 million adult population.[3] Tory strategists identified these voters as the only ones who even faintly mattered. To qualify for membership of this privileged category, Fox said, voters had to possess three attributes. First, they must live in one of the 167 target marginal seats, most of them in the central or west Midlands, which the Conservatives needed to secure if they were to claim election victory. Second, they did not vote Conservative last time. Third, they must be ready to toy with the idea of doing

---

* For example, according to Voter Vault, any US voter who drove a Volvo was almost certain to be a Democrat, while someone who owned both a dog and gun was virtually certain to vote Republican. In Britain, someone who has lived in the same house for more than ten years and has very low personal indebtedness is extremely likely to vote Tory. By contrast, heavily indebted people who have recently moved house are likely to fall into the category of swing voters.

so in 2005. Central Office strategists added that Voter Vault's precision – experts call it 'geo-demographic segmentation' – enabled them to identify every last one of these people.

The moment one of these individuals was unearthed, he or she was targeted with a pitiless accuracy. Election literature, focused on voters' special concerns, was remorselessly dispatched. These voters were called – in some cases repeatedly – from special Conservative phone banks. Armed with Voter Vault's insights, these well-paid staff showed an unnerving insight into the needs and preoccupations of the voters they spoke to.

What these voters could not know is that they are just dupes in a clever marketing exercise. Not long after the call was made he or she would probably receive further party literature, which would seem strangely sympathetic. Again, the voter was not to know that the literature had been specially tailored for voters like him or her.

All Tory policy-making was aimed directly at these swing voters in target seats, and this technique proved extremely effective. Though the party benefited only from a tiny national swing, the system of special targeting proved decisive in marginal seats. This enabled the party to win many more seats than its national performance alone would have suggested. In his final party conference speech ahead of the General Election, Michael Howard emphasised five issues – law and order, health, education, tax and immigration. These were the five points which, intensive research showed, most closely concerned the Voter Vault 900,000. New Labour embarked on an identical policy-making exercise, using similar technology.

It is this that explains the yawning boredom and lack of passion in the 2005 General Election. The political parties no longer took their ideas and beliefs from the aspirations of their membership, which had in any case largely disappeared. Nor did they refer back to their own underlying philosophies and beliefs. Instead they set policies only after remorselessly testing them on target voters in the key swing seats. Because all parties tried out their programmes on the same categories, their policies ended up being virtually identical, though strategists sometimes attempted to obscure this similarity by the use of rhetoric and deceit.

This obsession with swing voters in key marginals also helps to explain why politicians started to use the same language. One day during the 2005 election I accompanied Michael Howard as he went campaigning in the marginal seat of Winchester. I took with me the pledge cards of the three main parties. After Howard had left town I tested them on local people, asking them to match the pledges to the party leaders. Voters were unable to tell the difference. All the party pledges were carefully drafted to ensure they were inoffensive. The Labour Party's promises included 'your children with the best start', 'your child achieving more' and 'your family better off'. No one could disagree with these sentiments, but they lacked meaning. No one urges children to achieve less or campaigns for families to be worse off.

The poverty of aspiration lay with the Political Class. It did not want to engage in the sensible, civilised, grown-up conversation with voters that had been normal when Britain enjoyed a reasonably healthy democracy. It had debased the language of public discourse. Voters and politicians were no longer equals, sharing the same values, the same language, and a mutual respect. Indeed they very rarely engaged at first hand at all. The preferred method of communication involved marketing techniques drawn from the modern advertising industry, with everything that implied in terms of manipulation and deceit. To discover the views of voters, politicians had given up canvassing them directly. Instead political machines made use of so-called focus groups, closed occasions where experts seek to divine the attitudes and prejudices of 'representative' members of the general public. These events are controlled by the Political Class, which sets the agenda, asks the questions, and summarises the conclusions.

Modern elections do pay some acknowledgement to structures of the earlier period of representative democracy. There are still hustings, pamphleteering, election launches. But these are now carefully structured events, manipulated by strategists and overseen by operatives from the party machines. I saw this at first hand on the day Tony Blair launched the 2005 election manifesto, as I followed him to a leisure centre in the little town of Rushden in Northamptonshire.

Walkabout With Tony Blair

Everything that occurred that day was choreographed to make sure that those who saw the Prime Minister on the television news that night would assume he was mingling with ordinary voters. The cameras followed the Prime Minister as he appeared to make a speech to friendly voters, then lingered behind to shake hands and chat with local people. Tony Blair was at his most charming and accomplished as he basked in his warm reception.

The little scene looked like democracy in action. It sounded like democracy in action. It even smelt like democracy in action. But in truth it was nothing of the sort. The whole event was a fraud. Not one single ordinary voter was present in the leisure centre where Tony Blair spoke.

The event, I was able to establish, had even been kept a closely guarded secret from the public. The friendly crowd shown on TV screens were supporters who had been secretly alerted just hours before by Labour Party bosses. The Labour Party officials arranging the occasion tried to stop me getting in. When I got in, they tried to have me thrown out. When I tried to speak to the Prime Minister, they attempted to prevent me. Had any ordinary voter somehow got to hear that Tony Blair was in town and tried to meet him, he or she would also have been barred from what was a tightly guarded event, closed off to the general public.

Tony Blair had made sure he was among friends, so there were no worries about a hostile reaction, or even an awkward question. The media presence was strictly controlled, and confined to a select audience of regional journalists. This kind of fabricated and artificial public hustings was repeated hundreds of times up and down Britain during the 2005 election. There was no engagement with voters, just a piece of choreography designed to send a carefully chosen message to target voters through evening news soundbites.

This relentless focus on the manipulation of a tiny slice of the British electorate is a degradation of democracy. The lavish attention on just a few means the disenfranchisement of the majority.

The Consequences of Post-Democracy

The man who met me at Becontree station had fair hair, blue eyes, and the plausible air of a semi-educated man. As we shook hands, a passing car honked its horn in approbation, and the driver waved. My new friend took me to a local tea shop, which appeared to double as his campaign headquarters.

He told me his life story. His father was a corporal in the Life Guards, who became a chauffeur on retirement. His birth had been protracted, so his mother was asked to leave the hospital before he was born. She was told, or so he told me, 'We need the bed for people drafted off the boats.'

Richard Barnbrook was the campaign organiser for the British National Party in Barking and Dagenham. It was May 2006, and I was writing a story about the local elections. At the time of our meeting, there were no BNP councillors in the borough. It was instantly obvious this was about to change in a dramatic way. I would say that half the people Barnbrook met as he walked through the local estates either showed support, or friendly interest, in the BNP.

Phil, a shaven-headed man standing outside the front door of his house in a quiet crescent, told us this: 'I want to make a statement about what's going on. Half the world is getting dumped round here. I'm a retailer. I work fifty to sixty hours a week. I'm working my guts out. And I see people from nowhere getting a Mercedes cheap. My daughter was ill and it took us ten days to get to see my GP. People come in from Eastern Europe and get seen straight up.'

The next door we knocked on belonged to a travel broker. 'Dagenham isn't what it used to be,' he said. 'I'd certainly consider voting BNP. We're working-class. We've got two little kids.' He was a dark-haired man, standing in front of a nice, comfortable, well-kept family home. Surveys show that the typical BNP member is respectable working-class or lower-middle-class, some distance from the bottom of the heap. 'I don't know how I will vote, I haven't really considered,' he said to Barnbrook. 'My personal opinion is that family tax credits are no use to us whatsoever. I'd certainly consider giving you my vote.'

Over the road there was a man clipping a hedge. We strode across. Richard Barnbrook stretched out his hand. 'Labour wouldn't know a socialist view if it bit them in the backside,' said the man, putting down his clippers, 'and I believe in the working class.' For decades Dagenham and Barking had been heartland Labour. But the voters were switching to the BNP in large numbers because Labour no longer articulated their concerns. It was all too clear that the BNP had acquired the campaigning skills and ability to make a personal connection with the voters that the mainstream parties have forgotten.

The following Saturday I went canvassing with the local Labour MP, Jon Cruddas. Fewer than a dozen people gathered at the little community centre which formed our base, among them the famous old trade unionist Sid Kallar, whose first political experience was fighting Mosley's blackshirts in the East End in the 1930s.

Before moving to Dagenham in 2001, Cruddas worked as a special adviser inside Downing Street. The progress of most former Downing Street advisers has been stellar. Cruddas's colleague David Miliband, who worked alongside him in Number 10, is now Foreign Secretary and tipped as the next Labour leader.

I would judge that Cruddas could have gone just as far. But he chose not to. Cruddas turned down offers of ministerial jobs, and concentrated on his constituency, where there was a battle to be fought. As we drove around Dagenham, Cruddas pointed out to me the features of the area: the mainly derelict Ford works, which used to provide the local jobs; the crossroads site where the Bethel

Full Gospel Church is applying for planning permission to build a church to cater for the incoming African population by accommodating 2,500 worshippers; the 'for sale' signs springing up all over the borough, indicating that the whites are moving out.

Cruddas told me how New Labour had turned its back on its real supporters. He told me how the party had been 'hollowed out' by the modernisers, and its membership taken for granted. He described how the focus on swing voters had caused policy to be constructed for an aspirational middle class, which meant that Labour's core working-class vote was systematically excluded. In Dagenham this strategy deprived ordinary voters of the things they desperately needed: social housing, decent schools, a voice. He told how Dagenham had been offered one of New Labour's fashionable Academy Schools. When the borough turned it down, it was starved of government funding. What follows is a summary of what Cruddas told me as we walked around his constituency, dropping copies of the anti-fascist newspaper *Searchlight* into letterboxes:

The originality of New Labour lies in the method by which policy is not deductively produced from a series of core economic or philosophical assumptions, or even a body of ideas, but rather is scientifically constructed out of the preferences and prejudices of the swing voter in the swing seat.

It is a brilliant political movement whose primary objective is to reproduce itself – and to achieve this it must dominate the politics of middle England. The government is not a coalition of traditions and interests who initiate policy and debate; rather it is a power elite whose *modus operandi* is the retention of power. In short, the political priorities and concerns of a specific minority of swing voters in a highly select part of the country will become ever more dominant.

As a politician for what is regarded as a safe working-class seat, the implications of this political calibration are immense. The system acts at the expense of communities like these – arguably those most in need. On the one hand, we see a policy-making process that is driven by the preferences and prejudices of swing voters codified increasingly with reference to Conservative intellectual traditions and, on the other, the empirical realities of modern Britain, which demand an alternative set of policies in order to confront inequality.[4]

This book has many villains, and few heroes. Elizabeth Filkin and Sir Alistair Graham, who lost their jobs because they defied the Political Class and tried to sustain standards, are two of them. Jon Cruddas, a politician who fought for his constituents and defied his party machine, is another. In 2007 Cruddas fought a long campaign to be elected deputy leader of the Labour Party in an attempt to confront Britain's disastrous political culture. He failed, of course.

It was plain to me, walking through Dagenham with Jon Cruddas, that most of the defecting Labour voters were fairly decent people doing their best for their families: community-minded, law-abiding, hard-working, middle-of-the-road. They were victims of the Political Class who had been left with no one to speak up for them, and nowhere to go. Neither the Conservative opposition, nor the New Labour government, is capable of speaking for these people.

The same story is starting to repeat itself around Britain. The BNP in Barking and Dagenham, Dewsbury, Leeds and Burnley; Respect in Whitechapel; the SNP in Scotland: they are all engaged in a common insurgency against the Political Class. This estrangement between a tiny governing elite and mainstream British society is one of the overwhelming themes of our age, and it will only get more desperate, and more dangerous.

The Paradox of the Political Class

The immortal achievement of Sir Lewis Namier was to show in meticulous detail how politics actually worked. Previous historians, from Lord Macaulay to G. M. Trevelyan, had constructed an account of the eighteenth century that involved a two-party rivalry between Whigs and Tories, underpinning a constitutional monarchy, with a modern Cabinet system based on a majority in the House of Commons.

Namier demonstrated that this elaborately constructed account – the so-called 'Whig interpretation of history' – was a myth. Through remorseless attention to detail, and by focusing on the motivation and interests of individual ministers and MPs, he told a different story. He revealed that the idea of party was mainly a fabrication, that changes of government were no more than reshuffles among political cliques, and that politicians at the time were primarily motivated by venality and self-interest.

Namier's realistic account of parliamentary politics, and bleak assumptions about human nature, have upset many scholars, at the time of his writing and since. In the 1950s the historian Sir Herbert Butterfield sparked a famous controversy when he accused Sir Lewis Namier and his school of taking ideas out of history. Recently Butterfield recruited an ally in the shape of Gordon Brown, who denounced the Namierite school in the following terms: 'I studied history. It is fascinating. There is a Namier school of history, which suggests that everything is less to do with ideas or popular concerns and all to do with manoeuvrings of the elites. I do not accept that. I think that the real story of decision-making in politics is about ideas and ideals and is about the policies that reflect the concerns of people.'[5] Gordon Brown's criticisms, however, were based on a misconstruction. Sir Lewis had tried to portray politics as it was, and never set out to describe it as it ought to be. It should be borne in mind that Gordon Brown himself is most readily understood as a politician in the school of Namier, adroit at using patronage and connection to maintain a power base, operating most naturally through clients and retainers, happiest when striking private deals away from the public eye. Above all Brown has enthusiastically supported the modernisers' preferred methodology of triangulation, which deliberately drains the meaning out of political ideas by converting them into a tactical device.

The argument of this book is that the insights of Sir Lewis Namier have once again become relevant. The overwhelming fact about contemporary British public life is the collapse of political parties. Their continuing formal existence provides camouflage for the re-emergence of a system which has little in common with the comparatively robust representative democracy that served Britain during the first three-quarters of the twentieth century.

The primary purpose of General Elections is emphatically not so that the voice of voters can be heard. Indeed elections have regained their Namierite function as public stunts, whose primary purpose is an ostentatious affirmation of Political Class hegemony (see the powerful diagnosis from the political scientists Richard Katz and Peter Mair quoted at the top of this chapter). This in turn has led to the weakening or collapse of the adversarial party system taught in school textbooks. Instead British politics in the post-democratic era now bears many of the characteristics of a pre-democratic court. The characteristic figure of our age is the favourite – an Alastair Campbell under Tony Blair or an Ed Balls under Gordon Brown – who owes his status to influence and has limited political legitimacy beyond the all-important connection with a powerful patron.

This structure is designed to prevent political change and restrict the expression of popular discontent. This means that we should expect the same manifestations of anger from men and women deprived of access to the political system that were normal in the pre-democratic era. Britain is moving in precisely this direction. The Burnley riots of 2001 or the fuel protests the year before show that Britain is resuming the pattern of extra-parliamentary violence and disruption which dried up with the emergence of mass suffrage. The renewal of this method of political activity is the inevitable consequence of the triumph of the Political Class.

The problem with the Political Class is paradoxical. Its members care too much about politics. This single-minded fanaticism distinguishes the Political Class from earlier types of governing elites, which were grounded within civil society, and had a mass of loyalties, interests and affiliations that lay outside the centre of power. This fact that the political elite was rooted outside Westminster had several desirable consequences.

At a personal level, electoral rejection or loss of a ministerial job was less likely to be a disaster. There were other things that mattered in life, other places to go.* This mainstream sensibility explains, for example, the willingness of an earlier generation of ministers to resign from their jobs in cases of fault or dishonour.

The twenty-first-century Political Class, which embarks on politics as a career and is dependent on professional survival for material subsistence, is largely deprived of this perspective. Politics has become too important, and that has led to a besetting conceptual error: the confusion of success with virtue. Just as a businessman scores his performance by his market share, or an athlete is judged by the records he breaks, so a politician is today assessed on the rank he reaches, and the elections he wins. As Tony Blair defiantly remarked shortly before leaving 10 Downing Street: 'And anyway, like it or not, I have won three elections and am still standing as I leave office.'[†]

This rigorously professional viewpoint excludes both the moral purpose and the profound engagement with the nation at large which distinguishes politics from almost all other activities. Previous generations of politicians – Charles James Fox, Robert Peel, W. E. Gladstone, Churchill – all perceived that defeat or self-sacrifice could be honourable, and sometimes bring about much more lasting effects.

For the Political Class, victory alone has become the criterion of virtue. This means, for example, that it has become customary to fight elections by espousing ideas and beliefs politicians do not believe. This system of 'triangulation' was borrowed by New

---

* William Waldegrave, a Cabinet minister who had been tipped to lead the Conservative Party, but retrained as an investment banker after losing his parliamentary seat in 1997, showed an understanding of the wider possibilities of life of a kind that hints at an outlook which pre-dates the Political Class.

† This remark can be found in Blair's lecture on 'Public Life', delivered at Reuters in Canary Wharf on 12 June 2007. This speech received publicity for its attack on a 'feral media'.

Labour from Bill Clinton in 1997, and has since been adopted by the Tory modernisers under David Cameron. It is based on the idea that political leaders must occupy political territory in order to deny space to opponents. This strategic plan, while fantastically successful as an electoral ploy, has inevitably sucked grand ideas and passion out of politics. The client press has habitually awarded praise to New Labour and Tory modernisers when they abandon long-cherished beliefs. By contrast those politicians who go on fighting for causes they believe in out of principle and disregarding their personal interests, like the Tory euro-sceptics or 'Old Labour', are held in contempt. This is exactly the wrong way round.

Equally damaging, politicians have ceased to be squeamish about the methods they use in order to win. The contemporary obsession with success at all costs licenses fraud, deceit and the manipulation of voters. The use of these methods in turn causes the mutual distrust between the electorate and politicians to deepen further. Overall, the infatuation with the methodology of winning elections is a distortion of politics in very much the same way as the restless focus on short-term profits resulting in giant bonuses paid to City traders is a distortion of contemporary capitalism. Both are a result of a false set of values that cannot be sustained without inflicting grave damage on social and economic systems.

The obsession with politics has had a third debilitating consequence. The Political Class believes that all values are based in the political sphere. This insistence on the primacy of the political is dangerous. It is complacent, and factually wrong, to assume that democracy is the same as liberty, tolerance and fairness. The principle of liberty and tolerance was embedded in the British constitution long before universal suffrage and the emergence of what we think of today as democracy. Often – as we learned in 1930s Germany, when Hitler came to power with a popular mandate – democratic values can be profoundly inimical to freedom and tolerance. The example of German fascism is extreme, but it is by no means unique. Almost all democratic politicians in search of wide popularity come under ferocious pressures to oppress minorities and cancel ordinary freedoms.

This is why the presence of our great institutions – judiciary, Parliament, civil service, a free press and (in the private sphere) the family – have such profound importance. They offer protection against the populism that is such a potent feature of the democratic system. They stand for values – fairness, decency, protection of minorities, freedom under law – which inevitably come under strain in a democracy.

Members of the Political Class, as we have seen, regard civil society as a threat because it represents a giant area of the public domain which stands outside its control. Its earlier members reached adulthood in the 1960s. The prevailing teaching inside universities during that decade was that national institutions were instruments of oppression. Marxist thinking dismissed Parliament and the rule of law as 'bourgeois democracy' and instruments of class oppression, while the anarchist left claimed that they bore down on the naturally unfettered human spirit. Suspicion of what it regards as 'establishment' bodies remains to this day a powerful part of the intellectual ballast of the Political Class.

Conceptually, members of the Political Class seem unable to grasp that freestanding institutions embody individual freedom against the oppression of powerful individuals, corporations and the state. As a result the Political Class has turned on the institutions of civil society and attempted to destroy them. In doing so it has confounded the British system of representative democracy, and replaced it with a direct method of communication with the people, mediated mainly through a client media. This methodology of government – manipulative populism – is full of peril, and profoundly unstable. The weakening of institutions means that government today operates under fewer restraints than at any time since the brief attempt by James II to establish an absolute monarchy, untrammelled by Parliament or the rule of law, in the 1680s.

The Rebirth of a Ruling Class

Looking back over the political history of the past two or three hundred years, it is possible to discern three phases. The first period, lasting until the mid- or late nineteenth century, was characterised by elite rule and fragmentary political parties or factions. The great majority of the population did not possess the vote, and were excluded from formal political engagement. The mob nevertheless expressed its feelings through extra-parliamentary agitation, which often erupted into violence. There were a number of times during the pre-democratic period, above all the 1790s and 1820s, when this kind of activity became so widespread that the propertied classes feared revolution.

This alarm helped to hasten the extension of suffrage, a process which began with the Great Reform Act of 1832 and was only completed in 1928 when women were granted the same right to vote as men. This gradual extension of the franchise was accompanied by the emergence of a new phenomenon: mass political parties. This second phase of healthy civic engagement reached its fullest expression in the decade following the Second World War, when perhaps 20 per cent of the adult population was a party member.

We have now entered a third stage, the result of a very profound and rapid change in political structures. Our predicament today has almost nothing in common with the period of mass political participation of only fifty years ago. The resemblance, however, to the pre-democratic phase is uncannily close.

Once again the British system is defined by a sharp contrast between an arrogant and self-interested ruling elite and the mass of the population. In the eighteenth and for most of the nineteenth century this distinction arose because most people were legally denied access to the ballot box. Today the right to vote is universal but the methodology of post-democracy – manipulation, targeting, intra-party collusion – means that the great majority of voters have been disenfranchised in subtler ways.

In certain respects today's Political Class has a great deal in common with the elites that governed Britain before the widening of the franchise. Like the eighteenth-century aristocracy, it finds it hard to conceptualise the dividing line between the public sphere and private interest. It uses the resources of the state for private or factional advantage and is hostile to the bourgeois notion of personal privacy.

There is an important distinction, however. Members of pre-modern governing elites (with certain partial exceptions, such as Hippolyte Taine's emasculated French aristocracy in the pre-revolutionary period) owed their position to a territorial base, military strength, mercantile dominance, or some other source of status independent of the central power. By contrast the potency of today's Political Class is a pure function of the state, akin to the *nomenklatura* that dominated Eastern European states during the period of Soviet rule.

This means that in order to guarantee its survival into the long term, the Political Class has no choice but to secure a massive increase in the reach and scope of the centre. This means further emasculating Parliament, suborning the judiciary, consolidating its hold over a client press, widening the alliance with big business, strengthening the powers of the intelligence services, and sustaining the attack on the freedoms of ordinary citizens. In all these respects, the invasion of Iraq, and associated 'war on terror', has served the purposes of the Political Class exceptionally well.

Given this entrenchment it is almost certain, therefore, that the next great movement will come from outside the Political Class. Just as the Political Class has emerged from the wreckage of the party system, so it is certain to produce its own antithesis. At some stage a British politician may well discover a new language of public discourse and methodology of political engagement which communicates simply and plainly to voters.

It is by no means certain that such a politician would be a benign figure. If he is not, there is the frightening prospect that he will be able to adapt the techniques of manipulative populism to his own purposes. But even a new political movement intent on restoring individual freedom and the potency and independence of civil society may struggle to succeed. The Political Class is extremely well entrenched not merely at Westminster but in all the institutions of the British state, and is growing ever more accustomed to handling the machinery of power.

Epilogue

The appointment of Gordon Brown as Prime Minister in June 2007 led to an interesting and significant experiment: an attempt to renew the Political Class from within. Gordon Brown, as we have already seen, was one of the founding members of the Political Class. He was a career politician who both in opposition and during his long period as Chancellor of the Exchequer had been an enthusiastic and expert proponent of the techniques of manipulative populism. His disdain for the traditional structures and institutions of the British state can hardly be overstated.

However, within days of gaining power Gordon Brown was hard at work signalling an apparent rapprochement with the British Establishment. In a series of speeches the Prime Minister repeatedly showed that he understood how the governing methodology of the previous decade had corrupted British public life.[1] He promised to restore trust in British politics and bring back the integrity that had been lost during the Blair period in government.[2]

Most importantly of all, he made a series of very welcome, necessary and powerful moves that were aimed at restoring the integrity of the domestic civil service. He at once reversed the Order in Council which under the Blair government had given certain Special Advisers the power to give orders to career officials. This meant that there was no immediate attempt to replace Jonathan Powell, the shadowy Downing Street chief of staff who had played such a key role as broker between the international corporate elite and the domestic government machine. The new Prime Minister creditably made no attempt to find his own equivalent to Alastair Campbell, the legendary Downing Street press secretary who had been allowed to convert the morality, imperatives and deadlines of tabloid journalism into the driving force behind British government. The new Downing Street press secretary, Mike Ellam, was hired from the Treasury. Cautious and unostentatious, he was at all times open to the charge of dullness. However, he brought an immediate end to the culture of cheating, distortion, artifice and fabrication that had been the defining feature of Downing Street under Blair.

The winner from this new state of affairs seemed to be the civil service. The post of Cabinet Secretary, guardian of integrity in the British system of government, had atrophied under Tony Blair. Gordon Brown restored it, in part at least. Sir Gus O'Donnell, appointed (with the approval of Gordon Brown) in August 2005, less than two years before the end of the Blair government, was permitted to establish himself as a serious figure of some weight at the heart of Whitehall. If Sir Gus succeeds in bringing integrity back into government, he could in due course come to be regarded as the most significant Cabinet Secretary since Sir Maurice Hankey, the first occupant of the post.

O'Donnell did not secure backing for a new Act of Parliament to put protections for the independence of the civil service on a statutory basis – the measure for which his predecessor Lord Wilson had unsuccessfully lobbied five years previously. However, the Constitutional Renewal Bill, to be formally announced in the 2008 Queen's Speech, contained some of the provisions Lord Wilson had envisaged. Disappointingly, the first draft of the bill left ministers with very significant control over the employment conditions of civil servants, including promotion and dismissal. It allowed Special Advisers to manage and direct officials, and undermined the concept of 'fair and open competition' in both the Foreign Office and the Civil Service.[3]

In what seemed a remarkable admission that the Political Class had abused its connection with the security apparatus ahead of the Iraq War, Brown ordered that steps should be taken to halt the political use of intelligence material.[4] However, he kept in post Sir John Scarlett, the intelligence expert who had controversially been made chief of the Secret Intelligence Service by Tony Blair, despite his role in the preparation of the discredited dossier on Saddam Hussein's weapons of mass destruction. In mid-2007, according to reports, Gordon Brown quietly decided to renew Sir John Scarlett's contract as head of the Secret Intelligence Service.[5]

Attempts to undermine the monarchy, an intermittent feature of the Blair regime, ceased. The new Prime Minister abandoned the republican rhetoric that had been a feature of his own early days at the Treasury. He and his wife Sarah developed a warm connection with the Queen and other members of the royal family which contrasted sharply with the chilliness of the Tony and (in particular) Cherie Blair era. Prince Charles and the Duchess of Cornwall were invited, for example, to a private dinner in the Browns' Downing Street flat.[6] This event proved cheerful enough to stimulate a friendship between the new Prime Minister and the heir to the throne. The two men entered into a correspondence in which they discussed subjects of mutual interest including urban renewal, government plans for the creation of environmentally friendly 'eco-towns', youth volunteering and ways of helping the integration of immigrants into British society. Gordon Brown even set aside his long-standing aversion to the dress code of the British Establishment, consenting to wear White Tie – which suited him well – on state occasions.

In his early weeks in office the new Prime Minister announced a series of measures designed to help restore a more old-fashioned and scrupulous connection between the executive and the legislative arms of the state. He had promised to 'restore power to parliament in order to build the trust of British people in our democracy'.[7] He made international treaties and declarations of war subject to the approval of MPs, and indicated that he would return to the traditional system of making announcements to the House of Commons first.[8]

Personal integrity made a reappearance in the heart of government. The new Prime Minister and his wife did not demand special discounts from retailers, or use officials to run personal errands. They did not beg free holidays from chance acquaintances, such as the seedy billionaire and Prime Minister of Italy

Silvio Berlusconi. In 2008 Gordon and Sarah Brown announced that they would spend their summer holiday in a modest holiday resort in Suffolk.

Chancers such as Lord Levy, the music tycoon and prime ministerial tennis partner who helped arrange Labour's finances during the Blair era, were no longer conspicuous in Downing Street. Apparently resentful at his exclusion, Lord Levy launched a series of vindictive personal attacks on the Prime Minister.[9]

There were, at first, some signs that Cabinet government had returned. Many Cabinet ministers notoriously remained mute during the Blair term of office. On arrival at No. 10, Gordon Brown encouraged them to speak up. The first few Cabinet meetings of the Brown administration lasted much longer than the brief and truncated affairs of the Blair era. They were said sometimes even to run beyond the one o'clock lunchtime news bulletin, an almost unknown occurrence during the Blair regime. Government departments – with the notable exception of the Treasury – gained in autonomy and confidence. The Foreign Office, treated with naked contempt during the Blair era, started to perform more like a department of state under the leadership of David Miliband, arguably the most intellectually gifted Foreign Secretary since Douglas Hurd a generation earlier.

Another case in point was the Department for Work and Pensions (DWP). Under the Blair administration this Whitehall organisation lacked administrative competence, let alone intellectual courage. With the arrival of Gordon Brown in 10 Downing Street James Purnell, the competent and ambitious new Work and Pensions chief, used the power and clout of his department to propose a series of bracing reforms to the benefits system.[10] It would have been impossible for a Cabinet minister to exercise this kind of dynamic influence at DWP during the Blair era. Ironically, this was in large part because the Treasury during the period when Gordon Brown was Chancellor turned the DWP – along with other government departments – into its private satrapy.

In short, the incoming Prime Minister made significant steps towards restoring the integrity of government, which had been altogether lost during Tony Blair's term of office. Regrettably, however, Gordon Brown was not willing, or perhaps unable, to turn his back completely on all the governing techniques of the Political Class. He enthusiastically embraced the political system of triangulation. This meant that Brown refused to pursue political objectives with either clarity or authenticity. Instead he used ideas and policies as technical devices for electoral advantage. In the short term these devices worked brilliantly for the new Prime Minister, but in the medium term they played a role in discrediting his premiership.

The first sign that Brown was ready to make triangulation his hallmark in office came before he even reached 10 Downing Street, in the budget of March 2007. The ambitious Chancellor seized the moment to slash the basic rate of income tax by 2p to 20p in the pound. This move enabled Gordon Brown – who by then was probably already entertaining the idea of an election in the autumn of 2007 – to present himself to the country as a tax-cutting Chancellor, thus depriving the Conservative opposition of vital territory. The announcement of the tax cut was hailed the day after the budget as a brilliant stroke which would win middle-class voters over to the Labour cause. Only the most perceptive observers noted at the time that Gordon Brown paid for his showy tax cut by abolishing the 10p rate for lower earners. The future Prime Minister was financing his bribe for the middle classes through penalising Labour's long-suffering core supporters, a cynical strategy for which he would pay a heavy price when the Labour Party revolted against it the following year.

Brown, who looked impregnable during his early months of office, was determined – like Tony Blair before him – to forge a cross-party coalition at the centre of British politics. Upon becoming Prime Minister, he smashed through party lines to make a series of appointments that seemed to secure the centre ground. The formal naval chief Admiral West joined the Labour front bench in the House of Lords. So did Digby Jones, the former director-general of the Confederation of British Industry. Shaun Woodward, the one-time Conservative MP who had defected to the Labour Party under Tony Blair, was promoted to the Cabinet as Northern Ireland Secretary. Two Tory MPs, the former soldier Patrick Mercer and John Bercow, an ambitious though out-of-favour backbencher with little chance of party preferment, were persuaded to carry out work on behalf of the government in an astonishing transgression of normal party boundaries. The biggest capture of all, however, was the defection of Quentin Davies, a former member of the Conservative Shadow Cabinet under right-wing Iain Duncan Smith. Davies, a florid-faced former merchant banker and Tory MP of the old school, permitted himself to be convinced that politically he had more in common with the new Prime Minister than the Tory leader David Cameron.

The Brown administration of 2007 was a hegemonic project aimed at stifling political debate and squeezing out traditional party structures. By the late summer of that year Gordon Brown, with a clear eye to an autumn election, appeared to have shut his rival David Cameron out of the mainstream. His greatest triumph came when he persuaded Margaret Thatcher to visit Downing Street, a calculated repeat of a similar stunt pulled off by Tony Blair just three weeks after winning the 1997 election. Aides to the Prime Minister were exultant. In the medium term, however, this stunt turned sour. It came to be a seen as a bleakly cynical moment, not merely an affront to millions of Labour supporters who had always hated Margaret Thatcher but also a moment of calculating hypocrisy from Gordon Brown himself, who had made his early reputation by denouncing Margaret Thatcher as a moral reprobate in lethal terms. Seen in retrospect, the moment Gordon Brown welcomed Thatcher to No. 10 marks the start of his decline. He ceased to be seen as straightforward by the electorate as a whole, while the Labour Party turned against him.

Gordon Brown made one further fatal strategic decision. Like Tony Blair he allowed himself to become a client of the media tycoon Rupert Murdoch. Anticipating the premiership, Gordon Brown had been dispensing favours to Murdoch for some time. At one Treasury party for the media, thrown in the summer of 2006 while he was still angling to become Prime Minister, this special treatment was obvious. From ordinary newspapers, only political editors were present. But all political reporters from News International titles appeared to have been invited. Furthermore, it was bleakly noted by journalists from rival papers that News International hacks were allowed to monopolise Gordon Brown's company for the majority of the evening.

This favouritism became yet more blatant in late September 2007, when Gordon Brown delivered his first speech as leader to the Labour Party conference. Given a specially privileged set of seats close to the front were the most senior News International figures – executive chairman Les Hinton, *Sun* editor Rebekah Wade and others. Gordon Brown was placing News International executives in the same privileged category as elite members of the British governing party.

As the following week's Tory conference ended, the Prime Minister sought to deepen his friendship with News International yet further by inviting Rupert Murdoch to Chequers. The guest at this power weekend was Alan Greenspan, the former chairman of the United States Federal Reserve who received an honorary knighthood, at Brown's suggestion, in 2002.

These connections showed that Gordon Brown was determined never to turn his back on the international power elite who had provided the key buttress for Tony Blair in power. This strategic decision had a number of important consequences for the Brown premiership. Within months the new Prime Minister discovered the uses of government information as a method of paying tribute to his powerful patron. For example, on 14 November 2007 Gordon Brown trailed his statement on national security in the *Sun* newspaper. Though relations with Murdoch were doubtless sweetened, episodes of this nature meant that the new Prime Minister was breaking his promise to make important announcements through the House of Commons. Meanwhile relations between the News International boss and Downing Street continued to be treated as a state secret, as under Blair. Requests under the Freedom of Information Act for the publication of contacts between the Prime Minister and the newspaper tycoon were refused.[11]

The alliance with Murdoch did not merely mean that Brown carried on the Political Class attack on the institutions of the British state. The new Prime Minister provided continuity in other ways. Gordon Brown enthusiastically joined the Political Class attack on the rule of law. Forgetful that upon taking office in the summer of 2007 he had promised to protect civil liberties, the new Prime Minister sought to put the international terrorist threat to fruitful domestic political use. Just like Tony Blair he forged an alliance with the *Sun* newspaper, as well as certain elements of the security establishment, and developed a policy which, while intellectually incoherent, was designed to make David Cameron's Tory opposition look weak on terror. The Brown government sought to enlarge the time a terrorist suspect could spend detained without charge from 28 days to 42 days. Even though he failed to provide evidence that the measure was needed, it was narrowly forced through the House of Commons in the early summer of 2008.

The appointment of Jeremy Heywood in the vital coordinating role of Head of Domestic Policy and Strategy at the Cabinet Office gave certain grounds for doubt that Brown was serious about bringing back a new scrupulousness to government. Heywood had been private secretary to Tony Blair at the height of the so-called 'sofa culture' when normal systems of civil service administration, such as note-taking, had collapsed. Heywood was an important manifestation of the collapse of boundaries between the public and private domain. Since standing down as Tony Blair's private secretary in 2003 he had apparently been on 'unpaid leave'[12] at the investment bank Morgan Stanley, occupying the extremely senior – and far from unpaid – post of co-head of the investment banking division, which was heavily involved in making bids for government business.

Since returning to Downing Street, Heywood has probably become the closest equivalent to Jonathan Powell inside the Downing Street machine. Wisely he has avoided the Powell task of dealing with large party donors which so badly compromised the Blair administration. Instead he is said by insiders to be one of the key figures who have abetted the corporate takeover of the domestic civil service that has been such a feature of Political Class rule. Heywood, according to one minister, is a 'walking dictionary of public service reform'.

The insertion of this former Morgan Stanley banker at the heart of power was soon reinforced by other key figures from the global power elite. The most striking of these was Goldman Sachs banker Jennifer Moses as a Downing Street adviser. Stephen Carter, head of the global public relations consultancy Brunswick, was head-hunted to join Downing Street as chief of strategy and principal adviser to the Prime Minister. This appointment emphasised both the powerful corporate connections of Gordon Brown's Downing Street and the overwhelming importance of presentation.

Though Gordon and Sarah Brown's personal probity – in contrast to Tony and Cherie Blair – was a praiseworthy feature of their Downing Street incumbency, the new Prime Minister appeared to show no appreciation of the damage being done by the collapse in public integrity which was the inevitable consequence of Political Class government. The pattern of intermittent scandals concerning expenses claims by ministers and backbench MPs, such a squalid feature of the Blair regime, continued unabated. It peaked at the start of 2008 with the revelation that Derek Conway, a Conservative MP, had diverted thousands of pounds of parliamentary allowances to his son, a student at Newcastle University, for so-called research duties. However, there were no records of young Conway doing any work.

In private it was noteworthy that many MPs, from all parties, expressed the view that Conway had done little wrong and was simply unlucky to get caught. However, public outrage forced MPs to act. As national disgust grew ever more apparent David Cameron – not a moment too soon – stripped the wretched Conway of the party whip. Eventually even Speaker Martin, according to some reports a strong Conway sympathiser, was forced to admit that something had gone wrong. He addressed public fury by setting up a special committee review charged with tightening up MPs' notoriously lax expenses regime and making sure that the Conway episode would never happen again.

All main parties were represented: Labour's deputy leader Harriet Harman, the shadow leader of the House Theresa May, and Nick Harvey for the Lib Dems sat on this committee. After conferring for several months they produced two modest suggestions: that outside auditors should be employed to check up on MPs' expenses, and that MPs should put in receipts for all their expenditure.

Even if they had been put into effect in full, MPs would still have enjoyed a far laxer expenses regime than anyone else in Britain. Nevertheless, after a short debate in early July, these rather modest proposals were rejected. Some 33 members of Gordon Brown's administration voted in favour of the old corrupt system, including four Cabinet ministers: home secretary Jacqui Smith, culture secretary Andy Burnham, Shaun Woodward, and Paul Murphy. Both of Gordon Brown's parliamentary aides, Ian Austin and Angela Smith, also helped block reform. The Prime Minister himself failed to vote. At this point the prestige of Parliament reached a low point in modern history.

Observers noted that Brown's problem was a severe drop in authority. By the summer of 2008 there was mounting talk of a challenge to his leadership as opinion polls showed that his popularity had collapsed and that Labour was heading for a general election defeat. In these circumstances it was dangerous for an incumbent Prime Minister to risk a confrontation with backbench MPs and ministers over the abuse of Commons allowances that had become a systemic feature of Political Class rule.

The new Brown government was in certain respects the most egregious example yet of a Political Class in power. The new government boasted family connections more characteristic of aristocratic rule in the eighteenth century than democratic government in the twentieth. It included the first husband-and-wife team ever to serve together in Cabinet – Ed Balls and Yvette Cooper – as well as a rare case of two brothers in the shape of David and Ed Miliband. Not one of the Cabinet possessed significant business experience. By the end of 2008 Gordon Brown's attempt to reform the political system from within was paralysed. He had certainly obtained some improvements, and his personal conduct was a spectacular improvement on his predecessor Tony Blair. But the structural impediments to reform were proving too strong.

This inertia in New Labour politics meant that attention focussed more and more on the resurgent Conservative opposition under David Cameron. Cameron himself, as we have seen, was a creature of the Political Class. Yet from time to time – as when he led his party against 42 days detention without charge, or in his fine speeches in which he spoke of a revival for civil society – he spoke for a wiser and older tradition of political engagement. The most interesting question in British public life as the first decade of the twenty-first century draws to a close is whether David Cameron is capable of leading an insurgency against the Political Class – or whether he will in due course become no more than another manifestation of its alluring, corrupt and anti-democratic methodology.

Notes

Introduction

1. This argument is set out in Robert Neild, *Public Corruption* (London: Anthem Press, 2002).
2. 'Tories join battle to save MP Cormack', Press Association Regional Newswire, 2 March 2007.

Chapter 1: The Architecture of the Political Class

1. Michael Gove, *Michael Portillo*, p. 62.
2. Andrew Gimson, *Boris: The Rise of Boris Johnson*, p. 88. Johnson has always been too interesting and outspoken to be a satisfactory member of the Political Class.
3. Martin Amis, 'The Long Kiss Goodbye', *Guardian*, 2 June 2007.
4. See George Walden's important work *New Elites: A Career in the Masses* for an analysis of the emergence of an 'inverted elite' which affects populist attitudes in order to ingratiate itself with voters.
5. The civilians included a racing trainer, a wine merchant and several people from the City. See Peter Oborne, 'Table manners', *Spectator*, 16 December 2000.
6. David James Smith, 'Party political outcast', *Sunday Times Magazine*, 20 May 2007. This unusual piece of journalism is well worth reading in full for the deathly insight it brings to the hollow, exploitative world of the Political Class.
7. Private information.
8. Alastair Campbell, *The Blair Years*, p. 537.
9. Gaetano Mosca, *The Ruling Class*, p. 330.
10. My analysis here is rooted in Jens Borchert's important and illuminating essay 'The Concept of Political Class: From Mosca's

Ruling Class to the Self-Referentiality of Professional Politics', presented to the American Political Science Association Meeting, Boston, 29 August–1 September 2002. Borchert writes: 'During the fight against fascism and National Socialism the concept came across as banalising the real political conflicts of the day and their fundamental importance. After World War II, it was slightly too subversive for a political science that saw itself primarily as a science of democracy.'

11. A path-breaking essay by Richard Katz and Peter Mair asserts that the drift towards cartel party politics, strong in Germany and other European countries, was least noteworthy in Britain: 'Where a tradition of adversary politics combines with relatively limited state support for party organisations and where the possibilities for patronage, while growing, also remains relatively limited.' See 'Changing Models of Party Organisation and Party Democracy: The Emergence of a Cartel Party', *Party Politics*, Volume 1 (January 1995), pp. 5–28.

Chapter 2: The Political Class and the Destruction of the British Establishment

1. See for example Matthew Parris, 'The nonsensical world of New Labourspeak', *The Times*, 6 July 2002.
2. Colin Crouch, *Coping With Post-Democracy*, p. 17.
3. Peter Oborne, *Alastair Campbell and the Rise of the Media Class*, pp. 85–6.
4. Iain Dale, 'Labour MP: Don't You Know Who I Am', iaindale.blogspot.com, 27 April 2007.
5. See 'Flat for Falconer', *The Times*, 25 October 2006: 'Lord Falconer of Thoroton, the Lord Chancellor, has been given a grace-and-favour apartment by the Prime Minister. The property in Admiralty Arch – his sixth residence – was allocated after he gave up the job of Speaker of the House of Lords.'
6. Private information.
7. Quoted in Jeremy Paxman, *Friends in High Places*, p. 78.
8. Paxman, p. viii of the preface to the 1991 edition.
9. Jill Sherman, 'Blair outlines need for child benefit reform', *The Times*, 11 May 1996.

10. See 'Satirical fiction is becoming Blair's reality', *Guardian*, 14 February 2001.
11. Speech to the Institute for Public Policy Research, 14 January 1999.
12. Michael Young, 'Down with meritocracy', *Guardian*, 29 June 2001.
13. This account of Wellington's leadership style is based in part on John Keegan's masterful essay on Wellington. See Keegan, *The Mask of Command*, and in particular the section on 'Wellington and the presentation of self', pp. 140–5.
14. Quoted in Ferdinand Mount, *The Subversive Family*, p. 35.
15. Quoted in Anthony Sampson, *The Anatomy of Britain*, p. 62.
16. Ibid., p. 624.

Chapter 3: The Political Class and the Collapse of Public Standards

1. Geoff Mulgan, LSE Lecture, 4 May 2004.
2. Chris Blackhurst, *Evening Standard*, 15 May 2006.
3. Jason Allardyce and Jonathan Calvert, 'Prescott faces police probe into office sex', *Sunday Times*, 7 May 2006.
4. Jo Knowsley and Dominic Turnball, 'We made love in John's office', *Mail on Sunday*, 30 April 2006.
5. Toby Helm, 'Prescott accused of encouraging his lover to break Civil Service rules', *Daily Telegraph*, 31 May 2006.
6. For a description of the role played by Sedgwick and Toker see the *Sunday Telegraph*, 26 December 2004.
7. See for example Patrick Hennessy and Melissa Kite, 'The end of the affair? Not likely', *Sunday Telegraph*, 5 December 2004.
8. Joe Murphy, 'Blair under investigation over "leak"', *Evening Standard*, 13 September 2006.
9. Polly Toynbee, 'Labour should ignore the media, not appease them', *Guardian*, 22 December 2004.
10. Once Harold Wilson left Downing Street, however, Mary Wilson published her *Selected Poems*, which sold an astonishing 75,000 copies. See Ben Pimlott, *Harold Wilson*, p. 579.
11. Gordon Rayner, 'Cherie's regal tour', *Daily Mail*, 23 December 2005.
12. 'Cherie "crossed the line"', BBC News Online, 8 June 2005.
13. Private information.

14. Simon Walters, 'Cherie paid £25,000 for five hours' work at Bin Laden conference', *Mail on Sunday*, 25 March 2007.

15. Paul Ham and Jon Ungoed-Thomas, 'Cherie Blair set to earn £100,000 on charity tour', *Sunday Times*, 30 January 2005.

16. Greg Dyke, *Inside Story*, pp. 243–4.

17. Adam Nathan and Edin Hamzic, 'Cherie gags her discount frock designers', *Sunday Times*, 19 October 2003.

18. Private information. See also Simon Walters, 'Cherie: It's my human right to get perks', *Mail on Sunday*, 21 January 2007.

19. Paul Thompson, 'Cherie gives kids £2k designer gear spree', *Sun*, 26 April 2003; Lesley White later wrote: 'Apparently she offered to pay for her haul of 68 items. She was eventually required to reimburse the government.' See Lesley White, 'Going for broke', *Sunday Times*, 12 June 2005.

20. Stephen Wright, 'Police in dash for Cherie's passport', *Daily Mail*, 28 May 2005.

21. 'Diplomats shopped for Blairs', *Mail on Sunday*, 2 October 2005.

22. Lesley White, op. cit.

23. Anthony Seldon, *Blair*, p. 338. Seldon also quotes an unnamed senior Cabinet minister saying, 'He's not even vaguely "in the party". He's a clever bastard, but he doesn't have an ounce of political commitment.' Ibid., p. 345.

24. See for example 'Blair's advisers rebuff inquiry into their role', *The Times*, 5 July 2002; 'Alastair Campbell and Jonathan Powell, the Prime Minister's top political aides, have refused to give evidence to an influential committee about their role in Downing Street. The Wicks Committee on Standards in Public Life had summoned the two special advisers to appear before its inquiry into relations between ministers, officials and political advisers. Sir Nigel Wicks, the committee chairman, had planned to question the two men on their extra powers, which allow them to manage civil servants. It emerged last night, however, that Mr Campbell, director of strategy and communications, and Mr Powell, Mr Blair's chief of staff, had rebuffed the committee. A Downing Street spokesman said: "These officials do not generally appear before such committees."'

25. See the *Independent on Sunday* profile, 'Cuckoo flies the nest', 24 March 1991, which details that, 'Powell has always seen

himself with some relish as the "cuckoo in the nest" in Whitehall. "There are 800 of those buggers and only one of me," he once confided about his former colleagues in the Foreign Office.'

26. Nigel Lawson, *The View from Number 11*, p. 680.
27. Alan Clark, *Diaries*, p. 284.
28. Ibid., p. 227.
29. Seldon, op. cit., p. 338. Seldon cites his source for this intelligence as Lord Renwick, who was ambassador in Washington when Powell worked at the British embassy.
30. Ibid., p. 343. Seldon in turn seems to be relying on a *Times* report.
31. For example, Andrew Rawnsley says that Ecclestone 'appealed over the head' of ministers by asking Powell to arrange the meeting. See Rawnsley, *Servants of the People*, p. 93.
32. Ibid., p. 436. Rawnsley notes that 'despite the obvious bearing of this memo on the affair', the minute was not seen by the Hammond Inquiry. Alternatively, speculates Rawnsley, 'it was something else that was left out of the published report'. Rawnsley cites 'private interviews' as his source.

Chapter 4: The Financial Structure of the Political Class

1. The Cabinet ministers in question were the Lord Chancellor, Lord Falconer of Thoroton, and Stephen Timms, Treasury Secretary. See Sam Coates, 'Labour for hire – £1,500 to chat with a minister', *The Times*, 23 September 2006.
2. Private interview.
3. Christopher Hope, 'Bill for dinner with Cameron: £50,000', *Daily Telegraph*, 29 September 2006.
4. 'Dome woes haunt Blair', BBC.co.uk, 15 February 2001.
5. Sir Anthony Hammond KCB, QC, 'Review of the Circumstances Surrounding an Application for Naturalisation by SP Hinduja in 1998', published 9 March 2001, HMSO.
6. See 'The Price of Dishonour', a Bow Group policy brief by Chris Philp, 22 July 2006. The Bow Group is connected to the Conservative Party, but there was no reason to doubt the figures.
7. Sam Coates, 'MPs call for answers from police over cash for honours', *The Times*, 9 March 2007.

8. 'Blair aide: cash probe poisoning politics', *Observer*, 4 February 2007.

9. Vincent Moss, 'Blair probe "conspiracy"', *Sunday Mirror*, 4 February 2007.

10. 'No crime was committed at Downing Street, says minister', *The Times*, 9 February 2007.

11. *The Politics Show*, BBC One, 15 October 2006.

12. *Daily Telegraph*, 18 July 2006. I have found no previous example of this comparison being made.

13. Strapline to Martin Kettle's article in the *Guardian*, 3 February 2007.

14. Headline to Tim Hames, 'Why Blair must stay and resist jackboot justice', *The Times*, 5 February 2007.

15. Headline to David Aaronovitch, 'Was there a cash-for-honours crime? It's unlikely', *The Times*, 13 March 2007.

16. *Prospect*, March 2007.

17. Bagehot, 'The real Labour funding crisis', *The Economist*, 10 February 2007.

18. Leader, 'Let Tony Blair get on with his job', *Observer*, 4 February 2007.

19. Steve Richards, 'The police have turned this crisis into a drama', *Independent*, 8 March 2007.

20. Richard Stott, 'This is not Watergate', *Sunday Mirror*, 4 February 2007.

21. Michael White, 'John Yates – with the royal family', *Spectator*, 10 March 2007.

22. Philip Stephens, *Financial Times*, 23 January 2007.

23. Private information.

Chapter 5: The Ideology of the Political Class

1. My Channel Four documentary *Why Politicians Can't Tell the Truth*, shown in April 2005, carefully analysed how politicians from all parties evaded the large, long-term issues facing the nation.

2. See 'Comment is Free', *Guardian*, 25 September 2006.

3. See also David Miliband (ed.), *Reinventing the Left* (Cambridge:

Polity Press, 1994), for a printed example of the same phenomenon.

4. For an astute analysis of Clintonian triangulation see Martin Woollacott, 'The Hunting of the Quark of Politics', *Guardian*, 16 November 1996. Woollacott notes that 'the Morris kind of triangulation can only work when people have lost interest in the coherence of policies and are either happy with or unaware of contradictions'.

5. *Financial Times*, 5 June 2005.

6. According to one Conservative insider, David Cameron's strategy in his first year was 'all about triangulation – doing what you are not expected to do'. See David Cracknell, 'The changing face of Tory Boy', *Sunday Times*, 26 November 2006.

7. Private information. There is, however, no evidence that Allen was aware that he was acting as Conservative election strategist.

8. Michael Gove, 'I can't fight my feelings any more – I love Tony', *The Times*, 25 February 2003.

9. See Parsons' seminal works, *Structure and Process in Modern Societies* (New York: The Free Press, 1960) and *Systems and Modern Societies: Foundations of Modern Sociology* (New York: Prentice Hall, 1971), as well as the retrospective overview provided by Roland Robertson and Bryan S. Turner's *Talcott Parsons: Theorist of Modernity* (London: Sage, 1991).

10. See Norman Fairclough, *New Labour, New Language?*, especially the chapter 'Renewal, Modernisation and Reform', pp. 19–20.

11. See Neocleous' article 'Radical conservatism, or the conservatism of radicals: Giddens, Blair and the politics of reaction', *Radical Philosophy*, January/February 1999, pp. 24–34.

12. Ibid.

13. David Marquand, *Decline of the Public*, p. 140.

14. Alan Finlayson, *Making Sense of New Labour*, pp. 81–2.

15. Ian Hargreaves and Ian Christie (eds), *Tomorrow's Politics: The Third Way and Beyond*, p. 3.

16. Speech at Arrival Ceremony at the White House, Washington DC, 5 February 1998.

17. Speech to News Corporation executives, Pebble Beach, California, 30 July 2006.

Chapter 6: The Emasculation of the Civil Service

1. Peter Hennessy, *Whitehall*, p. 64.
2. Ibid., p. 65.
3. See Professor Kevin Theakston, 'The 1964–70 Labour Governments and Whitehall Reform', POLIS Working Paper No. 2, February 2004, p. 7. Harold Wilson's political aide Marcia Williams came to heartily share this view, attributing the failure of the 1964–70 government to civil service obstruction, and demanding a purge of senior civil servants.
4. Private interview.
5. See Norman Lamont, *In Office*, pp. 93–5, 316–18. Lamont insists there was political justification for the payment. He says that 'Peter Middleton, the Permanent Secretary, approached me and said that it was the considered view of the Treasury that it would be right for the Treasury to pay my legal bill'. Lamont insists he never raised the idea himself. In the end the Treasury contribution was downgraded to £4,700, said to relate to costs of expedited court proceedings and press enquiries, while Conservative Central Office picked up the remainder.
6. Private information. In the event Tony Blair never did so.
7. Geoffrey Robinson, *The Unconventional Minister*, p. 222.
8. See Frank Field's brief account of this conversation in the *Spectator*, 24 November 2001.
9. Committee on Standards in Public Life, 'Reinforcing Standards; Review of 1st Report of the Committee on Standards in Public Life', January 2000, p. 74.
10. Romola Christopherson, 'Goodbye minister', *Sunday Times*, 2 April 2000.
11. Sir Richard Wilson, 'Portrait of a Profession Revisited', speech at Admiralty Arch, 26 March 2002.
12. Peter Riddell and Jill Sherman, 'Mandarin from the Treasury plans a small revolution', *The Times*, 1 May 2002.
13. Max Hastings, *Editor*, p. 299.
14. Joshua Rozenberg, 'Harman and her sister in case papers blunder', *Daily Telegraph*, 24 March 2004.
15. Hugo Young, *One of Us*, p. 153.
16. Ibid., p. 155.

17. This process is described in the Appendix to Peter Oborne, *Alastair Campbell and the Rise of the Media Class*.
18. Private interviews. See the extremely useful account of these negotiations in Anthony Seldon, *Blair*, pp. 339–41.
19. Private information.
20. Private information. All of the quotes in this section are based on private conversations with very senior civil servants carried out during research for my Channel Four documentary *Gordon Brown: Fit for Office?*, screened in May 2007.
21. See Appendix 5 to the Select Committee on Public Administration Report on the GICS (HC 770, 29 July 1998).
22. Private information. Alastair Campbell's role in recruiting Woodward attracted public attention. However, it was the Downing Street press officer Lance Price who played much the larger role. See Lance Price, *The Spin Doctor's Diary*, pp. 164–72 and *passim*.
23. This account is based on my reporter's note on the visit to the *Express* building by Alastair Campbell and David Miliband, 28 July 1999.
24. For a useful account of the capture of British public administration by the management consultancy industry, see David Craig and Richard Brooks, *Plundering the Public Sector*.
25. See for example A. Doig and J. Wilson, 'What Price New Public Management?', *Political Quarterly*, 69 (1998), pp. 267–80; and C. Hood, 'A Public Management for All Seasons', *Public Administration*, 69 (1991), pp. 3–19.
26. Mandelson and Liddle, *The Blair Revolution*, p. 245.
27. Quoted in Sampson, *Who Runs This Place?*, p. 103.
28. These quotes are taken from Dr Catherine Needham, *Citizen-Consumers: New Labour's Marketplace Democracy* (London: Catalyst, 2003).

Chapter 7: The Fall of the Foreign Office – and the Rise of MI6

1. Lance Price, *The Spin Doctor's Diary*, p. 187.
2. See Andrew Sparrow, 'Vaz hosted private meeting with donor at Foreign Office', *Daily Telegraph*, 2 February 2001. See also Cathy Newman, 'Vaz under fire for resolving insurance claim', *Financial*

Times, 2 February 2001. The Foreign Office insisted that the ministerial code of conduct had not been broken. Paragraph 63 of the ministerial code insists that government property 'should not generally be used for constituency work or party activity'.

3. See for example Simon Walters, 'Cherie's £34 a night Bermudan mansion', *Mail on Sunday*, 11 May 2003.
4. Christopher Meyer, *DC Confidential*, p. 190.
5. Ibid., p. 202.
6. See 'Lord Levy's Diary, Overseas Trips and UK Meetings as the Prime Minister's Personal Representative' at www.fco.gov.uk.
7. See Peter Oborne, *The Rise of Political Lying*, pp. 52–6, for a full account of this episode.
8. See the highly informative paper by Dr David Morrison: 'What became of Blair's "several hundred" terrorists?', *Labour and Trade Union Review*, May 2005 and accessible at www.david-morrison.org.uk/counter-terrorism/several-hundred-terrorists.htm.
9. Private information.
10. See Michael Smith, 'The secret Downing Street memo', *Sunday Times*, 1 May 2005.
11. See my detailed analysis in *The Rise of Political Lying*, p. 191.

Chapter 8: The Political Class and the Rule of Law

1. Rodney Brazier, *Ministers of the Crown*, p. 176. I have partly relied here on Martin McElwee's 'Judicial Review: Keeping Ministers in Check, A Policy Brief for the Bow Group', February 2002.
2. Brazier, op. cit., p. 176.
3. *Guardian*, 24 April 2004.
4. Richard Ford, 'Afghan hijackers win asylum after six-year struggle', *The Times*, 11 May 2006.
5. 'Reid steps up the fight to kick out Afghan hijackers', *Daily Express*, 12 May 2006.
6. Ned Temko and Jamie Doward, 'Revealed: Blair attack on human rights law', *Observer*, 14 May 2006.
7. Joe Murphy, 'Law chief slaps down Reid', *Evening Standard*, 13 June 2006.

8. Alan Travis, 'Downing Street backs Reid', *Guardian*, 14 June 2006.
9. Andrew Porter, 'Reid wins support in fight with law chief', *Sun*, 14 June 2006.
10. Joshua Rozenberg, 'Farrakhan visit would pose little risk', *Daily Telegraph*, 2 October 2001.
11. Alan Travis, 'Blunkett fury at asylum camp ruling', *Guardian*, 8 September 2001.
12. Alex Carlile, 'Leave the judges alone, Dr Reid', *Independent on Sunday*, 18 June 2006.
13. Gaby Hinsliff and Mark Townsend, 'Critics turn on Blunkett chase for "cheap headline"', *Observer*, 30 November 2003.
14. 'Police killer gets 17 years for poison plot', *Guardian*, 14 April 2005.
15. Alasdair Palmer, 'Mr Blunkett belongs to a banana republic', *Sunday Telegraph*, 18 January 2004.
16. Ibid.
17. See Harry Snook, *Crossing the Threshold: 266 Ways the State Can Enter Your Home* (Centre for Policy Studies, 2007).
18. Home Affairs Select Committee, 11 October 2005, Q 73.
19. Hansard, HC Deb, 10 March 2005, col. 1801.
20. As quoted by Joshua Rozenberg, 'Not the usual channels', *Daily Telegraph*, 10 November 2005.

Chapter 9: The Monarchy and the Political Class

1. Anthony Sampson, *Who Runs This Place?*, p. 43.
2. Private information.
3. David Marquand, *Decline of the Public*, p. 81. Marquand's entire analysis is very telling.
4. Quotes taken from Black Rod's draft letter to the Press Complaints Commission.
5. Peter Oborne, *Spectator*, 12 April 2002.
6. Jackie Ashley, 'Duty bound but loath to keep taking the tablets', *Guardian*, 28 January 2002.
7. *Independent on Sunday*, 7 January 2001.
8. See Brown's comments to Mariella Frostrup during a platform interview at the Hay Book Festival, as detailed in the *Guardian*, 28 May 2007, as well as his keynote speech to the Fabian Society

Conference on the 'Future of Britishness', 14 January 2006; and the British Council Annual Lecture, 7 July 2004.

9. See Ruth Kelly and Liam Byrne, 'A Common Place', pamphlet published by the Fabian Society, June 2007: 'And these values are not merely abstract. They are embodied in our national institutions: not merely those to which Churchill assigned a "long continuity" but to new ones that encapsulate best what we like about Britain – like the NHS; fairness and decency in institutional form. It is why under this government new institutions like Sure Start centres say something about what we value as a society, alongside some of the more traditional institutions like the BBC, and our history of parliamentary democracy.'

10. Leader, *Sun*, 23 March 2001.

Chapter 10: The Attack on Parliament

1. Andrew Tyrie, 'Mr Blair's Poodle: An Agenda for Reviving the House of Commons' (Centre for Policy Studies, 2000), p. 4.

2. Quoted in Anthony Sampson, *Who Runs This Place?*, p. 79.

3. *Prospect*, May 2000, p. 41. I am indebted to Andrew Tyrie for this reference.

4. See Tyrie, op. cit., pp. 64–5, for a list of further examples.

5. 'Blair to unveil 1,600 cut in Iraq troop numbers', *Financial Times*, 21 February 2007; 'PM: Our job in Basra – Troops coming home', *Sun*, 21 February 2007.

6. Tyrie, op. cit., p. 10. To give one example, during the passage of the controversial Police (Northern Ireland) Bill in 2000, only three out of ten groups of amendments were debated on the floor of the Commons.

7. Sampson, op. cit., p. 28.

8. See Baroness Jay of Paddington, Lords Hansard of 26 October 1999, col. 277 and 14 October 1998, col. 923.

9. See 'Great and Good dominate the list of "People's Peers"', *The Times*, 27 April 2001.

10. Private information.

11. House of Lords debates, 10 May 2000, col. 1591. Warner was a long-term DHSS civil servant, notable for having cried when Barbara Castle was sacked by Jim Callaghan in 1976. Later he

formed his own consultancy company. Jack Straw (who had known Warner when he was political adviser to Barbara Castle as a young man) hired Warner as his special adviser in 1997. Warner was made a peer in 1998, and a government minister in 2003. His career demonstrates the ease of manoeuvre between officials and the Political Class.

12. Geoff Mulgan, *Good and Bad Power*, p. 84.
13. *Guardian*, 11 February 2004.
14. Quoted in Sampson, op. cit., p. 8.
15. Peter Riddell, *Honest Opportunism: The Rise of the Career Politician*, p. 120.
16. Andrew Adonis and Stephen Pollard, *A Class Act: The Myth of Britain's Classless Society*, p. 107.
17. Hansard, HC Deb, 10 August 1911, col. 1397.
18. Ibid., col. 1384.
19. 'Review Body on Top Salaries, First Report', Ministers of the Crown and Members of Parliament, December 1971, Cmnd 4836, para 26.
20. Ibid., para 41.
21. Hansard, HC Deb, 20 December 1971, Vol. 828, col. 1137.
22. Ibid., 8 February 1985, Vol. 72, col. 475.
23. Tom Baldwin and Philip Baldwin, 'Cabinet reaps a £280,000 windfall from second homes', *The Times*, 22 October 2004.
24. Benedict Brogan, 'Blair's £43,000 house expenses', *Daily Mail*, 22 October 2004.
25. Steven Swinford, 'Blunkett's £20,000 claim for cottage', *Sunday Times*, 23 April 2006.
26. Private information.
27. Kirsty Walker, 'MP claims enough expenses to drive twice around the world', *Daily Mail*, 15 February 2007.
28. See Peter Oborne, 'Why Gordon Brown hates Jack McConnell' and 'Parliamentarian of the Year – the winner: Special Award Elizabeth Filkin, QC', *Spectator*, 17 November 2001.
29. The details are complex. I am relying here on the academic Dr Robert Kaye, who writes: 'One aspect of Gorman's case – registration of an offshore trust – was comparable with the first Robinson complaint ... Robinson and Gorman both had the expectation of benefiting from the trust, Robinson more clearly

than Gorman. Whereas Downey had shied away from saying that Robinson should have registered his interest in an offshore trust, Filkin was explicit in upholding a complaint against Gorman for the very same reason, and the Committee found accordingly, citing the "considerable attention" that Robinson's had attracted outside the House. This differential treatment was not justified by the facts of the case.' See Kaye, *Regulating Westminster*, forthcoming publication.

30. Dr Kaye's original, extremely important and well-informed work is the most invaluable guide to the Filkin affair. Among other achievements, Dr Kaye demonstrates that the criticisms made by ministers and others of Mrs Filkin were unfounded.

31. Committee on Standards and Privileges, 'Twelfth Report: Complaint Against Mr John Prescott', HC 504, 17 May 2000.

32. Private interview.

33. 'Boothroyd hits out at "witch-hunter"', *Sunday Times*, 30 September 2001.

34. *Independent*, 22 March 2000.

35. See for example 'Prescott takes a pop at Mrs Sleazebuster', *Daily Express*, 18 May 2000.

36. Colin Brown, 'Minister attacks watchdog', *Independent*, 22 March 2000.

37. Interview with author, autumn 2006.

38. *Daily Express*, op. cit., 18 May 2000.

39. Private information.

40. 'Even MPs are entitled to be presumed innocent', Glasgow *Herald*, 21 December 2000.

41. Paragraph 2.9 of the Ministerial Code (Ministers and Appointments, Parliamentary Private Secretaries) states: 'Parliamentary Private Secretaries are not precluded from serving on Select Committees but they should not do so in the case of inquiries into their own Minister's Departments and they should avoid associating themselves with recommendations critical of or embarrassing to the government. They should also exercise discretion in any speeches or broadcasts which they may make outside the House, taking care not to make statements which appear to be made in an official or semi-official capacity, and bearing in mind at the same time that, however careful they may

be to make it clear that they are speaking only as Private Members, they are nevertheless liable to be regarded as speaking with some of the authority which is attached to a member of the government.' *Ministerial Code of Conduct: A Code of Conduct and Guidance on Procedure for Ministers* (Cabinet Office, July 2001).

42. Hansard, HC Deb, 13 February 2002, col. 243.
43. Kaye, op. cit.
44. 'Cook praises embattled watchdog', *Guardian*, 26 October 2001.
45. This point has been brilliantly established by Robert Kaye in *Regulating Westminster*.

Chapter 11: Client Journalism

1. 'Life's grand in redtop land', *Observer*, 6 March 2005.
2. Private information.
3. The former Downing Street spin-doctor Lance Price told a conference in 2001 that Downing Street had leaked the story to the *Sun*. See James Hardy, 'A spin too far', *Daily Mirror*, 25 October 2001.
4. For a description of this process see Peter Oborne, 'Why has there been a steady stream of leaked honours since 1997? Work it out for yourself', *Spectator*, 8 June 2002.
5. See for example *Trading Information* (London: Politico's, 2006); *The Control Freaks: How New Labour Got Its Own Way* (London: Politico's, 2001); *Sultans of Spin: Media and the New Labour Government* (London: Weidenfeld & Nicolson, 1999); and *Soundbites and Spin Doctors: How Politicians Manipulate the Media and Vice Versa* (London: Cassell, 1995).
6. Alastair Campbell, *The Blair Years*, pp. 89–90.
7. See Tony Bevins, '8 million jobs in jeopardy', *Daily Express*, 18 February 2000. Bevins' hard-hitting copy left *Express* readers in no doubt who would be to blame. 'Tony Blair,' he coolly informed readers, 'has said repeatedly that pulling out of the EU is William Hague's hidden agenda and the real motive behind the Tory leader's "Save the Pound" campaign.'
8. Campbell, op. cit., pp. 252–3. See also 'Brown rules out single currency for lifetime of this Parliament' and 'Brown: We won't fall into the Tory trap of "wait and see"', published on pages 1 and 2 respectively of *The Times*, 18 October 1997.

9. James Naughtie, *The Rivals*, p. 145.

10. Lance Price, *The Spin Doctor's Diary*, pp. 64–9.

11. *The Times*, 24 December 1998.

12. Price, op. cit.

13. For a more detailed account of this story see Oborne and Walters, *Alastair Campbell*, pp. 235–7.

14. See Bryan Appleyard's extremely important and original *Sunday Times* article of 18 May 2003, 'Don't believe a word they say about them', for an excellent exposé of how access was exchanged for favourable copy: 'The bigger point is that the virus of aggressive PR has compromised the claim that must underpin all the activities of the media – the claim that the story they are telling is true or an honest attempt at the truth. To my dismay, much of my profession can no longer make that claim.'

15. See Tom Bower, *Broken Dreams: Vanity, Greed and the Souring of British Football* (London: Simon & Schuster, 2003; new edition, 2007).

16. See the *Sunday Times*, 1 June 1986, 'Business Focus: Black velvet gets that extra fizz', in which following nearly 2,000 words of hyperbolic praise for Saunders' career and business acumen, Fallon slipped in the revelation that was to prove so contentious: 'Even now, Saunders feels the outside world has still not understood what he is about. 'There is this argument of whether we should be in St James's (the old Distillers London office) or whether it should be in Edinburgh. To me the issue is whether we should be in New York or Tokyo or Paris or even Frankfurt.'

17. For details of these persistent Downing Street attacks on *The World at One* see Oborne and Walters, op. cit., pp. 223–5 and *passim*. Downing Street used privately to label the programme 'Wankers at One'.

18. See for example Anthony Howard, *The Times*, 17 June 2003. Howard recorded Campbell's reaction in 1990 after being cited as an adviser to Neil Kinnock, then Labour leader: 'He jumped up and down and threw a wobbly. He was, he insisted, a totally independent journalist and I had injured his professional reputation by insisting otherwise.'

19. Private information. The journalist himself was in receipt of un-

authorised briefings from a senior Cabinet minister anxious to secure influential press support ahead of the Conservative leadership contest which, it was anticipated, would follow the 1997 election victory.

20. Andrew Neather, 'Confessions of a Labour Party spy', *Evening Standard*, 29 March 2005.

21. See 'Labour dirty tricksters spied and smeared for Attack Unit', *Sunday Times*, 29 September 2002. According to the *Sunday Times*, Attack Unit targets ranged from Michael Howard, then the shadow Chancellor, whose private life was investigated, to Ken Livingstone and John Prescott, Deputy Prime Minister. One of McMenamin's key achievements was helping persuade Labour election strategists to make Tory pension plans a central issue in the election. The Labour campaign, which insisted that the Conservative Party was planning to scrap state pensions, was entirely without foundation. See Philip Gould, *The Unfinished Revolution*, p. 379. The list of dirty tricks and subterfuges of which this enterprising New Labour apparatchik has been accused is too wearisome to list at length.

22. See Peter Oborne, *Alastair Campbell: New Labour and the Rise of the Media Class*, pp. 112–18 for a longer description of the social composition of the parliamentary lobby. See also Andrew Sparrow's lovingly researched *Obscure Scribblers: A History of Parliamentary Reporting* (London: Politico's, 2003).

23. For example 'A gay leader would be good for the party says Duncan', *Daily Telegraph*, 10 June 2005; 'We need a battle of ideas says the latest Tory hopeful', *The Times*, 10 June 2005; 'Wild Card' profile by Petronella Wyatt in the *Spectator*, 25 June 2005.

24. Lance Price, 'Rupert Murdoch is effectively a member of Blair's Cabinet', *Guardian*, 1 July 2006.

25. Andrew Grice, 'No. 10 refuses to release details of Blair's dealings with Murdoch', *Independent*, 23 May 2006.

26. Price, op. cit.

27. See the Commons Register of Members' Interests as updated 19 June 2007. The column was ghosted for the former Cabinet minister by Chris Buckland, a News International hack of long standing.

28. *Observer*, 29 March 1998.

29. John Rentoul, *Tony Blair*, p. 91.
30. 'Bush: I can't imagine the heartbreak of losing a child', *Sun*, 17 November 2003.
31. See account in the *Mail on Sunday*, 16 November 2003. According to a report in the *Washington Post*, the interview was 'done on the recommendation of Tony Blair'. The *Post* added that 'it is an obvious pay-off to the *Sun*'s owner, Rupert Murdoch, the conservative publisher behind many Bush-friendly outlets such as Fox News'. See 'Prez in topless tabloid; London paper nabs rare Bush exclusive', *Washington Post*, 15 November 2003.
32. Herman and Chomsky, *Manufacturing Consent*, p. xi.
33. Rentoul, op. cit., p. 99.
34. For evidence of this, see Peter Oborne, *The Rise of Political Lying*, p. 9.

Chapter 12: The Media Class and the Iraq War

1. See for example 'From the Editors: The *Times* and Iraq', *New York Times*, 26 May 2004. This article found 'a number of instances of coverage that was not as rigorous as it should have been. In some cases, information that was controversial then, and seems questionable now, was insufficiently qualified or allowed to stand unchallenged.' This observation is equally pertinent to the British press and broadcasting media during this period. Demonstrating an openness and self-reflection not replicated by British journalists and editors, all the *New York Times*' investigations into its coverage of the war are posted online at www.nytimes.com.
2. *Sun*, 23 January 2003.
3. I have taken this quotation, and used much of the very valuable and interesting accompanying analysis, from the Media Lens Media Alert on 14 January 2003.
4. Andrew Rawnsley, 'How to deal with the American goliath', *Observer*, 24 February 2002.
5. Rawnsley, 'Why war stirs the blood of Tony Blair', *Observer*, 8 September 2002. Rawnsley slightly misquotes the former Liberal Democrat leader. Ashdown actually quoted Blair as saying: 'I have now seen some of the stuff on this.'

6. Rawnsley, 'The voices of doom were so wrong', *Observer*, 13 April 2003.

7. Philip Webster, Roland Watson and Greg Hurst, 'Labour MPs split over Iraq dossier', *The Times*, 25 September 2002.

8. Michael Evans, Michael Dynes, Catherine Philp, Richard Beeston and Alice Lagnado, 'Uranium heads secret shopping list', *The Times*, 25 September 2002.

9. James Astill and Rory Carroll, 'Iraq dossier: African gangs offer route to uranium', *Guardian*, 25 September 2002.

10. All these quotes are taken from the brief summary of the contents of the dossier published on p. 4 of the *Guardian* on 25 September 2002.

11. David Rose, 'Hero of doves forgets when he was a hawk', *Observer*, 15 September 2002.

12. Rose, 'The Iraq crisis: Terror of tyrant's mistress in gilded prison', *Observer*, 8 September 2002.

13. Rose, 'Betrayed by this immoral war', *Evening Standard*, 10 May 2004.

14. Rawnsley, 'The voices of doom were so wrong'.

15. Con Coughlin, 'UN inspectors uncover proof of Saddam's nuclear bomb', *Sunday Telegraph*, 19 January 2003.

16. George Jahn, 'Countdown to war: Iraq nuclear data found in scientist's home', *Independent on Sunday*, 19 January 2003.

17. Coughlin, 'Britain finds Iraq's "smoking gun"', *Sunday Telegraph*, 25 May 2003.

18. Coughlin, 'Meanwhile, Saddam's secrets rise from the desert', *Sunday Telegraph*, 17 August 2003.

19. George Pascoe Watson, 'Brits 45 mins from doom', *Sun*, 25 September 2002.

20. *Independent*, leader, 19 March 2003.

21. David Hughes, 'No retreat', *Daily Mail*, 19 March 2003.

22. George Pascoe Watson and Nick Parker, 'Fiend to unleash poisons', *Sun*, 19 March 2003.

23. *Daily Express*, 19 March 2003.

24. Hughes, op. cit.

25. George Jones, 'Blair wins historic vote for war', *Daily Telegraph*, 19 March 2003.

26. 'Blair battles on after record rebellion', *Guardian*, 19 March 2003.

27. Among many others, see for example 'We're backing Blair because Saddam is a tyrant, says Duncan Smith', *Daily Telegraph*, p. 4; 'This is not the time to falter', *Daily Mail*, pp. 1–2; '"Shirkers" humiliated by Hague', *Sun* – all 19 March 2003. Compare to the tendency to outline anti-war arguments later on in the paper and with less fanfare: 'The House of Commons and House of Lords debate war on Iraq', *The Times*, p. 40; 'Blair and the day of destiny', *Daily Mail*, pp. 4–5; 'Wrong war, wrong time, wrong enemy, warns Labour rebel', *Guardian*, p. 6; 'Minister quits and Prescott wonders', *Daily Telegraph*, p. 5 – all 19 March 2003.

28. Trevor Kavanagh, 'Exclusive: PM's first interview since outbreak of war', *Sun*, 18 April 2003.

29. 'Leap of faith', *Financial Times*, 26 April 2003. But see John Lloyd's response, 'Now it's personal', *Prospect*, July 2003, and my reply in the August 2003 edition.

30. *News at Ten*, BBC1, 9 April 2003. Quoted in Media Lens News Alert, 18 April 2003.

31. Ibid.

Chapter 13: Manipulative Populism

1. See George Rudé, 'The Gordon Riots: A Study of the Rioters and their Victims', *Transactions of the Royal Historical Society*, 5th series, no. 6 (1956), 93–114.

2. Max Beloff, 'No better recipe for conflict', *The Times*, 9 August 1997.

3. See Peter Oborne, 'The Use and Abuse of Terror' (Centre for Policy Studies, 2006).

4. Ibid.

5. Terenia Taras and Paul McMullan, 'Does a monster live near you?', *News of the World*, 23 July 2000.

6. *News of the World*, 13 August 2000.

7. Vikram Dodd, 'Vigilantes defy calls to end paedophile protests', *Guardian*, 10 August 2000. See also the admirable summary by Simon Kelner in the *Independent*, 'Media – shame on you', 15 August 2000.

8. Nick Assinder, 'Why is Reid looking at new law?', BBC.co.uk, 20 June 2006.

9. Piers Morgan, *The Insider*, p. 176.
10. This account is based on the exemplary study by John Vidal, 'Never say die', *Guardian*, 25 April 2002.

Chapter 14: The Triumph of the Political Class

1. Private information.
2. Interview during the 2005 General Election.
3. Peter Oborne, 'The mean machine', *Spectator*, 20 November 2004.
4. Oborne, 'Beware: The voters Blair neglected are angry', *Spectator*, 15 April 2006.
5. Peter Riddell and Philip Webster, 'United we must stand on Europe, says Chancellor', *The Times*, 21 May 2003.
6. See Cabinet Office press release, 12 June 2007.

Epilogue

1. See Gordon Brown's speech on becoming leader of the UK Labour Party, Manchester, 24 June 2007: '... it is time for a new and better relationship between government and the British people – with government the servant and more power in the hands of the people ... The days of Whitehall ever thinking it knows best are over. We need government that does not overreach but reaches out; government as servant at all times putting opportunity in the hands of people. That's why I want a new constitutional settlement for Britain. And the principles of my reforms are these: Government giving more power to Parliament; both government and Parliament giving more power to the people; Parliament voting on all the major issues of our time including peace and war; civil liberties safeguarded and enhanced ...' Earlier in the year, during an interview for the BBC's *Sunday AM* on 7 January, Gordon Brown had stressed: 'We do need a new settlement over these next few years between, if you like, the executive, the legislature, and that is the power of Parliament and the House of Commons, and people themselves ... We've got to look at the relationship as a whole between the Executive and the law-making body which is Parliament, and the people themselves.'
2. In the speech marking the launch of his Labour Party leadership

campaign on 11 May, Brown delivered what appeared to be a barely veiled rebuff to Blair: 'As a politician I have never sought the public eye for its own sake. I have never believed presentation should be a substitute for policy. I do not believe politics is about celebrity. I want to lead a government humble enough to know its place.'

3. See *The Governance of Britain – Draft Constitutional Renewal Bill*, published March 2008 as Cm 7342-II and accessible at http://www.justice.gov.uk/docs/draft-constitutional-renewal-bill.pdf; my comments are informed by the memoranda of evidence submitted by the First Division Association to the Joint Committee on the Draft Constitutional Renewal Bill before its taking of oral evidence on 10 June 2008 – see HC 551-vii.

4. See 'Brown vows to make intelligence independent of politics', *Guardian*, 11 June 2007: 'I would like to see all security and intelligence analysis independent of the political process and I have asked the cabinet secretary to do that.' Brown later announced to Parliament: 'In line with the Butler Report we will separate the position of Chairman of the Joint Intelligence Committee from policy adviser to the Government. And so the sole responsibilities of the Chairman of the Joint Intelligence Committee will be to provide Ministers with assessments which have been formulated independently of the political process and to improve across Government the effectiveness of intelligence analysis.' Hansard, 25 July 2007, col. 841.

5. However, when asked to clarify the circumstances of Scarlett's continuation in the role, an FCO spokesperson stated: 'In recent years nobody has served for longer than five years, but there are no set rules for this position. As far as I'm aware there has been no formal extension of Sir John's appointment.'

6. Private information.

7. Labour Party leadership campaign launch speech, 11 May 2007. Brown continued: 'Government must be more open and accountable to Parliament – for example in decisions about peace and war, in public appointments and in a new ministerial code of conduct.' Once Prime Minister, Brown reiterated his intention, telling the Commons: 'All Members of this House and all the people of this country have a shared interest in building trust in

our democracy, and it is my hope that, by working together for change in a spirit that takes us beyond parties and beyond partisanship, we can agree a new British constitutional settlement that entrusts more power to Parliament and the British people.' Hansard, 3 July 2007, col. 815.

8. To prove the point, at least initially, Brown delivered his statement on Constitutional Renewal direct to the House of Commons on 3 July 2007 without prior briefing, the media being left to speculate on its potential contents beforehand. However, later that autumn Brown notoriously bypassed the House and announced the withdrawal of a thousand British troops from Iraq while in Baghdad on 2 October.

9. In an interview promoting his memoirs, Levy pointedly stated that he was 'saddened to see what's happened to the party now, I am saddened to see all of the bickering and I am saddened to see that somehow there does not appear to be that strong leadership that the Labour Party so desperately needs'. See the *Mail on Sunday*, 27 April 2008.

10. See the *Times* interview, 'Work-for-dole will force the benefit cheats to start earning their keep, says jobs minister', 5 July 2008, in which Purnell trailed his forthcoming Green Paper plans: 'There will be a very clear expectation that if there is work there people should take it, and sanctions to make sure that if they don't there are consequences.'

11. James Macintyre and Andrew Grice, 'Brown refuses to reveal contacts with Murdoch', *Independent*, 4 February 2008.

12. See Cabinet Office press release, 12 June 2007.

Bibliography

Books

Adonis, Andrew and Pollard, Stephen, *A Class Act: The Myth of Britain's Classless Society* (London: Hamish Hamilton, 1997)

Anderson, Bruce, *John Major* (London: Headline, 1992)

Annas, Julia, *An Introduction to Plato's Republic* (Oxford: Clarendon Press, 1981)

Ashcroft, Michael, *Dirty Politics, Dirty Times: My Fight With Wapping and New Labour* (London: Politico's, 2005)

Ashford, Nigel and Davies, Stephen (eds), *A Dictionary of Conservative and Libertarian Thought* (London: Routledge, 1991)

Barnett, Anthony (ed.), *Power and the Throne: The Monarchy Debate* (London: Vintage, 1994)

Bartholomew, James, *The Welfare State We're In* (London: Politico's, 2004)

Beck, Ulrich, *Democracy Without Enemies* (Cambridge: Polity Press, 1998)

——, *World Risk Society* (Cambridge: Polity Press, 2005)

Beckett, Francis, *Enemy Within: The Rise and Fall of the British Communist Party* (London: John Murray, 1995)

Beetham, David et al. (eds), *Democracy Under Blair: A Democratic Audit of the United Kingdom* (London: Politico's, 2002)

Beetham, David, *Democracy: A Beginner's Guide* (Oxford: Oneworld, 2005)

Beitz, Charles R., *Political Equality: An Essay in Democratic Theory* (Princeton, NJ: Princeton University Press, 1989)

Black, Crispin, *7–7: The London Bombings – What Went Wrong?* (London: Gibson Square, 2005)

Blake, Robert, *The Office of the Prime Minister* (Oxford: OUP, 1975)

Blick, Andrew, *People Who Live in the Dark: The History of the Special Adviser in British Politics* (London: Politico's, 2004)

Blunkett, David, *The Blunkett Tapes* (London: Bloomsbury, 2006)

Bogdanor, Vernon, *The Monarchy and the Constitution* (Oxford: Clarendon Press, 1997)

Booth, Cherie and Haste, Cate, *The Goldfish Bowl: Married to the Prime Minister, 1955–1997* (London: Chatto & Windus, 2004)

Boothroyd, Betty, *The Autobiography* (London: Century, 2001)

Borjesson, Kristina (ed.), *Feet to the Fire: The Media After 9/11* (New York: Prometheus Books, 2005)

Bower, Tom, *Broken Dreams: Vanity, Greed and the Souring of British Football* (London: Simon & Schuster, 2003)

——, *Gordon Brown* (London: HarperCollins, 2004)

Brazier, Rodney, *Ministers of the Crown* (Oxford: OUP, 1997)

Burton, Anthony, *William Cobbett: Englishman – A Biography* (London: Aurum, 1997)

Butler, David and Butler, Gareth, *Twentieth-Century British Political Facts, 1900–2000* (London: Macmillan, 2000)

Bywater, Michael, *Big Babies, Or: Why Can't We Just Grow Up?* (London: Granta, 2006)

Campbell, Alastair, *The Blair Years: Extracts from The Alastair Campbell Diaries* (London: Hutchinson, 2007)

Chippindale, Peter and Horrie, Chris, *Stick It Up Your Punter: The Rise and Fall of the Sun* (London: Mandarin, 1992)

Chomsky, Noam, *Hegemony or Survival: America's Quest for Global Dominance* (London: Penguin, 2004)

Clark, Alan, *Diaries: In Power, 1982–1992* (London: Weidenfeld & Nicolson, 1993)

Cobbett, William, *The Autobiography of William Cobbett: The Progress of a Plough-Boy to a Seat in Parliament* (ed. William Reitzel; London: Faber & Faber, 1947)

——, *Rural Rides* (London: Penguin, 1985)

Cockett, Richard, *Twilight of Truth: Chamberlain, Appeasement and the Manipulation of the Press* (London: Weidenfeld & Nicolson, 1989)

Cohen, Nick, *Cruel Britannia: Reports on the Sinister and Preposterous* (London: Verso, 1999)

Cole, G. D. H., *The Life of William Cobbett* (London: Home & Van Thal, 1947)

Cole, G. D. H. and Margaret (eds), *The Opinions of William Cobbett* (London: The Cobbett Publishing Co., 1944)

Colley, Linda, *Britons: Forging the Nation, 1707–1837* (London: Pimlico, 2003)

Craib, Ian, *Anthony Giddens* (London: Routledge, 1992)

Craig, David and Brooks, Richard, *Plundering the Public Sector* (London: Constable & Robinson, 2006)

Crick, Michael, *The Boss: The Many Sides of Alex Ferguson* (London: Simon & Schuster, 2002)

Dale, Iain, *The Blair Necessities: The Tony Blair Book of Quotations* (London: Robson, 1997)

Dalton, Russell J. and Wattenberg, Martin P. (eds), *Parties Without Partisans: Political Change in Advanced Industrial Democracies* (Oxford: OUP, 2002)

Deane, Alexander, *The Great Abdication: Why Britain's Decline is the Fault of the Media Class* (Exeter: Imprint Academic, 2005)

Driver, Stephen and Martell, Luke, *New Labour* (Cambridge: Polity Press, 2006)

Dyke, Greg, *Inside Story* (London: HarperCollins, 2004)

Edwards, David and Cromwell, David, *Guardians of Power: The Myth of the Liberal Media* (London: Pluto Press, 2006)

Edwards, Michael, *Civil Society* (Cambridge: Polity Press, 2005)

Eliot, T. S., *Notes Towards the Definition of Culture* (London: Faber & Faber, 1948)

Estlund, David (ed.), *Democracy* (Oxford: Blackwell, 2002)

Fairclough, Norman, *New Labour, New Language?* (London: Routledge, 2000)

Fielding, Steven, *The Labour Party: Community and Change in the Making of 'New' Labour* (Basingstoke: Palgrave Macmillan, 2003)

Finlayson, Alan, *Making Sense of New Labour* (London: Lawrence & Wishart, 2003)

Fish, Stanley, *Is There a Text in This Class?: The Authority of Interpretive Communities* (Cambridge, MA: Harvard University Press, 2003)

Foster, Christopher, *British Government in Crisis* (Oxford: Hart Publishing, 2005)

Gamble, Andrew and Wright, Tony (eds), *Restating the State?* (Oxford: Blackwell, 2004)

Giddens, Anthony, *The Consequences of Modernity* (Stanford, CA: Stanford University Press, 1990)

——, *Runaway World: How Globalisation is Reshaping Our Lives* (London: Profile, 2002)

Gilbert, Francis, *Yob Nation: The Truth About Britain's Yob Culture* (London: Portrait, 2006)

Gimson, Andrew, *Boris: The Rise of Boris Johnson* (London: Simon & Schuster, 2006)

Gould, Philip, *The Unfinished Revolution: How the Modernisers Saved the Labour Party* (London: Little, Brown, 1998)

Gove, Michael, *Michael Portillo: The Future of the Right* (London: Fourth Estate, 1995)

Gramsci, Antonio, *Selections from Prison Notebooks* (London: Lawrence & Wishart, 1978)

Grant, Wynn, *Pressure Groups and British Politics* (London: Macmillan, 2000)

Gunther, Richard et al. (eds), *Political Parties: Old Concepts and New Challenges* (Oxford: OUP, 2002)

Haines, Joe, *Glimmer of Twilight: Harold Wilson in Decline* (London: Politico's, 2004)

Harris, Robert, *Good and Faithful Servant: The Unauthorized Biography of Bernard Ingham* (London: Faber & Faber, 1990)

Hastings, Max, *Editor: A Memoir* (London: Macmillan, 2002)

Hayter, Dianne, *Fightback! Labour's Traditional Right in the 1970s and 1980s* (Manchester: Manchester University Press, 2005)

Held, David and Thompson, John B. (eds), *Social Theory of Modern Societies: Anthony Giddens and His Critics* (Cambridge: CUP, 1994)

Hellawell, Keith, *The Outsider: The Autobiography of One of Britain's Most Controversial Policemen* (London: HarperCollins, 2002)

Hennessy, Peter, *Whitehall* (London: Secker & Warburg, 1988)

——, *The Hidden Wiring: Unearthing the British Constitution* (London: Indigo, 1996)

——, *The Prime Minister: The Office and Its Holders Since 1945* (London: Penguin Press, 2001)

Herman, Edward S. and Chomsky, Noam, *Manufacturing Consent: The Political Economy of the Mass Media* (New York: Pantheon, 2002)

Hughes, Colin and Wintour, Patrick, *Labour Rebuilt: The New Model Army* (London: Fourth Estate, 1990)

Ingrams, Richard, *The Life and Adventures of William Cobbett* (London: HarperCollins, 2005)

Jenkins, Simon, *Accountable to None: The Tory Nationalization of Britain* (London: Hamish Hamilton, 1995)

———, *Thatcher and Sons: A Revolution in Three Acts* (London: Penguin Press, 2006)

Jones, Nicholas, *Soundbites and Spin-Doctors: How Politicians Manipulate the Media – and Vice Versa* (London: Cassell, 1995)

———, *Sultans of Spin: Media and the New Labour Government* (London: Weidenfeld & Nicolson, 1999)

———, *The Control Freaks: How New Labour Got Its Own Way* (London: Politico's, 2001)

———, *Trading Information: Leaks, Lies and Tip-Offs* (London: Politico's, 2006)

Kampfner, John, *Blair's Wars* (London: The Free Press, 2003)

Keegan, John, *The Mask of Command: A Study of Generalship* (London: Pimlico, 2004)

Kochan, Nick and Pym, Hugh, *The Guinness Affair: Anatomy of a Scandal* (London: Christopher Helm, 1987)

Koss, Stephen, *The Rise and Fall of the Political Press in Britain* (London: Fontana, 1990)

Kuhn, Raymond, *Politics and the Media in Britain* (London: Palgrave Macmillan, 2007)

Lamont, Norman, *In Office* (London: Little, Brown, 1999)

Langdon, Julia, *Mo Mowlam: The Biography* (London: Warner Books, 2001)

Lawson, Nigel, *The View from Number 11* (London: Corgi Books, 1993)

Linklater, Magnus and Leigh, David, *Not With Honour: The Inside Story of the Westland Scandal* (London: Sphere, 1986)

Lloyd, John, *What the Media Are Doing to Our Politics* (London: Constable, 2004)

MacArthur, Tom and MacArthur, Roshan (eds), *Concise Oxford Companion to the English Language* (Oxford: OUP, 1998)

Macintyre, Donald, *Mandelson: The Biography* (London: HarperCollins, 1999)

Mair, Peter et al. (eds), *Political Parties and Electoral Change: Party Responses to Electoral Markets* (London: Sage, 2004)

Mandelson, Peter and Liddle, Roger, *The Blair Revolution: Can New Labour Deliver?* (London: Faber & Faber, 1996)

Margach, James, *The Abuse of Power: The War Between Downing Street and the Media from Lloyd George to James Callaghan* (London: W. H. Allen, 1978)

——, *The Anatomy of Power: An Enquiry into the Personality of Leadership* (London: W. H. Allen, 1979)

Marquand, David, *Decline of the Public* (Cambridge: Polity Press, 2004)

Marr, Andrew, *Ruling Britannia: The Failure and Future of British Democracy* (London: Penguin, 1996)

Marx, Karl and Engels, Friedrich, *The Communist Manifesto* (London: Penguin Classics, 2002)

Mathew, H. C. G., *Gladstone, 1809–1874* (New York: OUP, 1989)

McSmith, Andy, *Faces of Labour: The Inside Story* (London: Verso, 1996)

Meyer, Christopher, *DC Confidential: The Controversial Memoirs of Britain's Ambassador to the US at the Time of 9/11 and the Iraq War* (London: Weidenfeld & Nicolson, 2005)

Miliband, David (ed.), *Reinventing the Left* (Cambridge: Polity Press, 1994)

Morgan, Piers, *The Insider: The Private Diaries of a Scandalous Decade* (London: Ebury, 2005)

Morrison, David, *Iraq: Lies, Half-truths and Omissions* (London: Athol Books, 2003)

Mosca, Gaetano, *The Ruling Class* (*Elementi di Scienza Politica*, edited and revised by Arthur Livingston; New York: McGraw-Hill, 1939)

Mosley, Ivo (ed.), *Dumbing Down: Culture, Politics and the Mass Media* (Thorverton: Imprint Academic, 2000)

Mount, Ferdinand, *The Subversive Family: An Alternative History of Love and Marriage* (London: Unwin, 1982)

——, *The British Constitution Now* (London: Heinemann, 1992)

Mowlam, Mo, *Momentum: The Struggle for Peace, Politics and the People* (London: Hodder & Stoughton, 2002)

Mulgan, Geoff, *Connexity: How to Live in a Connected World* (London: Chatto & Windus, 1997)

——, *Good and Bad Power* (London: Penguin Press, 2006)

Namier, Lewis, *The Structure of Politics at the Accession of George III* (second edition; London: Macmillan, 1982)

Naughtie, James, *The Rivals: The Intimate Story of a Political Marriage* (London: Fourth Estate, 2001)

Needham, Catherine, *The Reform of Public Services Under New Labour: Narratives of Consumerism* (London: Palgrave Macmillan, 2007)

Neild, Robert, *Public Corruption* (London: Anthem Press, 2002)

Norton-Taylor, Richard, *Truth is a Difficult Concept: Inside the Scott Inquiry* (London: Fourth Estate, 1995)

Oborne, Peter, *Alastair Campbell: New Labour and the Rise of the Media Class* (London: Aurum, 1999)

——, *The Rise of Political Lying* (London: The Free Press, 2005)

Oborne, Peter and Walters, Simon, *Alastair Campbell* (London: Aurum, 2004)

Osler, David, *Labour Party PLC: New Labour as a Party of Business* (Edinburgh: Mainstream, 2002)

Page, Bruce, *The Murdoch Archipelago* (London: Pocket Books, 2004)

Parry-Giles, Shawn J. and Parry-Giles, Trevor, *Constructing Clinton: Hyperreality and Presidential Image-Making in Postmodern Politics* (New York: Peter Lang, 2002)

Parsons, Talcott, *Structures and Process in Modern Societies* (New York: The Free Press, 1960)

——, *Systems and Modern Societies: Foundations of Modern Sociology* (Englewood Cliffs, NJ: Prentice Hall, 1971)

Paxman, Jeremy, *Friends in High Places: Who Runs Britain?* (London: Penguin, 1991)

——, *The Political Animal* (London: Michael Joseph, 2002)

Perryman, Mark (ed.), *The Blair Agenda* (London: Lawrence & Wishart, 1996)

Peters, B. Guy and Pierre, Jon (eds), *Politicization of the Civil Service in Comparative Perspective: The Quest for Control* (London: Routledge, 2004)

Piattoni, Simona, *Clientelism, Interests, and Democratic Representation* (Cambridge: CUP, 2001)

Pimlott, Ben, *Harold Wilson* (London: HarperCollins, 1993)

Plato, *The Republic* (London: Penguin Classics, 2003)

Pollard, Stephen, *David Blunkett* (London: Hodder & Stoughton, 2005)

Price, Lance, *The Spin Doctor's Diary* (London: Hodder & Stoughton, 2005)

Prochaska, Frank, *Christianity and Social Service in Modern Britain: The Disinherited Spirit* (Oxford: OUP, 2006)

Pugh, Peter, *Is Guinness Good for You? The Bid for Distillers – The Inside Story* (London: Blackstone Press, 1987)

Rawnsley, Andrew, *Servants of the People: The Inside Story of New Labour* (London: Penguin, 2001)

Rentoul, John, *Tony Blair: Prime Minister* (London: Little, Brown, 2001)

Richards, Paul (ed.), *Tony Blair: In His Own Words* (London: Politico's, 2004)

Riddell, Peter, *Honest Opportunism: The Rise of the Career Politician* (London: Hamish Hamilton, 1993)

Robertson, Roland and Turner, Bryan S., *Talcott Parsons: Theorist of Modernity* (London: Sage, 1991)

Robinson, Geoffrey, *The Unconventional Minister: My Life Inside New Labour* (London: Michael Joseph, 2000)

Rose, Jonathan, *The Intellectual Life of the British Working Classes* (New Haven, CT: Yale Nota Bene, 2002)

Runciman, David, *The Politics of Good Intentions: History, Fear and Hypocrisy in the New World Order* (Princeton, NJ: Princeton University Press, 2006)

Runciman, W. G. (ed.), *Hutton and Butler: Lifting the Lid on the Workings of Power* (Oxford: OUP on behalf of The British Academy, 2004)

Rush, Michael, *The Role of the Member of Parliament Since 1868: From Gentlemen to Players* (Oxford: OUP, 2001)

Russell, Meg, *Building New Labour: The Politics of Party Organisation* (London: Palgrave Macmillan, 2005)

—— (ed.), *Must Politics Disappoint?* (London: Fabian Society, 2005)

Ryder, Richard D., *Putting Morality Back into Politics* (Exeter: Imprint Academic, 2006)

Sampson, Anthony, *The Anatomy of Britain* (London: Hodder & Stoughton, 1962)

——, *Who Runs This Place? The Anatomy of Britain in the 21st Century* (London: John Murray, 2004)

Sands, Philippe, *Lawless World: Making and Breaking Global Rules* (London: Penguin, 2006)

Scott, Paul, *Tony and Cherie: Behind the Scenes in Downing Street* (London: Pan Books, 2006)

Scruton, Roger, *A Dictionary of Political Thought* (London: Macmillan, 1996)

Searle, G. R., *Corruption in Politics, 1895–1930* (Oxford: Clarendon Press, 1987)

Seldon, Anthony, *Blair* (London: The Free Press, 2004)

Seldon, Anthony and Kavanagh, Dennis (eds), *The Blair Effect: 2001–05* (Cambridge: CUP, 2005)

Senior, Ian, *Corruption: The World's Big C – Cases, Causes, Consequences, Cures* (London: Institute of Economic Affairs, 2006)

Short, Clare, *An Honourable Deception?: New Labour, Iraq, and the Misuse of Power* (London: The Free Press, 2004)

Smith, Michael, *The Spying Game: The Secret History of British Espionage* (London: Politico's, 2004)

Sopel, Jon, *Tony Blair: The Moderniser* (London: Michael Joseph, 1995)

Sowell, Thomas, *A Conflict of Visions: Ideological Origins of Political Struggles* (New York: Basic Books, 2002)

Sparrow, Andrew, *Obscure Scribblers: A History of Parliamentary Journalism* (London: Politico's, 2003)

Stallybrass, Peter and White, Allon, *The Politics and Poetics of Transgression* (Ithaca, NY: Cornell University Press, 1989)

Stephens, Philip, *Politics and the Pound: The Conservatives' Struggle With Sterling* (London: Macmillan, 1996)

——, *Tony Blair: The Price of Leadership* (London: Politico's, 2004)

Stewart, Graham, *The History of The Times: Volume VII, 1981–2002 – The Murdoch Years* (London: HarperCollins, 2005)

Stothard, Peter, *30 Days: A Month at the Heart of Blair's War* (London: HarperCollins, 2003)

Sutherland, Gillian (ed.), *Studies in the Growth of Nineteenth-Century Government* (London: Routledge & Kegan Paul, 1972)

Sutherland, Keith (ed.), *The Rape of the Constitution?* (Thorverton: Imprint Academic, 2000)

Sutherland, Keith, *The Party's Over: Blueprint for a Very English Revolution* (Thorverton: Imprint Academic, 2004)

Taylor, D. J., *On the Corinthian Spirit: The Decline of Amateurism in Sport* (London: Yellow Jersey, 2006)

Thompson, John B., *Political Scandal: Power and Visibility in the Media Age* (Cambridge: Polity Press, 2000)

The Times, *House of Commons 1955* (London: The Times Office, 1955)

de Waal, Anastasia, *Inspection, Inspection, Inspection! How OFSTED Crushes Independent Schools and Independent Teachers* (London: Civitas, 2006)

Walden, George, *New Elites: A Career in the Masses* (London: Gibson Square, 2006)

Walker, John, *The Queen Has Been Pleased: The British Honours System at Work* (London: Secker & Warburg, 1986)

Walker, Peter, *Staying Power: An Autobiography* (London: Bloomsbury, 1991)

Walters, Simon, *Tory Wars* (London: Politico's, 2001)

Weber, Max, *From Max Weber: Essays in Sociology* (edited by H. H. Gerth and C. Wright Mills; London: Routledge & Kegan Paul, 1977)

——, *The Vocation Lectures: "Science as a Vocation", "Politics as a Vocation"* (Indianapolis/Cambridge: Hackett, 2004)

——, *Political Writings* (edited by Peter Lassman and Ronald Speirs; Cambridge: CUP, 2005)

Weir, Stuart and Beetham, David, *Political Power and Democratic Control in Britain* (London: Routledge, 1999)

West, Nigel, *At Her Majesty's Secret Service: The Chiefs of Britain's Intelligence Agency, MI6* (London: Greenhill Books, 2006)

Wheatcroft, Geoffrey, *Yo, Blair!* (London: Politico's, 2007)

Willetts, David, *Modern Conservatism* (London: Penguin, 1992)

Williams, Francis, *Dangerous Estate: The Anatomy of Newspapers* (London: Grey Arrow, 1959)

Williams, Hywell, *Britain's Power Elites: The Rebirth of a Ruling Class* (London: Constable & Robinson, 2006)

Woodward, Bob, *Plan of Attack* (London: Simon & Schuster, 2004)

Wright Mills, C., *The Power Elite: New Edition* (Oxford: OUP, 2000)

Wyatt, Woodrow, *The Journals of Woodrow Wyatt: Volume 1* (edited by Sarah Curtis; London: Pan Books, 1999)

——, *The Journals of Woodrow Wyatt: Volume 2* (edited by Sarah Curtis; London: Pan Books, 2000)

Young, Hugo, *One of Us* (London: Macmillan, 1989)

——, *Political Lives: Intimate Biographies of the Famous by the Famous* (Oxford: OUP, 2001)

Young, Michael, *The Rise of the Meritocracy, 1870–2033: An Essay on Education and Equality* (London: Thames & Hudson, 1958)

Articles

van Biezen, Ingrid, 'Political Parties as Public Utilities', *Party Politics*, Vol. 10, No. 6, pp. 701–22

Borchert, Jens, 'The Concept of Political Class: From Mosca's Ruling Class to the Self-Referentiality of Professional Politics', essay presented to the American Political Science Association Meeting, Boston, 29 August–1 September 2002

Cruddas, Jon, 'Race, Class and Migration: Tackling the Far Right', published as Chapter 12 of *Rethinking Immigration and Integration: A New Centre-Left Agenda* (The Policy Network, 2007)

Davis, Aeron, 'Investigating Journalist Influences on Political Agendas at Westminster', *Political Communication*, Vol. 24, Issue 2, 2007

Doig, A. and Wilson, J., 'What Price New Public Management?', *Political Quarterly*, 69, 3, pp. 267–80

Foster, Christopher, 'Why Are We So Badly Governed?', *Public Management and Policy Association Report*, October 2005

Greenaway, John, 'Having the Bun and the Halfpenny: Can Old Public Service Ethics Survive in the New Whitehall?', *Public Administration*, Vol. 73, pp. 357–74

Hood, C., 'A Public Management for All Seasons', *Public Administration*, Vol. 69, pp. 3–19

Katz, Richard and Mair, Peter, 'Changing Models of Party Organisation and Party Democracy: The Emergence of a Cartel Party', *Party Politics*, Vol. 1, January 1995, pp. 5–28

Mair, Peter, 'Partyless Democracy: Solving the Paradox of New Labour?', *New Left Review*, March/April 2000, pp. 21–35

Morrison, David, 'What Became of Blair's "Several Hundred" Terrorists?', *Labour and Trade Union Review*, May 2005

Needham, Catherine, *Citizen-Consumers: New Labour's Marketplace Democracy* (Catalyst, 2003)

Neocleous, Mark, 'Radical Conservatism, or the Conservatism of Radicals: Giddens, Blair and the Politics of Reaction', *Radical Philosophy*, January/February 1999, pp. 24–34

Oborne, Peter, *The Use and Abuse of Terror: The Construction of a False Narrative on the Domestic Terror Threat* (Centre for Policy Studies, February 2006)

Robinson, Emily (ed.), 'Anti-Politics and Political Parties: The Case for State Funding, Dr Alan Whitehead MP', *New Politics*, April 2006

Rosewarne, David, 'Estuary English', *Times Educational Supplement*, 19 October 1984

Rudé, George, 'The Gordon Riots: A Study of the Rioters and Their

Victims', *Transactions of the Royal Historical Society*, 5th Series, No. 6, 1956, pp. 93–114

Theakston, Kevin, 'The 1964–70 Labour Governments and Whitehall Reform', *POLIS Working Paper No. 2*, February 2004

Other Materials

Alexander, Douglas and Creasy, Stella, 'Serving a Cause, Serving a Community: The Role of political parties in today's Britain' (Demos, 2006)

Blick, Andrew et al., 'The Rules of the Game: Terrorism and Human Rights – A Report by Democratic Audit, Human Rights Centre, University of Essex for the Joseph Rowntree Reform Trust' (York, 2006)

Boys Smith, Nicholas, 'True Blue: How Fair Conservatism Can Win the Next Election' (Demos, 2005)

Butler, The Right Hon. Lord, 'Review of Intelligence on Weapons of Mass Destruction: Report of a Committee of Privy Counsellors' (HC 898, 14 July 2004)

Cabinet Office Press Release, 'Reform and Delivery in the Civil Service – The New Structure for the Cabinet Office', 24 June 2002

Carswell, Douglas, 'Direct Democracy: Empowering People to Make Their Lives Better' (C-Change, October 2002)

Chapman, Jake, 'System Failure: Why Governments Must Learn to Think Differently' (second edition; Demos, 2004)

Clark, Greg and Mather, James (eds), 'Total Politics: Labour's Command State' (Conservative Policy Unit, 2003)

Commissioner for Public Appointments, Eleventh Annual Report, 2005/06 (OCPA, July 2006)

Committee on Standards and Privileges, 'Fifth and Sixth Report: Complaint Against Mr Robert Wareing' (HC 182, 29 July 1997)

——, 'Minutes of Evidence' (18 May 1999)

——, 'Ninth Report: Complaint Against Mr Peter Mandelson' (HC 611, 1 July 1999)

——, 'Thirteenth Report: Complaint Against Marjorie Mowlam' (HC 929, 10 November 1999)

——, 'Fifth Report: Complaint Against Mrs Teresa Gorman' (HC 260, 17 February 2000)

——, 'Seventh Report: Complaint Against Mr Ken Livingstone' (HC 342, 14 March 2000)

——, 'Twelfth Report: Complaint Against Mr John Prescott' (HC 504, 17 May 2000)

——, 'Second Report: Complaint Against Mr John Maxton and Dr John Reid' (HC 89, 22 December 2000)

——, 'Seventh Report: Complaint Against Mr Geoffrey Robinson' (HC 465, 4 May 2001)

——, 'First Report: Complaint Against Mr Geoffrey Robinson: Supplementary Report' (HC 297, 24 October 2001)

——, 'Sixth Report: Conduct of Mr George Galloway' (HC 509, 6 April 2005)

——, 'Seventh Report: Conduct of Mr George Galloway' (HC 1067, 26 April 2006)

Crouch, Colin, 'Coping With Post-Democracy' (Fabian Society, 2000)

Cruddas, Jon and Harris, John, 'Fit for Purpose: A Programme for Labour Party Renewal' (Compass, 2006)

Davies, Jon, 'The Future Doesn't Last Long', http://www.social affairsunit.org.uk/blog/archives/000716.php

Giddens, Anthony, 'Runaway World: Lecture 4 – Family', BBC Reith Lectures 1999, delivered in Washington DC

Goodhart, David, 'Progressive Nationalism: Citizenship and the Left' (Demos, 2006)

'Government Response to the Public Administration Select Committee's Fourth Report of Session 2002–03: "Governing by Appointment: Opening Up the Patronage State"' (HC 165, December 2003)

Green, David G., 'Civil Society: The Guiding Philosophy and Research Agenda of CIVITAS, the Institute for the Study of Civil Society', second edition, June 2005

Griffith, Phoebe and Leonard, Mark (eds), 'Reclaiming Britishness: Living Together After 11 September and the Rise of the Right' (Foreign Policy Centre, September 2002)

Gyngell, Kathy and Lewis, Ray, 'From Latchkey to Leadership: A Practical Blueprint for Channelling the Talents of Inner-City Youth' (Centre for Young Policy Studies, 2006)

Hammond, Anthony, 'Review of the Circumstances Surrounding

an Application for Naturalisation by Mr SP Hinduja in 1998' (HMSO, 9 March 2001)

——, 'Review of the Conclusions of the 2001 Review of the Circumstances Surrounding an Application for Naturalisation by Mr SP Hinduja in 1998' (HMSO, 9 March 2002)

Hansard, House of Commons Debates, 'Iraq and Weapons of Mass Destruction', 24 September 2002

Hargreaves, Ian and Christie, Ian (eds), 'Tomorrow's Politics: The Third Way and Beyond' (Demos, 1998)

Home Affairs Select Committee, 11 October 2005, Q 73

House of Commons Minutes of Evidence taken before the Liaison Committee, 18 June 2007 – to be published as HC 300-II. Uncorrected transcript of oral evidence can be found at: http://www.publications.parliament.uk/pa/cm200607/cmselect/cmliaisn/uc300-ii/uc30002.htm

The Hutton Inquiry, 'Report of the Inquiry into the Circumstances Surrounding the Death of Dr David Kelly CMG' (HC 247, 28 January 2004)

'In Praise of Ideology: An Inquiry Calculated to Draw the Timely Attention of Britain and America to the Necessity for "Ideology" and to the Inadequacy of "the Centre Ground"' (Centre for Policy Studies, 2006)

Kelly, Ruth and Byrne, Liam, 'A Common Place' (Fabian Society, June 2007)

Kirby, Jill, 'The Nationalisation of Childhood' (Centre for Policy Studies, 2006)

Leas, Ruth, 'The Larceny of the Lottery Fund' (Centre for Policy Studies, 2006)

Lodge, Guy and Rogers, Ben, 'Whitehall's Black Box: Accountability and Performance in the Senior Civil Service' (Institute for Public Policy Research, 2006)

McElwee, Martin, 'The Great and Good? The Rise of the New Class' (Centre for Policy Studies, 2000)

——, 'Judicial Review: Keeping Ministers in Check – A Policy Brief from the Bow Group', February 2002

McElwee, Martin and Tyrie, Andrew, 'Statism by Stealth: New Labour, New Collectivism', Centre for Policy Studies, March 2002

Mean, Melissa and Tims, Charlie, 'People Make Places: Growing the Public Life of Cities' (Demos, 2005)

Miller, Paul and Wilsdon, James (eds), 'Better Humans? The Politics of Human Enhancement and Life Extension' (Demos, 2006)

'Ministerial Code of Conduct: A Code of Conduct and Guidance on Procedure for Ministers' (Cabinet Office, July 2001)

Minogue, Kenneth, 'Civil Society and David Blunkett: Lawyers vs Politicians' (Civitas, 2002)

Morgan, Patricia, 'Family Policy, Family Changes: Sweden, Italy and Britain Compared' (Civitas, 2006)

——, 'The War Between the State and the Family: How Government Divides and Impoverishes' (Institute of Economic Affairs, 2007)

North, Richard D., 'Mr Blair's Messiah Politics: or, What Happened When Bambi Tried to Save the World' (Social Affairs Unit, 2006)

Philp, Chris, 'The Price of Dishonour: A Policy Brief from the Bow Group', 22 July 2006

Political Quarterly, Volume 77, Number 1, January–March 2006

'Power to the People – The Report of Power: An Independent Inquiry into Britain's Democracy, The Centenary project of the Joseph Rowntree Charitable Trust and the Joseph Rowntree Reform Trust' (Power Inquiry, 2006)

Public Administration Select Committee, 'Fifth Report: Mapping the Quango State', Vol. I, 'Report and Proceedings of the Committee and Annex 4' (HC 367 and HC 367–II, 21 March 2001)

——, 'Fourth Report of Session 2002–03: Government By Appointment: Opening Up the Patronage State', Vols I and II (26 June 2003)

Public Appointments to NHS Trusts and Health Authorities, 'A Report by the Commissioner for Public Appointments' (OCPA, March 2000)

Reinforcing Standards: 'Sixth Report of the Committee on Standards in Public Life, Chairman Lord Neill, Review of the First Report of the Committee on Standards in Public Life', Vol. 1 (HMSO, January 2000)

Robinson, Emily (ed.), 'The Future of Political Parties: Tony Robinson, Theresa May, Chris Huhne, Matt Carter in Conversation', Unlock Democracy, 16 January 2007

Saatchi, Maurice and Warburton, Peter, 'The Bad Samaritan: The

War of Independence Part Two' (Centre for Policy Studies, May 2000)

——, 'Poor People! Stop Paying Tax! The War of Independence: A Call to Arms' (Centre for Policy Studies, July 2001)

Select Committee on Public Administration, 'Sixth Report: The Government Information and Communication Service', HC 770, 29 July 1998

Skidmore, Paul and Craig, John, 'Start with People: How Community Organisations Put Citizens in the Driving Seat' (Demos, 2005)

Snook, Harry, 'Crossing the Threshold: 266 Ways the State Can Enter Your Home' (Centre for Policy Studies, 2007)

Standards in Public Life: 'First Report of the Committee on Standards in Public Life', Chairman Lord Nolan, Volume 1 (HMSO, May 1995)

Strengthening Democracy: 'Fair and Sustainable Funding of Political Parties, The Review of the Funding of Political Parties' (HMSO, March 2007)

Tyrie, Andrew, 'Mr Blair's Poodle: An Agenda for Reviving the House of Commons' (Centre for Policy Studies, June 2000)

Walker, David and Jones, Nicholas, 'Invisible Political Actors: The press as agents of anti-politics' (New Politics Network, 2004)

Whelan, Robert, 'The Corrosion of Charity: From Moral Renewal to Contract Culture' (Institute for Economic Affairs, 1996)

Index

POCKET
BOOKS

Peter Oborne

The Rise of Political Lying

'Brave and coruscating ... Anyone seriously interested in
the political culture of our time ought to read this book'
Sunday Times

Being 'economical with the truth' has become almost a jokey
euphemism for the political lie – a cosy insider's phrase for
the disingenuousness that is now accepted as part and
parcel of political life.

But is it now time to question the creeping invasion of
falsehood? What does the rise of the political lie say about
our society? At what point, if we have not reached it
already, will we cease to believe a word politicians say?

Peter Oborne demonstrates that truth has become an
increasingly slippery concept. From woolly pronouncements
that are designed merely to obfuscate to outright and blatant
lies whose intention is to deceive, the political lie is never
far from the surface. And its prevalence has led to a
catastrophic decline in trust, at a time when people are more
politicised than ever. Rigorous, riveting, and profoundly
shocking, this is a devastating book about one of the single
biggest issues facing us today.

ISBN 978-0-74327-560-6
PRICE £7.99